Anna Maria Islan

1940 - 1970

Tales of Three Cities:
From Bean Point to Bridge Street

Carolyne Norwood

Also by

Carolyne Norwood

The Early Days 1893 - 1940 *(4th Printing)*

Mary Ann Treadwell

Chronicles of the AMI Historical Society

Anna Maria Island

1940 - 1970

Tales of Three Cities: From Bean Point to Bridge Street

www.AMIHS.org

Anna Maria Island Historical Society Inc.
402 Pine Avenue Anna Maria, Florida 34216

First Edition : September 2010

ISBN 978 - 0 - 615 - 40050 - 1

Library of Congress Cataloging-in-Publication Date is availalbe.

Manufactured in the United States

Acknowledgments

This book is dedicated to my dear husband George, who gave me loving support and encouragement for 54 years, and to my faithful friends:

Jack Egan, cartoonist for Tales From the South Side
Andrew Clyde Little, consultant
Nick Norwood, photo editor and coordinator
Robert Reiber, artist, who designed the Island map
Christine Torgeson, The Boys of Winter
Melissa Williams, text consultant

Thanks a million to my wonderful proof readers who helped me immeasurably with this weighty tome.

Susan Anderson
Barbara Burda
Judy Hildman
Evelyn Hoskins
Linda Kinnan
Elizabeth Moss
Nicki Notaras Norwood
Evelyn Shinn
Betty Speare
John van Zandt

Betty Lou Backburn Huth was a champion skier at Cypress Gardens from 1955 - 1956.

Table of Contents

This book is dedicated to all the children who have lived on Anna Maria Island. Some of their tales can be found on the following pages

Introduction

Brisk sales of my first book, "The Early Days:1893-1940," now in its fourth printing, indicated the public's curiosity in the history of this unique island, a jewel on Florida's west coast. Readers were eager to discover how ensuing years affected this once primitive strip of land in the Gulf of Mexico. Almost daily I heard the question, "When is the next book going to be for sale?"

I have many to thank for helping me with this enormous undertaking. Don Moore, former editor of The Islander, had the foresight to preserve early issues of the newspaper which proved invaluable in my endless research. Many friends, who lived on the Island for 50 years or more, related fascinating tales of days past. I have interjected a few of my own adventures, which began in 1956 when my family discovered this Island paradise.

Of paramount importance was the support and encouragement I received from so many when the task seemed to be more than I could handle. To me it was truly a labor of love for Anna Maria Island and those who have lived here.

One

Remember When

Sanchez and his sons found Spanish silver under a shell mound in Bradenton Beach. Drawing by Jack Egan

Tales From The South Side: Pirates, Shipwrecks, Buried Treasure, Haunted Houses

Renal Hook, a native Floridian, was born in Homestead. At the age of four he was kidnapped by gypsies who spirited him off to the wilds of Michigan where he was forced to milk cows and slop hogs until he was old enough to escape and return to Florida. He told some "romantic tales" to members of the Island Historical Society, explaining they were neither fact nor fiction, but a combination of both.

"In the early 1800s, when Florida belonged to Spain, this area was the haunt of a vicious pirate by the name of Pascual Miguel. Pascual had a dirty, rum swigging, murdering friend- a counterpart of Jose Gaspar. Old Miguel had several vessels under his command; his flagship was a topsail schooner named Kayron, after the character in Greek mythology who ferried the dead across the river Styx.

"Miguel was credited with many acts of brutality, the most fiendish was the destruction of the British brig, Sunshine, off the south end of Anna Maria Island in 1809. The Sunshine was sailing north during the hurricane season, loaded with cargo and 28 passengers, including 13 women and children. The ship became becalmed off the southern tip of the Island when the barometer began to fall, and the captain became concerned the approaching storm would wash the ship aground.

"Then, as if by a miracle, a 10-oared longboat appeared from a Longboat Key inlet and offered to tow the ship to safety for 20 doubloons. The captain accepted, and the Sunshine was towed through the pass and northward along the bayside of Anna Maria Island—into the clutches of the waiting Kayron. The unfortunate crew and passengers were stripped of all valuables and beached near School Key.

"After Miguel decided none of the men, women or children aboard were worth taking as slaves, he locked them below the deck, had four kegs of dynamite placed in the cabin and set the ship on fire. There were no survivors.

"As a post script to this story, two of Miguel's most important henchmen were English. Although they were most certainly blackguards, even they could not stomach a deed this foul to fellow British and later reported the incident to the British Crown.

"Some years later, during the War of 1812, these two British pirates trapped old Miguel at the mouth of the Manatee River. They captured the Kayron, hung Pascual from the yardarm, locked his crew below the decks and set the ship ablaze. Again there were no survivors.

Strange things happened in the old, dilapidated, three-story house on Gulf Drive in Bradenton Beach. Neighbors said it was haunted. Drawing by Jack Egan

"After the appropriate demise of old Miguel, but before the purchase of Florida from Spain by the United States, there lived on the mainland a Spaniard by the name of Sanchez. He had three sons, and one of them settled on Anna Maria. One day while fishing in the Gulf, from what is now the north end of Bradenton Beach, the sons found Spanish silver in a sunken ship.

"Since the wreck lay in deep water, Sanchez waited for more favorable tides, and they retrieved an even larger stash of silver. He buried it in two locations: the larger amount in a mid-Island shell mound, located in north Bradenton Beach and the smaller 1,000 paces due west of the mound near the Gulf between two palm trees.

“Old Sanchez must not have had much trust in his sons, because he did not tell them the locations until he was on his deathbed. Immediately one of the sons erected a house in the area and laid claim to the land, but he never found either treasure.

“Much later, during the Spanish-American War, a man by the name of R. E. Cobb visited Anna Maria while stationed in Tampa. After leaving the military, Cobb homesteaded a large tract on the Island in the area where Sanchez’s son built his house. Although Cobb did not appear to have much money when he arrived, in 1906 he built a large hotel, bar and dance hall on the Gulf directly east of where the old treasure ship sunk.

“He named it The Club House, and some said he found and used part of the buried treasure to finance the building. If he did, Cobb never admitted it, even on his deathbed.

“In 1909 Cobb had his homestead surveyed, laid out streets and lots, and named it Ilexhurst. His dream of a grand development failed, however, because there was no bridge to the mainland.

“The Club House later became known as the Gulf Park Hotel, and when the first bridge to the Island was built in 1921 it became quite popular among Islanders and tourists.

“In 1950 when I first visited Bradenton Beach, Gulf Park was rather seedy, but the new owners promised to restore the old hotel to its former glory. By the time I bought my home in Bradenton Beach in the late ‘60s it had deteriorated considerably. It continued downhill from then on, sinking from a rock music hangout where the Allman Brothers played, to a scroungy biker bar named the Oar House, the bane of residents in the Sandpiper Mobile Resort across the street.

“One night it burned to the ground. Now, I ask you, was it really faulty wiring, a spaced-out hippy, or the ghost of old Sanchez’s son getting revenge for the hotel built on his land with his silver?

“An even larger development on the south side originated from the 1904 homesteading of 163-acres by Davis Roush to the south of Ilexhurst. In 1910 Wyman and Green, Manatee County’s first real estate firm, purchased the Roush homestead. The realtors laid out a development named Cortez Beach, which appears to have been the actual name of Bradenton Beach until the post office was established in 1941.

“Now we come to the haunted houses and sex. You’ll notice I saved the best for last. Some of you remember the old, dilapidated, three-story, cedar shake house on the west side of Gulf Drive about half a block north of the Gulf Drive Cafe. It had an equally dilapidated sign out front that read, “Romaine’s Unusual Gifts.”

“Romaine Thomasson was a nice lady, at least my mother said she was, and she should have known since she spent a lot of time with her, chatting and buying silver and turquoise jewelry. Even Mom admitted Romaine was rather strange. She felt the presence of ghosts and looked and dressed like a witch. Romaine wasn’t the really weird one, that was her husband, Glenn. He drank a lot! It was rumored he eventually was banned from every bar in Bradenton Beach for making obscene remarks to the female staff and patrons. The Thomassons claimed to have noticed strange things happening soon after they moved in.

“There was a sickly smell of orange blossom perfume, and peculiar events coincided with the demolition of the water tower, behind the house. Romaine surmised a spirit lived in the water tower and when they tore it down it moved upstairs in their house. Over the years other spirits came to the house. There was a seafaring ghost who smoked a pipe and whistled, and the ghost of Kelley Kenny who claimed she was Glenn’s wife in a previous life. Glenn was supposedly a wild Irishman at the time, which was in 1846. She was jealous of Romaine and only spoke to Glenn. Another spiritual guest was a child named Maria and her gentle Dalmatian, Domino.

“It was considerate of the spirits not to make their presence known when the Thomassons decided to sell the house and move on. The house sat empty for years. It deteriorated to the point where part of it began to collapse, and it was condemned. A young family bought the house and spent a great deal of time and money fixing it up. Unfortunately, the new owners replaced some of the old pilings, and the Department of Natural Resources took them to court and tied the house up in litigation. After sitting empty for several years, it began to fall into disrepair.

“The lesser known haunted house of Bradenton Beach was mine. We bought our place in late 1968, but were not able to move down from Maryland until the summer of 1970. In the meantime, we rented the second story to a German woman who had married a GI. Her husband was not around, but the renters downstairs soon informed us that many other men were visiting, and always one or two at a time. This was about the time the first news article on the Thomasson house was written. The downstairs renters sent us a clipping from a local newspaper. It was a very amusing article that ended something like this: 'So in Bradenton Beach when they say y'all come back they really mean it, dead or alive.'

"The German renter had decided our house was also haunted, and was after free publicity, but since our place was not zoned for commercial use we told her to take her business elsewhere. We were told she decided to move back to Germany and join her sister who was a professional prostitute, not an amateur.

A few years later we moved into our house, and a psychic appeared at the door asking questions about the spirits that haunted our premises. I informed him that I was sure no self-respecting ghost would stay in our house after we moved in with four kids and a dog. He left, and to this very day we have never been bothered by ghosts, psychics or prostitutes. We have heard noises in the attic, but those stopped when we put the cat up there."

Memoirs of Old Timers

This group met to swap stories from the past. Back row from left: John Van Ostenbridge, John Huth, Bob Hedgcock, John Adams, Bob Bayless, Jerry Ingram, Linda Ingram Wingard, Gwen Ingram Wilson, Laurie Adams, Peggy Blassingame Diamant, Jean Blackburn, Jim Adams. Front row from left: Elizabeth Moss, Daryl Van Ostenbridge, Betty Lou Blackburn Huth, Joyce Weersing Williamson, Dot Robertson Ingram, Carolyne Norwood.

About 20 folks who had lived on the Island for 40 years or more came to an informal gathering at the Baptist Church on April 21, 2008. Some had not seen each other for 30 years or more. It was grand hearing tales of the past. Laughter and interruptions of remembrances made the recording difficult to decipher. The following conversations took place:

Bob Hedgcock came to the Island in 1947: I remember making bird books at school. It was a requirement. This was at the old two-room schoolhouse on Magnolia.

Betty Lou Blackburn Huth arrived on the Island in 1936: My Aunt Lena Phelps was principal and my mother, Betty Blackburn, was the teacher. My father, J. Hartley Blackburn, was a teacher and then county school superintendent for 21 years. We thought the bird book was wonderful.

Daryl Van Ostenbridge came to the Island in 1947: I didn't want to go on the bird walk, so I had to stay behind and clean latrines.

Elizabeth Pierce Moss first came to the Island in 1920: I was a teacher at the new Island school built in 1950. We all respected Mrs. Phelps. She praised the kids individually, but when they misbehaved they had to bend over a chair and she gave them three whacks. Teachers all behaved too. We didn't want to get sent to the office.

Linda Ingram Wingard came to the Island with her large family in 1943: My dad, Jess Ingram, was the school bus driver. All he had to do was look at the kids and they would quiet down. He was involved in the community, was one of the founders of the fire department, city marshal and a county commissioner. On Saturday nights he called square dances at the community hall, and he was in some plays at the theater. He was stern, but well-liked by everyone. There was no air conditioning in the houses. At night we would use spray guns in all the rooms to get rid of the mosquitoes. The screens were black with them. Outside, the sand spurs were thick.

Gwen Ingram Wilson is Linda's sister: I rode Dad's bus. All he had to do was look in the mirror and the kids would be quiet. We felt blessed to live on the Island.

Bob Bayless came to the Island in 1947: My dad, Brim Bayless, built the first house on the north end of the Island after the Army moved out. For awhile seven of us lived in the small house, but then my brother and his family moved to the fire station. My brother called one day and said there was a rattlesnake in the fire station and for me to come and get it. I grabbed my shotgun and stuck it out the window while driving up the road at top speed. Constable Jess Ingram thought I was going too fast so he followed. I stopped at the fire station. He thought I was going to shoot my brother. I shot the snake, and the bullet ricocheted off an Australian pine tree. It was a peaceful Sunday morning, and the retort sounded like a sonic boom. None of the kids had driver licenses, and most of them drove. I was reprimanded many times. Jess would say, "Bobby, don't do that again or I'll have to tell your daddy." Jess had the first gas station on the Island. It was a Pure Oil station, and gas was 15-cents a gallon.

Jim Adams arrived with his family in 1946: Jess went in town for me and got my social security card, and

The Ingram family arrived on the Island in 1943; from left: Dot, Gwen, Maidee, Jesse, Linda, Gail and Jerry..

to this day my card says Jimmy Adams. Everyone on the Island showed up for those square dances.

Elizabeth Moss drifted over from Bartow, with her family, in 1920. In 1943 I bought my parents' house on the Gulf at Willow. Jess did favors for people. If someone needed a ride to town he would take them. I was in his station waiting to go to town with him when he got a call. He listened to the caller and then said, "Can't take you today. I'm taking another old biddy in."

Linda Ingram: We were forbidden to go in the Anchorage, the local watering hole. One day Jess was called when a fight broke out between two women. He backed off. "Oh no," he said. "Do you think I want to get in the middle of that?"

Dad told us kids to always hold our heads up high because we had a good name. He was very honest. We were excited about going to North Carolina on vacation one summer. We were packed and ready, but Dad had to wait for the milkman, since he owed him some money.

Bob Hedgcock: Ted Lundy was a carpenter. He cut the back off of his car and made a flat bed out of it. On Saturday nights he took all the Island kids to the western movies in town in his remodeled flat-bed car.

John Adams came to the Island with his family in 1946.

Joyce Weersing Williamson: When we arrived in 1947 we bought a house on Pine for $4,000 which belonged to Mitch and Anna Davis. It was between the Anchorage and the Roser cottage. The ceiling went up to the roof and my father added a bedroom upstairs. There were lots of windows in the sunroom which overlooked Tampa Bay. Mitch had made the two huge rocking chairs out of trees. We lived there until the '60s. Something went wrong, and my father walked out on the pier one day and said he would give the house to the first person to give him $5,000. Lefty Miller, the pier concessionaire, bought it and rented it out. I have pictures of this house.

The Anchorage was built in 1920. Charlie Hackney, his wife Leola, and her boyfriend, Dewey Adams lived there. Bands would play every evening, and rooms were rented upstairs. There were coconut palms along Pine Avenue, and a small building near our house where they smoked mullet.

Bob Bayless: The Island Baptist Church was built in 1948. Charter members decided to build a church at the first prayer meeting held at our house on North Shore Drive. There was no electricity in our house at that time. It took a month to get it and about four months to get a phone. In 1950 we built a house next door to our house on North Shore Drive.

Mr. and Mrs. Forrester gave the property for the church - and they were Catholic. My brother Bill designed the church. He, my dad and Rad Kermode built it. It was sponsored by the First Baptist Church in Bradenton. We met in the community hall on Sunday afternoons while the church was being built. The preacher came from Bradenton. I was driving the preacher back home one Sunday on Cortez Road, which was a dirt road. It had just rained, and it was a quagmire. We got stuck and had to wait until someone pulled us out.

Folks in Anna Maria were a close-knit family. They looked out for each other. There was no need to lock doors, and we left keys in our cars. John Adams and I were in the Naval Reserve. When a hurricane was coming we would get together and do what was needed. One time we were helping sandbag the log cabin on north Pine Avenue. We worked for 24 hours. The ladies were up at the community hall making sandwiches and coffee for us. When we went to eat, Josie Davis took our high-topped shoes and dried them out by the open fire. The next day when we put them on they fell apart. They disintegrated in the heat of the fire.

Jimmy Adams showed us how to knock down a pine tree. He ran the jeep, full speed, up the tree and knocked himself unconscious. My sister-in-law was a nurse, and she treated him for shock until he was rushed to the hospital.

Dot Ingram, Linda's sister: Someone drove a car right through the wall of the IGA store. The whole wall was gone, but nobody got mad.

John Huth arrived in 1953: My first day on the Island, I met Jess and Virgil Mora when they were collecting the garbage. They told my brother Danny and me if we helped with the pickup they would give us $1 an hour and all we could eat. The policeman, George Jordan, locked our house up one time while we were away, and when we got home I had to climb through a window to get in.

The Weersing family bought this house on Pine Avenue for $4,000 in 1947.

Laurie Adams came to the Island in 1947: Betty Lou and I skipped school one day and went to Betty Lou's house. Her mother was there and took us to school right away. Her aunt, the principal, was shocked at our behavior.

Jim Adams: Louis Melvin "Humbug" Cobb was everyone's friend. He was the son of an early homesteader, Louis Melvin Cobb, and had a brother Sammy. Humbug did not believe in maintenance. He had an Austin car. The headlights fell off, so he put them in the trunk. The fender fell off, so it went in the trunk. Then he cut the top off with a hacksaw. He worked with my dad, Sam, and made a convertible out of the Austin. Then he backed into a palm tree and both doors sprung open. The frame was bent and the doors would not close, so he tied them shut with a rope.

John Adams: I remember the hot rod races on the Holmes Beach field where the airstrip was. When the Sandbar burned in 1947, we only had a horse-drawn fire wagon, no horse and a tiny hose. They kept the fire engine at city hall on Pine. J. Hartley Blackburn pumped the water and Ernie Cagnina held the hose which shot about 25-feet, not even reaching the fire. Humbug turned the truck over once. That's when we decided we needed a better fire truck.

Jim Adams: It was the pavilion that burned, not the Sandbar. Ernie and Bennie Scanio watched it burn. They didn't have a horse to pull the wagon. Sam and the gang bought a fire truck. Sam was fire chief in 1947. There was a big celebration when the new fire engine arrived. Everyone piled on, and a loud siren blew at the fire station. From then on it blew every Saturday at noon.

Peggy Blassingame Diamant arrived in 1937: When Mitch Davis was mayor his son Howard, always wanted to make money. He was a little slow, but if there was a fire and you could find Howard he might be able to put it out. He had a decrepit truck. There were garbage cans filled with water in the back. He didn't have a phone, so it was hard to reach him, but if he came and there were others to help they would empty the cans of water on the fire.

Bob Bayless: We had summer celebrations at the Community Hall on Pine and Gulf Drive, now the Island Players. Barbecues and potluck dinners were popular. After the water system put some fire plugs in, we decided to have a water battle across the street from the hall. We blew the fire siren to get the people out of the way and backed the fire truck up to the hydrant. The fire truck had no brakes. Mrs. Forrester pulled out in front of the truck, and I turned and put it in reverse and pushed the fireplug over. The steel brake linings on the truck had rusted out because we drove it through the salt water on the beach. Fortunately, the ground was soft, and the plug just bent over. My dad gave me a good tongue lashing that time.

Jim Adams: A bunch of us set fire to garbage in the back of the school. Hughie and I drove the truck down the dirt road and got so stuck we could not move it. We heard about that.

Linda Ingram: Remember the time in the '40s when the Gulf washed over Bradenton Beach to the bay?

Joyce Weersing Williamson: The beginning of the Youth Center was at the old school on Magnolia. Parents took turns chaperoning. We had board games, movies sometimes, a basketball court but no net. Hughie Moore drove the truck used to transport fish and crabs, and a bunch of us would go to drive-in movies in town. We had to sit in the back where all the stone crabs had been. It was smelly. When we got to the drive-in, we jumped out and sat in front. One time I jumped out and sprained my ankle. Fifteen years later I found it had been fractured. It still hurts.

Once I was invited to the Davis home on Pine Avenue for supper. They had a galvanized tub in the center of the table full of stone crab claws. We had soda crackers and melted butter with the crab claws. It was a delicious meal. My mother was appalled when I described it to her. I have good memories of the Davis family. We lived next door to the Ingram family for a while. Every morning corn bread would be cooking on the top of the stove in a black skillet.

Jean Blackburn, Betty Lou Huth's sister, arrived on the Island in 1951: My life revolved around the water. I had 17 saltwater aquariums. I caught all kinds of sea creatures with a seine net, and used them as my science project. We swam all day and night. Even at midnight, we were in the water. My mother and I went clamming every weekend. Fishermen would dump their nets out on the beach and tell us to take as many fish as we wanted. There was a pram fleet for the kids.

Marie Scanio Franklin: There was a tornado in 1968 that hit the Bayou Marina and White Avenue.

Peggy Blassingame Diamant: All black workers had to leave the Island at sundown. There was one exception. A black man who did yard work lived in a shanty on Pine Avenue.

Jerry Ingram, Linda's brother: The city pier was our second home. We fished all day and slept on the pier at night. Lefty Miller would run us off the pier if we did something wrong, like running on the pier. We caught mullet, but the pelicans would take them. Tink Fulford came out with a shotgun and got rid of a pelican that was stealing our fish. At night it was so peaceful to lie on the roof and look up at the stars.

You had to be at least 13 to go to the Teen Club dances. After your parents dropped you off, the boys could go outside, but the girls could not. My sisters taught me how to dance. We did jitterbug and square dancing. I'd get all dressed up, and my sisters would say, "You can't go like that." Then they dressed me. (Jerry has four sisters.)

I made money by pulling tourist cars out of the sand. They would launch boats at the end of Spring Avenue, on the bay. I got $15 for pulling them out with my jeep. Bob Bayless said he only got $5 for

Island kids had great fun at festivals. The highlight of this event was a greased pole with a $5 bill at the top. The first one to climb the pole got the money.

doing the same thing.

Rick Adams, Roby Robson, Johnny Cagnina and me set the woods on fire. It scared us to death. When the crowd came to put it out, we were helping. They never knew we started it.

Snooks Adams, the policeman, had a Plymouth Fury. Parents of a boy our age in Bradenton Beach had one too. When we saw the Plymouth in front of us, we thought it was our friend and raced him all the way to Land's End on Longboat Key. Were we surprised when we found out Snooks was the driver!

Linda Ingram: We made coquina soup and seagrape jelly. My mother had a business selling tiny baby cup shells which were bought by a shell factory in Port Charlotte to make jewelry. All five children helped sort shells. It was a great life.

Jim Adams: Bill Corsen ran the city pier before Lefty. He liked kids and let us ride our bikes out there. He would go to Mullet Key and catch jewfish which he would sell. They weighed from 500 to 700 pounds. He would catch some and tie them to the pier. There were always three or four jewfish tied up. Also known as goliath grouper, Hughie Moore would catch them with balls of dough.

Jerry Ingram: We played baseball on the field where the airport was laid out in 1948. Stu Hawkins worked with the kids. Lots of baseball greats lived here. Warren Spahn was here in 1948. He was instrumental in building Scanio Field by the Youth Center, and operated the bulldozer to clear the field. He played catch with the kids and sent them to baseball camp in St. Pete. Warren gave Linda a baseball with all the players names on it, but it didn't mean much to her. Players from the Milwaukee Braves, Cincinnati Reds and Detroit Tigers were here.

The first TV on the Island was at John Holmes' house. We would wait and wait for the test pattern to come on. Hugh Holmes had a hard-top car and told us if we washed and waxed it we could use it. We worked all day on it and double dated in it that evening.

Joyce Weersing Williamson: One Sunday we were baptised with our Easter hats on, and the water ran off our hats. Daryl had water dripping off her nose. On Saturday nights we would go to the Youth Center and walk across the street to Marion Colman's house to play her piano and practice singing for Sunday choir.

The group had so much fun they decided to meet a few weeks later to share more memories.

John Adams: Did you hear about the time Humbug borrowed Betty Lou's father's sailboat to rescue a boat out in the bay? It belonged to a man who kept it at Humbug's marina. He was fishing around Egmont Key, and the boat would not start, so he swam to shore. When he told us about the boat, Hugh Holmes, Humbug and I went out to get it. It was a long sail back, and when we got to the city pier we decided we needed a drink. We got back in the sailboat. The wind had changed and was blowing the wrong way. It was blowing us into the pier. We attempted to sail away from the pier and were about to crash when Humbug jumped in the boat and tried to start the auxiliary motor. There must have been 100 people out there laughing at Humbug, who held a beer in one hand while cursing and trying to start that motor with the other.

Ernie Cagnina, co-owner of the IGA grocery store, knew a lot of important, influential people. When Jimmy Carter won the presidency, guess who was sitting about six rows down from the front at the inauguration ceremony? Ernie! Ernie and Senator Chiles went to Washington and got money for the first beach renourishment on the Island. Bradenton Beach and Holmes Beach turned it down, and Senator Chiles got so mad he moved off the Island.

Does anyone have the picture of the turtle caught off the city pier? We used to see some huge turtles. I parked on the beach at the end of 83rd Street. It's rather high there, and I was in the jeep trying to stop this huge turtle. My front wheel went up on its back, and the turtle dragged the jeep and me into the water.

Jack Egan arrived in 1965: I'd like to know if anyone knows how my condemned home at 711 North Shore Drive got there. Some think it came by boat, others say they heard it crossed the bridge. It belonged to Mr. Baskam in Lakeland.

Judie Egan, Jack's wife: The Avon lady told me about the boy who worked for Norm Rosedale and every day after he came home from work they had to pick the sandspurs off of him. The house came by barge, and they rolled it up the beach on logs. It was a rumor that it came by road.

Bob Hedgcock: I don't think they could have gotten it across the drawbridge with that weight and width.

Bob Bayless: Back when the mackerel were running, the city pier was crowded with people sitting on the edge and standing. I had an old rowboat, and Jack Fiske and I decided we would get outside of that area and catch mackerel from the boat. Jack got so excited about catching the fish he threw his line sideways and wrapped it around me, but didn't hook me. "I said, Jack, I think that's enough fishing for the day." We had fun. We would get the coon oysters south of the marina. That was when the water was clean. There's a big difference now.

Carmen Cagnina arrived in 1945: We had ballroom dancing classes in the old school house and etiquette classes. My parents gave me a 16th birthday party at the Youth Center. There were so many teenagers and lots of activities for the girls. We didn't use cars, and walked to church and youth activities. The boys had bikes, and girls walked everywhere and kept our weight down. On Saturday mornings we caught the Trailways bus on the Island, and would go to the movies in town. We would always hit the bakery between the bus stop and the movie, and we always had the same driver, Ernie.

Bob Hedgcock: Our school bus driver was Mr. Ernie Johnson. Twenty years ago he lived in the same retirement home as my mother. He was just the same Mr. J. He remembered us and was always glad to see us. I believe he was a retired policeman from New York. We gave Mr. J. a retirement party.

Joyce Weersing Williamson: If I wasn't on the corner by the pier, Mr. J. would beep the horn in front of our house. Mother would run out and tell him that I was not going to school. I remember he would stop in front of Maxine Davis' house. She was always late and would come running out with her hair in curlers with buttered toast in her hand. He was the neatest guy. If it was raining, he would stop at our house. I remember at the end of the school year Daryl and I took up a collection and we bought Mr. J. two shirts. Everybody on the bus chipped in. He was so thrilled that we bought him those presents.

Daryl: He would park the bus on Pine and Tarpon. Several times the bus would not start. I was dating John at the time, and he had a big dump truck. We would all get in the truck, and he would take us to school. Remember that place in Bradenton Beach where the water covered the road? The kids at school would make fun of us because we were the only bus that came to school with seaweed all over it. They were jealous. The girls alway took over the back of the bus.

Johnnie Cagnina, Carmen's brother: There was a flagpole by the Community Hall, where City Hall is now. I remember fundraisers held there. They would put lard all over the pole and a $5 bill at the top. All week long all the kids would try to climb up.

"Humbug" Cobb was a friend to everyone on the Island.

Finally, all the lard was worn off and someone got the $5. Another big gathering was Beachcombers Week. They sold straw hats and everybody was wearing them. The kids decided to have a water battle using the hose from the fire truck. The water pressure damaged one boy's eyes so we couldn't do that anymore.

Jack Egan: Does anyone know how Humbug got his name? At one of my class reunions, Blue Fulford mentioned how Humbug got his name. Seems Humbug was in a fourth grade Christmas play at Cortez School. His one word was "humbug." From then on he was known as Humbug.

Jack Fiske: I was here during the early '40s, and there was evidence of WWII on the Island. McDill Air Force base would send planes down over Passage Key and drop bombs. Airplanes would fly with targets behind them for other planes to practice shooting. One Sunday morning, from our house on 840 South Bay Boulevard I could see white plumes on each side of the fishing pier where bombs were hitting. One bomb landed near the Hazzards' house, where the Waterfront restaurant is now, and blew all the windows out. They had crash boats tied up at the city pier to pick up any downed flyers.

Bob Hedgcock: We would go to Egmont Key on the weekends. I don't know why, but we would always run around naked over there and scare the sunbathers. We had a lot of fun. We were the original streakers.

Joe Hutchinson's family arrived on the Island in 1952. Joe was born in 1953: There were lots of trees along Beach Avenue where Torgesons lived. A great horned owl would always be sitting up in a tree. My brothers said I couldn't go out at night 'cause it would get me. It was so big, and I was about 3.

Chris Torgeson was crowned Miss Florida in 1966.

The "in group" was always having fun in the '40s.

Chris Torgeson arrived in 1947: A rattlesnake was killed on Cortez Road, and my dad saved the rattles. After being gone all summer, we would come back to the Island in the fall. We would always kill three or four rattlesnakes in our yard after the men cleared out the bushes. We collected the rattles and displayed them on a plate in the main hall of our house. My dad and Fred Hutchinson built a screened house in the back of the house near the barbecue pit. There was a big party going on one night. Everyone was drinking, singing and having a great time. Rick Hutchinson was always the instigator. We each got some rattles. Rick, Jack, me and my brother hid outside the screen behind bushes and started shaking the rattles. That really stopped the party. I don't know how we ever played in all those jungles without a bite. We even rafted over to School Key, now Key Royale. Dr. Huth took care of stingray bites, snake bites, delivered babies and cured feet infected from sandspurs.

Joe Hutchinson: I never saw a snake, maybe a water snake. The big thing for us was following the fogger. I don't know what kind of chemicals they were spraying for mosquitoes, but we would run behind it thinking it was great fun.

I remember there was an alligator that wandered out into the Gulf. Everyone on the Island who had any kind of gun met on the beach. I was about five years old. There must have been 40 people with different kinds of guns from the war. They lined up, and then all at once everybody shot the alligator. That poor thing, it flipped up and spun around.

Johnnie Cagnina: The dentist, Rex Lee, would take Roby Robson, Rick and me to School Key to shoot. I had a 9-millimeter P38. Dr. Lee was always with us when we went target shooting on School Key. He would reload everything, and he taught us to be careful. I remember seeing Roby walking down Marina Drive carrying his 22-rifle. Nobody said anything.

Joe's father, Fred, and Warren Spahn would hang around the IGA. They were always cutting up. They would throw eggs back and forth and have lots of fun. My dad probably had more cigars on display than any store, since he was a fan of cigars. I got my one and only award in 1947 for dressing up like Johnny, the Phillip Morris mascot.

Rick Adams and I would sit on the front ledge of the store. When the ice cream man came by, he would give us ice cream bars, and we would sit there and eat them.

Mrs. Phelps always had something grand going on at school. She was very organized. She and J. Hartley Blackburn were great educators. Even to this day, the Island school has a good reputation. They all worked together to make a wonderful ballpark next to the Youth Center. Dr. Huth took my tonsils out, and took good care of my family.

Rick Hutchinson is the son of Fred Hutchinson, manager of the Reds.

Joe Hutchinson remembered the alligator in the Gulf.

Gwen Ingram Wilson: My dad and sister Dot did several plays together. I decided we should have a play and open it up to the community. The Community Hall was never locked. All the kids were in the show. Everybody came to see it, and we filled up the Community Hall.

Most of our activities as teenagers were with the youth group at Roser. Remember when Mrs. Maskiell's dog ate someone's cake. She asked me to compete in the Miss Jeannie With the Light Brown Hair contest for Manatee County and I won. They gave me a beautiful gown to wear when I sang in the state competition. It was wonderful.

I just found out my father's grandmother was related to President Roosevelt.

Linda Ingram: Marie Scanio and I were good friends. Her father was part-owner of the IGA grocery store, and they lived behind it. We ate dinner at each other's house every Sunday after church. When we got tired of spaghetti at Marie's we would go to mine and eat Mama's fried chicken. I was always at the IGA store. When Ernie and Bennie saw me walking through, they would ask me where I was going and I'd say to see Marie. They would tell me I had to sing first. So there in the middle of the IGA, I'd sing.

There was a boat someone kept in the lagoon, north of Pine Avenue. My sister and brother, Dot and Jerry, were playing there and

Baseball greats, Fred Hutchinson and Warren Spahn would hang around the IGA grocery store acting rowdy.

Mama sent me to get them for supper. I wanted nothing to do with the lake since it was polluted with snakes. I was standing on the old broken dock with my feet in the water and I looked down and saw a cottonmouth snake with an open mouth full of babies. I was petrified. Babies were all over my feet. I ran home so fast. I don't understand why we're all alive today. Our precious Lord kept us alive.

Johnnie Cagnina: A big bird-dog named Joe was at our bus stop every day. He would run around the Island during the day during hunting season. My dad and Melvin Davis would pack him up with their gear to go hunting. Joe came to the bus stop every morning and stole our books. We'd chase him. Finally, just before the bus came he'd bring the books back with slobber all over them.

Across from the Feagles' house, on Magnolia Avenue, near the Gulf lived a Doberman pinscher named Major. His owner was a major in the Army, but he never was in combat. That dog was always in the front yard. We'd have to walk on the other side of the street. We were told he was only mean if you stepped in his yard, but his bark scared the living daylights out of us.

Linda Ingram: Suppertime was when Daddy came home. We were sitting around the table one day and someone asked, "Where's Gail?" We looked everywhere and could not find her. Nobody had seen her. Finally we found her locked up in a room at the school.

How did Mrs. Phelps get the nickname name Leapin' Lena? Nobody knew.

Dot Ingram: In our backyard we grew lady-finger bananas, papayas, oranges, grapefruit, guavas, tangerines and vegetables. We were little when we got here, and Daddy said we had to learn to eat what's here. Daddy would say the water tastes better than it smells. We never got cavities. A dentist told me you must have been raised on sulfur water because your teeth are yellow but strong. We put water in the fridge to try to get rid of the taste and smell. Daddy finally broke down and bought water.

Bob Hedgcock: There was a well on School Key. There was so much sulfur in the water there was white stuff hanging down all over the well. A farm was out there too.

Dot Ingram: Cedar trees grew all over the Island. They were our Christmas trees.

Elizabeth Moss: My husband Gene and I were judges for a Teen Club dance contest. Johnnie and his sister, Carmen, danced and danced and won top prize. We were honored to be the judges.

Johnnie Cagnina and Rick Adams enjoyed fishing off of the Anna Maria City Pier in 1946.

Chris Torgeson: Mrs. Moss was my fourth grade teacher, and we had the best time. We had studies in the morning and Spanish and square dancing in the afternoon. Johnny and Carmen Cagnina won the grand prize when they danced at the Teen Club dance contest. She always said I was in her best fourth grade class.

I am part of the baseball family on the Island. In 1947 my dad played for the Braves in Fort Lauderdale spring training. The next year the Braves started training in Bradenton, so this is how we came to the Island. Both my parents were from small towns. My dad was from Washington, and my mother came from Minnesota, and they loved small towns. We came past the reptile farm in Cortez Plaza, out the long, sandy Cortez Road, over the rickety bridge and up Gulf Drive. We rented cottages for several winters, and then my mother saw the house on Beach Avenue. She said not only was this the most beautiful place in the world, but that was the most beautiful house, and my dad bought it for her.

Johnny and Carmen Cagnina won the grand prize when they danced at the Teen Club dance contest.

Elizabeth Pierce Moss was Chris Torgeson's teacher when she was in the fourth grade at the Island School.

Chris Torgeson, her mother and father, Norma and Earl, are pictured in front of the Dixie Grand Hotel in Bradenton during spring training in the '40s.

Then he was traded to the Phillies. Their spring training camp was in Clearwater, and when he went with the Tigers it was in Lakeland, so the Island was a convenient place. After he was traded to Boston in 1952, we made this our home year-round. We had to go north in the summer where Dad was playing ball. This meant closing up the house, packing up the station wagon, driving up Route 41 to Philly, Detroit or wherever he was. If he got traded again, we'd pack up the house and start school late. I always wanted to stay here for the summer and eventually I did.

My parents divorced in 1961, and my dad remarried. I am close to my dad's second family. My stepmother used to rent The Mound, until it sold. I have two sisters in that family, and they come down in April.

Just lately one of them asked me, "Didn't you have any structure in your life when you were young?" Structure, I said. When we got off the bus we had freedom. We threw our shoes in the house and took off. We didn't come home until we were hungry. You don't get in trouble here, you just keep doing stuff.

My girlfriend Kathy had a boat. That was great. We would ski up and down the canals until we got to the end, then we had to slow down. There were no houses around. When Jordan, the police chief, was around we could see him coming. Someone would holler, "Here comes Jordan!" and we would run away. We thought he never slept. He would follow the school bus and would drag you off the city pier if you were there too late. This was a wonderful place to grow up. I loved the school experience. Joe will tell you our families were very close. After the baseball season was over my dad would come home, and he and Mom would have great get-togethers.

Gwen Ingram was a contestant in the Jeannie With The Light Brown Hair contest at the Stephen Foster Memorial.

We had bonfires on the beach, while crabbing, and the mosquitoes stayed behind the smoke. Sometimes my dad would invite the whole team out to the house for a cookout and have Maine lobsters shipped in. They would all enjoy the feast, but didn't pick up afterwards. Then the 'coons came out, and lobster shells were left scattered all over the street.

Mrs. Phelps took us on bird walks. We learned so much about the Island birds on those walks. It was wonderful. Talk about the good old days. Mosquitoes were so bad that we ran as fast as we could to the water. They would swarm.

Remember that sulfur water? It was an awful smell. I think I smelled like sulfur water until I was 25. Oh yes, stuck in the sand! Who here has not been stuck in the sand?

Jess Ingram bore a remarkable resemblance to Abe Lincoln.

The volunteer fire department was on Oak Avenue. When they rang the siren, everyone would get in their car and go to put out the fire - if they weren't stuck in the sand.

I loved going to Pete Reynard's (restaurant) and having a Shirley Temple. There were mangroves and a little bridge so it looked like Pete Reynard's was on an island. I have wonderful memories of the Youth Center and Roser Church. They were the center of our activities. The Hawkins showed movies at the Youth Center on Saturday nights. The Van Ostenbridges put in a cement slab so we could roller skate. On Saturdays, garage bands would play at the Youth Center.

When Benjie Scanio died, his father Bennie went to the school board and was instrumental in getting property for the baseball field as a memorial to his son. He got professional baseball players to help with the field. Even Warren Spahn was there driving the tractor. They made a high-quality baseball field. The kids had professional baseball players starting them on the way to baseball. It was only the boys, though. The girls called their own games, got our own teams together, and played until dark. The boys were more organized.

I've had 40 years living down my title of Miss Florida. It was a fun time. The Island supported and encouraged me. My mom worked for Dr. Huth and Dr. Deam at that time, so we did not have much money. Lots of people gave me checks and clothes.

I tried to get my classmates Sherrie Tripp, Mary Kaekel, and Joan Gunther to come to the meeting today, and I'm sorry they could not make it.

Daryl Van Ostenbridge: My kids played Little League baseball. Some of the boys in town thought it was a big deal to come out here and play under the lights. It was a Class A field.

Chris Torgeson: We raised a baby raccoon. We gave him Karo syrup and milk until he got big. He followed my brother to the bus stop every morning. My brother would take him to spring training camp in Lakeland where he usually would cause a disturbance. Joe's sister, Patty, and I had a gopher turtle farm. We collected gopher turtles.

Daryl Van Ostenbridge: Sylvia Lundy and I confiscated an old rowboat and paddled out to Passage Key using a broom and dustpan. We came home with magnificent shells and bomb shell fragments. My mother never knew about this. It was a seaworthy boat. We had no life jackets, but it worked well.

Joyce Weersing Williamson: In this old Islander I found information on Humbug Cobb. Allan Haines' column mentions several girls we all know. Daryl and I once dropped aspirin in Cokes trying to get intoxicated. We tried it at the Youth Center. We thought we were drunk. Rumors went around that we had been drinking. All this and more are written in an article in this paper dated 1951.

Here's a picture of me when I was 15, which is embarrassing since I had Mr. Ingram's policeman's cap on and his holster and gun on my hip. I sent the photo to a boyfriend in Michigan thinking I looked so sexy. He wrote back asking what kind of firearm I had on. That was a downer.

I went to the Stephen Foster Memorial on the Suwannee River with a group to hear Gwen Ingram sing in the Jeannie contest. We went to the beach called The Rocks, down from the IGA on Magnolia Avenue, every day after school and on weekends.

On New Year's Eve we'd have a house party. All of us would chip in and rent a house on the beach. The chaperones never showed up.

Linda Ingram: That's because my daddy was up the street watching.

Jack Fiske: It was so hot. Sand flies and mosquitoes were terrible day and night. An attic fan saved us by bringing in cooler air.

I remember when the rum barge sank in a squall off Mullet Key. Prohibition had just been lifted. The barge was sailing from Cuba to Tampa. When it sank, barrels of rum floated into the ship channel and came ashore on the Island between the city pier and the Bayou Marina. Cap Ohlson retrieved one barrel. The Coast Guard offered a bounty of 75-percent of the value of the barrels, which would then be auctioned off in Chicago. Cap turned his in, but lots of people on the Island did not. They opened them on the beach, dipped saucepans in and took plenty of rum home. Cars were hitting the old wooden post office and other obstacles. Drivers had been drinking too much rum.

Mrs. Lena Phelps and her students are shown front of the old school house on Magnolia Avenue, which is now the Island Community Center.

My Childhood on The Island

By Janet Hyde

In the fall of 1940, my mother and father pulled a Silverdome house trailer across the wooden drawbridge from Cortez to Bradenton Beach on Anna Maria Island. As soon as we got off the bridge, we spotted the Pines Trailer Park, and we decided that would be our home for the winter months. We parked the trailer to the right of the unpaved road where it intersected with another road named Spray Street. The park road was a circle lined with pine trees ending with a frame clubhouse with an outdoor shuffleboard court. The clubhouse was a center of activities where bingo, dances and potluck suppers brought the residents together.

We could not wait to inspect the Island. Where Bridge Street met the Gulf beaches there was a rundown outdoor concrete bowling alley. You needed your own pin boy, but the balls were free. I was fascinated.

On Bridge Street, the Island Market, the post office, a bait and tackle shop and a bar were popular spots. To the right on the main road was the Mira-Mar Seafood restaurant. Just past that, out from the beach, within swimming distance (if you were a brave and good swimmer) was a rusty old molasses barge partially submerged. The beach was absolutely gorgeous. The white sand, sunshine and azure water lured us to walk daily. A few frame homes on the main road led to the Gulf Park Hotel and the Gulf Trailer Park.

Several years later my Aunt Betty and Uncle Mac visited and liked what they saw so much they sold their home in Cincinnati and built East O' The Sun Motel, smack dab on the beach. It consisted of three, one-story concrete block cottages and a two-story apartment. They lived on the top floor and rented the rest. After the front cottage was destroyed in a hurricane, they built more cottages behind the two-story one. My father built a concrete, one-floor duplex across the street. I have great memories and a few treasured photos of East O' The Sun.

As we traveled toward Anna Maria (City) we came to a bend in the road where a house sat in a grove of trees. This is where the Cobbs lived. Mrs. Cobb kept the school bus in her driveway and drove the children to the Island school and back home every day. A little way on the right was the lovely home of Kathleen Donovan, the music teacher.

After we got to Anna Maria City, we saw the community building which was used for many activities. When the little frame schoolhouse was too crowded during the winter months, classes were held in the community hall. I recall dressing as a majorette and leading my classmates on to the stage singing, "When Johnny Comes Marching Home." We learned Polish folk dances there.

We saw the Anna Maria Jail, which had no bars, no doors and no prisoners for years, Roser Church, the pier and a saloon. Nearby was Tampa Bay where I swam during the school's swimming lessons and Girl Scout outings. Many good-sized fish were caught on the pier. It housed a small eatery and many boats were tied up there.

Next we drove around the streets and came to a dead-end street where a small frame building was the Anna Maria School. It had a front porch, two bathrooms, a sulfur water drinking fountain and two classrooms. In the school at that time grades one through three were in one room and four through six in the other. I entered grade two with Mrs. Betty Blackburn as my teacher. Her husband, J. Hartley Blackburn, became county school superintendent. There was one row of traditional desks for each class. I really enjoyed my class. I became a good student and was rewarded in grade three for helping the winter enrollment crunch by tutoring first graders in a house across the street. Actually, I was a winter enrollee quite often since we left in April and returned in October. I was a student in eight different elementary schools.

In fourth grade I was in Mrs. Lena Phelps' classroom. There was a row of desks with inkwells. Mrs. Phelps' desk and two recitation benches were in the front of the room. There was a hectograph on the back table. This was a gelatinous pad with a specialized pencil which made copies. I loved to be asked to make copies. An old piano sat against the wall. Each student had a Golden Book of Song and we learned old folk and patriotic songs. Mrs. Phelps let us sing at Roser Church services, and we memorized all three verses of the Star Spangled Banner. I am convinced that my fifty years as a choir singer were inspired right there.

Recess was a fun time. The playground was all sand, and we played softball with home plate by the school steps with Mrs. Phelps as the umpire. Climbing the large tree behind the school and swinging on the bag swing was thrilling for us.

We brought our lunches. I had a lunch box with a thermos since I choked and gagged on the sulfur water. After lunch, Mrs. Phelps would read to us. I really enjoyed hearing "The Yearling" by Marjorie Kinnan Rawlings. We had art classes too, using chalk and crayons. On Fridays students had custodial jobs. Cleaning the bathroom went with the job, but we enjoyed that too. When school was over we all got on the bus and shared the honor of holding the red flag out the window when the bus stopped.

I spent three years at the Island school and made a few friends. I remember Petey Moore and Peggy Blassingame. Peggy was slightly older than me so I did not know her well, but I recall the book, "Island In The Sun" that someone in her family wrote. There were the Nokes girls and my good friend, Carolyn Meeker. She had a brother, Stuart, and I think they started a trash collection business on the Island.

When Pearl Harbor happened I was eight years old. I was apprehensive when I heard about it on the radio, and as time went on I began to understand that it could affect us. I knew Hitler, Mussolini and Hirohito were bad people. During the war the Air Force practiced bombing on Egmont Key. At school we practiced going outside and hiding in the palmettos when the planes went over. Miraculously, no one was bitten by a snake. Once a plane miscalculated and dropped a bomb in Anna Maria City. It did no damage except for a large crater.

Living in our house trailer home in the Pines Trailer Park was a memorable experience, and our neighbors were friendly. Some of them were carnival workers enjoying their time off in the winter. There were Bingo Bill and Mabel, the trapeze artists. They all loved me, and Mabel made me a blue taffeta dress for Easter. Mrs. Burst knitted a short-sleeved sweater for me and used flamingo tongue shells for buttons. Frank Horton brought his granddaughter, Genevieve, south for the winter, and we became playmates. Uncle Frank was 20 years older than my parents. He was a retired policeman from New York, and he and my parents played cards almost every evening. Years later he became my loving stepfather.

The bay was a stone's throw from our trailer, and we kept an outboard motor boat tied to the dock. I had a carefree life climbing pine trees and playing on the docks. When the kids heard the horn sound for the drawbridge to open we raced out to the middle of the bridge and helped turn the crank that opened the bridge sideways. We were fascinated watching the boats go through. My mother did not worry about me getting into trouble. I could ride my bike up and down the Island with my friends. We would jump off the docks into the bay. I was not a good swimmer, but I could stay afloat and I saw such interesting sights when I opened by eyes under water.

My mother and I walked the beach every day. South of 12th Street a large iron pipe spewed sulfur water onto the sand. Shells were varied and plentiful. We gathered scallops, cockle shells, bleeding tooth shells and many others. Especially rare were angel wings, genonas and lions paws. When we rounded the point across from Longboat Key, we walked around South Pass to the bay if it was low tide. There was no bridge to Longboat Key. We preferred live shells because they were shiny and more colorful. Most shells we took home to remove the mussel. A large group of fiddler crabs made holes in the sand flats. I liked watching the male fiddler raise his claw when the female passed by. We took quarts of coquinas home and my mother made soup. She convinced me coquina soup was a delicacy, so I ate it.

I had a marine education. The men fished daily for our supper. If they didn't catch fish we had to rely on canned dried beef or Spam. In the evening we went shrimping after dark. The men donned rubber waders and dragged a 60-foot net along the bottom. Mom and I would pick the shrimp out of the net and put them into a metal pail by lantern light. We never ate the shrimp. They were used for bait and some were sold to the boathouse in Cortez. We found eels, octopuses, seahorses and lots of fish. Raccoons stood very close to steal the shrimp out of the bucket.

Mom was hooked. She preserved all living creatures in quart jars of formaldehyde and stored them under the trailer. She donated all her creatures to the science department at Richfield Springs High School in New York. Mom became interested in making shell jewelry. She used everything. She painted a nasty face on a horseshoe crab shell and called it Hirohito. One time, she discovered a dead porpoise and made a necklace from its teeth.

I fought a war of my own with the mosquitoes. I was pale and skinny, and even though I wore citronella constantly I was a mass of mosquitoes bites. Someone found DDT to be effective, and they sprayed the park at night while we were sleeping.

As I think back on my days living on Anna Maria Island, I know I learned a great deal. Out of the eight grade schools I attended it is obvious to me I was taught more and better in the little one-room schoolhouse by Mrs. Phelps than any other teacher in my life. In addition to the basic subjects, I learned respect and responsibility. As my life went on, I remained a good student with high grades. I graduated in the top ten-percent in a class of 480 and spent three years in nurses training, graduating with a cash award for high student performance. I passed the state boards in 1954 and began an exciting 31-year career as a registered nurse.

My husband and I will celebrate our 50th wedding anniversary soon. We have three grown children and seven grandchildren. Back in the '60s we took our children to Anna Maria Island. We went over the new concrete bridge. The old Cortez Bridge was half gone, and the remainder had been turned into a fishing pier. The kids enjoyed fishing and heard many tales of the old days. In 1986, we went to Siesta Key, and drove north to Longboat Key. I was amazed. When I lived on the Island there was no development on Longboat Key and we could only get there by boat. We drove north on Anna Maria Island. The old tanker wreck was missing off of Bradenton Beach. Change is difficult for an aging lady, so I began to sing the song Mrs. Phelps taught us:

Anna Maria, isle of the sea,
Anna Maria, all hail to thee
Home of the happy, the brave and the free
Beautiful Anna Maria.

We are a family of committed Christians, and I want to thank the Lord for directing my life to Anna Maria Island. J. Hyde 5/10/2004

Stories by Historian

By Jack B. Leffingwell

Uncle Ike lives up in Parrish, known to be a mendacious liar, he now and then tells the truth. He swears this is a true story:

Uncle Ike fired up his foul old pipe, which he lovingly called his gumbucket and we began to talk of old times. The subject of fishing came up and I asked the old gentleman if he had ever heard of the giant octopus that inhabits the old wreck in the Gulf off the Mira Mar pavilion.

"Yep," replied Ike. "He ain't got but seven laigs, he got foul with the propeller of a fish boat and lost one, when he was young. But, let me tell you about the time the gov-ment hired me and Capt. Charlie Moore to chase loggerhead turtles off Passage Key so the birds would have room to nest.

"You see them old loggerheads was so numerous that in laying season they practically covered the island and the poor birds was fluttering and flying around trying to find a place to set down and lay their aigs."

"Hold on Ike," I said. "We were discussing an octopus."

"As I was saying," continued the old man, "Me and Charlie was hired to chase off the turtles and it shore was keeping us bumping. Every time we would chase off a turtle or two more would crawl ashore. We finally licked them. We brought a bottle of turpentine and made a couple swabs and every time we would tackle a turtle we would apply a dose of turps where it would do the most good and man oh man, you should see those critters take for Pass-a-Grille and points north.

"Here's a true story about the octopussy. Way back yonder about 1890 me and a fellow named Dick Harris was shark fishing down at Longboat Pass. One day we set a line in that deep hole on the west side of Jewfish Key. We was setting and fighting skeeters when we got a bite and he sure was a sockdolger.

"We hauled and hauled for about an hour, then he gave up and we hauled him out on the bank. No, Jack, it warn't no shark. It was the durndest, biggest octopussy I ever did see. The critter had arms 20-feet long and his head was as big as a flour barrel. As I said, we got him up on the bank and there he sat, hissing at us and spitting ink.

"Every time we went near him he would begin waving his laigs and we would retreat. This kept on for about two hours. Then the octopussy reached out with a couple of his laigs and fastened himself to a mangrove stump. Me and Dick grabbed us a couple clubs and charged him. Right at that minute the durn thing jerked the mangrove stump out of the ground and using it as a club killed us both. Goodbye, Jack." The old man jumped out of his chair and made for the door. *Anna Maria Key News, Nov. 30, 1950*

It's mysterious music, said Jack Leffingwell. May, June and July are the only months of the year it can be heard up the Manatee River and then, only in the dark of the moon.

What caused the strange phenomenon has never been explained. It was a humming sound, like that of an Aeolian harp or the hum of a telephone pole. It emanated from the water and often times accompanied by a distinct vibration which at times would cause a large boat to tremble.

I cannot guarantee the music will perform, but I have never failed to encounter it when all conditions are right. You cannot hear it from the shore. You must be in a boat and go in the dark of the moon. Just before moonrise is the best time. *Anna Maria Key News May 25, 1950*

The Magic Of Anna Maria Island

Chris Kachudas came to the Island in 1930. Doctors were sure he would not live long. There were three reasons why he grew strong and lived: his wife, Norma, his daughter, Connie and the health-restoring climate of peaceful Anna Maria Island.

Bob and Connie Hoffman, on right, with Island friends, Janie and Free Hiscox.

Within five years, Chris was busy in the real estate business and civic affairs on the Island. He helped get the first street lights and a bus to the Island on a regular schedule. Chris could have become wealthy, but a staunch sense of honor prevented him from acquiring land by paying pennies in defaulted taxes to acquire properties.

Harry Varley, editor of *The Islander* in 1952, said without Chris the newspaper would not have existed. "He brought us to the Island, found us a place to live, when we had not seen a vacancy sign for miles, cared for us when we were sick and some years later selected the house we live in today."

By the '50s, Chris had slowed down. His real estate business was managed by his daughter, Connie, and her husband, Robert Hoffman. Bob and Connie purchased a house on Avenue F in Holmes Beach in 1946 and drew up plans for a home and office complex. Bob presented plans to Kay Rowlett, who turned them down since he had never built a two-story Florida home. Aaron Van Ostenbridge, Sr. agreed to be the builder. The house was on Gulf Drive, just south of the original Duffy's Tavern near the public beach.

Silent screen star, Wilna Hervey, was over six feet tall.

The Hoffmans had three children. Bob was honored to be chosen to portray Hernando Desoto in the annual DeSoto Celebration in 1969. The firm of Kachudas and Hoffman flourished until Bob and Connie retired in 1981.

Few people who live on the Island can say they were born here. Mrs. Thomas P. Murphy first saw the light of day at her grandfather's homestead near the North Point, which was later named Bean Point after her grandfather. Her mother was Mary Bean Hall, and her famous grandfather was George Emerson Bean, who was the first Anna Maria Island homesteader in 1893. She attended the first school on the Island at the site of the present Island Community Center on Magnolia Avenue. At the age of six she left the Island, but the family came back to vacation. After marrying Thomas Patrick Murphy, she lived in Santa Barbara, California. In 1952 she persuaded her husband to move to the Island permanently. They bought a house in Sportsman's Harbor, near the Catholic church in Holmes Beach, and soon became active in community affairs and Roser Church activities.

When anyone falls in love with Anna Maria Island it becomes a faithful unto death affair. Sometimes it was love at first sight. Such was the case of F. P. Stanley in November of 1952. He bought land and joined the Holmes Beach developers and opened an insurance office in the Island Shopping Center.

A silent screen star lived on the Island in the '60s. Wilna Hervey was over six-feet tall and best known for her portrayal of Powerful Katrinka in the Toonerville Trolley movie series. She and her close friend, Nan Mason, wintered on the Island beginning in 1934 and in 1960 purchased a home at 112 Willow Avenue where she and Miss Mason lived from the end of October until May of each year. They summered at Miss Mason's farm in Bearsville, N.Y.

When Wilna was a girl, her family moved to Far Rockaway, New York, and it was there that she got her start in movies. Miss Mason, whose father, Dan Mason, played the motorman in the Toonerville series, said when the originator of the series saw Wilna he said, "My gosh, you are the original Katrinka."

The Whittaker childrens' playground was the water surrounding the Island.

She played the role of a powerful woman who could lift the trolley back onto the tracks or pull clothesline poles out of the ground. She made 48, two-reel Toonerville films, and from 1921 to 1923 she teamed with Dan Mason, as he conceived plots built around her strength. She played in the Plum Center Comedies directed by the young Frank Capra. After four years in movies, Miss Hervey and Miss Mason bought a farm in New York and developed it into a colony for artists. Miss Hervey became an accomplished artist and, after moving to the Island, became active in Longboat Key, Sarasota and Bradenton art associations, taking many prizes for her work in enamel on copper.

Miss Mason recalled the first house they rented on the Island in 1934 on the end of Willow Avenue. They paid $25 a month. "We paid $1 for a maid for three hours. In 1936, Miss Hervey bought a new car. She wanted a garage to put it in, so they found a beach house for $40 a month.

Growing Up on A Houseboat

Dorothy Whittaker, on right, and her friend Elsie Prothero.

Dorothy Raymond Whittaker was the grandniece of 1895 homesteaders, Sam and Annie Cobb. She was seven when her family moved from Cortez to Anna Maria Island, where her father had grown up. In 1924, her father, Elmer "Sugarfoot" Raymond, bought a houseboat. It had no engine so he had it towed by barge to his Uncle Sam's boatyard. The Raymonds' water-borne home added four people to the small colony at Cobb's Corners, in the central part of Holmes Beach.

"The houseboat was a great big thing," Dorothy recalled. "It had a deep bilge and was roomy for a houseboat. We had a wood stove, a built-in toilet and rainwater barrels. The beds and kitchen were partitioned with curtains. The large entertainment room was also the dining room.

"My brother Steve and I would come home from the Anna Maria School, which was on Magnolia Avenue in Anna Maria, and before we were off the bus we'd start undressing. Everything was off by the time we got to the gangplank except the bare essentials. We'd grab our bathing suits, pull them on and jump off the porch into the water.

Shirley Brownell and the plane, her stepfather, Charlie Whittaker, built for her.

"The bay was our front yard. The flats went out for miles to the steamer channel. All the shorelines were covered with mangroves, and the grass flats went on for miles. On the bayside, east of Gulf Drive, everything grew abundantly. You could drop a tomato down by the bay in the grass and it would grow. The other side of the road, the Gulf side, was all prairie. There were sea oats, cactus, Spanish bayonets, beautiful blue lupine, gopher holes and rabbits everywhere you looked.

"I remember we could walk out to the beach and look in both directions and not see a soul. We had to slide down a high bluff with sea oats to get to the water. The beach went out for a quarter-mile, and we would get tired walking through the sand to the water. But it was not all paradise.

"We had mosquitoes and sand flies, and had to paint our screens with kerosene to keep them out. Some would crawl right through the screens. We'd keep smudge pots going all the time. Rattlesnakes were all over the Island. I don't think I ever went off the boat that I didn't run into one. We always watched where we walked. There were stingrays in the water. But it was all part of living on the Island, and we loved it."

"Sug" Raymond and his granddaughter, Shirley Brownell.

Dorothy's father was a fisherman who fished for himself as well as on a crew out of Cortez. He taught Steve and Dorothy to fish, and they would go out with him often. They would take their catches to Cortez to sell.

"Dad made my brother and me a boat and we could go all over the bay, but we were not allowed to go in the main channel. A lot of my boating experiences are in the book I wrote. The descriptions in *Angels In The Swamp*, such as snakes falling into the boat, are authentic."

Dorothy and Steve spent their summers harvesting shellfish at low tide. Every day they would pedal their bikes to Anna Maria City to make deliveries to regular customers. They caught mainly scallops and how the tourists loved them. They got 50-cents a quart for small white scallops, not bad for Depression times.

"It has been said fishermen and farmers fared better than most during the Depression years because they had food on the table. We found this to be true, although with money so tight, we had our problems too. The most widely used medium of exchange in those days was bartering, not hard cash. We had no competition selling shellfish because most of the youngsters on the Island had no access to the backwaters like we did, or they were reluctant to put their feet in the water, where dreaded stingrays were prevalent.

"Shell fishing made an important contribution to our family income, though it hardly seemed like work to us. Our mother put aside the money we earned and doled out only enough for one small ice cream cone for each of us during our deliveries.

"The rest of the money went toward our visits to the dentist and for school clothes in the fall. My brother and I felt fortunate to be able to contribute to the family. It made us feel important and part of the solution to our problems. If nothing else, the Great Depression brought families like ours closer together."

About the time Dorothy went to Bradenton High School, her father acquired the nickname of Sugarfoot, after spilling a sack of sugar while unloading a boatload of supplies. He decided to build a house on 52nd Street, about a block from the Gulf. When the family moved in, Dorothy wanted to know why he didn't build right on the beach.

"We're close enough," he said. He knew the unpredictable ways of the weather. Dorothy and her husband, Charlie, lived in that same house until their deaths.

In 1993, Dorothy wrote *Angels in the Swamp*, a book in the American History Series by Walker and Company. The book took more than ten years to complete, and she gave credit to Island writer Wyatt Blassingame and his wife, Jeanne, for encouraging her to persevere.

The novel, set in 1932 on Florida's west coast, draws the reader into the lives of two runaways and an older teenager. They meet by chance in dismal and treacherous Crane's Bog and travel 100 miles to deserted Pelican Island. Dorothy used her knowledge of early Florida to enhance the story. Her description of the lush, mysterious wilderness captures the reader's imagination. Tension mounts when snakes fall from the trees in the dark, dense mangrove swamps and rattlers float by ready to strike. The accounts of the sea's bounty, such as fishing, shelling and using nature's materials for shelter, protection and food could only be told by one who had experienced that life on the Island years before. Dorothy autographed her books at the newly established Island Historical Museum in 1992. In the book she gave to the museum she wrote, "With love and support to the Island Historical Society." This was her first novel, however, she penned two successful "how-to" books, *How To Cook and Catch Shellfish* and *Stalking The Stone Crab*, both published in 1972.

Charlie and Dorothy Whittaker, in the center, with John and Daryl Van Ostenbridge.

Snippets From The Islander

December 11, 1952: The Bradenton couple who dove through the Cortez Bridge railing and went swimming forgot one trifling detail. They forgot to take off their car.

August 13, 1953: James Clifford Hardy, 22, of Bradenton decided to go for a ride in his car last Sunday. It was a little early, 3 a.m., when he hit the old, rickety, wooden Cortez Bridge. His car went out of control as he entered the Cortez end of the bridge and took 75-feet of rail with it before it came to rest in 22-feet of water.

Hardy got out and climbed onto the bridge and walked to the nearby trailer camp. In the meantime, Bradenton divers were summoned to search for bodies in the car and fire trucks from the Bradenton and Bradenton Beach fire departments stood by with emergency equipment. They soon learned no one was in the car and Hardy was finding new friends in the trailer park.

August 21, 1958: Ken Fellows stopped by *The Islander* office and informed the editor someone had just thrown a baby off the Longboat Key Bridge. He said the baby had long hair and had screamed on its way into the deep water of the Pass. Upon further investigation, the police found there was no baby and no screams. The final verdict from deputy sheriffs, Adams and Ford, was that somebody threw a bag of garbage from the bridge. Though the rumors were as tenuous as a spider's web, all the Island forces went into action. What an Island!

May 15, 1958: There was a quick, unpredictable blow last Sunday and a large object sailed across the Island. The weather station announced the radar screen was not working so no advance warning could be given. Islanders were glad it was not a 90-mile an hour hurricane, but just a 60-mile windstorm.

The wind picked up a large, yellow, rubber raft from Cobb's Marine Works in Holmes Beach and sent it flying high over the Island. This plea was issued by the Cobbs: "Please let us know if you find the raft."

June 23, 1955: Teenagers who lived on the Island, Cortez or Bradenton were invited to the Holmes Beach Yacht Club from 8:30 to midnight every Thursday night for dancing. They were encouraged to bring their favorite records. Pete Reynard, congenial restaurateur and former professional dancer, gave free rumba lessons for half an hour at each dance. The dances were chaperoned and no bathing suits or shorts were allowed.

January 13, 1955: Some Islanders who moved from the north to Florida wondered what Christmas decorations would be appropriate for the Sunshine State. Lyman Christy, who spent many years in South American countries, borrowed an old Spanish custom and decorated his Spanish bayonet plant, on Palm Avenue, with egg shells stuck on the needle-sharp points of the plant. His neighbors contributed eggs shells they had saved for weeks.

October 7, 1954: Lyman Christy excitedly reported seeing a quail with six offspring crossing the lot across from his house in Anna Maria. He said they were the first he had seen in many years. He was glad the Island was a bird sanctuary and firearms could not be used within the city limits.

September 22, 1955: Children playing on the patio of the Rod and Reel Pier Motel heard loud noises and thought someone was shooting off fireworks. No, a fire had started in one of the units. A tackle box lying on a Bermuda couch had caught fire and in the box were shells for a 22-rifle. When they became hot they shot around the room. What started the fire? Spontaneous combustion was charged.

Harold Igo, a Yale graduate and director of the Island Players, owned a pet raccoon.

This story is by Mrs. Fred Rolle who lived on Beach Avenue in Anna Maria in 1972:

"My neighbor in back of my house was Harold Igo, a graduate of Yale and director of the Island Players. One morning we heard a tremendous explosion. Our lights and air conditioning went off. The electric company came out and told me someone had touched the 15,000-volt wire in the transformer and it had blown a fuse. At the foot of the transformer pole we saw a tailless raccoon that appeared to be dead. By the time the FPL repairman put on his spikes to climb the pole the raccoon vanished. Later in the morning, Harold Igo came to my door asking if I knew what caused his pet raccoon to lose its tail. He had just cooked a chicken for his unusual pet. A few months later the same thing happened, but this time the raccoon was dead. Harold came over again and asked me to pray for the raccoon. I was shocked at the request, but said nothing. Every week he visited me and asked if I had been praying for his deceased raccoon. Finally in desperation, I said I had prayed. I hope the Lord forgave me for that lie."

Startling headlines were in a late '60s newspaper: "Police Chief Shoots Himself." Snooks Adams was mowing his yard when the mower ran over a bullet which went straight into his foot.

February 6,1958: Dr. Roy Gunther had a parakeet that would not talk, but was very fond of music. When Mary Gunther played the piano, the bird perched on her head. The trouble was the bird only appeared to like Chopin. Dr. Gunther bought a bird-lesson record to try to improve the bird's mind and encourage him to talk. When they played the record over and over the parakeet ruffled its feathers and flew away or went to sleep.

May 5, 1958: The Lions met. They ate! No Speakers, no guests, no business worth mentioning.

May 15, 1958: Virgil Mora picked up garbage in Holmes Beach and Anna Maria. He was supposed to pick up just what was in cans, but for no extra charge rubbish near the cans was also picked up. One lady left a package of laundry next to the can. The boys put it in the truck. Luckily, the loss was discovered in time.

An Island man was eating watermelon and took out his false teeth and wrapped them in a Kleenex. His wife threw the Kleenex, with the teeth, away. They had already been consigned to the dump when Virgil was notified. He and a helper spent most of a day searching in the dump, to no avail. Virgil Mora said he might be compelled to make a rigid rule that only trash in cans be collected.

July 23, 1953: Miss Carolyn Meeker is going to marry Bruce L. Meeks. In honor of her impending marriage Carolyn was given a bridal shower at the bayside home of Mrs. C. M. Bayless. Many Meeks and Meekers attended. Carolyn could not wait until her name was Carolyn Meeker Meeks.

September 8, 1960: Three Island couples were lost at sea. Mr. and Mrs. George Norwood (that's me), Mr. and Mrs. Bob Hynton and Mr. and Mrs. John Van Ostenbridge went for an evening cruise in a 16-foot outboard motorboat leaving the Island about 7:30 p.m. When they failed to return by 1:30 a.m., Daryl Van Ostenbridge's brother, Bob Hedgcock who was babysitting, called the Coast Guard. The Coast Guard helicopter sighted the drifters at 3 a.m. about two miles off the North Point of the Island. They had been stranded because of motor trouble. This was the account in The Islander.

This is the real story. The boat belonged to John, and he forgot to bring extra gas. Yes, the boat ran out of gas, and he was too embarrassed to tell the truth. While drifting in the Gulf, we heard a loud noise coming closer and closer. It was the Coast Guard helicopter. When it was directly overhead it felt like we were in the middle of a hurricane. The tumultuous wind and waves were frightening. Then a rope came down from the helicopter. John, the boat captain, said, "I'm not going up!" We finally decided the helicopter pilot meant to fasten the rope to the boat. But, we wondered, what if they pulled the boat out of the water. As it turned out, the plane pulled the boat closer to the Island, and Bob and Aaron, John's brother, towed the outboard to shore.

September 15, 1955: Jungle hammocks were the latest craze among boys of the Island in 1955. They were cleverly designed hammocks with mosquito-proof nets. The boys preferred to sleep in the unique swings instead of ordinary beds which were fine for old, tired people, but without the appeal of the jungle hammock. In brave defiance of wild animals, they had the joy of sleeping under the stars.

December 15, 1955: Though it was cold and rainy, 200 members of Wally Byam's trailer caravan came to the Island as guests of the Chamber of Commerce and were served a fish and hush puppy dinner at the Public Beach pavilion. It rained, but they were not concerned. That was just one of the hazards of the road. Charles Schaldenbrand, Island resident, was a member of Wally's caravan and had gone to Mexico with them on a recent trek. He was responsible for having them visit the Island. A good time was had by all.

July 10, 1958: Charlie Thompson from Ohio found that collecting shells on Anna Maria beaches was a pleasant diversion. He had a special rig for washing shells and set himself up on the south end at night with a harvest of 12 bushels. Sheriff Paul Ford spotted Thompson's abundance of shells and gave Charlie an invitation to municipal court on the charge of violating an ordinance that prohibits taking shells and sand in large quantities from the beach. Charlie did not know about the law, but ignorance of the law was no excuse.

September 10, 1953: Fortunately for two women who could not swim, Monroe Lee was surf casting in the Gulf in front of his home when he heard cries for help. He spied two figures out in deep waters gesticulating wildly. Luckily, he was a husky and powerful swimmer. He plunged in, swam to the women, and was able to get them to shore. The elder of the women was violently ill, so Dr. Ed Huth, who lived nearby, was summoned and administered first aid to both women. The elder woman was taken to Memorial Hospital. Both women recuperated.

Monroe Lee, a Yale graduate, was a retired cattle rancher in Colorado and an expert fisherman. He and his wife, Josephine, had been living on the Island for three years.

June 27, 1957: This is a believe it or not tale. Betty McKinney of East O' The Sun was asking if anyone had lost a seal. "A what?" was their reply. She explained the kind of seal that balanced a ball on its nose, blew a trumpet and performed in the circus. "There's one in the Gulf just off-shore," she told *The Islander* editor. "It comes in close and barks the way seals do." Before the photographer could get to the spot darkness had fallen and the seal had disappeared by the next morning. The end of the story was that the large white heron, that had been hanging around the editor's house, stood just outside the open window not five feet away, and appeared to be listening intently to the long phone conversation about the seal.

December 18, 1958: "If Mambo, Pete Reynard's dachshund, jumped in your car or boat near the Yacht Club please call Pete," *The Islander* ad read. Mambo's mother was unhappy, but her sadness was nothing

Pete and Eleanor Reynard enjoyed cruising with their dachshunds.

compared to Pete's and Eleanor's. A liberal reward was offered with no questions asked.

June 4, 1953: It had been two weeks since young Dan Huth lost his Arbalete spear gun and he was still hoping, through some fortuitous circumstance, it would be returned to him.

He lost the gun in a most unusual way. He was riding his motor scooter, with his cherished weapon aboard, when suddenly the chain on his scooter snapped. As he dismounted to inspect the damage, a heavy leather strap swung out of the window of a passing car. He was struck on the side of the head and knocked unconscious.

When he came to, he started to push his scooter home, forgetting his gun. Again, the same car passed and he was given another blow with the strap. By that time he wanted to get home as soon as possible. The next morning he went back to the spot of the accident, and his gun was gone. Anyone seeing the gun was asked to call Danny Huth immediately. Everyone knows a gun is a boy's most important possession.

This was an Associated Press release that appeared in the *New York Herald Tribune* on November 18,1952: Anna Maria Island, It Happened On The Beach: Douglas Seba, 11, was kicking his football to Dale Alderton, 12, when it veered into the Gulf of Mexico. Four or five dolphins playing offshore made a beeline to the ball. They batted it among themselves with their heads, all the time rolling, diving and coming up to bounce it again. The dolphins finally disappeared and so did the purloined football.

October 9, 1958: Mary Andreen, daughter of the owners of Andreens' Island Sundries, wrote a letter in 1956, put it in a bottle and threw it into the Gulf. More than two years elapsed before she received a letter from England.

"I am writing to say on Oct.1, 1958 I picked up your bottle on the seafront at Angmering-on-Sea, Sussex, England. Your note had been wandering around for about two years. You asked me to write and tell you where I live." Following an informative letter, the writer asked Mary to write and send a photo.

It was signed: Gerald Andrews, East Preston, Nr. Littlehampton, Sussex, England. We wonder if that was the beginning of an international friendship.

August 22, 1957: A tourist on the Island, Victor Woodward of Chicago, was very tired. He had been driving under difficulties. Trees, people and cars were getting in his way, even the highway would not stay where it belonged, so he parked his car in the middle of the road and lay down outside the car, and went to sleep. When the deputy sheriff was called to the scene, he could not arrest the man for drunken driving, but he did arrest Victor for parking his car in the road and for being intoxicated. The fine for illegal parking was $100, and for the rest, $40. Quite a price to pay for napping on the main road.

December 18, 1958: A shopping party, for men only, was held on December 19 at LeAnn's Dress Shop in the Holmes Beach Shopping Center. The idea was that the men should come to the shop and buy Christmas presents for their wives, daughters and sweethearts. The genius behind the idea was LeAnn, who had a sizable list of what many of the women on the Island wanted, complete with sizes and colors. Not as a special inducement, but strictly as selling propaganda, beautiful girls modeled bathing suits, lingerie and dresses in the shop.

The date conflicted with a meeting of the Island Garden Club, but the women who ran the meeting arranged to have a short business meeting so the men could depart for LeAnn's

December 9,1954: W. W. McKinney invented a grill-in-a-wheelbarrow. Using a few cement blocks and half-inch metal bars, "Mac" could wheel it to any of his tenants cottages, so one grill served all. The patent had not been applied for and the name not determined. The McKinney Wheel-It-Where-You-Want-It was suggested.

December 4, 1958: Here are two excerpts from the column entitled Mish-Mash in *The Islander*: A man was floating on a rubber mattress in the waters off the Public Beach. The sun was warm, the waters calm so he closed his eyes and dozed off. All of a sudden he felt a thud on his body. A large fish jumped out of the water and landed with a thwack on his stomach. He was so scared he quickly paddled to shore and went home.

A fine-looking woman was walking along Gulf Drive in a slight drizzle. In one hand she held a leash. At the end of the leash was a magnificent boxer. In the other hand she held a fly swatter. Mosquitoes were numerous.

August 30, 1957: Mrs. G. E. "Lula" Colman, the daughter of the first homesteader, George Emerson Bean, is observing her 93rd birthday. The grand old lady was guest of honor at a party given by her good friends in the Anna Maria Readers Club, at the home of Mrs. J. E. Raymond in Holmes Beach. Her daughter, Marion, was one of the many attendees.

May 22,1952: Wade Botkin and George Harris, Jr. were skiing off Cobb's Corner in the bay when suddenly the gas tank in the boat sprung a leak. George was on skis and Wade was steering the boat. They were about half a mile from shore when a bolt slipped out of the gas tank and the trouble began. Wade stuck his finger in the leak and George took over the controls. The gas kept flowing and soon flames erupted. Wade dove into the water and George followed. George made a valiant effort to save the boat, but Wade said it would explode so they let it go down. Asa Pillsbury of the Pillsbury Dragline Company saved the day by hauling the boys and boat to shore. The boys were fine and there was little damage to the boat.

March 18, 1954: P. D. Wright, former mayor of Anna Maria City, accused the editor of stealing papers from the city office. The Islander Publishing Company issued a statement saying they would pay $5,000 to him or anyone else with proof that the editor stole a single paper from the city office.

December 1952: It is unclear when the Never Be Lonely Club started, but the basic thought was no one should be eating dinner alone on Thanksgiving and Christmas. The club was open to all with each paying for his or her own dinner. We do not know the place, but it was assumed the dinners were held in homes of the "lonely." There were 14 at the Christmas dinner in 1952. Wine flowed freely and the spirit of friendship prevailed. Roger Stonehouse, when asked to say a few words, said, "Many years ago, a few of us, guided by mutual affection, drifted into dining together on Sundays. Then it was inevitable we should celebrate the glad days, Thanksgiving, Christmas and Easter together. We never had organization, officers, or speeches, just a vast goodwill. The joy of that fellowship was so rich that the idea was born to open our circle to any and all, that they might know they were welcome here, where love is and no heart is lonely."

July 3, 1958: An unidentified man drove from Bradenton to the Island in a 1958 Chevrolet. He had imbibed too much and when he decided it was time to go home he took a short cut. He drove down South Bay Boulevard and just kept going. After running into a couple of trees, he got stuck in the sand. If he had kept going he would have taken on water. The thoughtless driver was stuck with a $50 fine and whatever it cost to repair the car.

All these stories are proof that truth is stranger than fiction.

Ernie Smith, Bus Driver Extraordinary

Ernie drove the only bus from Bradenton to Anna Maria Island in 1953 and his kindness and extra duty services were known to thousands. He stopped anywhere, helped children and old ladies off and on the bus, carried packages to houses, mailed rush letters to town, took packages back and forth, chaperoned busloads of teenagers to football games, shopped for people and made bank deposits. In other words, Ernie did any and all services within his power and schedules.

Jim Zerby was the most colorful mayor in the history of Holmes Beach.

Once he helped disarm a would-be murderer of a woman about to board his bus. The man received a 10-year sentence. On another occasion, Ernie saw two women in trouble in the surf in Bradenton Beach. He stopped the bus, jumped in the water and dragged the unconscious women out of the water. When neighbors came to help, Ernie climbed back in the bus, soaking wet, and caught up with his schedule.

Friends tried to nominate him for the Carnegie medal for bravery, but no one could identify the women he saved or find witnesses, so the nomination failed. He deserved the medal, but Ernie had something more important – the affection of hundreds of residents and visitors.

Jim Zerby Loved Island Life

At a meeting, held in the early 1990s, Anna Maria Island Historical Society members enjoyed hearing Jim Zerby reminisce about his years on the Island.

"In the early '30s, shortly after I arrived on the Island, I became city clerk in Bradenton Beach. The city hall was a storefront and my desk was by the front window. For air conditioning I would open the window. Every morning at 9 a.m. a brown "Heinz 57" dog named Tag would put his paws on the windowsill and sing his song. I brought biscuits for him every day. He was the nicest dog I ever knew.

"It was quite a tumultuous time to be city clerk. I was fired seven or eight times because I felt they were not doing things right, and of course they didn't agree with me. It was a tough go.

"I lived on 13th Street, and late at night, when cars were coming out from the mainland, you could hear those boards on the old wooden bridge rattling. It was kind of eerie, but an old familiar sound like the Gulf, always rolling. Most people don't realize the Gulf is always moving. I wasn't aware of it until one time I left the Island and it took me a week to get to sleep without the Gulf and bridge noises. It was surprising to know the surf was my lullaby.

"Then I moved to Holmes Beach and became involved with the Island Players. Director Harold Igo asked me if I would read for a part in a play. I said no, I was not interested. He insisted, so I did and then I got the bug. I acted in some of the plays and then directed Bus Stop, Man In The Dog Suit and several others. I also became involved with the Manatee Players. Those were exciting times for me.

"You didn't need newspapers, news by word of mouth worked great. I got my news from Rich's Drugstore in the Holmes Beach Shopping Center. One time I was sitting there having a cup of coffee, complaining to the guy sitting next to me about an Airwick I bought that didn't work. 'It's the most lousy stuff I ever saw,' I said. 'Shhhh,' he said, 'the man sitting next to me invented it.' The next week I got a case of Airwick.

"One day sitting around the marina yakking and a man kept staring at me. Finally I asked him if we had met somewhere. By the process of elimination we discovered he was the sea captain of a tanker in the Mediterranean that picked me up after I had been shot down in the war.

"Another incident happened when a fisherman landed a huge jewfish off the old wooden Cortez Bridge. He was hollering and raising cane trying to get someone to help him get it out of the water. We finally had to get a wrecker to pull it up. The fisherman was a little guy, weighed about 120-pounds, and that fish weighed more than 600-pounds.

"We were sitting around the marina, with a black setter dog named Midnight, drinking 'grape juice' that had been in the jug too long, when we heard a splash off the dock. We thought the dog had fallen in, but discovered he had caught a fish. He swam to shore and put the fish at his owner's feet, so we cleaned it, cooked it and ate it.

"Then there was this little white cat named, Damn It. Everyone asked how on earth he got that name. The lady who owned him said he liked to jump on the couch and she would holler, 'Damn it, get off the couch.' The name stuck. He liked rose petals, and my neighbor raised beautiful roses. She would put the roses in a vase on the table and when the petals started to fall, Damn It would eat them. It got to the point that she would just put them in a bowl and let the cat eat them.

"There was my friend, Roger, the squirrel. He would crawl up my shirt onto my shoulder and go into all my pockets looking for corn and peanuts. He was a great fellow and would scamper to the roof of the garage, and when I walked by, he'd jump on my shoulder.

"One time, while I was mayor of Holmes Beach, we got a call from the school. They had snakes. Mike Grace, the policeman, called me and asked me to go to the school with him. I told him no, I didn't like snakes. He said he didn't either, but something had to be done. Even though I was scared of snakes I went with him. A rattlesnake, about five-feet long, was trapped in the corner of one of the classrooms. Mike had a wire hoop and got it around the snake's neck and we carried it out. An Islander reporter took our picture with Mike holding the wire hoop around the snake's head and I held the tail. We were both a dark shade of grey. We hated that snake.

"When I was mayor the Holmes Beach Council did not exactly agree with me. If I said white all five of them would say black. I was the municipal judge at one time, and one of the rumors flying around was that I was using city funds to buy judge's robes. This was not true. I would not be caught dead in a judge's robe.

"I wanted to build sidewalks, and the council didn't go for it. I found out the government would help, but I felt anytime you take something from the government there were strings attached. I figured out a way to get labor from them, and my city crew built miles of sidewalks. That was one of the things I am most proud of. Many people thanked me for the sidewalks. It's hard to remember what I am most proud of during those four years. I had the police communications building constructed out of the old sewer plant. Most of the materials were donated and it had three-foot thick walls.

"To relax I would go eight to ten miles out in the Gulf in my boat. The Australian pines along the coast were my land markers. Now the storms have taken most of the trees down, and developers have taken the rest. Hurricane Donna in 1960 took out a lot of them. I lost my boat in that storm. I had moved it to Cobb's Marina on the bay and tied six, one-inch lines to it. Those lines snapped like strings, and the 32-foot boat beat itself on the seawall dock and sunk in the bay. Many pine trees were lost on Coquina Beach from 15th Street to the south end, and several small rental cottages in Bradenton Beach were swept into the Gulf."

Zerby closed his talk to the historical society by saying, "People are the fabric that makes the Island what it is. We need a dedicated group to keep the Island just as it is now."

Mort Clark Arrives

In 1955 Morton Clark, a retired business man from Lima, Ohio, arrived on the Island with some radical ideas about development. He purchased lots from 69th to 70th Streets on Holmes Beach Boulevard which was one of the worse mosquito breeding mangrove swamps on the Island. He turned it into a beautiful expanse of white sand, large trees and two artificial, spring-fed lakes. The two lakes were excavated and connected by a channel. The water came from a well 78-feet deep and natural springs which existed in the lakes. The water was 10-feet deep, except at one end where a gradually sloping beach was made for children. The swimming was fine, and the waters were stocked with mullet, redfish and trout.

The interesting feature of the development was every lot owner automatically became a member of the Aquatic Club, which elected its own governing body and controlled the use of the lakes. The development, named Clark Spring Lakes Estates, consisted of 12-acres. The Clarks built their home on the peninsular between the two lakes. Owners of each lot became stockholders in a company which would hold the lakes in perpetuity.

Marion Colman, on the left, stands with her mother, Lula Colman. Lula was the daughter of George Emerson Bean, the Island's first homesteader.

Early Settler Turns Nonagenarian

Lula Colman, the daughter of the first homesteader, George Emerson Bean, had memorable birthdays every August. She received many cards and gifts, but one card was especially exciting.

It read: "It is a privilege to have the opportunity to extend hearty congratulations and best wishes on the occasion of your 91st birthday. I know Friday, August 19, will be a day of celebration as all Islanders pay tribute to one of their beloved citizens." It was signed by Governor LeRoy Collins.

As a matter of fact, according to her daughter, Marion, the celebration began several days earlier, and the mail box fairly bulged with cards, gifts and letters of congratulations from the three mayors, the Woman's Club, Garden Club, Bradenton Beach Civic Club and Roser Church, all of which she was a charter member. One of the highlights of the day was a birthday dinner at the home of Miriam Murphy, her niece. Even nature joined in by providing the opening of almost forty night-blooming cereus in the Murphys' backyard.

Mrs. Colman had lived on the Island since 1930. She came with her father and lived in a tent near the North Point, which is also known as Bean Point. In 1960, Mrs. Colman celebrated her 96th birthday. She said she had no formula for her longevity, and still took an active interest in Island events. In the '40s, she was a member of the all-woman Anna Maria City Commission and Roser Church, where she was treasurer for a number of years. At 96, she attended Sunday services every week, regardless of the weather.

Mrs. Colman's sister, Mrs. Mary Hall, and her niece, Mrs. Luther Ennis, built a home next door to the Colmans. Mrs. Hall spent her childhood in the family home on the North Point. After her marriage, she lived there for eight years, and four of her five children were born during this time. After moving away, she returned to spend vacations on the Island.

Sherlockians Converge

Pleasant Places of Florida, the local Scion Society of the famed Baker Street Irregulars, held a gathering in Lowe Hall at the Church of the Annunciation in May of 1979. Devotees of Sherlock Holmes from along the west coast of Florida were making their annual trek to the place of the master's namesake, Holmes Beach, where a complete Sherlockian display of assorted incunabula was exhibited.

Following traditions in Sherlock Holmes books, canonical toasts, provided by the Criterion Bar, were proffered and an elegant luncheon was served from Mrs. Hudson's kitchen. Hosting the gathering was the Rev. Dr. Benton Wood, rector of the Holmes Beach Church of the Annunciation

The Rev. Dr. Benton Wood was head of the local chapter of the Baker Street Irregulars.

and head of the local chapter of Baker Street Irregulars. He was to be invested in the Baker Street Irregulars in New York City in January of 1980. The group was founded about 1940 by such noted Sherlockians as Christopher Morley, Franklin Roosevelt and Robert Benchley.

Billie caught a 122-pound jewfish while fishing off of the shores of Bradenton Beach in the '40s. Billie is standing on the right.

Billie Martini, Fisherwoman

Billie Martini grew up as a Navy brat and somewhat of a rebel. She was named Billie because her parents liked the name and was taught at home until she was 11. The family lived in the Philippines, Panama and on the island of Samoa. "My mom taught me using a home study course. When we lived in Samoa and I was supposed to be doing my lessons, I often climbed out the window and went fishing. It's a wonder I learned anything, she said.

Billie began her formal education in San Diego and graduated from San Diego High School. In 1944, her father retired from the service and the family moved to Anna Maria Island, first to Bradenton Beach, and then to Holmes Beach.

Billie worked at various jobs. She was a clerk in the Bradenton Beach drugstore, a bookkeeper and a clerk in the Holmes Beach Post Office. In 1951, she married Bob Martini, and the couple became active in Island life. He was one of the original members of the Bradenton Beach Volunteer Fire Department, a councilman, vice mayor and served as mayor from 1955-1957.

Meanwhile, Billie became a licensed boat captain, took flying lessons and helped build the family home. She once caught a 122-pound jewfish while fishing off the shores of Bradenton Beach. Quite a feat since she only weighed 98-pounds. "It was a real fight to bring that fish in," she said. "It took two hours and ten minutes, but I won."

When her daughter entered the Island school in 1966, Billie became active in the Parent Teachers Association. With the help of her husband and mother, Daisy Greenwell, she organized numerous school carnivals and in 1971 became a teacher's aide. Years later she donated $32,000 to build a covered playground at the school where she had spent so many years. "It's a wonderful gift from a peach of a person," said Principal Jim Kronus. "Billie has always been a giver and would help anyone in need."

Martens-Steffen Cottages

For four decades Caroline Martens was an Island businesswoman. She and her husband, John H. Martens came to the Island in the mid-'30s from Buskirk, N.Y., and purchased beachfront property on 32nd Street and the Gulf. They built rental units that eventually became Martens-Steffen Cottages. By the early '40s, the Martens owned 13 units, and in the mid-'50s they sold the complex. Mrs. Martens became a realtor and worked with Jack Marshall and Jack Holmes, Sr. In 1968, after the death of her husband, Mrs. Martens moved to Seaside Gardens in Holmes Beach and branched out on her own in real estate until she retired in the '70s.

Billie married Bob Martini at Roser Church in 1951. They were known as "The Two Martinis."

Times Change

"We used to back out onto Pine Avenue without even looking," recalled Aladine Davis, who settled in the sleepy village of Anna Maria in 1938. Aladine and her husband, Melvin, came from Parrish where he was born and raised, and bought a house on Pine Avenue. At that time there was barely a house between Anna Maria and Bradenton Beach.

The Davises lived on the second floor of a concrete block house, and one of the three garages downstairs housed the fire truck. Melvin was the first chief of the Anna Maria Fire Department. When they moved into the partially furnished house they found, wedged in a bureau drawer, a yellowed brochure printed in 1912 by the Anna Maria Beach Development Company. The deteriorating paper extolled the benefits of living on the Island.

"It brought back memories of the early days on the Island," Mrs. Davis said. "We had well-water back then. It was so hard I couldn't cook tender beans. How I wish I still had my rainwater tank."

The wheels of progress have made dramatic changes

The Martens-Steffen cottages in Bradenton Beach were built in 1947. A seawall was built in 1950.

in the seven-mile-long Island since the young Davises settled across the street from Roser Church, the oldest church on the Island. Now the street is a hub of activity.

"I used to hold my breath when we crossed that old wooden bridge to the mainland. I've been through four big hurricanes, but none directly hit the Island. Every summer I would fix a hurricane shelf with water, staples, flashlight and candles. When they announced mandatory evacuation for Hurricane Elena, I panicked. We left the Island, and I not only forgot to take anything on my hurricane shelf—I forgot my toothbrush.

Centenarian Celebrates

Mrs. Elizabeth Chase of the Sandpiper Mobile Home Park in Bradenton Beach observed her 100th birthday on May 9, 1953. She was born in 1853 and remembers seeing Lincoln, who she thought was a fine man. Her mother lived to be 103 and her sister was 90 when she died. Elizabeth outlived two of her seven children. She played the piano for the reporter and recited "Glow Worm," which she thought was of the prettiest pieces ever written.

When asked how long she expected to live, she replied, "A long time, there's nothing wrong with me. I don't have a pain or ache in my body."

As the photographer got ready to take her picture, she stated adamantly, "Now why would you want to take my picture with all these wrinkles?"

"Do you enjoy life?" the reporter asked. "Oh yes, I love people, flowers and music," she said.

Short and Sweet

A lady visiting the Island described the Island like this: "It's a place where you wear little, do less and enjoy life."

Growing Up In The '40s

By Laurie Thaden Adams

"I moved to Bradenton Beach in the 1940's with my parents, Anne and Lu Thaden, and my younger sister, Joan. My father was in real estate with Jack Marshall. Our first house is still there, but has been painted blue and turned into apartments. We also owned and rented out the house next door. The huge rainwater tank between the houses supplied most of our water except for drinking. I can still remember how soft the water was. I think we should still have rainwater tanks.

"Ours was the last house on the Gulf across from Fourth Street South. We had porches all around the house. Upstairs they were called sleeping porches.

Island Brownies, Laurie Thaden, on the left, her sister Joan Marie on right and their friend Vera in the center. The photo was taken in 1947.

No one had air conditioning. The homes were built to catch the breezes, and we sometimes slept on the porches at night. They were great for slumber parties. When it was late and we were too loud, my dad, the ghost, would sneak around on the porches covered in a sheet and scare us to death. That was our signal to quiet down.

"There was no Coquina Beach. That area was full of beautiful mangroves. Annie Silver's grocery store was across the street. Every weekend we went to the movies for ten cents at the community house in the Bradenton Beach Trailer Park (now The Pines) near the old bridge. I lost track of how many grade-B westerns we saw.

Laurie Lu and Norma Ford in their 1949 Easter outfits.

"The nights were quiet. The only noise was the gentle rolling waves and clattering of a car now and then across the old bridge. We could tell whose car was coming from the different sounds they made. How we would wish for the bridge to go out on school days. If it did, we either stayed home, or most of the time a boat would pick us up and take us across to catch a bus in Cortez. This took a while, so we missed part of the day at school with an excused absence.

"Two years later we moved mid-Island to Holmes Beach, across from Cobb's Marine, where the insurance office is today. I thought we were moving to the end of the earth. I remember lots of trees and having to push a lawnmower through what seemed like acres of sandspurs.

"Humbug Cobb lived across the street. He was older and many of the girls had crushes on him. He took us for rides in his small racing boat, about the size of a jet ski, but with a flat bow. We sat on the bow and flew across the waves. I don't remember how we held on or whether we were more thrilled at the dizzying speed or being close to Humbug. I'm sure he thought we were pests, always begging for rides.

"When I compare what our children and grandchildren have to deal with today, Island life was idyllic. Some of us had less than ideal home situations and tragedies, but we felt very protected by our surroundings. Life revolved around family, church, school, chores, the beach and bicycles. If things were bad at home, there was always a caring friend or family to visit. We spent hours in the water, on the beach or walking back and forth to homes of friends.

"I started attending the Anna Maria School in the fifth grade when it was just two rooms in what is now the Island Community Center. Mrs. Phelps was the principal and teacher. Betty Lou Blackburn Huth was my classmate and a good friend, and she still is. I remember the excitement the day our teacher, Mrs. Blackburn, had to leave to have a baby. Jean is now a well-known artist.

"Often we didn't wear shoes to school or took them off when we arrived at school. At recess we would swing from a bag tied to a big tree. We would climb to the highest limb, grab the bag, shut our eyes, leap out and go swishing through the air.

"I remember sitting in the corner on a stool as punishment for chewing gum. Mrs. Phelps was the perfect combination of kindness and discipline. As I look back, I remember many people who cared for us and gave of themselves.

"When there were too many students for the small school building, classes expanded to the Community

Hall, which is now the Island Players Theater. In the morning we had math and several subjects at the schoolhouse and then walked two blocks in the afternoon to the Community Hall for geography. That was an adventure and now I realize it was a big responsibility for the teachers.

"My dad was not well, so we sold the house in Holmes Beach and moved back to Bradenton Beach where we lived until I graduated from Manatee High School in 1954. Graduation day was also the day my father died. Change and growth were beginning on the Island and for us."

Bayless Family Builds First House on North End

By Bob Bayless

"Our first visit to Anna Maria Island was in 1945 while we were living in Tampa. My family moved to Tampa in 1942 so Dad could work in the shipyard. There he met James Reynolds who owned property in Bradenton Beach. We visited the Reynolds family in Bradenton Beach and Dad became interested in moving to the Island. Soon he bought property north of the city park in Anna Maria. The Army had just moved radar and artillery fortifications from the North Point where they had protected Tampa Harbor during the war.

"While living in Tampa, we met Mom and Pop Ernest and their son Richard. In 1947, my brother Bill returned from the Navy. He and Pop Ernest camped out under the Australian pines near the north tip of the Island and built the first house in the area by hand. Dad and I would come down on weekends to bring supplies and help out. I'm not sure which was worse, the mosquitoes or Dad's snoring.

"In the fall of 1947, the house was finished and we all moved from Tampa to the Island. There was Mom, Dad, Bill, his wife, Mona, their first child, Sylvia, and me. It was a real pioneer experience: no phone, no electricity and plenty of mosquitoes. I enrolled in Manatee High School and the fun began.

"Soon a second house was added, and then Dad began to build houses for sale or contracted to build custom homes on the Island. We made friends and life was good. We didn't have a lot of money, but you didn't need money to enjoy Island life. There was lots to do: fishing, swimming, community activities, barbecues, volunteer for the fire department, square dances, an occasional hurricane and the winter invasion of those visiting the Island. Snook were plentiful, it was legal to gig, and mullet were abundant. While working on the houses, we would spot schools of mullet and yell to the Cortez fishermen who were fishing in the Gulf near us. They would holler for us to come and help pull up the nets and help ourselves to a mess of fish. We always had a good supply of fish and friends.

Bob Bayless first came to the Island in 1945.

"While one of the hurricanes was offshore, we worked as a community to save houses that were in danger of being washed away. Once we worked all night sand bagging and saving a log house north of Pine Avenue on the Gulf. The women were in the Community Hall serving food and hot coffee and had a fire roaring in the fireplace. Johnny Adams and I got radios from the Naval reserve and set them up in our jeeps for communication on the Island during the storms.

"There were rattlesnakes all over the Island. We could find them everywhere and they were big. While my brother's house was being built, he and his family were living in the fire station. A snake had been in the station all night and my sister-in-law called us and said she smelled a strange smell and heard a rattle every time she opened the refrigerator door. When they moved to the North Point she could smell snakes there too.

"Jesse Ingram was the real pioneer on the Island. He ran the first gas station, the only one on the Island, and was the only law officer around. I always respected him. If one of us was not driving properly, he gave us a warning before he went to our parents.

"I learned to drive on the Island before I had a license. First, I had a '35 Chevy and then a '47 Willys Jeep. Petey Moore and I took our driver's test in the Jeep in 1949. We drove to Bradenton without a license, passed our test, and the officer said, 'You can drive home now.' Petey had a Chevy chassis with orange crates for seats, and we drove it on the beach. It would hold about ten kids. Humbug Cobb was one of the best drivers, but also the wildest. In the '40s, the road did not go around the North Point. That didn't slow down Humbug. He knew how to drive over soft sand without getting stuck. Johnny Adams' dad had a Jeep, and we put double two by fours out the back of our Jeeps and skied from the canal, north of the City Pier, all the way around the North Point. That was before his daddy built the Rod and Reel Pier. Mr. Moore had stone crab traps from Anna Maria all the way down to Longboat Key. We often pulled up the traps and took them to Miami in his truck and brought back lobsters for local restaurants. We always had plenty of stone crab claws and lobsters.

Jess Ingram owned and operated the first gas station on the Island.

"Mom and Pop Ernest's son, Richard, and his wife, Florence with their daughter, Mary, moved to Anna Maria and built houses. Richard was elected mayor of Anna Maria City. During this time, we would all gather on the North Point about dusk, build a large fire, have dinner and listen to Pop Ernest and Dad Shryock talk about the old days. Pop grew up in Oklahoma in a sod house and Dad Shryock was raised in Ohio. These were treasured times.

"Ted and Kathleen Lundy played records and teenagers learned to square dance at the Youth Center. It was truly a community center and the center of many activities. The City Pier was another busy place.

"In 1950 my parents, along with others, decided to start a Baptist Church on the Island. A prayer meeting was held in a pioneer house with the help of the pastor of the First Baptist Church of Bradenton, the Rev. Frank Anderson, who had been our pastor in Tampa. A mission was started at the Community Hall. It has been more than 50 years since the Island Baptist Church was founded. My family was instrumental in its start and growth.

"Richard Ernest built a house for Florence and Woodie Pace, who were from Polk County. One day Richard introduced me to their daughter, Emily Pace. In 1954, Emily and I were married. Richard's other daughter, Mary, married Petey Moore about the same time and we double dated a lot.

"Humbug Cobb went into the Army about 1950. He went to a small boat school and operated boats until he was discharged. In 1951, some of the local guys signed up with the Navy during the Korean War. The Navy promised not to take us until school was out in June. I had graduated, but most of my friends were seniors. In April, we were called, and 12 of us from Manatee and Sarasota counties left for boot camp. I never made Anna Maria my home after that. My parents lived on the Island 35 years, and in 1979 Emily and I moved to Terra Ceia. It was a lot like the old Anna Maria. Everyone knew each other and helped out when there was a need. My parents moved off the Island to Terra Ceia to be closer to us in their old age.

In the late '70s, I worked as a civil engineer for a large marine construction company in Tampa. A man came up to me one day and said that Louis Melton Cobb had applied for a job as tugboat skipper and said he knew me. They wanted to know if they should hire him. I had no idea who it was until I saw "Humbug" written on the application. It was the first time I knew his full name. He was one of the best skippers the company ever had. Another Island resident, Richard Kermode, worked for the same company. His father had been a block mason in the '50s on Anna Maria and he had worked for my Dad.

"The years I spent on Anna Maria were good years, no TV, no movies, without a long trip to town, but lots to do with good friends. I recall going to a city meeting with my dad and there was a big discussion as to whether a law should be passed banning neon lights in Anna Maria. It must have passed.

Tripps Settle in Anna Maria

In 1950, Ted and Paula Tripp pursued their dream. They built three duplexes on the northern end of Bay Boulevard and called it Tripp's Court. They had previously lived in Washington, D.C., where Ted was in the advertising business, but they were tired of the fast-paced living and ready for a change They traveled to the Fort Myers/Sanibel Island area. "We were interested in sand-spits," Ted recalled. In 1949, an inland lot in Fort Myers was about $2,000. On Anna Maria Island, they discovered lots were $200. "We were going to semi-retire and run a hotel. That part turned out to be a joke. I had a family to feed," he said.

Ted and Paula Tripp, on the right, with their friend Rho Welsch

For a few years he worked for the Bradenton Chamber of Commerce as advertising director. Then he went into truck trailer sales, a job that allowed him to have an office at home when he was not traveling.

Ted served as Anna Maria's City's 12th mayor from 1952 to 1954. "Paul Carlisle, builder and owner of the Anna Maria Motel, realtor H. B. Miller and contractor Norm Rosedale came to me and told me about the city's bond and indebtedness that dated back to the '20s. They said the city was behind the eight ball and they wanted me to run for mayor.

"Their agenda was to get someone in office who would really go to town to sell some of the large amount of land the city owned dating back to the Depression to pay off the bonds. The interest was killing us."

The bonds had been sold by the city in 1924 for city improvements. When the Depression hit many were bought for two cents on the dollar by wealthy Islander Ruth Eddy and a Mr. Wright from St. Petersburg. Ted agreed to run for one term to get rid of the bond and indebtedness. He bought back the bonds from Wright and worked out a deal with Miss Eddy to deed her a swale in front of her Gulf front home in exchange for the bonds she held. The city began advertising to auction off big plats of land it held.

Ted accomplished what he set out to do, and when his term was over Paul Carlisle became mayor, and Ted took over Carlisle's job as president of the Anna Maria Chamber of Commerce. Jerry Cigarran founded the Chamber in 1949 and George Morris was the first president.

Carlisle and Tripp joined ranks to get one good bridge to the Island. State legislators had a bigger scheme that included a new Cortez Bridge, a new bridge to Longboat and a Manatee Avenue bridge to the Island. The ultimate plan also included two bridges in Bradenton. Ted said Islanders could not see the need for the Manatee Avenue bridge or a way through the Palma Sola jungle, but the state boys got their way. The development on the Island took off after that.

Ted was involved in the push to incorporate the Island cities into one in the '50s. Because of some shenanigans the first referendum; that was supposed to be a simple Island-wide, majority rules vote, was lost due to the opposition of unincorporated Holmes Beach. By the second referendum both southern cities were opposed to the incorporation and that was the last time the idea of one city was talked about, according to Ted.

Ted was involved with the Island Lions Club, which was responsible for leasing the old schoolhouse on Magnolia Avenue from the school board. "We worked our tails off fixing it up and turning it into a youth center," he recalled.

While being interviewed in the early '90s, Ted agreed the Island had really changed. "It's like watching a child grow. You don't see the change day to day even though it's happening." Ted recalled some of his favorite tales about how it used to be.

"There were two taverns in town, the Sandbar cocktail lounge on the Gulf and the Anchorage across from the City Pier. Paula and I and the kids would stroll down to the Anchorage. I'd like to get a beer and some smoked mullet. The kids would play outside while we relaxed. Often we would see a couple, the wife in a mumu, and the husband in an old pair of khaki pants. He said he was a shipper. One day we received an invitation, from the couple, to Mr. Emil Ludwig's yacht for cocktails. The yacht was the largest in the world and it had just pulled into the City Pier.

"Just to show you what a cosmopolitan group we were, we joined the Ludwigs, along with the garbage man and his wife, and Island sales clerks and their wives. There just were not any big shots on the Island," Ted said.

The Ludwig home stands to this day on the Gulf end of Oak Avenue. At one time, Ludwig was reported to be the richest man in the world.

Ted remembered there were a group of about eight men who were designated as sandbaggers in the '50s. They were on call when the storms came in.

"One night," he related, "the Gulf was really whacking the Sandbar restaurant. By the time I got there, the whole porch was in the Gulf. Pat Holmes, the owner, turned to us and said, 'I'll give you the whole thing and the back house for $10,000.' I don't think we had $10,000 between us so it was no deal. That's the way things were back then."

Ted stepped onto his deck facing Tampa Bay and pointed to the bayfront property where they built their first home. Now living across the street, he said, "Everything we've done since 1950 has been within a city block - and it's been a good life."

Why The Island?

By Carolyne Norwood

Ruth Mahar, one of the Island's top realtors in the '50s, made this observation: "It is a story all Islanders know so well. People come to the Island, and get Island fever, which is totally incurable."

One visitor I met on the beach said she loved the Island. "You can wear anything you want, and I don't even have to dye my hair."

Many of the people who settled on the Anna Maria Island came because they had friends here. The most asked question when you met someone for the first time was, "How did you find Anna Maria?"

I believe my story is unique. My husband, George, and I were born and raised in Baltimore. We married in 1948 and soon had three children. In the early '50s, we moved to Silver Spring, Maryland because of George's job. I was a stay-at-home mom and we lived from paycheck to paycheck. We could only afford a small house in a development where the houses were alike and three or more kids in each. Frequently, I counted 15 kids playing in our small yard. Needless to say, I did not like the housing arrangement and George was dissatisfied with his job. Then I became pregnant with our fourth child.

It was about this time we received a phone call from a man George had worked with in Washington, D.C. Reds Whitener was a gregarious redhead whom I had met once.

"Come on down," he shouted. "Where are you?" George asked. Reds had suffered a mild heart attack, so he quit work and had moved to Florida.

"I'm on Anna Maria Island," he stated. "I'm going to open a restaurant and you can be my partner."

Well, George knew nothing about the restaurant business and he laughed at the absurdity of it. He told Reds, no thanks, and after hanging up the telephone told me what a crazy guy Reds was. I started to think how wonderful the Florida sun would feel. It was November, cold, damp, and muddy in Maryland, and the children had one cold after another. I knew we would be housebound for months. It was so depressing. We had just about forgotten about the sunshine state when we heard from Reds again.

"Come on down," he urged. "I'm buying a gas station." This perked George's interest. He was mechanical and loved cars, so he told Reds he would think about it.

"Please, I want to go," I pleaded, with visions of orange trees and palms waving in the warm breezes dancing before my eyes. "If I have this baby here, we'll never go." I finally convinced George we would be so happy and content in Florida. We would practically be living outdoors. What a place to raise a family: no heating bills, no heavy clothing and no one would ever get sick.

Neither George nor I had ever been to Florida, but what was not to like, we thought. We loved the outdoors, sun, surf, boating and fishing. So we agreed to pull up roots and move.

The Norwood boys and their pets, from left, Nicky and Rosemary Cooney, John and Blackie, Billy and Fuzzy.

I often think how fortunate we were. We knew one person in the entire state and he lived on Spring Avenue and Gulf Drive in Anna Maria City, across the street from the old post office.

When our families gathered for Thanksgiving in 1956, we broke the news. Our friends and family thought we had lost our minds. We told them George had a job and we had a place to live, both lies. I was in seventh heaven and didn't notice how distressed our relatives were.

When a neighbor asked me where we were going, I replied, "I don't know where it is exactly because we've never been to Florida. The only person we know lives on an island in the Gulf of Mexico." My friend's mouth opened in shock. "Do you mean to say you are pulling up stakes and moving to a state you have never visited?"

Finally the night arrived. The children clutched their suitcases and we drove to the airport. It was so exciting. None of us had ever been on an airplane. George stayed behind to sell the house. He watched until the plane was a small red dot in the black sky.

"That red light represented my whole family," he told me later. "I really felt quite alone and sad."

When we arrived at the Tampa airport at 4 a.m., a blast of hot air hit us as we walked out of the plane. The children quickly peeled off their coats and sweaters. Reds and his wife, Mary, met us and drove us to the Island. I often think if they had lived in Ruskin, Ellenton or Bradenton that is where we would have settled. When we started over the rickety bridge, which led to Bradenton Beach, I held my breath. Fortunately nothing was coming toward us. I could not imagine how two cars could pass in such a narrow space. In a few days I was driving back and forth across the dilapidated bridge in an old panel truck Reds had loaned me.

It was about 6 a.m. when we arrived at the Whitener house, a concrete block structure built in the '40s. The children were surprised to find they could pick oranges for breakfast from a tree in the back yard. Reds and I took them to the Island school. Linda was in the first grade and Nicky was in kindergarten. John was three and stayed home with me.

We were greeted by the congenial principal, Lena Phelps, who took each child to his or her classroom. They did not miss one minute of school in the transition and adjusted beautifully to their new location, the teachers and made new friends immediately. It was November, and the school children were wearing shorts and open-toe sandals. The playground bordered on Sarasota Bay - unbelievable!

"This is truly paradise," I wrote to George that night. "Hurry down!" It took longer than we had expected for him to sell our house. I made an appointment with Dr. Ed Huth right away and he said the baby was due in several weeks. My letters to George were full of enthusiasm for our new home. After a week living in the Whiteners garage, I found a small rental cottage across the street from the Youth Center on Magnolia Avenue. Our next-door neighbors were relatives of the first Island homesteader, George Emerson Bean. His daughter, Lula Colman, and her daughter, Marion, were wonderful neighbors. They had many cats, and sometimes Marion would kill a rattlesnake and nail it to a tree. My children thought that it was great fun. I wasn't so sure.

I was positive George would appear by Christmas and we were ready for him. The boys went up the street and chopped down an Australian pine tree for our Christmas tree. It was huge, and we kept cutting branches off so it would fit into the sparsely furnished cottage. One day Nicky mentioned the tree had been growing in George Wagner's yard, but I guess he never missed it. The children made a variety of colorful holiday decorations to hang on the tree. It fell down several times, but we were determined to leave it up until George arrived.

One night, about the middle of January, George appeared at my bedroom window. He was holding our dog Rex, who got carsick if he went a block. Billy was born on Jan. 31,1957 at Veterans Memorial Hospital, which is now Manatee Memorial Hospital. We began Island living with zest and the days were full and happy.

We became active at Roser Church. The pastor, Rev. Richard Wiggins, and his wife, Mae, became our good friends. Their children were the same ages as ours and they lived close to us on Pine Avenue. George was hired by Karl Francis Karel, owner of the Island Water Company, and came home for lunch every day. He would always drive by the beach first to see if we were there. If we were, he would kick his shoes off and take a swim before lunch. Life was good and to this day we never regretted our move.

After the children finished Anna Maria School, they attended Walker Junior High School and graduated from Manatee High School. I became a stringer (reporter) for the St. Petersburg Times for two years and then was hired as editor of the Manatee County Women's Section for the Sarasota Herald Tribune. I held that position for three years, but never liked the in-town work.

In 1970, Don Moore, publisher of *The Islander*, offered me a job as photographer/reporter, a position I held and enjoyed for 20 years. Pat Copeland, another Island journalist, and I came up with an idea of preserving historical facts and artifacts pertaining to the early Island days. We formed the Anna Maria Island Historical Society in 1990.

The organization grew from a small, enthusiastic group to several hundred members. Today, dedicated docents give tours in the old icehouse on Pine Avenue, which was renovated into a charming museum. I worked in various capacities for 15 years, encouraged by supporters and visitors. In 2003, I wrote my first book, "*The Early Days, 1893-1940*." I started *Tales of Three Cities* in 2004 and now, in 2010, I am still working on it daily. It has been truly a labor of love.

I lost my dear husband, George, in 2002 to cancer. He was my wonderful helpmate for 54 years. No matter what projects I undertook he was always beside me, encouraging and lending a hand. On October 6,

2002, a month before his death, he wrote: The Luckiest Man Alive: "I praise God for leading me to Anna Maria Island where my wife, Carolyne, and I raised our family in a safe, healthy environment of sand and sea.

"Then, there was a wonderful bonus of the Island school and Roser Church. What a childhood the children had growing up, and I was working in this paradise. We met great people, went to picnics, dances, fishing trips and other fun activities. Who could have had it better?

"When I got bored with my job I decided to retire. Just imagine, 18 more years of heaven. The tennis we played, the fish we caught, smoked and enjoyed eating. Folks, I have had absolutely the best life and I invite you to celebrate it with me. God bless you all, George."

This message was included in the order of worship at George's memorial service held at Roser Church on December 7, 2002.

My children have all settled in Florida, all but one are nearby. My daughter, Linda, created a scrapbook on our 40th wedding anniversary. It was filled with notes and pictures from friends far and near. Nicky, my oldest son, who is a professional photographer and lives in Miami, wrote: "Thank you for bringing us to Anna Maria Island, so we did not have to grow up on the streets of Baltimore." That just about sums it up.

Linda is married to Joe Kinnan, the head Manatee High football coach. They have a son, Jo-Jo, and grandson, Jay. A teacher and librarian, Linda expressed her love of close-knit Island friendships and the casual Island community. "I benefitted from older family friends who took an interest in me and influenced my life. In particular, I have fond memories of Helen Clark, Miriam Murphy, Marge Tritt, Richard and Mae Wiggins and the Van Ostenbridge family. We were sheltered and insulated to some extent and that was a good thing."

"This is what living on Anna Maria Island has meant to me," John wrote. "It meant experiencing a casual and carefree lifestyle, full of fun and good friends. I enjoyed playing on the beach, swimming, fishing, boating, water-skiing, camping out and sports, like baseball and football, at a very young age. It was nice knowing everyone you saw each day, since we lived in such a small community."

John lives just off the Island now, in Palma Sola, and boasts he can be on the Island, at my house, in less than 15-minutes. He is married to Nicki Notaras, a native of London, England, and they have a daughter, Lilia. He is also the father of Tina, John and Seann, and at this writing has six grandchildren. John owns an electric service company.

Billy, who prefers to be called Bill, lives in Bradenton and is an electrician. He is married to Connie and they have one daughter, Candida, and two grandchildren. Billy said, "Growing up on the Island meant I had freedom to run anywhere in the city. Everyone knew each other. The weather was great. I had many friends and there was so much to do. I never had a boring day. Of course, no one ever locked their doors."

Fun and Games

This was overheard in the Anna Maria post office: Bud and Gretchen Edgren threw a cocktail party years ago to welcome Joan Zak and Bob Dancy to the Island. Howard and Betty Carr were among the guests. Howard asked the hosts if they had a blood pressure machine. When it was produced, the party-goers passed it around taking each others blood pressure. Only on Anna Maria Island would such a party be considered normal. Gretchen, the former senior editor of Playboy magazine, wrote five books on the Playboy empire.

The Teddy Bear Lady of Park Avenue

Virginia Archer came to the Island with her parents in the late '40s. She was a stunning beauty and soon became interested in the Island Players theatrical group, which had just been organized. While performing on the Island stage, a young man, named Stephen Walker, became enamored with the attractive actress and waited for her at the stage door many evenings.

Virginia married her admirer in 1956. He bought Miss Ruth Hart Eddy's house on Beach Avenue as a wedding present for his bride. The unique manse was filled with Italian and Spanish furniture and colorful mosaics. Soon she decided she did not want to live in the Spanish-style mansion with the red tile roof, and insisted they build a house on the next street, Park Avenue.

When she was young, Virginia liked teddy bears, and in the 1970s she renewed her love for the furry, cuddly stuffed animals. Soon it became an obsession. She and her husband traveled around the world and she met teddy bear collectors from foreign countries and attended numerous teddy bear rallies. The soft toys became real to her.

While visiting London, Virginia spotted a bear in Harrods's Department Store window. It was love at first sight. She named him Eggie. Soon he was joined by Cissie and Ollie, who were engaged.

When the Walkers returned to the Island, she talked her husband into adding an apartment to their home, which she named Teddy Bear Towers. Three large rooms were filled with bears of all sizes. Huge stained glass windows in each room depicted the four seasons with bears as focal points. One room was completely white. A group of white bears were gathered around a shimmering white Christmas tree.

Tommy Tyrrell cuddles up to the teddy bears.

A large merry-go-round was in the center of another room. Of course, bears were riding on the horses. There were bears sitting on chairs at tables set with china, bears asleep in beds and bears sitting in baby carriages. Virginia told rambling stories about all of her bears. She loved to entertain in Teddy Towers, and was especially well known for her Christmas parties. Parting gifts for her guests were coffee mugs, pens and tee shirts, decorated with pictures of Eggie and Cissie, her favorite bears.

Over the years she developed a friendship with Peter Bull, an English actor who was smitten by her extensive bear collection. Their favorite bears "corresponded" regularly.

As a reporter for *The Islander*, I visited Teddy Towers several times. The first time I arrived at the house, on the Gulf end of Park Avenue, I searched everywhere for Teddy Towers before I discovered a winding stairway inside the garage. Virginia was waiting for me at the top of the stairs. She was a large woman with curly brown hair and wore a multi-colored smock decorated with teddy bears. A large bear amulet hung from a heavy chain around her neck.

As we entered the first room, I could not believe my eyes. There were bears everywhere. She started telling me about each one. As we moved around the rooms, I took many pictures and decided the next time I interviewed Virginia I would bring a child. At first, Virginia was not sure her bears would be safe with a child, but I convinced her I knew a young boy who was very well behaved.

Several weeks later Tommy Tyrrell and I paid a visit to Teddy Towers. The visitation went well and I took excellent pictures of a cute youngster cuddling the bears. When we left, I felt like we should be saying goodbye to the bears, as well as Virginia. She knew how to make the furry toys come to life.

The Eddy house deteriorated over the years. Vandalism and rodents left the ornate furniture unrecognizable. The city told the Walkers they must restore the historic home or tear it down. When the wreckers took over, residents mourned the loss of the once beautiful landmark.

The city proposed the land be turned into a public park, but the Walkers would not hear of it. They wanted privacy, and did not want people or houses near their beachfront home.

Stephen Walker died in 2001 and Virginia passed away in 2004. Virginia was survived by a sister in Arizona, a niece in California and a nephew, John Chapman, in Texas. Some family members took a few of the bears, others were donated to museums or sold. About a year after Virginia's death, a three-day estate sale was held at the Walker home. Buyers and the curious arrived in throngs to view the mysterious abode.

John Chapman said his aunt was vivacious, whimsical and had a good sense of humor. "She loved Anna

Maria and had a wonderful life here," he said. "She enjoyed herself tremendously."

The Boys Of Winter

By Christine Torgeson

Professional baseball players have been called, "The Boys of Summer." During the glory days when many baseball players were known to live and play on Anna Maria Island, back in the late 1940s, '50s and early '60s, they were actually "The Boys of Winter."

Spring training may have begun in Florida in the 1870s, but in 1930 the St. Louis Cardinals began a seven-year stay in Bradenton. It became known as the most colorful period in spring training history, with Dizzy Dean's "Gashouse Gang" well-known for their antics. Casey Stengel brought his Boston Bees to Bradenton after

Members of the Boston Braves were keeping cool while waiting for the start of spring training. Pictured from left: Sibby Sisti, shortstop; Frank McCormick, first baseman; Tommy Holmes, right-fielder and Earl Torgeson, first baseman.

World War II for a couple of years, then in 1948, the Boston Braves (with their name changed from the "Bees") invaded the area.

It was a good year for the Braves. They were a very close, proud team, a gathering of new players, rookies and a blend of older players. That year they went on to win the National League pennant and play the Cleveland Indians in the World Series.

The Braves team was full of outstanding players and future Hall of Famers. Out of this team came the slogan, "Spahn and Sain and pray for rain." The roster included my dad, Earl Torgeson, Warren Spahn, Johnny Sain, Vern Bickford, Alvin Dark, Red Barrett, Bobby Hogue, Eddie Stanky, Sibi Sisti, Tommy Holmes, Phil Masi, Connie Ryan, Frank McCormick, Jeff Heath and Bill Voiselle. Others included Johnny Antonelli, Bob Elliot, Sid Gordon, Clyde Shoun, Jim Russell, Bill Salkeld, Mike McCormick, trainer "Doc" Lacks and manager Bill Southworth.

No one was happier about the Braves coming to Bradenton than Ernie Cagnina and Bennie Scanio, co-owners of the IGA grocery store in Anna Maria City. Although they lived in Anna Maria, the Cagninas and the Scanios had lots of family and deep roots in Tampa, also home to Boston Braves president, Lou Perini. They were all part of the community of Italian families in Tampa and over the years became good friends. Lou Perini, his sister, and her family rented a place on the Island for spring training that year. They loved being close to their old friends and enjoyed Ernie's Italian specialties. The Cagninas and Scanios loved their relationships with the Braves; Ernie even got box seats at the World Series that year.

My family came to Bradenton that same spring. It didn't take long for my parents, "Torgie" and Norma, to find their way to Anna Maria, past the reptile farm at the corner of Cortez and US 41, the "Tamiami Trail." We stopped there for a Coca Cola and a look at the cages of rattlesnakes and the pit with big alligators. We rode out the long, sandy Cortez Road, over the rickety wooden bridge that groaned and swayed while the cars slowly made their way across. My mother and dad saw that beautiful beach, and they knew that the Island was where they wanted to live.

Chris and Andy, with their father, Earl Torgeson, at the start of spring training.

They first rented a little cottage on the beach from the Gutierrez family, just south of what is now the Martinique. It was a long drive to town for my dad to play ball, but it was worth it.

My dad was from Snohomish, Washington, and he first signed to play professional ball with the Pacific Coast League (PCL) when he was 15. Like so many players of his era, he spent time in the war. He thought he was being groomed for the Yankees, but in a fox hole in Germany he learned the Braves had bought his rights for a record sum of $100,000. His first year in the big leagues, he earned $25,000. Dad said the best years of his 15-year career were with the Braves. Even though he was with two other pennant winners,1948 was the first. "Your first years in the big leagues are always the most memorable," he said He went to the Phillies in a five-player swap six years afterwards, and later was traded to the Tigers, White Sox and Yankees. He had the unique distinction of having been in three World Series, on three different teams, in three different decades.

About that same time, Fred and Patsy Hutchinson and their kids, Rick, Jack and Patty moved to the area. Fred already knew Dad from Seattle, when they were both part of the PCL.

Fred signed with the Seattle Rainiers, went on to win 25 games that season and was named the PCL's Most Valuable Player. He came up to the big leagues in 1939 when he was sold to Detroit for $100,000. He had one of the great major league pitching careers while with the Tigers for 11 years. He was known for his amazing control, his natural sinker, and a consuming desire to win, and was elected player representative in 1947.

Thanksgiving at the Torgeson home with the Hutchinson family.

In the summer of 1952, Fred was named new player-manager for the Tigers. He was one of a handful of ex-pitchers in baseball who have successfully made the transition to manager.

He turned down a Tiger contract, went to back to Seattle and was named PCL Manager of the Year after a wildly successful season. He then went to St. Louis to manage the Cardinals, and back to Seattle. In 1959 he managed the Cincinnati Reds until his career ended. In 1961 his Reds were picked for sixth in the league, but Fred led them to a pennant. As the National League Manager of the Year, Fred believed, "The ones who work hardest are the ones who make it, the ones who win."

While Fred was playing with the Tigers, he and Hoot Evers were roommates. After one season, the Hutchinsons did not want to go home to Seattle, back to a rainy climate and a wet winter.

Hoot lived in Bradenton with his wife, Nancy, and daughters, Chris and Kay Ann. He told Fred, "If you want to come down here, my father-in-law is a real estate agent, and he'll find you a house."

The Hutchinsons rented a house in Bradenton their first year. "But being in town was like being in any town anywhere," said Patsy.

Nancy's dad told Patsy, "I think I know what you want," and he took them over the old wooden bridge to the Island.

Once she saw the beach, Patsy said, "Now, this is what I am talking about." The Tigers trained in Lakeland, but the kids loved the beach and that was more important.

"You can't live out there year round," they were warned, "with hurricanes and all."

But Patsy and Fred built a house with a great beach view. Their youngest son, Joe, was the only one in the family born in Bradenton. Their house has grown and changed over the years, but Patsy still makes that house her home.

Warren Spahn, his wife, Lorene, and their son Greg were also on Anna Maria for the first time in 1948. "Spahnie" joined the Boston Braves in 1946 and stayed with them for 20 years. Considered one of baseball's best, he was a Hall of Fame pitcher, known for his high kick.

They rented a small cottage on the north end and fell in love with the beaches and the Island. Warren said Anna Maria had "the most beautiful beaches I've ever seen." A couple of years later they bought two little cottages on the beach on Tuna Avenue and named them "The Infield" and "The Outfield."

The Spahns had a ranch in Oklahoma, but Warren had an eye for a good investment, and he wanted more land on the beach. He bought a tract of beach front land on Cypress Avenue and the beach from Clyde Phelps for a whopping $10,000 in 1953. Eddie Matthews also wanted land on the beach, so Warren let him buy in for $5,000. Spahn built "The Mound" on that land, and Matthews built a cottage nearby and named it "Home Plate."

Patsy Hutchinson remembers a night when the Spahns had a fish fry for some baseball players and their wives. Warren had a big tub of oil over a fire in the back yard, and he was standing about five feet away, tossing the breaded fish filets into the hot oil.

Warren "Spahnie" Spahn was a Hall of Fame pitcher

Patsy walked up and said, "Warren, why are you doing it that way?"

"I don't want to get burned," he told Patsy.

"But what if you miss?" she said.

He turned to her and said, "Patsy, I am NOT going to miss."

The Spahn family owned "The Mound" until 2008, when it was sold for $1.65 million.

Families of Vernon Bickford, Johnny Logan, Eddie Matthews, Walter Dropo, Walker Cooper, Doc and Eileen Lacks and many of the Boston Braves rented places on the Island during those years

Pitcher Ernie Johnson joined the Braves in 1950. For his first spring training in Bradenton he came without his family, but his family joined him the next year, and they rented a house in Palmetto. My dad said, "What are you doing way over there? Come on out to the Island." From that time on he and his wife Lois rented on the Island.

Pitchers reported earlier than the others, but Ernie said, "We'd find some excuse to get down here even earlier because we had so many good times on the Island."

During spring training of 1953, the owners of the Braves announced they would not be going back to Boston for the season. "They moved the team to Milwaukee and it took all of us by surprise," Ernie said.

Ernie went to the World Series with the Braves in 1957. When his playing career ended, he joined the Milwaukee broadcast team, and was known as one of the "Voices of the Braves," the first to have their games broadcast nationally via cable. He and his family still visit the Island every year.

Our family continued to rent until I started school at Anna Maria Elementary. That year, we bought a house. My mother fell in love with the "Castle Cottage" on Beach Avenue. It was a magical stone house with a winding staircase that led to a tower. Big cypress beams were in every room and even the heavy doors were made of pecky cypress. We could see the Gulf from our bedrooms and hear the waves coming in. We'd lie in the tower at night and look at the stars. Upstairs was a big screened sleeping porch, which was a good thing to have because there was no air conditioning. We were home.

The Torgeson home on Beach Avenue, Anna Maria, was called The Castle Cottage.

Our house was always full of people. Mom was from a big family and she was used to having people around. My dad's parents came from Washington State many times to spend most of the winter.

Spring training meant every bed was full. Connie Ryan and his wife, Iris, and their three kids stayed with us too. Ryan had a 20-year career in the major leagues, but is remembered mostly for a game one rainy night in Boston when he wore a yellow slicker and carried an umbrella to the on deck circle. While they lived with us, I got the chicken pox. I don't know how we managed, but none of the other kids got sick.

The Hutchinson house had ballplayers staying with them on and off. Dizzy Trout slept upstairs sometimes and bumped his head every time he came down the stairs.

One of the first years that we were in our house, Peggy and Red Marston lived with us. Red was a broadcaster of the Braves games in Boston and a sports writer for the Boston Herald. Red was looking for a change, a native of Maine, a salty sort, he dreamed of taking a boat down the East Coast of Florida.

In the summer of '53, Red and Peggy launched a 36-foot, refit lobster boat, the Sea Scribe, in Cape Ann, Massachusetts. They made their way down the East Coast, facing three hurricanes. During one storm, Red tied off at a large shrub, and when the water receded found it to be a 25-foot sycamore tree.

One day that fall, my mom said, "Peggy and Red ought to be here soon, let's go out in the boat to see if we can see them." We took our boat out in the bay, and there they were! They were idling their way along, looking for the right anchorage. The Sea Scribe had arrived!

We led them into the Bayou Marina, now home to Galati's Marina. Peggy and Red moved in with us, and Red got a job writing for the Bradenton Herald. That same year, Peggy gave birth to their son, Glenn. Red went on to become the outdoor sports editor for the St. Petersburg Times, a position he held for many years. He followed the America's Cup Challenge and wrote for many sailing publications.

When we moved to Anna Maria, life was different from today. During the early years, before I started school, and when the baseball season was over, Dad's first job was to whack back the weeds in the yard that had grown unmolested for four or five months. He usually found two or three rattlesnakes in the first cut. Dad kept the rattles as souvenirs and put them in an alcove in the house.

I rode home from Bradenton with my dad one day down Cortez Road. We came upon a farmer, standing in his bare feet trying to kill a good-sized rattler, over six feet long. Dad helped him kill the snake. We got the skin and added the rattles to our collection. By far, those rattles won the prize.

Fred and Dad built a barbecue pit and a screen house in our back yard so we could cook out and get away from the fierce mosquitoes. This was the scene of some great parties. Patsy and Fred were always there with Hoot and Nancy Evers who lived in Bradenton. Doc and Eileen Lacks, the Lew Burdettes, Connie and Iris Ryan, Lois and Ernie Johnson, Vern and Jean Bickford were renting on the Island and were regulars too. "The Boys" and their wives all loved to sing the old songs and harmonize, tell stories and have a big time. Lois Johnson was easily coaxed into sitting down at the piano to play a few oldies wherever she was.

My dad was known to walk up on the stage when he was in a club with live music, grab the microphone and sing. Fred had a great voice too, and he would sing "I Understand." Connie Ryan had the best line-up of Irish songs. They sang, told jokes, laughed and sang some more.

Patty Hutchinson, who was my age, stayed overnight with us many times while our parents sang, ate, partied and had a big time in that little screen house. She and my brother and I remember nights when we sat up in my room and peered down at the parties, listening to the laughter and stories.

One night all the Hutchinson kids stayed at my house. Patty and I were in my room and the boys were on the sleeping porch, which would sleep eight. Rick, the oldest Hutchinson son, sneaked downstairs and got the rattles Dad had collected from the snakes. He gave one to each of us, saving the largest one for himself. He led us out through the family room to the big powder-puff plant near the screen house. Oh, it was a great party with lots of singing and laughter. On Rick's signal, we all started rattling the rattles. Now, that was a party stopper! Silence. Then our laughter gave us away and we scattered.

My dad loved Maine lobster. Red introduced him to it when we lived in Boston during those summers with the Braves. I think lobster is probably what he missed most about moving South, so at least once a year in the spring, Dad ordered a big barrel of Maine lobsters, and had it shipped to Anna Maria for a cookout with "The Boys."

The first time we feasted from the lobster barrel, the raccoons had a party, and they invited a crowd, too. There was clanging and banging of garbage cans and a 'coon-screeching really good time was had. In the morning we saw lobster shells strewn from Gulf Drive to the end of Beach Avenue.

Dad and Fred often got ribs and steaks. Mom and Patsy, of course, did most of the work, including the preparation, cooking, and

Members of the Boston Braves team. From left, Earl Torgeson, Connie Ryan, Alvin Dark and Lew Burdette.

cleaning up after everyone went home. After the 'coon incident, they put everything tightly in the garbage cans and said, "Good night."

Dad's friends from the Braves were there, and a few years later, after Dad went to the Phillies, the Phillies came for some of his ribs, too. Robin Roberts, Del Ennis, Granny Hamner, Eddie Waitkus and Curt Simmons were some of his teammates. Connie Ryan was also playing with the Phillies those years. When Dad went to the Tigers, he invited his teammates Ray Boone and Harvey Kuenn, along with the rest of the team, to drive over from Lakeland to see the Island, feast on stone crab, eat some ribs and join in the harmony.

Dad and Fred built a fire pit at the Hutchinson house. Over the years the cookouts continued at our house or the Hutchinsons. They had some great parties with ball players and their new friends who lived on the Island. Fred and Patsy hosted the Cardinals and the Cincinnati Reds. Fred managed the Cardinals during years when players like Stan Musial, Alvin Dark, and Ken Boyer were stars. When Fred was with the Reds, he had a roster of players such as Vida Pinson, Frank Robinson and Don Blasingame.

Throughout the 1950's, members of the Braves came out to the Island to rent during spring training, including players like Phil Payne, Chet Nichols, Jack Differ and Jim Wilson.

Ernie and Lois remembered parties with the Braves at the Sandbar. Lois was always looking for a piano. She could play about anything and get everyone singing. One night she got everyone in the whole place dancing the "Bunny Hop." They emptied the tables and everybody joined in a long line and bunny-hopped their way out to the beach and back.

You really had to watch where you were driving in those days. You'd turn down one of the side roads and could be up to your axle in sand. But coming home to the Island after training games, the players followed each other and loved racing down the long Cortez Road. Jim Wilson swore he got up to 80 mph until he got to the old bridge.

Most of all, as kids, we loved the big bonfires right on the beach in front of the Hutchinson house with just our families. Sometimes Hoot and Nancy Evers would come out from town and join us. Fred would come home for dinner and ask Patsy, "What are we having with our sand for dinner?"

We collected driftwood and dry palm fronds, which could really get a fire going, sit in the damp sand and huddle near the fire. If you sat on the smoky side, there were fewer mosquitoes. When the fire burned down to embers, they cooked stone crabs, hot dogs, hamburgers and those delicious roasted marshmallows. What memorable days and nights. If it was Sunday night, we ate early so we kids could get back to the house to watch Lassie and Bonanza.

We all loved stone crabs. Dad and Fred took the kids to the south end of the Island to hunt for stone crabs. Now it is Coquina Beach, but in those days it was just mangroves and sand. There was no bridge to Longboat Key. We went after dark, and the hunt was an adventure for us, with elements of mystery. The little kids got to ride on our dads' shoulders. We'd take turns with the nets, the buckets and holding the lantern. We got to go only if we promised not to get tired.

One afternoon when all the kids were swimming in the Gulf in front of the Hutchinson house, my brother Andy was running down the beach, warning people, yelling, "There is a gator out there!" Patsy and my mom thought he was kidding. Rick ran to the water and he started getting the kids out. Mom and Patsy took a closer look and saw the 'gator's big tail come to the surface of the water.

Once the kids were out of the water, Patsy called Mitch Davis, who was the local wildlife expert. He told her that 'gators sometimes got disoriented and would make their way into the salt water. Dr. Ed Huth, Island doctor, and Rex Lee, the Island dentist, came down with their rifles and shot the 'gator. It washed up on the beach on Longboat Key a couple of days later.

Andy, loved being outside on the beach and in the water. One day, when he was about nine or ten years old, he wandered up to the beach in front of the Sandbar and just sat on the rock groins outside the bar, listening to what was going on inside. In those years the Sandbar was just a wooden building with big, screened windows. The windows were covered with sheets of plywood propped up on the outside by a stick in the sand to let the breeze in. There was a long bar, and the only entertainment was a table-top shuffleboard game. Andy was just sitting there when something came hurtling through the window and landed on the sand. A man came out and asked Andy if he saw anything.

Andy pointed where it landed and asked, "What's the deal?"

The man answered, "Fred got mad. Now he wants his puck back."

Another favorite hangout was the back of the IGA grocery store where Sunday afternoon poker games were held with Bennie and Ernie. Dad and Fred were there and Islanders Jess Ingram, J.D. Webb and Roy Gunther sat in on a few of those games.

If Dad, Fred and Warren or any of the other ball players were in the IGA, lettuce, tomatoes or anything within reach suddenly would be tossed around the store. Johnny Cagnina recalls a time they started playing catch with a dozen eggs. Boys will be boys, even if they're grown men.

In the off-season, ball players had other jobs. In Boston, my dad sold real estate, had a weekly radio talk show and was part owner of a sporting goods store. Warren Spahn owned a restaurant close to the Braves Field in Boston.

Exhibition games, including some in Europe and Cuba, speaking dates, winter baseball meetings, public relations, scouting new talent, and winter ball kept Dad and Fred on the road a lot in the winter. My mom and Patsy volunteered in the school clinic, served in the school lunch room, made Halloween costumes, drove us to school, and generally just tried to keep all of us kids out of trouble.

My mom was a Brownie troop leader for a few years, and the Brownies met in the game room of our house. We learned to weave palm fronds and made hats, baskets and "sit-upons." Once my mom and Patsy each drove a car full of little Brownies to St. Pete to be on the TV show, Captain Mac's Adventure Trails, on Channel 38. The trip involved riding the car ferry across Tampa Bay.

Patty and I anticipated the fall arrival of the carton from the Topps Chewing Gum Company that produced our dads' baseball cards. We tore open the packages to chew the bubble gum and had contests to see who blew the biggest bubble and kept it full the longest. Andy pinned the baseball cards to his bike tires with clothespins.

Patsy, Mom and Nancy Evers headed for the golf course at the Bradenton Country Club as often as they could. They were all beautiful golfers.

Dad and Fred were both very competitive on the field and known to have big tempers. Fred often threw things when he was mad. Dad was known to clear a few benches in his scuffles during a game or two. They were both pretty easy-going off the field, but the game of golf also brought out their competitive spirit.

Fred was playing a round of golf with his old friend Birdie Tebbetts. Birdie was a catcher with the Tigers when Fred pitched his first year in the big leagues. Fred hit a bad shot and threw his club straight up in the air. Birdie told him, "That club's going to come right down on your head."

Fred replied, "It wouldn't dare."

On the golf course at the Bradenton Country Club, Fred had been having a particularly frustrating round. He teed off on the 16th hole and hit his ball into the water. He tried another and hit that one in the water. So he hurled his club into the water and then grabbed his bag from the caddie, lifted it over his head with all the clubs in it, threw the whole thing into the water and walked off the course.

At that same hole, in the same pond on New Year's Day, Fred, Patsy, Bill McChesney and a fourth were playing. They saw some kids teasing a snake. Bill, who was coming up behind Fred, was a southerner and yelled to him, "That's a cottonmouth, get those kids away from there!"

Fred grabbed a club and ran down to the pond. The snake turned as he raised his club and struck him on his upper thigh. He was wearing an old pair of baggy woolen pants.

"He got you, Hutch! Take off those pants and see if he bit you," McChesney yelled. The snake missed Fred, but his fangs were hung up in his pants. So Fred grabbed the snake and killed it.

The kids were standing there wide-eyed, and then they ran home. Their mother called the Hutchinsons later and said, "One of my kids said your husband took his pants down on the golf course."

Fred told the woman, "You tell that kid he is lucky to be alive."

When Hutch was asked what club he used to kill the snake, he said he just grabbed the longest club in his bag.

Once, Dad and Fred challenged each other to a car race to Pete Reynard's Yacht Club, where they were meeting friends. They tore off down sandy Gulf Drive. Fred followed the road to take a left into the parking lot. Dad took a shortcut by the shopping center and crashed into the only big shade tree in the middle of the parking lot. Fred won.

Travel to and from Anna Maria Island wasn't all that easy. When we traveled by plane, we would land in the tiny Tampa airport, use the car ferry to shuttle across Tampa Bay, and drive down US 41 to the Island.

When we could, and if the weather was good, we would fly from Tampa in a little single-engine plane piloted by an Island neighbor. When my dad flew in, the pilot would buzz the house, and Mom would get in our car and pick him up at the airstrip.

The airstrip was nothing more than a sandy path with a windsock at one end. There were fiddler crabs all over the end. If a plane was due later in the day, close to sunset, Island residents would line their cars, with lights on, to light the runway.

Andy and his father, Earl Torgeson.

One fall, Rick Hutchinson flew to Tampa a little earlier than the rest of the family. His parents told him to go into the terminal, ask around and find the pilot who would take him to the Island. In those days the Tampa airport was about as big as a house. The plane landed, Rick looked around and went to the lunch counter. A man called out, "Are you Rick Hutchinson? Come over and sit down. Are you hungry? We'll leave as soon as I finish breakfast."

After the regular season in the mid-1950s, Dad came home and said that he had a job managing winter ball in Managua, Nicaragua. My mom thought this would be a great adventure and a good education for my brother and me. Dad had a team there made up of eight minor leaguers from the United States. There were a total of four teams in the Nicaraguan League. Johnny Pesky, of the Boston Red Sox, managed one of the other teams, made up primarily of local talent.

Patsy and Fred came down for a visit. There were only three hotels in town. Managua had been destroyed years before by a terrible earthquake, and it really hadn't recovered much. The only hotel in town with air conditioning was three stories high and had a pool. General Somoza, brother of then President Somoza and future President of Nicaragua, came every morning to have breakfast in the large open-air dining room. He snapped his quirt on his boot top as he marched into the dining room and his steps echoed through the hotel.

Fear won over air conditioning after a couple of good tremors sent things flying off the shelves, and my dad moved us out of town to an enclave of little houses where John and Ruthie Pesky and their son, David, lived. David, Andy and I went to the American School. Tremors often sent kids running from the schoolroom to the yard. We caught on pretty quickly.

Each year, spring training came and the "Boys of Summer" arrived on the Island and began to ease their way into shape. Players often arrived overweight and out of playing condition. It was not like today, where players are fit and work out all year. Back then, players arrived at spring training to get in shape. Spring was a time to get the knots out, a time for fans and players alike to bask in the warm sunshine and enjoy the game before the serious playing started. It gave managers time with the rookies and to work new players into the lineup. They spent the four weeks getting ready to play. Some people say that they really didn't care who won or not.

My dad loved the game of baseball and the fans. When he hit a home run he would run around the bases waving his hat above his head, and occasionally came back out of the dugout for an encore. The fans loved it, and he loved playing to the crowd.

Sometimes called "Boston's Jesting First Baseman" or "The Earl of Snohomish" by the sportswriters, Dad was always ready with a good story or a joke. He also had the nickname, "Superman." Dad wore horn-rimmed glasses, and the kids thought he looked like Clark Kent. Some said it was because you never knew what to expect next from him.

Injuries were always a big part of his life. He was known for his head-first slides which more than once dislocated his shoulder. A host of other injuries plagued him his entire career.

During spring training of 1948, Dad was out with an injured finger, and one teammate after another started nursing their own aches and pains. He held a "Courageous Athletes Derby" for the plagued Braves. Dad and Connie Ryan made up a chart and awarded points for various ailments such as: five points for a sprained back, three points for a twisted knee, two points for a blister, four for a twisted ankle or charley-horse, and so on.

Dad claimed he was in the running with his infected finger until Jeff Heath rushed in at the finish, producing two blisters, a crooked sacroiliac and a hangnail. He solemnly declared Heath was the champion. Their slogan became, "It's not whether you win or lose, but how much tape you use." He then awarded a Badge of Merit to veteran pitcher Red Barrett, "Because he dared to pitch without having anything to throw."

After spring training, all the "Boys" headed north to Boston, New York, Philadelphia, Cincinnati, Pittsburgh, Washington D.C., Detroit, St. Louis, Chicago, Milwaukee or wherever they were playing.

The families all stayed in Florida until school was out. Then Mom would close up the house, pack the old Mercury station wagon with us and our dog, Duke, and head north on old US 41 or US 301.

Some years, we took the train. Since the road trips the team took were long, we tried to time our arrival in town so that we could see Dad while he was playing in a home series.

The second season my dad played for Philadelphia, we had just settled into our rental accommodations in Philly when Dad learned he was traded to the Detroit Tigers. He flew to Detroit, Mom packed up the old Mercury again and headed down the Pennsylvania Turnpike in a heat wave. A few miles out of town, we heard a noise and looked out the back window to see the rack flying off the top of the car and our stuff all over the highway. We got it all packed into the car and started up again. The engine blew in Harrisburg and we spent three days in a hotel. Thank goodness there was a nice house waiting for us outside of Detroit.

Patsy's sister, Bobbie, rode north with Patsy and the kids, and they took two weeks to get to Cincinnati. Well, they were just taking their time, thinking they would arrive in town when the team did. When they got to the station, the players told her, "Wait till Fred sees you! He hasn't known where you were for a week!"

Another year Patsy and their family took the train to Cincinnati, they thought. Suddenly, Patsy and the four kids and the two dogs were put off the train in Lincolnville, Kentucky, because that was as far as that train went with dogs. She had to hire a car to drive the family to the ballpark in Cincinnati.

It was really nice when you moved into a new town for just a few months and you could live near the other players families. While their husbands were on the road, the baseball wives supported one another. The kids played and the families had fun together. If one of the kids got sick, or they needed someone to watch the kids, or if they just wanted company, it was really good to have each other.

Once we got older, school started before the end of the baseball season, and we had to leave the team early. Mom packed up the car once again and headed south down that long road to Anna Maria Island. It felt so good to cross that rickety bridge and feel the salt air and see our Island. "Safe at home, again!"

Amidst the hot, humid, fall air, every year our moms, by themselves, opened up the houses, got the bugs out, aired everything out and got us settled in for the school year.

So we were growing up. The boys were into sports, and they played pick-up ball wherever there was a field. The Island Baptist Church parking lot was good for football and baseball for a while. Andy remembers playing there until the church put up short, white concrete pilings to designate parking areas. So the boys used them as bases and home plate. That worked unless you slid into one, or if you were up to bat, swung at a low ball, and hit the piling instead. That would be a real stinger, and it could wreck your bat.

Earl Torgeson made a spectacular catch in the 1948 series. Ernie Cagnina, with cigar, can be seen in the background and John Ringling is on the right.

Jo Ann Ryan, who owned Key Sundries, lived in a house adjacent to the church parking lot on Archer Way. "She was really nice at the Key Sundries, but she was not happy when a ball went into her yard," Andy said. He admitted he was one of the boys who carved his initials into the brand-new shiny tin lids on the canisters she had on the counter top at her store.

The boys played ball in the Roser Church parking lot, but eventually that got to be too small. So Rick, Jack, Johnny Cagnina, and brothers Bobby and Tommy Hawkins started playing down near the end of the airstrip in Holmes Beach.

John Cagnina said: "The area we wanted to use as a field was tidal with hundreds of fiddler crabs, so they dragged it, and then we picked all the shells off the field. We built a backstop, but there wasn't any fence, so when you hit a ball, it just kept rolling. John remembers one particular ball my dad hit went out of sight. Remembering the years of baseball on the Island, Rick and Johnny said, "We all just had a lot of fun. The Island really was a magical place."

Bobby Hawkins was at bat the day his father threw a nice ball over the plate. Bobby whacked it and hit his father straight on and Stewart fell flat on his back. When Dad and Fred were in town, they worked with the boys to teach the fundamentals of baseball, and joined them in pick up games.

Birdie Tebbetts was manager of the Braves in 1962.

"Stewart Hawkins was most instrumental of all in pulling us together to play baseball. Stewart was with us all the way up," said Rick. "He got us together, found us a place to play, formed teams and played ball."

Patsy and Fred could see there was a real need for a field to play ball, so with Bennie Scanio, they appeared before the city commission to make them aware that land for a public playground was getting scarce.

"The commission agreed, and a deal was made with the school board to allow the school property, on Magnolia Avenue, to be used as a playground. City land that had been used as a garbage dump was swapped for land adjoining the school," wrote Wyatt Blassingame in his article, "The Youth Center History" on July 2, 1961. "Walter Hardin donated a lot. Captain Bill Davis swapped land he owned for some elsewhere, and the entire block, containing the school building, was set aside for a Youth Center."

The property was still largely mangrove and jungle for a few years. The playground developed slowly, and some land was cleared for a rough ball field. Mrs. Clyde Phelps taught in the old school house on the property in 1934. Stewart Hawkins, Melvin Davis and Richard Ernest kept the building open and showed Saturday night movies.

One night in 1956 was proclaimed "Freddy Hutchinson Night," honoring Fred for his professional career and his work with the Island kids. A testimonial dinner was given for Fred at Pete Reynard's, with proceeds going to the Island playground. Guy Bagley, television sports commentator, was master of ceremonies, and Al Lopez was the guest speaker.

In late 1959, Bennie Scanio's six-year old son, Benji, died of leukemia. Everyone knew the Scanio family, part-owners of the IGA grocery store. Benji's death broke the hearts of our Island community. Bennie Scanio poured himself into the dream of completing the Youth Center in memory of his son.

Fred and Patsy Hutchinson, Dr. Roy and Mary Gunther, J.D. and Jackie Webb, Lew and Mary Burdette, my dad and mother were among many who worked at raising money. Money started coming in from all over, even the Atlantic Coast Line and Seaboard Railroads contributed.

"We went door to door for contributions. We had auctions and fish fries. Even people with very little were giving," recalled Patsy.

When Bennie heard the old Manavista Hotel in Bradenton was being torn down, he personally bought timber and hauled it to the Island in his own truck. The old Ringling winter quarters in Sarasota was being abandoned. Bennie brought the light and tent poles from the circus, tent poles that once toured the world were placed around the Youth Center field. The backstop was part of a lion cage; the barbecue grill was a bear pen and part of the fence had been a monkey cage.

Clay from Tampa came by train and was off-loaded into pick up trucks. Island contractors and carpenters donated materials and labor. The Van Ostenbridge brothers, George Wagner, Father Lowe, Earl Mowry, Johnny Jackson, Stewart Hawkins and others, all worked tirelessly. Their families gave help wherever it was needed. Anna Maria's Volunteer Fire Department had drills on the field, so the field would get watered. Cub Scouts pulled weeds and sandspurs out of the field.

Fred Hutchinson was known as "The Bear."

Marie Scanio Franklin, Bennie's daughter, remembered people coming together. She said, "In those days, if there was something to be done, everyone helped." Fred got every ball player on the Island that spring to pitch in.

"Fred and Warren Spahn both loved being on the tractor," Patsy said. "I had to bring Fred his lunch and hand it to him on the tractor because he just didn't want to give it up to Warren."

And the kids on the Island had a place to play baseball.

Birdie Tebbetts was manager of the Braves in 1962 when he and his wife Mary, their three daughters Sue, Betty, Pat and their son George, moved to Anna Maria. They rented the house across the street from us on Beach Avenue. Once again, the Island's close proximity to the spring training camps was the draw. Birdie also liked being close to his lifelong friend, Fred Hutchinson, and his family.

Birdie had an astounding 53-year career in baseball. He came to the big leagues with Detroit, played with the Red Sox and Cleveland Indians and was a member of four all-star teams. Birdie was manager of the year in 1956 when he was with Cincinnati. He later managed the Cleveland Indians. He was on the field, during spring training with the Indians in Tucson, when he had a heart attack. Birdie returned to limited duty and then resigned as manager in 1966. He scouted for the Mets, Yankees, Orioles and Marlins for the rest of his life-long career.

Mary traveled with the kids from the Island to Milwaukee and then Cleveland where Birdie was manager of the team. She remembered heading north from Anna Maria the first time. She called Birdie and told him she was leaving the next day for the long trip north, and he told her to call him when she stopped for the night.

She finished closing up the house, packing for four kids, loading their possessions into the car, and the next day she drove north. She found a great motel to stop for the night with a pool for the kids. She checked in, gave the kids their swim suits, put her feet up and called Birdie.

"Where are you?" he asked.

"Clearwater," was her reply.

Birdie traveled, scouted and was sought after as a guest speaker. He was a graduate of Providence College, majoring in philosophy, and was a pensive, intelligent man with a great sense of humor.

While Birdie continued traveling, Mary, who had experience working in politics for the governor of New Hampshire, went to work as the Anna Maria City clerk, working with their old friend Ernie Cagnina, mayor of Anna Maria.

When Birdie retired after his lifetime career in baseball, he spent many hours with the Island kids working on their baseball skills. In 2001, the new field by the old airport was named after Birdie in recognition of his work in baseball and contributions to youth on the Island.

"The night the Reds took the National League championship, winning their first pennant since 1940, was the greatest night of Fred's life," recalled Patsy. "In a city rally to celebrate the surprise pennant victory by the Reds, Fred was raised aloft on the shoulders of the delighted fans. They were heading to the World Series to play the New York Yankees. Nicknamed 'The Bear,' and known as the most imposing leader who ever took part in Cincinnati sports, Fred was twice named Manager of the Year. His No.1 jersey has been retired in Cincinnati."

Fred managed three more seasons. In early 1964, he was diagnosed with lung cancer and fought a courageous battle. With fans gathered at Crosley Field for his birthday that summer, he announced it was his last day in uniform. He died later that year.

Baseball greats crowded the tiny Roser Memorial Church to mourn his death. Memorials poured in from across the nation. The field at the Island Youth Center was rededicated, and the name was changed to the Hutchinson-Scanio Memorial Stadium in 1966 at a ceremony attended by baseball commissioner Gen. William Eckert. Members of two major league teams, the Cincinnati Reds and the Kansas City Athletics, attended. Island little leaguers got to shake hands with many big league ball players.

Also present for the ceremony were: George Selkirk, general manager of the Washington Senators; Joe Brown of the Pittsburgh Pirates; Dick O'Connell of the Boston Red Sox and John Quinn of the Philadelphia Phillies; Al Dark, the field manager of the Athletics; Danny Murtaugh of the Pirates; Bob Prince, Pirates broadcaster; Paul Florence, Houston Astro scout; Pat Mullen of the Detroit Tigers and Don Heffner of the Reds.

My father's last year as a player was in 1961 for the New York Yankees. My parents separated, Dad remarried and moved back to the Seattle area. He managed some AAA teams in Arizona and New Jersey for a couple years and left baseball for a career in politics. He died in 1990. My brother and I made our home on the Island with my mom who worked at the Island Medical Center for years.

The era of the Braves came to an end in Bradenton and Anna Maria in 1963. A new roster of players started making Bradenton their home in the winter and spring. When the now "Milwaukee" Braves moved their spring training camp to West Palm Beach, that city built a new stadium to say, "Welcome."

The Braves Field in Bradenton was renamed "McKechnie Field" for the much-loved resident "Deacon" Bill McKechnie. The Hall of Fame manager had a 25-year managerial career with teams including the Pittsburgh Pirates, St. Louis Cardinals, Boston Braves and the Cincinnati Reds.

The Athletics trained in Bradenton for the next five years, and in 1969 Bradenton began its love affair with the Pittsburgh Pirates. The Pirates signed a 40-year lease which has been renewed for an additional 30-years.

The Youth Center has grown into the Anna Maria Island Community Center, providing cultural, education, family support, recreational and social programs for more than 1,200 youth and 2,300 adults in our community each year. The center has one little league baseball field, two soccer fields, a gym, three tennis courts, playgrounds, classrooms, a library and family counseling areas.

Dr. Bill Hutchinson started the Fred Hutchinson Cancer Center in Seattle named in memory of his brother. The center has grown to be a world-class cancer research center, home to researchers and Nobel laureates.

So, whenever you see the Island Community Center, or hear the crack of the bat during spring training in

Bradenton, now you'll know of the tremendous legacy of the "Boys of Winter" who called Anna Maria home.

Christine Torgeson has made her home on Anna Maria Island since 1948.

In 1956 Fred was honored for his professional career and his work with Island kids. Shown from left J. D. Webb and Holmes Beach Mayor Pete Niles congratulate Fred, Patsy and Joe.

Anna Maria Mayor Vanishes

Maxwell L. Woodland was elected mayor of Anna Maria City in February of 1959, to serve a year of the unexpired term of Mayor William Brier, who had resigned. Woodland was reelected to a two-year term in 1960.

In early May of 1961, Mayor Woodland mysteriously abdicated and disappeared. It was rumored he spent a year in Hong Kong and then returned to his native Australia where he died of a heart attack at the age of 39. He left his wife, Marguerite, sons Christopher and Dale and daughter, Melanie, on Anna Maria Island.

Maxwell Woodland was born in Sydney, Australia in 1924. After graduating from high school, Max rode horseback 1,500 miles through the wild country of New South Wales to work at ranches of relatives. He became a drover, which is similar to a cowboy. Drovers are responsible for driving thousands of sheep hundreds of miles to the railroads.

In 1941, at the age of 17, Max enlisted in the Royal Australian Air Force. The next year he was sent to Canada for training as a bomber pilot. Here he met a lovely blonde, Marguerite, and they were married in 1943. He made 33 night-bombing flights over Germany and came back to England with three broken vertebrae in his spine.

After the war, he and his bride returned to Australia where he studied engineering. They decided to settle in Canada, her homeland, and for five years he worked in St. Johns for one of the world's largest accounting firms. In 1953 he accepted the position of comptroller for a large corporation in Texas which operated a chain of stores. Max had always been interested in living in Florida, so several years later the family went south pulling a trailer. He landed a job with an accounting firm in Sarasota, and in 1957 bought a spacious Gulf front home in Anna Maria.

His children, Chris, 12, Dale, 10 and Melanie, 8 lived the good life, swimming, fishing and sailing. On weekends Max would bring the boat around to the beach in front of their home, and he and the children would ski back and forth in front of the house all day. Marguerite brought sandwiches out to the beach at noon. They seemed to be the perfect family. The children were graceful and attractive. Max dressed strikingly and drove a convertible with a mobile phone.

In May of 1959, Max was serving his second term as president of the Anna Maria Elementary School Parent Teacher Association. He was vice president of the Manatee PTA Council and treasurer of the Island Kiwanis Club. In August 1959, the Key Look-Out magazine featured his picture on the cover with the caption, "Man of the Keys." The inside story went on to say, "Max Woodland, 35 years old, has come a long way. He is a successful businessman, an important community leader and a dedicated family man. He lives the life he planned in exactly the place he planned to live. He is imaginative, humorous, likeable, has movie-star good looks and a stern sense of duty to the community."

However, there were problems, but they were kept private until Aug. 24, 1960, when Max had Marguerite committed to the mental health unit of Sarasota Memorial Hospital. She remained hospitalized for 21 days. She was sedated and given 10 or 12 shock treatments. Her friends and children were sure she was not insane. Her daughter said it was a "put-up job." Friends thought surely someone could not be committed and given shock treatments merely at the urging of an unhappy husband. Melanie and Marguerite both said it was to get her out of the way.

The Woodland children, from left, Chris, Melanie and Dale.

Then one day, he was gone. People recalled Max acting strangely months before he disappeared. He started carrying a gun and moved to a place of his own. Local papers wrote about him when his car was stolen. He was arrested for drunkenness in public and charged with non-support of his family. A few days after the arrests, he relinquished his half interest in the Sarasota accounting firm, told Marguerite he was returning to his friends, and vanished.

Years later the St. Petersburg Times ran a story entitled, "A Love Lost." Marguerite had called the newspaper with a complex tale of foreign intrigue woven around a handsome man who disappeared, seemed to have died, but according to her, did not die. She had approached the reporter calmly, prepared with an array of dates, facts and documents. The papers were about the man who walked away from being mayor of a Florida town, gave up a good business, a political office, his family and the respect and admiration of many people. There was talk of another woman.

Marguerite was consumed by the notion that her husband had ditched his family, fled to Australia, faked his death and returned to America and made millions. Why was she so obsessed with this? "Money," she said. Glenn Braswell was a rich man and if he was Max Woodland she had the right to become rich too.

How did Glenn fit into the story? In 1977 she saw a picture of a man named Glenn Braswell in an ad for body care products. Immediately she told anyone who would listen that it was Max. A Bradenton photographer said the picture of Glenn looked a lot like Max, but it could be a coincidence. She even wrote to Braswell in Macon, Georgia, but never received a reply. The federal grand jury was investigating Braswell's mail order business. If he was indicted, Marguerite said she would be there to look him in the face.

Mayor Maxwell Woodland was a drover in Australia.

Meanwhile, the Woodlands' lovely home on the Gulf was in sad disrepair, cluttered with boxes, papers, photographs, yellowing newspapers and cats. Marguerite never threw away anything, thinking there might be a clue to explain what had happened to her since the day she met Max. She could not afford to spay and neuter the two cats she took in, so they turned into almost two dozen cats. The ceiling was moldy and there were leaks in the roof. The yard was overgrown, and the house, once filled with a happy family, was faded on the outside and falling apart on the inside.

It took Marguerite almost two years to track Max down. She discovered he had been issued a passport in Miami, and then traced his wanderings to Hong Kong, Chicago, the Philippines, Hawaii and Australia. She caught up with him on May 3,1963, through Sydney police who had advised him he had fallen far behind in his support payments. Three weeks later a telegram from Australia to the Anna Maria police read: "Maxwell Lloyd Woodland died in Sydney on May 25, 1963. Please ascertain from his wife funeral arrangements." She took the news with relief. By return telegram her instructions were to bury him in Australia, half a world away, "We all said, Thank God he's dead."

Marguerite wrote to Max's family in Australia asking about the circumstances regarding his death. There were never any replies. Nine years later in 1972, Christopher made plans to visit Australia. A few weeks before, he was scheduled to fly with friends to the Bahamas. The single-engine plane crashed, killing all five people on board. According to the report, the right wing fell off and the plane spiraled into a thick stand of trees and exploded. Marguerite grieved, but her grief soon turned to suspicion. Why would a wing fall off? Was it just a coincidence that he died just a few weeks before going to Australia?

There were many unanswered questions. A psychic told Marguerite that Max was alive and had something to do with the crash. Each of us may supply a different ending to this story. Some believe Max Woodland died. Others believe he is living, agreeing with Marguerite who is possessed by the man she no longer loves, but cannot forgive or forget.

Marguerite Woodland believes Max is alive.

Anna Maria Island in 1958 looking north from Bradenton Beach.

Two

Island Wildlife

Jamie and Drew Adams feed their raccoons by the "coondiminium" while their pup seems bored with the whole transaction.

Wild Animals Roamed The Island

Anyone who loves animals should have been here many years ago. Living on Anna Maria Island in the pre-developmental days was paradise. Alligators, snakes, armadillos, porcupines and deer were just a few of the creatures roaming around. One little known fact, reported by Capt. Mitch Davis, Anna Maria's first mayor, was that Harry Ditmas, the postman, raised turkeys.

Before the bridge was built in 1921, everything and everybody came to the Island by boat. Horses and cows swam across at the narrowest part of the bay between Cortez and Bradenton Beach.

In a speech to the Anna Maria Star Club in 1945, Marion Colman, granddaughter of the first homesteader,

George Emerson Bean, told about animals on the Island in the early days.

"There was plenty to eat for the taking," she said. "Lots of clams, oysters, fish, turtles, rabbits, deer, ducks and other game birds, and turtle eggs were all easy to find. I remember the big rooster that chased all the children and the goat that would butt anyone over who tried to milk her. The Halls thought goat's milk would be good for their baby, who was not thriving. Even without the milk the baby got along fine. He grew up to be the well-known writer for *Reader's Digest*, Clarence Hall."

Wyatt Blassingame, prolific writer and animal lover, arrived on the Island in the 1930s.

Island writer was a naturalist

Acclaimed Island author Wyatt Blassingame and his wife, Gertie, arrived on the Island in the late '30s. He put Anna Maria Island on the map after his article "Anna Maria, I Love You" appeared in the *Ford Times* in 1957.

'George, Island heron, becomes local celebrity

ANNA MARIA CITY — Wyatt Blassingame, the Island's illustrious author, has an article in the current issue of Ford Times, the Ford owner's magazine. Color illustrations are by Eric Von Schmidt of Sarasota.

"George, the Great Blue Heron," is a delightful story about "a big bird with personality-plus." Islanders should be touched by the narrative since Blassingame's meeting with the 'great blue' took place by a canal in Key Royale.

Pearl referred to in the tale is Pearl McCoy, the sister of his wife Jeanne, who now lives on Hammock Drive, Anna Maria.

George is well known by residents along the canal and is kept well fed with chicken necks and other delicacies. Writing of their first meeting, Blassingame says, "He stood well over three feet tall. The blue-black crest on his head was partly raised. His eyes were golden circles with jet centers. He looked at me

Drive. The one George stalked and stabbed. "He jumped back, staring at the thing in amazement. And then — I'll swear to it — he turned his head in embarrassment. At least I think he did," wrote Blassingame.

The prolific writer is now working on a book about crows, one of the Dodd, Meade and Company series for third through sixth grade readers. He has completed books on alligators, raccoons and frogs. His research covers a variety of areas. Information on crows he has gleaned not only from books, but also from Pam Stewart, the well known bird lady of Bradenton.

"Pam had a crow for 17 years," said Blassingame. "She has a young one, just a year old, which she is giving me. I'll keep it as a pet on the porch as soon as my friend, Harry Rife, can get the cage built."

Most consider crows boisterous and overbearing but actually they can be

GORGEOUS GEORGE — George, the great blue heron become a celebrity since his story appeared in the Febr

"We rented a house on the bay, with no nearby neighbors. It had two bedrooms, a living room, a dining room, kitchen, bath, three mice, several giant Florida spiders, a chameleon and a blacksnake.

"Our first morning when I went across the road to swim. The blacksnake, which was basking on the front step, went with me. Gertie, watched from the window. When I got back she was packing. She was, she told me, on her way back to New York. She didn't go."

An account in *The Islander* in 1955 explained it this way. "This is Anna Maria Island where robins become intoxicated, a dolphin steals a rubber ball from bathers, five kittens were born in a grandfather clock and a group of boys and girls are raising two-day-old 'coons." All facts were verified in this report turned in by Mrs. Frank Dunham.

Rambunctious Rascals

The following articles appeared in several issues of *The Islander:* "Raising raccoons is a new fad on the island. Seven boys, one girl and one cat are raising a litter of baby 'coons. Richard Kermode's dog unearthed a nest containing five baby 'coons while on Fiddlers Flats. The mother 'coon attacked his dog and the dog ran into the water with the mother 'coon attached to his rear. The dog came back, but the mother disappeared leaving the babies. Danny Carnahan is feeding an infant 'coon, with its eyes shut, using a medicine dropper. Danny's mother found a baby doll bottle which works better. The 'coon sleeps nestled in soft cloths in a parakeet cage. The other 'coon babies were cared for by Richard, his brother Rusty, Jackie Ehrenzeller and Bobbie Cable.

"Freddy Asher got one on a trade from Roby Robson. The 'coon was traded for a model airplane and an old lawn mower motor. Jerry Ingram found a tiny 'coon in a stump and brought it home. He feeds it baby formula four times a day. When it was three-weeks old, Mrs. Ingram said it was time for the 'coon to leave the foot of

Jerry's bed and sleep outside. The first night out the 'coon caught cold, but seems to be recovering. Last night the 'coon slept with a two-month-old kitten, and they got along very well.

"A two-day-old 'coon was presented to the Ernest family. Their cat, Long Sam, just had a litter of kittens in the antique grandfather clock. When the cat and her five babies were later moved into a box, Long Sam was given the baby 'coon whose eyes were not yet open. The 'coon nuzzled up to the cat and started nursing. The cat licked her the same as she did her own kittens and accepted her as one of her family."

Back in the '50s, raccoons were numerous on the Island and were annoying residents because they turned over trash cans and scattered the contents. In September of 1954, the Bradenton Beach City Council heard a letter from a concerned citizen: "The city has not picked up rubbish and garbage and 'coons are playing with it." Everyone was warned not to approach them, especially in the daylight hours, since they might be rabid.

Oscar Ohlson, an Island character, had many pets. In 1957, he was raising two small 'coons, one adolescent 'coon and many kittens and cats. He said they were all more trustworthy than people.

In 1957, *The Islander* carried a photo entitled: "Ohlson and Friends." The caption read: "It would not be possible to gather all his speechless friends into one picture. Here we see him with a baby 'coon. A larger one was taking a bath in a rowboat. Cats and kittens were all over the place. Oscar Ohlson is between 80 and 90 and has the heart of a teenager with the wisdom years bring. His little cottage, or rather his small patio, is the real Holmes Beach Town Hall."

Oscar Ohlson lived in a shack near the Holmes Beach City Hall and raised a variety of pets.

In another *Islander* article a pet raccoon was featured. It read: "Bobby Cannon of Anna Maria has a baby 'coon and his name is Salty, because Bobby's dog is named Pepper. All three are good companions. The 'coon climbs up Bobby's legs and curls around his neck. Like Mary's lamb, it follows him to school ambling alongside of him. However, the 'coon is uncomfortable walking with climbing claws on paved roads."

Also in the newspaper was the story about Jamie and Drew Adams of Anna Maria who had an eight-week old raccoon named Sneaker. It had the run of the house, showered with the boys, and played with the two dogs. Sometimes Sneaker curled up in bed with the boys, but most nights were spent in his own "coondiminium." The Adams family raised about a dozen raccoons.

My family had many experiences with raccoons. My sons came home with a treasure one day. An infant raccoon had fallen from a tree and been abandoned. They talked us into letting them keep it and we named her Rosemary Cooney. We found a tiny baby doll bottle to feed her, but the trouble began when she started eating. As Rosemary grew so did her appetite. She would scurry around the house looking for handouts, and if no one fed her she would help herself.

Many times I caught her on the dining room table scooping up sugar out of the bowl. Her front paws were

Drew Adams and his pet raccoon, Sneaker.

like hands and very functional. I would pick her up, and toss her out the kitchen door, only to have her race around to the front door rip the screen and come right back.

The day came when I had had enough. I told the children they would have to find another home for Rosemary who had grown huge. The Misner family ran a marina on Pine Avenue and were glad to give our wayward 'coon a home. In fact, they gave her a room of her own, and she dined on scrambled eggs and bacon every morning.

The late Wyatt Blassingame wrote *The Wonders of Raccoons*, which featured a photo taken by the first police chief of Holmes Beach, Snooks Adams. It shows dozens of raccoons which gathered in his yard every evening. Some residents had flood lights installed and fed the "bandits" as entertainment for their guests.

The tale of Racky is about a baby raccoon adopted by John Prothero's mother. The Protheros had rental units in the '50s. They bred love birds and gave geranium plants to everyone. Racky lived at the end of a 10-foot chain and slept in half a barrel in the yard. One day he curled up in a tree enjoying the sunshine when suddenly he started to scream. Mrs. Prothero ran out and saw a bald eagle a few feet from Racky anticipating an easy brunch. Racky was quickly pulled away and neighbors were called to verify the presence of an eagle. The story had a happy ending with Racky safe in the barrel enjoying the aroma of Old Forrester whiskey. An account of a mother and baby 'coon that came daily to the Theodore Patzke house on Pine Avenue, next door to Roser Church, was written up in the Christmas Eve issue of *The Islander* in 1953. The pair would show up at 6:45 every night, so Ted rigged a ladder. On the top, a can was nailed to an upright board. Below was another can for food and on the ground two trays of water.

The entire scene was illuminated by a floodlight so it was possible to sit in the kitchen less than six-feet away and watch the cute animals perform. They washed and ate, ate and washed and came and went as if there were no humans or enemies within miles.
The 'coons were clean with coats combed and brushed as if they had visited a beauty parlor. It was inconceivable that they would knock over garbage cans and eat refuse, not as long as Ted provided fresh bread daily and encouraged them to partake. They were a joy for Mrs. Patzke, who had been confined to the house while recovering from a serious illness, to watch.

Donna Girard loved all the animals on the Island. She had raccoons, kittens, chickens and other critters that wandered by her home.

Gen. Taylor phoned an *Islander* reporter to tell him he forgot to take in a bowl of sauce and cooking utensils from his barbecue grill. The 'coons came after dark, emptied the bowl, and departed with a long fork. The reward offered for the fork was an invitation to the next barbecue. Gen. Taylor wondered what a 'coon would do with a barbecue fork.

In the late '50s our family moved into an old house on Spring Avenue. It was like a barn since it had not been entirely finished. We were glad to have the low rent and stayed until our house near the North Point was built. As soon as we moved into the old wooden structure we heard noises at night. When we went outside we saw raccoons on the roof. There was a mother and her babies plus several large males. In the daytime they lived in the attic.

Mae Wiggins, wife of the pastor of Roser Church, the Rev. Richard Wiggins, remembered a raccoon experience. "Richard and I were living on Pine Avenue in 1955. In those good old days no one locked their doors. We were sleeping one night when I awoke to hear scraping, scratching sounds coming from the kitchen. I awoke Richard and whispered that someone was trying to get in the house. He made a muffled sound, turned over and resumed snoring. I shook him again, but got the same response.

"Since I could not sleep, I got up, tiptoed down the hall and flipped the kitchen light on. Lo and behold there was Chico, the neighborhood raccoon. He was carefully going through scraps from supper in the trash can. Chico was as surprised as I. We looked at each other; then he dropped the snack and went out the screen door that he had opened. I crawled back in bed to hear the sound of someone in a deep sleep."

Coondiminium Constructed

By Judy Adams

We have always had animals around our house. Most were orphaned and in need of special care. There were snakes, parrots, skunks, possums, turtles, squirrels, rabbits and assorted birds, to name a few. Bringing us the most joy were the raccoons. It was satisfying to raise them until they were old enough to be released.

One pair got us into a building mode in 1960. It was probably Anna Maria's first and only condo and we called it the "coondiminium." It was complete with several floors, decks, an old hollow log and running water. We placed it on the upper deck of our Gulf front house to give the occupants a better view and Gulf breezes, and it was once featured in the Island newspaper.

We named one pair of raccoons Double and Trouble, because they were. Jim found them abandoned among the mangroves and brought them home. Our two young sons were delighted to have wild animals around. Learning to feed, care and play with them kept the boys busy. Raccoons are not laid back animals. They move and play all the time. When they matured, we released them at the spot where they were found. We had many similar happy endings with orphaned animals. My very favorite was a raccoon we named Mini. She was found in an attic close to our home and appeared to be about a day old. We fed her goat's milk through an eye-dropper and she survived.

Mini was like a cat and lived with us for almost 18 years. She had all her shots and was spayed. Mealtime was whenever Mini wanted food, and of course, she had to have water to dip it in. Bedtime was an event. She slept with my son, Jamie, on her satin pillow, and when he was away she slept with me.

One of her favorite activities was watching fishermen on the beach and waiting for the right time to steal their catch from a bucket and run. Our cat picked up this fishing strategy. Once a fisherman caught her swiping his catch and chased her off the beach. She soon returned to try again.

After a few years we built another coondominium, larger and with all the comforts of home. We found there was something special about sharing part of your life with wild creatures. The rewards of watching them grow and providing special care were some of our finest moments.

One time, we had a renter who brought home everything he could catch. We had a torrential rain one night. He collected and brought home more than 150 frogs. The frogs croaked so loud we had to suggest he take them elsewhere. The same man came home a day later, with a small horse and tried to convince us to let it stay at our house. This renter stayed long enough to have the horse's picture in the newspaper, and then they both moved on.

Alligators were spotted in the Gulf and Island canals in the early days.

Astonishing Alligators

This is the tale of an alligator as written in *The Islander* on August 15, 1957: "This is exactly what happened, although you may read a less intimate story in the daily papers. Saturday morning at 11:30, Mrs. Ken Coles telephoned the newspaper office. Some men were trying to shoot a 10-foot alligator in the Holmes Beach Yacht Basin. The *Islander* staff photographer hastened to the scene.

"All was quiet! Joe Hicks, with a rifle fitted with a telescopic sight, was talking to Mr. and Mrs. Pete Reynard, managers of the Yacht Club. The alligator was gone, submerged, annoyed at a couple of Joe's shots that were near hits. Nobody knew if the beast would surface again, so Joe handed the unloaded rifle to Pete with a box of ammunition. 'Keep these for me, Pete. If he should show again I'll come back,' Joe said.

"Well, in about 10-minutes Mrs. Reynard spotted the alligator. He came up a few yards from the dock and was eyeing Pete's two dachshunds. Quickly Pete loaded the rifle and took careful aim. But he did not know how to release the safety catch. Several times he tried but the alligator just looked up and grinned, his mouth watering as he eyed the tasty 'hot dogs.' Pete spied Joe's car and his wild yells brought him back to the scene. Joe checked the rifle to see if it was loaded. Balancing the heavy weapon on a dock piling he aimed and shot once. The monster jumped, turned over and was dead."

Later, the alligator was measured, he was exactly eight feet long. Ken Coles came to the Yacht Club with part of the dressed tail and some steaks. He asked Pete to cook them at his restaurant, since he claimed they tasted as good as frog legs. Pete took one look at the alligator steaks, turned a pale green and exclaimed, "Cook them? Not in my pots."

The very first alligator tale I heard was the one about the alligator that chased Clyde Phelps up a tree. He had a nursery on Pine Avenue, where he and Lena lived. Lena was working in the kitchen one morning when she heard a commotion outside. She opened the front door and saw Clyde up a tree across the street by the canal and a large alligator looking up at him hoping he would drop down. The 'gator had a young one nearby and kept Clyde treed most of the day. Finally someone had to shoot the 'gator so Clyde could go home to supper.

My son recalled Dickie Wagner had a pet alligator that swam in the pool with his family in Bradenton Beach.

Roaming Rodents

We were awakened in the middle of the night by splashing water. "It must be Chester getting a drink out of the toilet," my husband groaned, "I'll have a look." He stumbled into the bathroom, switched on the light and then slammed the door. He had seen a huge water rat climbing out of the toilet. In the morning he went outside and peered through the window. The rat lay still on the floor. Its head was caught in the door.

One other rodent invaded our home before George installed a valve, so nothing could come through the pipe to the house. We were sound asleep. I awoke when George gasped and sat up. "A rat just landed on my head and ran down the length of my body," he said.

I jumped out of bed screaming. I would not go back into the bedroom until he caught the rat. He slid a trap under the bed and soon we heard it snap. We told our rat story many times. George marveled at the velvety softness of the rat's feet. Since George had sparse hair, he felt the little feet on his head. I trembled to think what would have happened if it landed on my head and got tangled in my hair.

Our neighbor Rosemary hollered for help one day when two rats came up into her toilet bowl. George and our son, John, got rid of them. I didn't ask how. Flaps were installed in her pipes also.

Prized Pets

"Island dog owners of pure bred dogs together with residents of Manatee County, similarly afflicted, are invited to attend a meeting at the Chamber of Commerce at the Bradenton Memorial Pier to establish a permanent organization of Manatee County dog lovers. Among those expected to be present is the English and American champion white bull terrier from St. Pete. He will bring his owner with him. Dog lovers should not miss this groundwork meeting of what will probably become the Manatee County Kennel Club." This announcement was in *The Islander* on Sept.17, 1953.

Many exceptional dogs lived on Anna Maria Island at this time. Bambi was a magnificent Llewellyn owned by Conrad Clevers of Anna Maria. Folks who lived along the Gulf from the post office to the North Point used Bambi as a water thermometer. Every morning Bambi would go to the beach. He would step daintily into the water. If it suited him, he would plunge in and swim half a mile. But if Bambi refused to go in the water, there wasn't much sense in putting your bathing suit on. It meant the water was too cold and you better wait a day or two.

It was the early '60s when Glenn and Vivian Carlson's dog gave birth to a bunch of black and white pups in their Holmes Beach home. When they asked if we would like to have one, we didn't hesitate saying yes. We named him Chester and brought him home in a shoebox. There was never a dull moment at our house after Chester moved in. He grew to be a medium-sized terrier and was wonderful with the children and our assorted pets. One thing Chester did not like was to be confined. In those days, there was no emphasis on male dogs being neutered. Chester and Pee Wee Jones, who lived on North Shore Drive, were known far and wide as the Romeos of the Island.

One evening, George and I were attending a party in Holmes Beach. The police came to the door looking for George. He disappeared with the officer, and when he returned he had a wild story to tell.

Chester was seldom still, except when a camera was in front of him.

It seems Chester escaped from the house, which was almost a daily occurrence, and discovered a Doberman pinscher in heat on North Shore Drive. When he began digging under the fence to get to her, the owner called the police. By the time George and the officer arrived, Chester had dug a huge hole and was just about to go under the fence. George picked Chester up and as he turned to leave the owner yelled, "Your dog is oversexed!" Everyone at the party thought it was hilarious.

The next time Chester got out of line, it was not as funny. We would take Chester to the Holmes Beach airstrip to run. It was a large, usually deserted field. Sometimes I would drive slowly in the car and Chester would run along in the field. One day the unexpected happened. I saw him look up, and then I saw a small plane coming in for a landing. I knew what was on his mind. *A big bird for me to chase!* I called him to no avail.

The plane got closer. Chester ran out to meet it. You guessed it. The plane hit him. He rolled over and lay still. My only thought was get him off the field. When I got to him, the school bus had just stopped to let the children off. They couldn't believe their eyes. Somehow I picked him up and got him to the car. He was hurt and looked at me soulfully. The closest veterinarian was Dr. Butler in town on 17th Avenue. When I got there I jumped out of the car, ran in and asked the receptionist if the doctor was in. When she said yes, I turned, and ran out the door saying, "Chester was hit by a plane." I heard her holler, "A what?" as I headed to the car. Chester was treated for a broken pelvis (I still have the x-ray) and he was fine in no time.

We tried to keep Chester tied up or in the house, but with four active children it was easy for the intrepid canine to escape. Another romantic adventure led him down Bay Boulevard in front of the Parrish home. A frantic Marilyn called me exclaiming, "You have a vicious dog. Come get him right away. He's terrorizing the neighborhood."

There was a poodle in heat next door to her, and Chester was running up and down the street barking, chasing people and cars, just showing off. Chester was severely reprimanded when we got him home, but soon he was off again.

Our good friends, Helen and Bill Clark, lived directly across from the Bayfront Park in Anna Maria City. To Helen's surprise, she saw Chester peering in her living room window one day. He was not alone. The security man, who patrolled the park, was with him- stick in hand.

"Do you know who this dog belongs to," he asked Helen. "Of course," she said, "it's Chester, the Norwoods' dog." Seems Chester had figured out that if he toured the Bayfront Park, especially on weekends, he could get tasty tidbits from the picnickers. When the patrolman held up a stick, he said Chester became violent. We thought he just wanted to play. Nevertheless, Chester was arrested.

We had to appear at the Anna Maria City Court, which was held in the old icehouse on Pine Avenue. Mayor Harvey Meyer fined us $25, which was a lot of money for us in those days. Soon after this, I purchased a Yashica camera and became a reporter for the *St. Petersburg Times*. I earned a measly 10-cents an inch for my writing, but soon I discovered I could earn $5 for every picture I took that appeared in the paper.

Chester was a great subject and soon paid back the $25 fine. One Saturday I had five photos in the paper. Whoever picked out the pictures at the *St. Petersburg Times* liked dogs, children and beach shots. What a fun job.

Rev. Richard Wiggins, pastor of Roser Church in the '60s, told this tale: "It happened in the mid '40s when we were spending the summer on the Island in the family home on Spring Avenue. The Blackburns lived just around the corner on Pine Avenue, across from Roser Church.

"My brother Jim and I befriended a wandering bull dog. It was the ugliest dog we ever saw. He was obviously lost and in need of water. Our mother decided the dog needed a temporary home until the owner could be found. Little did we know the dog slept on his back and snored louder than any human being.

"Decisions... Decisions" was the caption of this picture of Chester that went across the country on the Associated Press. The picture was taken on the Holmes Beach field where hundreds of fire hydrants were lined up waiting to be placed throughout the Island.

"He was quickly relegated to the small back porch, but could still be heard all over the house. It was a great relief when his owner claimed him after several days. We often wondered how a dog with such short legs could have made it from Bradenton Beach to the north end of Anna Maria Island. We credited my special friend, Humbug

Cobb, for spreading the word about the lost dog."

The Van Ostenbridge family had an unusual cat. He was a neutered tomcat, and they named him Baby Sister. He loved water in any form. Frequently he fell in the toilet and bathtub and would stalk fish along the seawall. Baby Sister would fall or jump in when he thought he could catch a fish. When he wanted to go outside at night he ran up and down the piano keys. Vicki Van Ostenbridge was three when she dressed the cat in baby clothes, complete with bonnet and bottle, and entered him in the DeSoto pet contest. He won for being the funniest.

The Van Ostenbridge family also owned a pet pig. They named it Arnold. He was perfumed, sported painted toes and was trained to walk with a harness and leash. "He still smelled like a pig," Vicki's mother, Daryl, said. "Within three weeks we gave him to a petting zoo."

Other pets in the fun-loving family were "male" gerbils that proceeded to reproduce rapidly. A few were sold, then they gave some away and finally they begged people to take the rest. Butch's science project of a homemade incubator produced two hens and a rooster. The rooster attacked anything female and chased Daryl around the yard more than once.

Creeping Critters

One evening while watching television I saw something out of the corner of my eye. It hopped across the living room floor. Without a sound I lifted my feet. It was an enormous toad. My reaction came from years of experience living with boys. You do not scream or in any way act afraid of any animal large or small because you might get it in your lap. Since moving to Florida, I had become accustomed to many crawling things. I had heard bugs grow larger in the tropics, and I agreed.

My first encounter with the larger variety happened soon after arriving on the Island. I yanked a bureau drawer open and came face to face with a mammoth spider. The body was as large as a walnut with legs extending to about five inches. I shrieked!!!

Later that day, I was on the beach chatting with a neighbor who was a native. She asked if I had a housekeeper. "Oh no," I replied. "I've always done my own housework." She laughed and explained that the large spiders that lurk in drawers and other nooks were referred to as housekeepers since they disposed of many bugs.

In the Christmas issue of *The Islander*, on Dec. 20, 1951, a headline proclaimed "Pets, Dogs and Children!" There was an upcoming pet and doll show, with an exhibition and contests to be held at the Youth Center. Dogs, cats, ducks, pigeons, dolls, lizards, and an alley cat named Highway excited the children and parents who filled the center. Mary Ernest brought her singing dog. Some of the dogs were obscure with mixed breeds and no pride of ancestry, but with energetic designs for posterity, according to *The Islander* reporter. In the article was a story about an exotic visitor named Squeaky, since that was the sound he made. It was an 18-month old prairie dog, owned by Marshall Davis who was vacationing from Tampa with his family at Playa Encantada in Holmes Beach. Squeaky won two ribbons and the grand prize in the Skyway Playground Show in Tampa. He was uncooperative with The Islander photographer, since he had just had a bath and was mad at the whole world.

Private Phew

"If you want a pet that is both a friend and companion, a pet that you can feel affection for and be sure that it, in turn, feels affection for you, get a dog. Do not get a skunk," wrote Island author Wyatt Blassingame in his book entitled, *Skunks.*

"But, if you want a pet that will make people stop and stare, a pet you can't be sure of from one minute to the next, one that is always interesting then, maybe a skunk is the pet for you," he continued.

"By nature a skunk is a wild animal. Even when born and raised in captivity it remains basically a wild creature. It may adapt to life with human beings; it will learn very quickly where its food comes from. In its heart it stays wild and independent. It is this very quality that makes the skunk such an interesting pet for some people," according to Wyatt.

The Egan family named their skunk Private Phew. Erin Egan Kosfeld tells the story: "I was searching through the classified ads for a pet. 'No dogs', my father said."

Since the Egan homestead on North Shore Drive sits directly on the Gulf, that would be too tempting for a canine. Erin and her sisters had owned guinea pigs and hamsters, but she wanted "more of a pet."

She spied an ad for a baby descented skunk and so Pvt. Phew came to live with the Island family. They brought him home in a paper cup and soon he became paper trained and friendly, but one characteristic was most disruptive. Skunks are nocturnal, and Phew would wander around the house at night awakening the family by the clatter of his sharp claws on the floor. One night he nipped Erin's father's toe, so Jack did not think much of him. "He was a joy, but he was a wild animal," Erin's mother, Judie said. Pvt. Phew was about four when he died of a tumor, which is common among skunks, according to Island veterinarian "Doc" Stevens.

A Glistening Bug

On March 13, 1958 Paula Duba came to *The Islander* office with a gold bug in the palm of her hand. It was a beetle-type insect, a half-inch long and appeared to be carved from solid gold. Through a jeweler's glass it was even more beautiful. Part of the gold bug was solid, glistening gold and the rest was translucent gold with a unique under-pattern. Those who saw it hoped the local agriculture agent could give them information on the unusual beetle. We found it was a golden tortoise beetle, often called a goldbug. Both the adults and larvae feed on the leaves of all members of the morning glory family, leaving numerous small holes which give a lacy effect to the leaves.

Dog And Bird Are Buddies

An unusual camaraderie existed between Frisky, a fluffy brown and white terrier, and Ichabod, a large jet-black crow. They were the fascinating pets of the Hugh Holmes family on Sunrise Lane in Holmes Beach. Frisky accepted the bird, which was affectionately called Ikkie, by the family. The two pals collaborated on catching bugs and other pests, and kept all animals out of the yard.

The crow had been found by Mrs. Robert Moses in her yard on 49th Street. She cared for the featherless infant for four weeks and then presented it to the Holmes family who had experience in caring for injured and abandoned birds.

They kept it in a cage for a few weeks, and then the large crow was free to come and go as he pleased. He never ventured out of the bayfront yard except for an occasional visit to the neighbor's bird bath. Ikkie measured about a foot in length with a wing spread a little more than a foot. His favorite spots were under a large shade tree, the porch and seawall where he kept an eye on all the action.

Erin Egan Kosfeld had a most unusual pet with a strange name, Private Phew, the skunk.

Sometimes Ikkie joined the children for a swim, but the house was off limits. Several times he flew into the house and caused a major commotion.

Scary Squirrel

The account of L. H. Dosh walking under a grapefruit tree when a squirrel fell or jumped on him was documented in *The Islander*. The unexpected blow knocked Dosh to the ground. Both were frightened. The squirrel bit Dosh's ear and scratched his face. Then the Doshs' dog, Pooch, came to the rescue and caught the squirrel which was taken to the vet for examination. Dosh visited the doctor for a tetanus shot.

There's A Rattlesnake Under The Hood

By Jim Adams

During the early years, Anna Maria Island was inhabited by a variety of critters. The diamondback rattlesnake was the most dangerous. One summer day my brother, John, and Pete Moore ran over a six-foot rattlesnake. It was slightly injured, so they picked it up with a shovel and placed it under the hood of the car. They decided they would go to the gas station and yell, "There's a rattler under the hood!"

The proprietor of the gas station was Jesse Ingram, who wore many hats in the community. When he heard there was a snake under the hood he raised the hood and took a look. The snake, very irritated by now, took a strike at Jesse and narrowly missed him. His loud proclamations could never be repeated, and Pete and John remained clear of the gas station for several days.

Anna Maria Cobb Recalls The Wild Cat

According to records, Anna Maria Cobb was the first white baby born on Anna Maria Island. She was born in 1897. In an interview, just before she died, the *Bradenton Herald* gave this account of her life in this virtually untouched paradise:

"My parents told me not to ride my horse on the bluffs, but I would do it anyway. We would ride over the sand bluffs that were more than five-feet high. One day, while walking with my brother and sister, we came upon a sleeping wild cat. He woke up and stretched like a cat sticking out his long, sharp claws. We ran away screaming, jumped in a row boat and rowed out into the bay," she recalled. She also remembered close calls with rattlesnakes, seeing deer, rabbits and gophers.

Jack Moore, Bard Of Stone Crabbers

By Jim Adams

J. A. Moore Sr., Pete and Hugh Moore, my brother, John and I stuck together during the early days. One of the most colorful characters on the Island was John Allan Moore, Sr., one of the earliest stone crabbers. He was huge man, weighing more than 300-pounds. He could consume a six-pack of beer at one sitting and not even show the effects. He ran a stone crab business across south Florida from Tampa to Miami.

A very patient man, he treated the Island kids with great kindness. All of us often went with him on his trips to Fort Myers and Miami. He would stop the truck along the Tamiami Trail so we could see the alligators and otters running along the banks of the canals. Our fondest memories were pulling up the crab traps.

Mr. Moore would go on for hours reciting word for word the works of William Shakespeare: "Midsummer Night's Dream," "Julius Caesar" and "Hamlet," he knew them all.

He would quote Hamlet speaking to Laertes or some other character using the old English inflections. He entertained us with tales that we knew nothing about. In later years I learned Jack Moore had a Harvard education.

Blackburns' Pets

In the '40s, the Blackburn family lived in Cozy Corner, a house on Pine Avenue across from Roser Church. They owned a horse that Betty Lou rode all around Anna Maria City. "He was crazy," she recalled. "I would hang on when he'd run to the beach. He liked to roll in the sand and it was frightening. I would have to jump off his back quickly to avoid being crushed." When they moved from Cozy Corner to White Avenue they had a colt named Billy. He was a much calmer horse and liked to go swimming.

Betty Blackburn, a devoted bird lover, and her parrot.

Pattie Welsch with Humprey the armadillo.

Armadillo Palm

An account in the July 21, 1955 *Islander* tells of an escapade experienced by Lil (Mrs. Ed Huth) and her son Danny. They were driving along 67th Street in Holmes Beach when they saw a dark object near the street. It was not moving. Francis Welsch arrived and identified the creature as an armadillo. Their theory was that a visitor had brought it to the Island. It must have been a family pet that got away and could not find its way home. It was buried under a royal palm, which was then named the Armadillo Palm.

Cop Kills Bobcat

A wild bobcat, 33-inches long, hung around the Anna Maria toll bridge plaza frightening employees, according to an article in the June 1,1960, *Islander*. Deputy "Snooks" Adams shot the intruder.

Was It A Panther?

In *The Islander* on Oct. 12, 1967 these headlines shocked the populace: "Is There A Panther On The Island?"

The story read: "A resident, who wanted to remain anonymous, called the police and told officers that she had seen a big cat, possibly six-feet in length, jump into a tree and grab a blue heron. First she was awakened by the squawking of a bird and snarls of a wild animal and said she saw something that looked like a panther's tail going through the brush."

After this story appeared in the paper, Glen Gantz of Holmes Beach called the newspaper office to say he found some large animal tracks, too large to be a dog's, near one of his cottages. The reporter went to the scene and found tracks more than four inches across, and the stride of the animal was 27-inches.

Mrs. Gray Houston, a former Island resident, wrote to the newspaper: "I was extremely interested in your news items on the big cat stalking the wilds of Anna Maria. I am so glad someone else saw it. When we lived in Bradenton Beach, I saw a huge animal slink across the yard and up a tree. It was dusk and not enough light to see plainly. It was much too big to be a raccoon. Its actions were of a big cat."

Lt. Bud Hammock of the Holmes Beach Police Department said there was a panther in Palma Sola. Police Chief "Snooks" Adams said five years before, he kept getting reports of a panther crossing the road near the tollgate on the Anna Maria Island Bridge. Pat Green said he had seen a panther crossing the road near the

The Blackburn family always had a dog. Pictured on their boat, from left, Gina, Betty and J. Hartley, Jean, Christiaan and Betty Lou Blackburn Huth. Samson, the Great Dane, was the center of attention.

tollgate a couple of times. The chief said he had complaints from the tollgate attendants about cats bothering them. Adams waited near the tollgate one night and shot a bobcat.

Jesse Ingram, owner of the Anna Maria Texaco Gas Station, spent many hours hunting in this area and considerable time hunting bobcats. When asked, he replied with a smile, "I don't say it's impossible there's a bobcat or panther on the Island."

Professor J. G. Montgomery, head of the biology department at Manatee Junior College, said there are mountain lions in Florida which are eight or nine-feet long , including their tails, and weigh up to 200-pounds. Florida is the last natural range for these cats east of the Mississippi River.

Grampus Sighted

Norman Duncan brought a strange looking creature to *The Islander* office. The story and picture appeared in the Aug. 22, 1957 issue of *The Islander.* " The body of this specimen was two-inches long and the tail was that long also. The front claws were sharp as needles, and it smelled worse than it looked.

"A visit with Colonel Ball down the street revealed the following information. The insect, called a grampus, is fairly well known, according to Louis Cobb, who told the colonel of a grampus killing a chicken and another story of a baby calf found dead with a grampus hanging on his nose. The girl, ironing clothes in the next room, heard us talking and said she heard of a child killed by a grampus. She said the grampus is definitely poisonous."

The grampus (*mastigoproctus giganteus*) is a giant whip scorpion found in the southern United States. A specimen can be seen in the Anna Maria Island Historical Museum.

Be careful if you see a grampus. It's a killer.

A Ferret's Folly

I ran into my neighbor Don Masson at the post office in the '60s, and he asked me if I owned a ferret. On his morning trek to the fishing pier he encountered an animal in the street and stopped his car to have a look. The ferret ran over to him, climbed up his leg and on the way down it bit Don on the ankle. Concerned over

A ferret was spotted on Holly Road in Anna Maria City.

the broken skin, he sought medication and received a tetanus shot at the doctor's office.

My son, John, came by when he heard about the unusual creature in our neighborhood. He took it home to his family in Palmetto. They thought it should have a name. The name Ferret Fawcett-Majors came up, but when it was determined it was a boy, monikers such as Frank Ferret and Freddie the Ferret were suggested. They decided to call him Critter, but they did not keep him for long. " He bites a lot," John said. The last we heard, the original owner found him at the SPCA and took him home.

Domesticated in countries far from its native Africa, the old-world ferret is a variety of polecat used for centuries to drive rodents and rabbits out of their holes. Ferrets are members of the weasel family.

Protecting The Turtle

In 1950, William Marchand, Sr. was walking along the beach when he came upon tracks as straight as those of a tractor. He followed them up the beach near the edge of some tangled growth of bushes and found a huge turtle furiously digging her nest. As he watched, she began to lay the eggs. They left her body as fast as bullets, making perfect circles in the nest with each emission. When she completed her task, the nest was filled with eggs in a hard, compact circle. Marchand went home and told his friends about the miracle on the beach, never thinking they would swarm back with him.

Earl Murdock discovered a large loggerhead turtle that had washed up on the beach in the '50s

He told an *Islander* reporter: "I saw the crowd coming and was determined neither the nest nor the turtle should be molested. I scooped sand over the nest and camouflaged it until no one could find it. The men offered me all kinds of money if I would show them the turtle and the nest and, failing that, permission to take the turtle itself. I told them this turtle is going back to the Gulf of Mexico if I have to stand bodyguard over her every step of the way."

The people finally went away, and the turtle returned to the water. Later, Marchand went back and took some of the sand off the nest so it would be more like she left it. He often wondered how large a family left the nest Sometime later, he found there was a heavy fine for molesting turtles on the beach.

Years ago turtle patrol members would place the eggs in styrofoam boxes. When the eggs hatched they would release the baby turtles into the Gulf at night.

"If I had let them take the eggs, I could have gotten into a lot trouble," he said.

Many Islanders saw the big turtle that washed up on the beach in front of Schaldenbrand's home on March 19, 1955. "It was not the waste by-product of seine fishermen, but one of those mysteries of the deep. Another turtle of the same species washed up on the sand at the public beach about a year before. It measured 48-inches long, 28-inches wide and 17-inches high," according to *The Islander* story.

A reporter for the newspaper removed the shell of the dead turtle with more elan than skill. For a while, it served as a house for Sally and Joe Duprea's dog. It should be noted the turtle came not to lay eggs and create life. It had been mortally wounded, perhaps by men blasting for oil.

Slithering Snakes

In 1956, soon after my children and I moved into a little house on Magnolia Avenue across from the Youth Center, now Island Community Center, they came running into the house yelling excitedly, "Quick, come look!" They led me to our neighbor's house. Miss Marion Colman, the first Island homesteader's granddaughter, was a middle-aged spinster. She and her mother, Lula, lived in a typical beach cottage with a large screened porch shaded by many trees and bushes.

The children showed me a tree near the house. I was horrified to see a six-foot rattlesnake nailed to the tree. Marion had killed it with a shovel. I was amazed such a quiet, shy woman was so brave. My children were fascinated with the reptile and examined it closely. I warned them not to get too close as some venom might be in the air. The snakeskin now hangs in the Island Historical Museum.

Miss Colman was involved in another rattler adventure as told in the October issue of *The Islander* in 1958. She heard the rattling of 14 castanets and looked out to see a large rattlesnake in her yard. She called her neighbor Willoughby, who shot it. He was pictured holding it high with a hoe because it was "still dangerous."

This story appeared in the Island newspaper about the same time: "About once a year comes the report of

Rattlesnakes were plentiful on the Island before the building boom in the late '50s.

a rattlesnake killed on the Island. The latest was last Sunday when a six-foot rattler was disposed of by Ray Glennon and George Engel on 72nd Street and Marina Drive, in Holmes Beach. To the knowledge of this reporter, only one person has been struck by a rattler in the history of the Island and that was many years ago when a man was cleaning up some brush and stepped on the snake. He did not die.

"If rattlers were the only things to worry about on the Island, life would be more peaceful. Each year the haunts of snakes are cleared. They are not a general menace, nor something to fear."

Still another story was told to the Island editor, Harry Varley. "While Colonel Sherman sat on his porch sipping a pale, amber beverage, he spied a small rattlesnake swimming around in the canal and called John Holmes, Jr. who lived nearby. John brought his 22-rifle, and as the snake started to swim away John drew a bead on the serpent's upheld head and at 35-feet killed the critter with one shot. A swimming snake is a hard target, and Col. Sherman commended the rifleman."

In June of 1950, headlines in the *Key News* paper proclaimed: "Rattlesnake shot six times in back of the IGA store." Jack Chaney, the hunter, hung the snake on a tree in front of the community hall, now the Island Players theater. It was six-foot, three inches long with a girth of ten and a half inches and was viewed with awe by many residents. The news report claimed many snakes were being caught due to the amount of clearing going on.

Headlines in the *Anna Maria Island Reporter* in April of 1952 read: "Rattler Bonus! "Some months ago, to prove the rarity of rattlesnakes on the Island, the *Reporter* offered a bonus of $10 for each snake caught or killed on the Island. Readers may recall one bonus was paid for a small snake about two-feet long.

"The offer is now withdrawn to discourage adventurous teenagers who plan to hunt rattlers on Perico Island and other swamp areas. The bonus was cancelled not because of fear the boys would find a rattler, but because a rattler might find them, with dire results."

"Rare Rattler" was the eye-catching headline of a story in the September *Islander* in 1957. On September 3rd, Mrs. Robert Grace of 34th Street, Bradenton Beach, saw a five-foot rattler on her lawn. Out came Mrs. Grace and speared the reptile only to be closely followed by her niece, Mrs. Barbara Art, who shot the rattler with a 22-rifle. The snake had 14 rattles. It was the first to be reported in months.

About 1960, a controlled fire was raging on Egmont Key. Residents along the bay saw hundreds of snakes swimming toward Anna Maria Island. They came up on the beaches and were easy to catch because they were so tired. My son, John, remembers going to Egmont Key with his friends and stepping over a large stick on the pathway. After they all crossed it, they heard the ominous rattles.

Another snake episode occurred in our family. My son, Nicky, had a small ring-necked snake he kept as a pet. It was usually in his shirt pocket or his top drawer. It was cute, but I did not want it near me. One evening George and I went out, and the babysitter let Nicky sleep in our bed. I checked the drawer to make sure the snake was there. It was not.

"I'm not getting into bed until we find the snake," I said emphatically. I pulled back the sheets and moved the pillow, and there it was curled up right under my pillow.

With an abundance of wild critters on the Island during the early days, there was never a dull moment. Whether the creature moved on all fours, flew or traveled through the water, the curious were watching. The bountiful wildlife provided Island young people a close-up, hands-on education in zoology. Fortunately, most of the adults were willing to accommodate these animals, at least for awhile.

Daisy Greenwell holds a six foot rattler.

Mosquitoes Plague Islanders

"We used smudge pots in the house, and you hoped you would not choke to death on the fumes," an early Islander said. "We wore long pants and long sleeved shirts all the time."

Mosquitoes swarmed in such large numbers that it was difficult to avoid inhaling them. Sometimes breathing masks were necessary. Houses were screened, and a palm frond, called a swisher, was kept by the door to swish the mosquitoes off before entering. It took hardy people to grin and bear the pesky insects.

"We put kerosene and moth flakes in a Flit gun to kill them," Peggy Blassingame Diamant, who arrived on the Island in the '30s, recalled. "One man attached a fogger to his lawn mower."

In an interview, Amelia Gonzalez told the reporter that they always slept under mosquito netting.

"The abundance of mosquitoes in the '40s resulted in my dad buying our Spring Avenue house," recounted Richard Wiggins, who later became pastor of Roser Church. "We found a house-for-sale by owner during a visit to the Island and we checked it out. I remember standing in the yard as the owner and my dad discussed the price and terms. I watched that poor guy, from somewhere north of the Island, swatting mosquitoes with a branch from a tree. I was amazed how they attacked him with vigor but left my dad and me alone. We were born in Florida.

"It was obvious the seller of the house and the mosquitoes were not compatible. The longer my dad delayed, the better the deal became. Dad could never pass up a bargain, so they finally agreed on a price which included the contents of the house and a boat. The only condition the owner made was that the sale must be closed the next day, with cash, so he could catch the bus and head home with only the clothes he could get in two suitcases."

Richard told another mosquito story, actually told to him by his first cousin, Blake Whisenant, who created the popular Earth Box, known for growing prize vegetables. "Blake and his family spent at least one month each summer during the mid '40s on the Island, near the City Pier. He went fishing with my dad in the bayou on

South Bay Boulevard before it was developed. It was a good place for cast netting.

"They were wading late in the afternoon, and he told me my dad's bare back was black with mosquitoes. Dad was not even flinching. You can't hold a cast net, stalk mullet and swipe mosquitoes at the same time. Seasoned fishermen at that time chose to catch mullet. Blake, who was along just to carry the sack of mullet, splashed himself with water to ward off the mosquitoes."

Ellen Marshall, editor/publisher of the *Key News*, wrote in the August 1950 issue: "Two fogger trucks were used during the night, and a new Buffalo turbine was thrown into the battle against the varmints."

John Holmes spoke about the importance of ditching at the Island Chamber of Commerce meeting. He said, "There is nothing much we can do about the water collecting in palmetto trees, but there is no need for stagnant pools of water on private property. If ditching could be done by individual property owners, a great source of breeding mosquitoes would be eliminated, and spraying would be of great assistance."

Dr. Ed Huth came up with the idea how to eradicate mosquitoes in 1957.

In 1952 Bob Kemp, director of the county mosquito control, told members of the chamber that mosquitoes were breeding on School Key (now Key Royale). During clearing and construction, it was difficult to get heavy equipment to School Key, since there was no bridge. J. R. Miller suggested temporary fill could be thrown across to the Key. Dynamite had been used with great success in some areas to clear the land. Constant spraying was another suggestion, but had to be done under perfect weather conditions with no rain in the forecast and no wind.

It was agreed that every resident must be enlisted in the war against mosquitoes. Since the female laid eggs in water, preferably dirty, stagnant water; an overall comprehensive plan was made with every citizen cooperating by spraying and fogging on a grand scale.

A helicopter skimmed low over the Island in late 1952 carrying a photographer who took aerial photos of marsh areas where mosquitoes bred, to determine locations where water should be drained off. Drainage was believed to be the most effective method of eliminating the ubiquitous mosquitoes. Approximately five miles of ditches had been dug on Anna Maria Island by Feb. 21, 1952.

However, it was soon discovered mosquitoes were building a resistance to the spray. Another fogging truck may not have been the answer to the Island's mosquito problem, according to Leon Stafford, police chief and fire marshal of Bradenton Beach in 1953. He felt more could be accomplished toward curbing the mosquito scourge by drainage and larvicide than attempting to "smoke 'em out."

Malaria and yellow fever had been eradicated in Florida, so mosquitoes were not infected with diseases man could catch. There was one disease, passed on by the mosquito, the dreaded heart worm, that was fatal to dogs and cats.

Luckily the winter tourist season and mosquito season did not coincide. No one would question the fact that if the Island was free of mosquitoes, sandflies and other biting insects, more people would stay year-round and the general prosperity of the Island would increase.

An article in the June 25, 1953 *Islander* told of a hitch-hiking mayor. "Bradenton Beach mosquitoes were given a brisk workout Friday night when the city garbage truck, with foggers attached, and Mayor Jack Jones aboard, set out on a mosquito hunting safari so folks in Bradenton Beach could live in comfort. The mosquitoes were said to have suffered heavy losses."

In February of 1954, Harry Varley, editor of *The Islander*, made a treacherous journey through the impenetrable jungles of School Key with Peder Mickelsen, who owned about half of the Key. Varley described the sojourn in a jeep through underbrush, fallen trees, and deep sand, worse than riding a bony horse. The purpose of the trip was to see the work of the Mosquito Control Commission.

A main canal had been dug which led to open waters, and ditches cut a swath through the Key. Mickelsen said the theory was to let minnows, which inhabited the canals by the millions, devour the mosquito larvae. The fresh-water, flowing well on School Key was diverted into the main canal. It was hoped these projects would greatly reduce the mosquitoes on Anna Maria Island.

An editorial in *The Islander* drew smiles from readers: "It was known that the blood-sucking beasties would come following the high tide of July 8-9, 1954. They arrived! They seemed to be a more vindictive crowd than their predecessors. These late visitors bite as if trying to emulate New Jersey mosquitoes. There are no more ferocious insects anywhere. The new ones carry spurs as well as spears. If the boys keep fogging, it will be only a matter of days when an Islander can walk or sit outside after sundown and never hear the hum or feel the thrust of the mosquitoes' vicious swords in his epidermis."

"This Was A Swamp" was the caption under an aerial photo in *The Islander* on Aug. 12, 1955. The area between 69th and 70th Streets in Holmes Beach was pictured. The story read: "There was no worse mosquito-breeding mangrove swamp on the Island. Now, the beautiful stretch, which appears in white in the photo, was transformed. Morton L. Clark, a retired businessman from Ohio, was the owner and developer. Two lakes were excavated and connected by a channel. The water came from a well 78-feet deep and natural springs that existed in the lakes. The water was 10-feet deep, except at one end where a gradually sloping beach had been made for children. Swimming was fine, and the waters were stocked with mullet, redfish and trout.

An interesting feature of the development was that everyone who bought a lot automatically belonged to an Aquatic Club, which elected a governing body that controlled the use of the lakes. The development, named Clark Spring Lake Estates, consisted of 12-acres. Clark and his wife built their home on the peninsula between the two lakes.

The stretch of land, east of Snapper (Gulf Drive) from the Island Baptist Church to the firehouse on Oak Avenue, to the bayou in Anna Maria City was known as "Mosquito Haven." The breeding marsh was called an eyesore and disgrace to the city. In March 1955, the property was sold to Fred Archer. Immediately he had bulldozers working to clear, level and drain the acreage and dig a channel from the bayou so there would be waterfront lots. The property was next to Bimini Bay, and the two owners cooperated in making it a fine residential section.

In 1956, citizens were complaining about fumes entering their homes when the fogger truck rumbled by. Some suggested a siren be sounded to warn folks when the fogger was approaching. "The thundering roar of the fogging machine sounds like a detachment of mobile army artillery with iron wheels driving down a cobbled street," one angry onlooker complained.

Residents were torn between leaving windows open so the insecticide would kill mosquitoes in their homes or closing the windows to prevent the fumes from damaging their respiratory systems. Children thought the fogger was great fun and, when unsupervised, would run and ride their bicycles behind it.

Airplane spraying was tried in 1956, but proved to be ineffective. Residents complained of residue left on their cars which damaged the finish. Bird lovers said the insidious poison was killing birds, bees and beneficial bugs. *The Islander* carried an article about airplane spraying, saying it was presumably for medfly control. The reporter wrote there had never been a report of medflies on the Island. A large number of irate citizens, whose cars were speckled with the chemical, called the newspaper. They wanted to see if anything could be done to stop the spraying. They thought if spraying was intended for citrus trees, it would be better to send a man with a Flit gun to each tree. There were only a few back-yard citrus trees scattered over the seven-mile Island. This would save the expense of the plane, pilot and expensive chemicals.

"Mosquitoes Subdued in the Island," and "Successful Battle Against Mosquitoes," were welcome headlines in *The Islander* by the end of 1957. How did this miracle take place?

Dr. Ed Huth praised the work of many volunteers who had worked diligently to rid the Island of the pests. At a Chamber of Commerce meeting, he informed the public of his simple solution. He caught mosquito larvae in ditches and put them in a quart of water. The meeting hall was packed, and the jar was passed around so all could inspect it. Then Dr. Huth put one drop of kerosene on the water and placed it on the podium so all could see.

He told them how the French had failed in building the Panama Canal, because they lost more men to mosquito-carried illnesses than in all the Franco-Prussian wars.

Dr. Huth held up the jar, and to the surprise of the audience all the larvae were dead. He went on to explain how the United States had taken over the building of the canal, but before they began they sent Army troops in with dippers and pails filled with kerosene. Kerosene was poured on every bit of stagnant water in the Canal Zone. During the time it took to complete the canal, there was not a single mosquito-related fatality.

"Why don't we do the same thing here?" he asked the audience. There was a roar of applause and approval. Before the meeting was over, leaders for each district on the Island had been appointed. The county provided barrels of kerosene which were placed strategically around the Island for residents to spread in ditches of stagnant water. In three weeks there were no mosquitoes on the Island, and the real estate boom began.

Everyone on the Island was talking about the absence of mosquitoes. They could sit outdoors all day and evening and walk to the beach without the constant buzzing in their ears. In July of 1958, *The Islander* received a letter to the editor which read: "I have never seen the Island so free from mosquitoes at this time of year. Congratulations."

Anna Maria Island: A Bird Sanctuary

It was a well-known fact that Anna Maria City had been designated as a bird sanctuary, although no document attests to this fact. The Anna Maria Island Branch of the Manatee County Audubon Society was formed in 1954 with Mrs. Talbot Brewer of Anna Maria as chairman. She noted, at this time, an unusual concentration of perching birds was occurring on the Island caused by a north wind which blew spring

The most popular, and most often seen bird on Anna Maria Island, is the seagull.

migrating birds off normal courses. Mrs. Brewer observed a rare Sutton's warbler, a Kentucky warbler and a golden-winged warbler. In the first eight years of the bird count on the Island, a total of 182 varieties of birds were seen. One of the rarest birds, seen during this time was the cattle egret. This was the only record of this bird north of Okeechobee. Bird watchers found Gulf beaches and the mud flats of the bay made good hunting grounds for the birds.

An account in *The Islander* on Nov. 11, 1955 read: "A group of 20-odd men and women from the Manatee County Audubon Society came to the Island last Saturday under the guidance of the Talbot Brewers. They wandered along the bay shores to see what eyes plus binoculars could show them of bird life on the Island.

They should have come a week ago when a flock of white pelicans, ibis and cranes provided a fascinating spectacle for Islanders."

"It's For The Birds" was the headline in the June 21, 1956 *Islander*. The story went on to say Mr. and Mrs. Talbot Brewer for the past two years conducted a bird census on the Island with the help of bird enthusiasts. They timed the count to coincide with the peak of the migration in April. The census, in addition to recording many rare and beautiful transients, showed permanent Island bird residents as well. The notes that follow refer to land birds, songbirds and others which nested on the Island:

Frank Cavendish took care of injured birds on the Rod and Reel Pier.

"The most numerous species are red-winged blackbirds and mockingbirds. Other year-round residents were ground doves, mourning doves, cardinals, crested flycatchers, grey kingbirds, towhees, red-bellied woodpeckers, flickers and blue jays. Besides these familiar and frequently seen species, nighthawks, Chuck-will's-widows and meadowlarks were seen each year. The first two have been known to breed on the Island, but keep well concealed in the daytime. Meadowlarks are more common on the mainland, but undoubtedly some nest here."

In 1957, according to *The Islander*, 103 species were seen in the second annual spring bird count on the Island. This was an increase over the 90 species seen the year before. Twenty field workers were assigned to 11 Island districts. They checked from the southern tip to North Point and used boats to reach School Key (Key Royale) and the mangrove shores on the bayside. They counted 103 species with 43 shore birds. Strong winds from the west blew some birds off their route, such as the indigo buntings, blue grosbeaks, Baltimore orioles, rose-breasted grosbeaks and a variety of warblers.

Frank Cavendish, genial proprietor of the Rod and Reel Pier in the '50's, frequently nursed injured sea birds back to health. A pelican with an injured wing captured his fancy, and he advertised a contest to name the bird. A woman in Bradenton was proclaimed the winner. She named the pelican, Juan Wing.

American ornithologist, naturalist, hunter and painter, John James Audubon, described the great blue heron as, "Extremely shy, ever on the watch, with sight as acute as the falcon and its hearing keen and so wary that it takes wing at the sight of a man half a mile ahead."

That was written in 1832. Since then the great blue has learned that man can often be put to use. A heron is apt to be seen on every bridge, pier and beach waiting for a handout from people who are fishing. If there are two herons, they stand far apart. The great blue heron is a loner, except during the mating season.

While waiting, the bird may stand as motionless as a statue. When someone hooks a fish, the great blue walks or trots toward the fisherman. It prances with excitement until the fish is landed.

"George, This Great Blue Heron," is a delightful story about a big bird with personality-plus by Island author Wyatt Blassingame. The article appeared in the *Ford Times*, a publication for Ford owners. "I met George when I was sitting on a neighbor's porch. He stood well over three feet tall. The blue-black crest on his head was partly raised. He was staring at me through the screen. His eyes were golden circles with jet centers, and he looked straight at me down his long, golden nose that would have put Cyrano de Bergerac to shame. Raising one foot, he began to scratch gently at the screening which he could have ripped to pieces without much effort.

"My friend went in the house and got a chicken neck. George went half galloping, half stumbling around the corner and stooped in front of the screen door. When he raised his head, his neck seemed to stretch longer and longer until he could see inside. His feet began a tap dance. Everybody up and down the canal buys these necks for George, my friend explained. The butcher said he could not keep up with the demand. She put the chicken neck on a newspaper on the floor and opened the door.

"George came in. He stalked the neck as he would a living fish. He raised each foot gently and eased it forward and put it down. His head was extended and his neck half extended. About two feet from the paper he stopped. Several times his head moved forward and back. Then he struck.

"He whammed it! Next he 'killed' it by snapping his bill on it several times. George turned the neck so he held it by the end and swallowed. In his skinny neck the shape of the chicken neck was visible. He raised his head, stretched his neck, bent it into various shapes, and the chicken neck went down."

When George came to live at the Blassingame's home on Hammock Drive, Anna Maria, he spied a small ceramic frog in the garden. "He stalked and jabbed it. Then he jumped back, staring at the thing in amazement. And then, I'll swear to it, he turned his head in embarrassment and walked away," Wyatt wrote in his book.

Wyatt befriended two other birds, a great white egret he named Ichabod and a great blue heron named Stalker. Wyatt would carry a bucket of pinfish around the yard and Stalker would follow. If the bird did not get fed right away, he would make noises like an old-fashioned automobile horn.

When Wyatt began the book, *Wonders of Crows*, he had spent a lot of time watching and studying crows. He contacted Pam Stewart, the "Bird Lady" of Bradenton and asked if she had a crow. She did. Pearl was not a year-old yet and had been shot. Wyatt brought her home and placed her in a large cage with food and water. Terrified, the bird fluttered back and forth. When she flew into a swinging perch and her foot got caught in the bent wire, it took awhile to get her free. She never got over being afraid of Wyatt, in fact Pearl was afraid of all men, especially if they carried a stick. Perhaps it was because a man shot her. If she saw a man working in the yard with a rake or hoe, she became frantic. She would fly back and forth and hurl herself against the bars of her cage.

On the other hand, she was never afraid of Wyatt's wife, Jeannie. Jeannie would bring Pearl crackers coated with peanut butter, and the bird would sidle up to the edge of the cage and eat out of her hand.

"If Jeannie leaned close, Pearl would ruffle her feathers, bend her neck and make soft cooing noises. But never, even for peanut butter, would she take food from me," Wyatt said.

The first time the cage was put outside, Pearl refused to come down to the ground until newspapers covered the grass. Then she came down, tore up the newspapers, and from that time on happily accepted the grass floor.

Wyatt and Jeannie decided they would teach Pearl to talk. Wyatt wanted her to say, "Nevermore" and Jeannie tried to teach her to say, "Pretty Pearl." Pearl would cock her head to one side and yell, "Caw-w-w!" Pearl never learned English words, but Jeannie could talk good crow.

Perhaps it was Pearl's lusty calling that attracted wild crows. Sometimes half a dozen would gather in trees near the house making loud noises.

After three months it seemed time to give Pearl a chance at freedom. The cage was opened outdoors, and Pearl came out and sat on top of the cage. A strong wind was blowing and she started to fly, but the wind pushed her back. She turned and went with the wind going higher and higher. She flew back over her house and clung to a swaying pine tree. A grackle began to dive-bomb the crow. Pearl took wing with the grackle close behind. Suddenly, another crow appeared and was chasing the grackle. The three birds flew up the canal and disappeared. Pearl's cage was kept in the yard with the door open and food and water inside.

A variety of birds would go in and out, but Pearl never came back to her cage. Whenever a crow flew low over the yard, Jeannie dashed out, waving a cracker, calling, "Pearl." Sometimes, a bird would answer and Jeannie would say, "That was Pearl. I know it was."

One September morning students at the Island school heard a knock on their classroom window. When they looked closely they saw a crow. Stuart and Jimmy Anderson, from the other side of the room, hollered, "That's our crow Johnny!" Mrs. Clyde Phelps, teacher and ardent bird lover, knew about Johnny and told the children to let Johnny in. Johnny flew across the room and landed on Jimmy's desk. Then he flew to the teacher's desk, picked up a sheet of paper, walked across the desk and dropped it in the wastebasket. He turned, cocked his head to the side and eyed Mrs. Phelps.

Mrs. Phelps told the class that crows were very intelligent birds. The children were curious, so she decided to give the class a lesson about birds, and crows in particular.

George, the great blue heron, became a celebrity when his story appeared in the *Ford Times.*

One student told a story of his friend, Whitney, in Delaware who sang in the church choir. Whitney was sitting in the choir loft listening to the service. The minister had just announced his sermon when, from an open window, a voice shouted, "Hot Dawg!" The minister opened his mouth to speak but nothing came out. The congregation sat in silence. No one knew where the voice came from, but Whitney had an idea. That morning, he forgot to fasten Andy, his pet crow, in his cage. Whitney saw the church window was open from the top, and perched in the opening was his bird, Andy. The minister began his sermon. Andy listened, and then roared, "Quiet! Quiet!"

It was a long service for both Whitney and the minister. When it ended, Whitney found Andy perched on a car in the parking lot surrounded by admirers. "I never enjoyed church so much," one of them said. Whitney vowed he would never again forget to fasten Andy in his cage on Sunday.

Students at the Anna Maria Elementary School became interested in their surroundings, especially the wildlife on the Island. They took walks with their teachers and learned to recognize many winged friends. Allen Haines was the teenage editor for the *Anna Maria Key News* in 1951. He wrote about events on the Island involving school children. Mary Stuart Gushill penned this column entitled "Elementary School: Our Bird Walk."

"The date was April 19th. On the way to Mrs. Phelps' house we saw some redstarts, which was unusual. Walking down Spring Avenue we saw a Pied-billed-Grebe, and while we rested we saw two turtles and a brown swamp rabbit. In Mrs. Phelps' garden, we learned how the plant called the travelers palm got its name. If you stick a knife in it, drinking water will spurt out. We saw about 60 birds on our trip: warblers, flickers, woodpeckers, cardinals, mockingbirds, herons, egrets, doves, blackbirds, a man-of-war and a flock of white ibis. Then we had ice cream at the drugstore and took the 11 o'clock bus back to school."

For students attending the two-room schoolhouse on Magnolia Avenue in the 40s, making bird books was a requirement every year. Teachers Lena Phelps and Betty Blackburn were bird enthusiasts. Betty Lou Blackburn Huth recalled overnight trips to Myakka State Park with her teachers.

"It was primitive camping, and we loved it. We looked for birds, fished and rode horses. Feral pigs were rooting and tearing up the ground, so the hunters would shoot one, roast it on a spit and we would eat it along with swamp cabbage. It was a wonderful experience," she said.

For years, all fourth graders in the new Island school, built in 1950, continued the tradition of making bird books. They drew pictures of birds they had seen and wrote about them.

Betty Blackburn, the well-known and loved teacher, was an avid birder. As she was driving along Gulf Drive one day she spotted a most unusual bird in a field. She jammed on the brakes, grabbed her binoculars and headed to the field. Her car was left in the middle of the road.

Sam Schiek, a principal of the Island Elementary School, lived in a woodsy setting on Los Cedros Drive in Anna Maria. His passion, other than his motorcyle, was his beloved bonsai trees, which he tended with loving care. Sam's pet parrot, Hector, was in a playful mood one day and took a chunk out of Sam's chin. Maybe it was a kiss, but it required immediate treatment. Hector lived to be almost 50.

Mrs. Thomas Hyatt of Bay View Drive was a bird lover in the true sense of the word. About 100 wild parakeets landed in her yard one day, so she and her husband put out feeders, and the birds stayed. Her hobby had begun. She became more interested in the colorful birds after finding an injured bird, which she took into her house and nursed back to health. Soon neighbors brought her birds needing care. The larger ones she would take to Frank Cavendish at the Rod and Reel Pier or Pam Stewart in Bradenton. Mrs. Hyatt had 16 birdcages hanging from the ceiling in her living room. The birds were not allowed to fly in the house since she had three cats.

"The cats watched them and would get them if they had half a chance," Mrs. Hyatt said. "One time I took a cage down, the cat came too close and the bird pecked him on the nose."

Along with birdseed, she gave them vitamins and chalk cake and provided playthings like mirrors and ladders in their cages. After the birds became well, she would put them outside. Some stayed in the yard, some left and others would come back to visit. The entire neighborhood was full of bird lovers. The man across the street from the Hyatts had 29 birdhouses.

The most unusual bird the Hyatts ever spotted was an Indian parakeet. It was as large as a parrot, had a red beak, red eyes and a necklace to match. A band of 40 muscovy ducks roamed through the yards. The Hyatts agreed it was a good life.

The Islander editor reported: "I had to see it for myself to believe it. Above Cortez Road, a small bird, about the size of a mockingbird, chased a huge buzzard. Back and forth they flew, with the little bird actually coming to rest for seconds on the back of the large one. The buzzard did not seem to object, but tried to get away from his tiny assailant. He could have gobbled him up in one gulp."

The editor said he had seen this happen on several occasions and once stopped his car and watched the birds for 15 minutes. He thought the buzzard must have robbed the nest of the smaller bird and was amazed at the courage of such a small bird attacking something 20-times as large.

In 1955 Maud Holmes phoned *The Islander* photographer and asked if he would take a photograph of white pelicans in front of her home. By the time he arrived, the birds had moved, so he drove south to Sportsman's Harbor and got the pictures. Aided by nature expert, Carl Scott, they counted: 75 wood ibis (curlews), 110 white pelicans, 20 brown pelicans, three cormorants, two blue herons and one Ward's heron. News spread by the Island grapevine and many saw the temporary visitation of the birds.

A flock of red-winged blackbirds was the pride and joy of General Buck and Nita Taylor. He was the mayor of Holmes Beach in 1953. It was a fascinating sight when Buck or Nita rattled a can containing corn. This instantly brought the entire flock of several hundred birds to the feast. They were quite tame and let the Taylors walk within a few feet of them while they ate the kernels from the ground. The birds bitterest enemy was a hawk which once in awhile swooped down to have one of them for lunch.

There were many bird-feeding stations on the Island at this time. The Allen Davis' backyard was full of birds and sounded like a birdhouse at the zoo. The birds were a picturesque addition to Island life and personal pleasure to all who took care of them.

In the past hundreds of robins visited the Island and enjoyed the berries from Island trees and bushes.

"Little Pigeon Lost" was the title of a short story in *The Islander* on March 21, 1957. A homing pigeon flew into the yard of Jerome Vitts of Anna Maria. On one leg was an aluminum band inscribed with numbers and

"Miami" and on the other leg was a band with 9942Z imprinted.

The Islander called the *Miami News* staff, but all they could do was to point out that the bird belonged to the Pigeon Union. They tried to find the owner. The next week *The Islander* continued the story. *Associated Press* editors thought the episode was interesting enough to send to all papers using their service. It turned out to be national publicity for Anna Maria Island. The bird's owner, Miami Fire Capt. H. L. Owens, said the bird was released with several others in Palmdale, about 100 miles from Anna Maria, in the center of the state. He guessed a hawk chased it and got the pigeon confused. There were seven other birds released at the same time, and they came back to Miami in two hours. The mixed-up bird made the rest of the trip in a box shipped to Captain Owens.

Our concrete block home was built in 1960. Later, we added a wooden garage. I was in the house one day when I heard hammering on the outside of the garage. I wondered what my husband could be hammering, and when it got louder I went out to look. To my surprise I saw a large pileated woodpecker hitting the wood so hard I was afraid the wood would split.

It is common for birds to see their reflection in mirrors and windows. A friend who lived on the bay placed rubber snakes on all her windowsills hoping to prevent birds from crashing into the glass. I have a stained-glass bird inside in a window. For days a bird fluttered around the window before it gave up hope of the pretty red bird ever coming out.

It was July of 1955, when Annie Silver's parakeet, Billy Boy, took off through a partly opened door and vanished. She advertised in *The Islander* and results were immediate. Allen Davis told Annie that the bird had joined a flock of red-winged blackbirds at his house.

Delighted, Annie hastened to the secluded garden, which was the Davises' private bird sanctuary. She saw her Billy Boy and called his name several times. He knew the voice and cocked his head side-to-side. Then, chirping his defiance, he flicked his tail and flew away never to be seen again.

On Jan. 13, 1955, robins had been seen on the Island for 10 days looking for something to eat. The next report was that the visiting robins were intoxicated, as drunk as sailors on a binge. They teetered back and forth on the telephone wires, fell off, and fluttered feebly to the ground. Many lost control and flew into cars. The roads were strewn with their dead bodies. Those that stayed on the ground could not walk in a straight line.

Robins by the hundreds were eating fallen fermented berries of the seagrape and Brazilian pepper bushes, which seemed as potent as Kentucky moonshine. In a similar invasion 10 years before, robins were so numerous the telephone wires were packed solid, and those who wanted to perch had to wait their turn.

In January of 1955, Harry Varley, editor of *The Islander*, received letters about hundreds of robins all over the place. The next week they all disappeared except one on a wire. Varley deduced the bird either didn't like crowds, didn't know which way the others went, was a rugged individualist, or a hermit who wanted to be left alone.

Richard Wiggins, pastor of Roser Church in the '50s, had two memorable encounters with birds in his early teens. "Both times I happened to be hunting, so I had my shotgun in my hand. I saw a lone female quail running through low bushes. As I watched her disappear, a fox came tracking her. She was doing what birds often do when they have nests on the ground. She was luring the fox away, and when it was safe, she flew back to the nest.

"The second encounter happened when I was sitting in an oak tree over a creek near our Ellenton home looking for fish. We would often shoot into a school of mullet and then jump in the water and collect stunned fish. Mullet were part of our staples in the depression years. An eagle flew to the limb just above me. He never saw me, for I was under him. I was excited to have a good, long look at our national symbol before he resumed hunting for food."

The Wiggins family moved from the Island, many years later, to a home on a river in New Port Richey. They were constantly entertained by many river birds. Beauty was a great egret or American egret which often visited the Wiggins family. A very large bird, the egret has jet-black legs and a yellow beak. The egret is very common in Florida, except in the Florida Keys, where the great white heron is frequently seen. For positive identification, check the leg and beak color.

Richard told a tale of his friendship with Beauty: "Beauty was always looking for handouts down at the dock.

Then the bird became braver and would sit on the rail of our patio to get my attention. I began to buy chicken necks and cut them when I didn't have any fish scraps. Beauty learned quickly to take them from my hand, but I had to make sure my finger would not be near his beak. A cut finger resulted several times when I carelessly held the fish or chicken. One day I was on the patio when Beauty arrived. I went inside to get the chicken necks and accidentally left the outside door open. My brother-in-law was sitting in the river-room reading. He called to me softly, and I looked back to see Beauty walking into the room. Beauty panicked when he saw Bill and flew up on the card table where Mae and her sister, June, were working on a puzzle. Then he flew to the couch. Beauty was so nervous that I had to help him find the door. He visited most days for years and then disappeared for almost a year. Soon a younger egret took his place. The young one would never trust me enough to eat out of my hand, but he did sit on the patio rail.

Beauty, a great egret, visited the Wiggins family often. This picture was taken in their living room

"One day Beauty showed up in elegant breeding plumage and brilliant green in front of his eyes, all part of the breeding changes. The young one disappeared. I knew it was Beauty because of his actions as well as appearance. Beauty would recognize me when I walked through the kitchen. Even when he sat on the top of our pontoon boat he would fly to the patio railing. I learned that nature had provided him with marvelous eyes. The glare on windows or in the water did not affect him.

"On his first day back, Beauty took the first piece of food right out of my hand like he had never been away. I don't know why he disappeared for so long, but I do know he disappeared for several days at a time during nesting or mating season. Sometimes, when I fed him, he would fly away immediately to his roosting area. I suppose he was taking food to his mate. When he came back I left the door open several times and he came into the house, even when our grandchildren were in the room."

This eagle sighting was reported in *The Islander* on Sept. 29, 1955: "A full-grown eagle spent several hours in a tree on Fiddlers Flats," the editor wrote. "I would not have accepted this from one observer. It is conceivable that, after a couple for the road, someone might have mistaken an odd-shaped branch for an eagle. The story was confirmed by a lady who does not imbibe. Isn't this the wrong time for eagles to appear in these parts? I must ask Mr. Michaelson, who has an eagle's nest near his orange groves. He thinks more of his eagles than his fruit trees."

Charles L. Broley was known as the "Eagle Man" after an incident was reported in the March 12, 1953 issue of *The Islander.* "Broley attempted to place a metal band on the foot of an eaglet in Michaelson's Grove, Holmes Beach. As he approached the aerie the fledging flew to a nearby tree. High above, the adult birds circled and watched the performance, screaming all the time. Broley catapulted a string over a high branch, pulled up a rope and fashioned a rope and wood ladder. When he was close enough to reach the bird with a fishing rod it took off, soaring up and off majestically. At least a dozen Islanders witnessed the attempt to band the bird. Some asked why the eaglet should be banded. 'A sign of slavery?' one asked. Broley's bandings decreased each year. Some say this proves the eagles are getting scarce. Others offer a simple explanation, Broley is getting older. He is 73."

In October of 1957, a phone call to *The Islander* claimed an eagle came down on the Alvin Blacksmith lawn. Photographer David Cooper was delegated to take an action picture. With the camera focused, he waved his arms at the bird and shouted. The bird spread its five-foot wide wings, opened its claws and headed for David. David ran using the camera and tripod as defense. The action picture he took was a blur and the camera was broken. The next day Don Brackin found the bird dead a short distance away. It was an osprey, not an eagle.

The osprey is a large, fish-eating bird of prey that is frequently mistaken for a bald eagle because of its white head. Even more obvious is its white breast. Eagles are dark underneath. Ospreys build large nests, which they expand and improve year after year. Some of these can be seen on the causeway to the Florida Keys. Most nests are built in tall trees, but the osprey is adaptable and will also use man-made structures such as telephone poles. This bird co-exists well with man and seems unconcerned about cars and people.

We found an osprey at the corner of Holly and Iris streets in Anna Maria. It was dead. It was a magnificent bird, large and beautiful. Days later I heard of other ospreys which were electrocuted when the fish they caught touched the power lines. Island residents living on canals watch ospreys as they plunge feet first into the water and grab fish with their sharp claws. Sometimes, when a fish is too large to carry, the osprey is unable to let go. One theory is that the excitement of the catch stimulates a locking mechanism in their claws. Some people think the claws simply sink into the bone and get stuck. Whatever the reason, fishermen have reported catching large fish with osprey feet attached. Those unfortunate birds perished by the same ability that enabled them to survive.

"How To Catch An Owl," was the headline in the May 15, 1952 *Islander*. The story read: "Much confusion was aroused at the Anna Maria Post Office this week when a baby owl flew down the chimney and ended up in the heater. For two days before the invader was found, Postmaster Frances Warttig said she had heard queer noises. Last Monday Art Riles looked into the heater and thought he saw a kitten. Upon closer inspection he saw a beak. Finally, after much waiting, a little five-inch, yellow-eyed owl came out, but refused to leave the post office.

"When Harold Igo came for his mail, Mrs. Warttig asked him if he knew a way to catch an owl. He threw the mail bag over the bird's head, took it outside, and the diminutive owl flew away."

There are no better-fed seagulls than on Anna Maria Island. The birds on the Gulf beaches grow fat on a mixed diet. Restaurants on the beach have problems with the gulls pilfering food. They swoop down and carry off sandwiches, french fries and any other edibles they can grab. When offered a morsel by hand, they will take it, to the delight of the giver.

The osprey, a majestic bird, can be seen diving into canals for fish.

There are about 45 different kinds of gulls. Even though gulls have webbed feet and can swim well, they rarely go far out to sea. Many follow boats in hopes of getting food, but most of these birds do not fly far. Gulls may fly more than 100 miles a day going between feeding and nesting sites. They depend on their long wings to catch drafts and glide. At sundown the birds can be seen heading off to their nests. Many on the Island fly north to Bird Island, off the North Point of the Island.

For more than 20 years Pam Stewart of Bradenton took care of wild and domesticated birds that were injured, sick, or too young to take care of themselves. Her house was a big aviary for birds of all sizes. There were almost 100 birds in the Stewart house most of the time.

Once Frank Cavendish and Dr. Ralph French caught an injured bird on the Rod and Reel Pier and delivered it to Pam for treatment. The left wing of the four-foot tall great blue heron was drooping at a peculiar angle. It was obviously broken. The "Bird Lady," as she was known to many, examined the bird and decided the wing had been broken by flying into a power line. It needed a veterinarian, so she took it to Dr. Henry Stevens at Bayshore Animal Hospital. Pam named the bird Charlie, and it convalesced at her bird hospital for four months. She later released

Charlie in Bradenton Beach at the water's edge. He waded along in shallow water in the bay until he spotted a walkway leading to an old, dilapidated dock. Stepping cautiously to the end of the dock, he stood still as a statue except for an occasional quick turn of his head. Pam watched the bird for awhile and then turned and walked down Bridge Street to her car. She glanced back once. Charlie was still standing motionless. "Bye Ol' Charlie," she said out loud. "I think you'll make it."

The skimmer is a interesting bird which has special feeding skills and equipment. The adult skimmer develops a lower beak which is much longer than the upper beak. The long beak is dragged through the water to catch food. Islanders who walk along the beach at sunset are fascinated by the graceful flying skimmers as they scoop fish from the water's edge. Each year, starting in late March, beach-nesting birds come to Island beaches to raise their families. Black skimmers can be seen nesting in colonies on Anna Maria beaches near the North Point. Nesting areas are off limits to beachgoers, and watercraft is not allowed near the shore. If the birds are bothered constantly, they sometimes abandon their nests and the young will die.

A few semi-tame peacocks or peafowl were brought to the Island in the '60s. In the '70s more than a dozen roamed in Holmes Beach in the vicinity of 50th Street. It was quite a sight to see a flock of the colorful birds crossing Gulf Drive. Traffic would stop. People would get out of their cars with cameras to record the phenomenal sight.

The few peafowl soon grew into a herd and wandered around the school and shopping center in Holmes Beach. Residents in the surrounding neighborhoods found the birds a nuisance. Loud and eerie mating screeches in pre-dawn hours jolted many out of their beds. Screens on porches were shredded by peacocks in search of peahens.

Astonishing headlines in *The Islander* in 1970 proclaimed, "Mating Fervor Drives Peacocks Into Headlong Attack on Glass." The explanation continued. "It's spring and the grass is growing. Flowers are springing out of the ground and the peacocks are beating themselves to death against glass doors. Every spring peacocks perform their mating ritual. The males grow elegant tail feathers and parade in front of demure females. A glass door, reflecting a primping male, looks like another primping male. In the case of one bird on 51st Street, the male attacked the other male he saw and bashed himself against the glass. Mrs. Walter Stewart was the owner of such a bloodied door."

"The birds are so beautiful," Mrs. Stewart said, "but look what they are doing to themselves."

Blood glistened on the concrete driveway, evidence of the bird's ferocity in the attacks. The SPCA was called and promptly picked up the injured bird. A wildlife expert advised Island homeowners to coat their windows with white glass cleaner or hang sheets over their doors and windows for a few weeks to stop the birds from seeing their reflections until the mating fervor was over.

"Crafty Peafowl Outwit Holmes Beach Trappers," was the headline in the Aug.17, 1978 issue of *The Islander*. The Holmes Beach City Council ordered a peacock deportation plan. A large cage, stocked with cornmeal, was placed on an empty lot in the 50th Street area, not for the birds to eat, but for their capture. For two weeks, eight of the colorful birds were lured into the cage and carted away to Sarasota Jungle Gardens in Sarasota and a farm in Arcadia. The farmer was delighted with them since they made excellent farm birds. They mixed with wild turkeys, ate undesirable insects and their calls served as watchdogs, warning the approach of a stranger.

However, the remaining dozen peacocks got smart and did not go in the cage. One theory was they had human friends who scattered feed outside the cage to keep them from being captured, or when captured would let them out. Peacock lovers stormed city hall with more than 400 signatures on petitions demanding a halt to the trapping practice. A veterinarian eventually sedated the birds and transported many of them to a farm in eastern Manatee County. Some can be seen at the Red Barn in Bradenton, and Longboat Key became the home of a large flock.

An article in the *Sarasota Herald Tribune* described the birds eloquently: "The great, beautiful birds are indigo blue, with shimmering eight-foot tail feathers that spread out in an unbelievable kaleidoscope of brilliant colors. They have claimed the northeast end of the Key as their own.

"At times their number has reached 100. Where they came from is a mystery. Back in the '70s no one had

When the peacocks spread their eight-foot tail feathers the effect was spectacular.

heard of a peacock on the Key. All of a sudden between 30 and 40 were walking down the streets and across the yards. Older residents tell you that the birds had been on Anna Maria Island and people there were fed up with their mess and noise, so they trapped and released them on Longboat Key. Some residents love them, others hate the sight of them. They are dirty birds. They amble across streets with no concern for traffic."

"I've seen 10 cars stopped waiting for a couple of peahens to cross," said Michael Drake who became an unofficial game warden.

"A large number of residents," Drake concluded, "delight in their presence. The novelty is one thing, but mostly it's the thrill when a peacock unfurls his tail feathers to display breathtaking colors. In addition to their plumage and mating calls, males in the peacock world are responsible for building the nests. It's the way they attract mates. Because the birds have been so prolific and have been around so long, the Longboat Key Council has enacted a specific law protecting them. It's called The Peafowl Ordinance."

A seven-year-old boy went into the business of selling peacock feathers and food packets to people who wanted to feed the peacocks. He started because he wanted to financially help a cousin who was stricken with leukemia.

A guide booklet, compiled by the Audubon societies of Sarasota, Manatee and Venice areas, attests to the fact that monk parakeets and budgies were typical of the exotics that escaped, survived and bred successfully in the wild and were seen on Anna Maria Island. Parakeets and warblers were found nesting in the public beach restrooms. Monk parakeets were seen nesting in the palm trees on Bay Drive off of Bridge Street in Bradenton Beach. Monk parakeets, or Quaker parrots, sport beautiful bright green upper parts with orange bills. The forehead and breast are pale grey with dark scalloping and a belly of light green or yellow. The remiges, or flight feathers, on the wings are dark blue, and the tail is long and tapered. This parrot builds nests in trees. Their calls are loud and throaty and many residents are annoyed by their ear-piercing screeches. This species is considered adept at learning, and those kept as pets develop large vocabularies and are able to learn scores of words and phrases.

During winter months, white pelicans can be seen along the bay at the southern end of Bradenton Beach.

Island police were kept busy rounding up the pesky peacocks in the '70s.

Low tide is always the best bird spotting time. Ground doves, rails, reddish egrets and yellow crowned night herons can also be seen. In Cortez, brown and white pelicans hang around the fish houses. Across the water to the southwest on Cortez Key, there is a roosting area for frigates, wood storks and pelicans. In addition to birds that live in this area, several hundred species pass through during spring and fall migrations.

The Pelican

A peculiar bird the pelican,
His beak can hold more than
his belly can.
He can take in his beak,
Enough food for a week!
But, I'm dammed if I see how
the hell he can!

Dixon Lanier Merritt, a southern newspaper editor and president of the American Press Humorists Association, penned this famous limerick in 1910.

Three

Communities Emerge From Jungles

School Key Becomes Key Royale

When Peder Mickelsen of Minneapolis decided to heed the doctor's advice and head south for the winter, he had no intention of continuing his career in land development. While visiting Florida's east coast, a friend told Mr. and Mrs. Mickelsen about Anna Maria Island. When they arrived, they liked what they saw and made the

Island their permanent winter home in 1946.

According to the *Minneapolis Sunday Tribune* on Oct. 30, 1955, Mickelsen had too much energy to remain idle and started looking around for something to keep him busy. He discovered 160-acres of palmetto jungle in Holmes Beach. This became the Bay Palms subdivision from 77th Street southward.

"Even after I bought it, I didn't know what I had," Mickelsen said. "Ten feet from the road it was impassable."

He hired a local pilot to fly him over the tract, but the pilot flew so low Mickelsen was more concerned about the plane clearing the tops of trees than what was under them. He tried to inspect the land from the water, but a storm blew his boat off course. Finally, he sent a bulldozer crashing through the palmettos to clear a pathway

School Key (Key Royale) in it's natural state early in the '60s.

through the dense growth of plant life.

Several years later, the Florida attorney who handled Mickelsen's purchase confessed he was ashamed to take his client's money because he thought he was just another northern sucker getting fleeced by Florida real estate.

As soon as part of the land was cleared, the developer quickly turned it into building lots with streets and utilities. He built a few houses and sold them to get the development going. Since waterfront lots were highly prized, Mickelsen dug canals and built boat anchorages for buyers of lots that did not touch the bay.

It was 1947, when he started the development. In 1955 the largest part was not completed, for digging canals and building sea walls took time; however, many lots were sold then and homes were built. Leveled and cleared of brush and alligators, the former jungle property commanded premium prices. Locals remembered hearing about Mickelsen capturing a five-foot alligator. He took it home to his wife, but no one knew her reaction.

Then Mickelsen became interested in a small island east of his development. The 150-acres, which were covered with an impenetrable tangle of brush and palmetto, were known as School Key. Mickelsen and his partners, Harry Gustafson, a Minneapolis attorney and William B. Lee, Mickelsen's partner in a Sioux Falls construction business, paid $25,000 for the island. The cost of basic clearing and development of the acreage was estimated to be about eight times the original cost. In the summer of 1955, equipment was sucking up sand from the bottom of the bay to provide fill for construction of a bridge to School Key and to smooth the jagged shoreline.

The small isle was a mosquito-infested mangrove swamp and a prolific breeding place for rattlesnakes. Only fishermen and boaters ventured out to the tropical jungle. They found it delightfully isolated. The island was named School Key since the government had approved a school on the site for the first homesteaders. No document has ever been discovered validating the school; however, old timers remember seeing a dilapidated

Key Royale in 1965.

shack in the underbrush at the southern end.

Elmer Raymond said the early homesteaders received a grant of land, with the understanding that a portion would be assigned for a school. He said there was never a school on School Key, but there was a flowing well.

"It was a deep artesian well," recalled Jack Fiske. "I would paddle my boat over there with Cap Ohlson and we'd fill up our jugs with good drinking water. The well was where Dundee Lane is now."

In 1875, the United States Surveyors Department placed a cypress post on School Key to establish a section line corner. The starting point was Cobb's Corner, a mile away in the center of the Island, and another marker was a mile from there to Oscar Russell's place.

A document written in 1961, revealed the history of the land. It read: "All the old timers in the area know the 150-acre key lying to the east of Anna Maria Island at 66th Street as School Key. It has been renamed by the developers and now will be called Key Royale. Audrey Lee, wife of William B. Lee, one of the developers, named the island. Heavy machines started last week to transform the rough terrain into one of the finest residential sections on the west coast of Florida. Draglines are digging the first of 12 canals. About 50 of the 400 lots will face Tampa Bay with a view of the Sunshine Skyway Bridge. Most of the remaining lots will be on canals with access to the Bay and Gulf.

"The head of Key Royale, Inc., is Peder Mickelsen, who came to Anna Maria 12 years ago. Other members of the group are William B. Lee, a builder from South Dakota, and Harry Gustafson, a Minneapolis attorney. The firm has already developed a 40-acre tract on Anna Maria leading to Key Royale. A 72-foot bridge has been constructed, and a foothold tract of 10 lots on the tip of the key is now ready. The first phase of development will take in one-third of Key Royale. The developers expect to move 400,000 yards of dirt from the bay bottom to the island. In excess of $2-million of the finest residential property will be added to the tax rolls of Manatee County upon completion of this property."

Since Mickelsen began his Anna Maria development, several others began developing land on the Island. A quote from the *Minneapolis Sunday Tribune* read: "The Island newspaper, edited by a crusty, ex-advertising man from New York (Harry Varley) takes a dim view of most of them, but rates Mickelsen as a great developer."

Varley wrote in the *Anna Maria Island Reporter*, Jan. 16, 1962: "This reporter has a profound admiration for the way Peder Mickelsen develops. Whatever he does takes courage, foresight and vision, of which he has plenty, and a fundamental respect for the ethics of his chosen occupation."

The Islander on Oct. 6, 1955 showed a photograph of Mount Mickelsen, the highest mountain on Anna Maria Island. An explanation of the phenomenal hill was that it was man-made. The volcanic shape was due to nature's arrangement when sand was dropped from a dragline. Peder Mickelsen was building stockpiles of sand for raising the level of School Key.

Using this ingenious method, he was able to acquire tremendous quantities of fill. First, he blocked off Sarasota Bay with two dams several hundred feet apart between School Key and the Island. Then, the water was pumped from this artificial lake and the fill was obtained from the bed of the pass. Later, plans for a bridge to span the pass were formulated, and the dams would be destroyed.

This was a gigantic development for an island as small as Anna Maria, but Peder was accustomed to doings things in a grand manner. This invitation to residents of Manatee County was extended: "To see where jungle swamps were weeks ago there are now beautiful home sites. This is no longer a beach, it's an Island for large homes."

The *Bradenton Herald* ran a picture of the new home sites on Nov. 10, 1963. The caption read: "The 60 new home sites created in the Key Royale and Bay Palms developments on Anna Maria Island are shown. They appear as light fingers on opposite sides of the waterway."

Many fishermen and old timers on the Island expressed a fear that the waterway between the Island and the Key would be closed. They were assured that it was closed temporarily to facilitate work, and a bridge with a 44-foot span and 12-foot height from mean low tide to the bridge would be built.

The first development plat for Key Royale was approved by Holmes Beach in May of 1957, the same year the bridge to the Key was built. Several development practices, followed by the Mickelsen group, helped make their work unique. One was the installation of seawalls on their home sites, which eliminated any possibility of erosion. Another was the installation of concrete gutters and curbing along the road edge of each lot. Every possible effort was made to save the native palms.

The neighborhoods of Bay Palms and Key Royale represented more than 250-acres of low-lying mangrove swamplands. The developers carved channels throughout the property and raised the elevation with materials taken out of the waterways. They created open living space, privacy and sea-walled home sites bordering on navigable waters which provided fishing and boating activities in the homeowners backyards.

Headlines in the *Bradenton Herald* proclaimed, "Key Royale: A Dramatic Development." An aerial photograph taken in 1957 of the front of Key Royale, and the back of Bay Palms shows a dramatic contrast to the other photograph taken in 1970. The development in 13 years was astounding. No houses were visible in the first shot and the second showed houses on every finger of land.

One of the most popular sections of the Key Royale community was the nine-hole golf course. Built in 1964, it was owned and operated by Key Royale stockholders. Included in the complex were a lake and stream twisting through the 29-acre layout, a large clubhouse with pro shop, snack bar and lunchroom.

The orderly growth and upgrading of Bay Palms and Key Royale was a tremendous Manatee County success story. It represented one of the finest waterfront communities in this area. Front-page headlines in *The Islander*

Canals were dug and sea walls were built.

on Jan. 30, 1964 broadcast this news: "World's Fair Model Home At Key Royale." Key Royale had been selected as the site for the Florida version of the 1964-65 New York World's Fair Model Homes, one of two to be built on the west coast of Florida.

The home built by the Richmond Construction Corporation of Sarasota, was a public attraction until November 1965, when the World's Fair closed. The home exemplified the latest design, methods and materials in building and furnishings for modern homes. More than 100,000 persons were expected to visit the Florida model during 18 months. It would be erected on Lot 6 of Key Royale's Fourth Addition. The site had 110-feet of seawall along the water and overlooked the Skyway Bridge and Tampa Bay.

In 1964 Key Royale sales were booming. The opening of the Formica World's Fair house, removal of bridge tolls, and the survey to see what interest there was in a nine-hole golf course on the Key had affected sales, according to Howard Adams, sales manager of Key Royale Homes, Inc. "We are operating at least a sale a week and have been for four months," he said.

"In those days there were less restrictions on dredging canals and filling in land areas, so we could move a little faster," Adams said a few years later. "It took 12 years to complete 500 homes. We sold bayfront homes for $50,000 each, including the lot, in the early days. There was no pre-arranged financing. After you made a sale, you'd take the buyer in hand to the bank. Money cost about six percent, which seemed a little high at the time. The economy was lively and most of our customers were well-financed, and able to live almost anywhere they wanted."

Nell and Howard Adams were among the early residents of Key Royale. Their home was at the end of a street with a view of the new Manatee Avenue Bridge leading to the Island. "My associates claimed I selected that lot so I could watch the bridge for prospects," Adams said.

A major decision was faced when the developers were asked by residents to build a nine-hole golf course at the northern end of Key Royale. "This took 80 lots away from sales," Adams recalled. "We debated a long time whether this would improve business enough to offset the loss of land."

By August of 1965, work on the clubhouse had started. The grand opening of the golf course was held in September of 1966. Initial membership was limited to 225, but over the years this was increased several times. There were many golf events, such as club championships, women's handicaps and mixed couples championships.

Most of the social events were sponsored by the Key Royale Golf Club Women's Association and included monthly scramble luncheons, Christmas parties, Octoberfests, bridge and bingo games and annual awards dinners and dances. The club became so popular there was a waiting list for new members. Memberships were sought by many Island residents.

Seaside Gardens

Apartment homes on the canal at 63rd Street in Holmes Beach were a new concept designed by 74-year-old builder, Jack Holmes. He came out of retirement in 1962 to launch one of the most successful housing developments to hit Florida.

The construction of the first five units of Seaside Gardens started in January of 1962. At that time, cooperative apartments were being built in other communities in the bay area. Rather than following the co-op pattern, he chose to build one-story units with each owner possessing the land and the unit.

In March of 1962, he opened the first five units for inspection. They all sold that first day. Twenty-four units were built the first year. Jack kept the prices low, so the average middle-class couple could afford to purchase a home. He offered the finest waterfront view with a place to dock a boat. Each apartment had central air conditioning and heat and was equipped with an electric kitchen, screened porches and sliding glass doors, to bring the outside in.

Prices ranged from $8,950 to $10,950, depending on the size of the unit. By combining three, four and five homes under one roof they became apartment-homes.

By January 1964, half of the 100 units were sold. During the next few years Jack Holmes continued to sell and build additional units. He turned more of the responsibilities over to his son, Hugh G. Holmes, Sr., who continued to build duplex units on the property until the development was complete. Most of the units were sold to permanent residents or those wanting winter homes in the area. The development concept was very

A waterfront view and a place to dock your boat were the selling points of Seaside Gardens.

successful, according to Hugh, and brought many new residents to Holmes Beach.

Shell Point

In the late 1970s, development of the Shell Point Condominums began. Six acres, which bordered on Anna Maria Sound at the north end of Flotilla Drive in Holmes Beach, had previously been purchased by the Holmes family from the state and was adjacent to the uplands owned by the developers. Fill, dredged from the bay, was used to raise the elevation above the mean high-water line sufficiently to enable the development of the property to proceed.

The land was covered under the existing zoning ordinances, along with several other parcels within the City of Holmes Beach. During this period, the city was in the process of revising the zoning ordinances and zoning maps. Consequently, the Holmes family requested and received zoning that would allow the construction of condominiums on the property.

Hugh Holmes, Sr. drew up the preliminary design of the units and developed a site plan. When all the plans were complete they were presented to the city for approval. Permits were issued and construction commenced. A legal firm in Bradenton was appointed to prepare the condominium documents as required by the state. Hugh selected a firm in Bradenton to handle the preparation of the documents and the application to the state. A model apartment was constructed for the sales office and realtor George Wagner handled the sales. Eventually Hugh's wife, Jean Holmes, acquired her broker's license and handled sales and management through her own office. All the work was done by the Holmes Construction Company.

Construction continued for several years until 44 units were completed. A recreation building, tennis courts, swimming pool and putting green were added to the complex. Then the management was turned over to the association.

"The board of directors has managed the association and deserves credit for a commendable job," Hugh G.

Holmes, Sr. said.

Undeveloped Shell Point can be seen in the middle of the picture. Taken in 1957, the Key Royale Bridge had just been built.

Four

Three Cites Take Shape

The volunteer firemen gave Island kids a cool time when they attached the fire hoses to the water supply.

Historic Anna Maria

The rugged individualism of pioneer settlers, the vision and enterprise of developers made Anna Maria City, which was incorporated in 1923, the first resort community on the west coast of Florida.

On Feb. 22, 1951, the *Anna Maria Key News* came out with an entire page dealing with the history of the northernmost city on the Island. The following is part of that informative article.

"The City of Anna Maria has grown rapidly in the last five years. Because this section has been incorporated for so many years and has kept zoning restrictions, it has been kept attractive and no development can harm it. In fact, the growth that has come to it, and the Island as a whole, is mostly in the way of increased services for the convenience and comfort of its citizens.

"The first school on the Island was in Anna Maria and was used until last February, when a modern school was constructed mid-Island. The old school, on Magnolia Avenue, has been turned into the Island Youth Center, which is sponsored by the Island Lions Club.

"The Community Hall, on Gulf Drive and Pine Avenue, is where most organizations hold meetings. The new school has taken some of the strain off the hall, but it remains the home of the Island Woman's Club, the Island Players, and last year the first Island art exhibit was held there.

"The City of Anna Maria has had its own water system since the incorporation, but through the years it became inadequate and a new one has just been installed and dedicated. The new, pure water system is one of the city's greatest assets. Anna Maria will institute shortly its own refuse disposal, which is a modern convenience enjoyed by few small communities.

"The City Pier has been famous for many years and is known to fishermen all over Florida. At the height of the season you can meet visitors from almost every state in the union and foreign countries as well. There have been many times when anglers lined up shoulder-to-shoulder to catch thousands of mackerel. Many of them cast over electric wires where the lines, hooks and bait became entangled and were abandoned. The wires, festooned with curious debris, looked like a new form of Spanish moss.

"Leading out to the bay is the man-made Lake LaVista which is what happens to a jungle swamp when a real estate man, bulldozers and dredges go to work to make beautiful homesites.

"Roser Memorial Community Church, the first public building on the Island, is one of the most beautiful structures in the city. It has been enlarged, but still retains its original simple, charming lines and recently acquired a new Hammond organ.

"John Roser was an excellent example of the first type of visitor attracted to Anna Maria, and each year retired business and professional people, artists and writers, add to the year-round population of the community and are a tribute to the substantial character of the original homesteaders and developers of this hamlet.

"There is now a second house of worship in the city. The Island Baptist Church has just been completed on Gulf Drive at the border of Holmes Beach. The Rev. Eugene Baxley is the pastor.

"The hub of activity in the city of Anna Maria centers around a tiny structure on Pine Avenue (now the Historical Museum) which is not as beautiful as the churches, but as quaint a city hall as can be found. Affable Mayor Richard Ernest, who was elected to office in February 1950, is a builder on the Island and carries on the business of city administration. The mayor is assisted by two commissioners, vice mayor James Forrester, whose native land is Scotland and Sam P. Adams, who is proud to be called a Florida cracker.

"The tourists have made the city famous. Pioneer settlers and developers gave it character, but the present citizens give this beautiful little city warmth and personality that make visitors feel that at long last they have found everything they ever wanted in the way of a peaceful, quiet, but exhilarating life."

Another article in *The Islander* newspaper read: "There was little else to discuss at the town meeting on Tuesday, February 5, 1952, so an open forum on dogs developed. Mrs. Woods said there were too many dogs in the city. Mr. Jones claimed dogs went to the IGA store where Benny and Ernie would give them bones, which the dogs buried in his yard and the neighbors' gardens. Mrs. Woods came back with, "All dogs should have tags on their collars, and the city should have a dog pound."

"Jess Ingram, a city worker, seeing where the discussion was heading, demanded recognition and refused point-blank to become a dogcatcher along with all his other chores.

"Mr. Jones did not see how a license tag would stop the dogs from digging up gardens, and Mrs. Woods said you could train the dogs not to go into people's gardens and bury bones. "You punish them with a newspaper when they do wrong," she said.

Paul Carlisle, owner of the Anna Maria Motel at the North Point, topped the discussion with a speech on regimentation. He explained how rules and regulations were coming from Washington threatening the smallest communities with loss of freedom.

"The dog licensing business was evidence that regimentation was rearing its ugly head amongst us and endangering the free and easy, happy-go-lucky, friendly life on Anna Maria," Carlisle said. "As for the dogs, there are a dozen playing around my motel every night."

The newspaper article continued: "Each morning, armed with stick and shovel, Paul Carlisle gathered up what the dogs had left and spread it around the roots of his oleanders. They bloom in great beauty and have an extraordinary lovely odor which permeates the air with a sweet effulgence around the Anna Maria Motel, all which could probably be traced to an itinerant retriever or a visiting Airedale. That ended the dog session, with Mayor Ernest promising to look into the matter."

A typical beach cottage in 1955.

In 1952, the city dedicated the Bay Front Park property as a park to the people. The city was growing in a haphazard, disjointed fashion, and some owners were disregarding the law to make money. Praises went to Mayor Ted Tripp and his commission for approving a plan by Al Robson for plantings in the Bay Park in 1953. Plans included curved walks winding around a series of Tahitian huts, seagrape bushes and pine trees for shade. The Garden Club suggested a Memory Avenue of palms. Citizens were encouraged to donate palms and plants as symbols of affection for loved ones.

According to a brochure produced by the Anna Maria Beach Company in the early 1900s, a small group of men bought a large part of the city. A search though city archives revealed there were sidewalks throughout the city and when excavated were found to be in good condition. They dug wells for water, built an ice plant, a community hall, a post office, a church and the pier. After the town was incorporated, electricity came to the Island.

East and west avenues were named for trees. Some still remain. They are: Oak, Cedar, Willow, Palmetto, Palm, Magnolia, Pine, Elm, Cocoanut and Spruce. The north-south streets were named for fish. Three main streets ran from the north to south border: Grouper, Snapper, which is now Gulf Drive, Shad, which is Crescent now and Tarpon, the only one remaining today. Many of the 40-foot access streets to the Gulf and Bay were closed and turned into building lots.

In the early 1920s, the city borrowed $40,000 and, due to repeated default in interest payments, the total indebtedness represented by the issue reached the formidable total of $100,000. In October 1953, the commission heard the indebtedness was largely liquidated through the sale of city land.

On January 1954, headlines in *The Islander* were: "Carlisle Unopposed For Mayor of Anna Maria City." The article read: "Paul Carlisle has a heavy burden thrust upon his shoulders. He has the courage and now the opportunity to clear away some rubbish, solve some problems and make Anna Maria City a fine example of good government."

Paul Carlisle was elected in 1955 and died while in office in 1956.

Looking south from Pine Avenue to the newly-developed Bimini Bay in the mid-'50s.

During February of 1954, the papers were full of aerial photographs of Bimini Bay Estates, which promised to be the finest residential section in Anna Maria City. Water channels from the bayou to the main road provided waterfront lots and boat docks. Ads read: "You can catch your breakfast fish every morning without leaving your lawn." Perhaps the best thing for the city was that in one fell swoop this large tract was now free of mosquito-breeding marshes and opened up a vista from bayou to the Gulf in place of the mangrove swamps where raccoons and snakes were known to thrive and multiply.

A special bond-burning celebration took place Nov. 9, 1963 at the Bay Front Park. The bond-burning symbolized the retirement of bonds issued by the city during the days of the Florida boom in 1924. State Senator Ed H. Price Jr. was the principal speaker. Mayor James O. Ferguson emphasized the end of Anna Maria's bonded indebtedness. Ralph Parrish was in charge of the fish fry, and Dr. Ralph French caught many of the fish.

Houses were frequently moved down the beach.

An installation of electronically operated camera equipment, to be used in conjunction with an Eglin Air Force Base Gulf test, was in operation in 1963 on the beach at the north end of Bay Boulevard. A similar operation was going on at the same location in 1961. According to the technicians, the installation was not a missile-tracking system. One-third of the triangulation system was used to calibrate radar systems which tracked guided missiles. The equipment was owned and operated by Vitro Corporation of America, a private contractor for the Air Force. Cameras were used to take still pictures at night of airborne flashing lights. Stars were used as the background for reference points to establish time and space position. All data gathered was classified.

In January 1955, the board of commissioners voted unanimously to put 24 lots in Fiddlers Flats on the

Anna Maria Bayfront park was a popular place for picnics.

market. This wide expanse of land was named after the ubiquitous fiddler crabs which roamed the flats by the thousands. The crustacean is named for the fiddle-shaped large claw on all males. During courtship, the males wave their oversized claws high in the air and tap them on the ground in an effort to attract the females. They are found along sea beaches, brackish inter-tidal mud flats, lagoons and swamps.

In 1953, the land was valued at $3,500, and in 1955 the evaluation was $5,500 with a firm cash offer from a resident in Delaware. Engineer Frank Giles estimated it would cost $8,400 to clear, drain, raise the level with a two-foot fill, put in streets and prepare the land for building. At that price a buyer would acquire one of the 24 lots, close to the Bay, for $580 each.

On March 21, 1955, Fiddlers Flats, the last sizeable piece of city property, was sold to Lacios and Lardas for $6,280 at a commission meeting. A $5,000 performance bond accompanied the bid to assure the land would be filled, cleared and graded to the level of the adjourning, Bimini Bay Estates, which was five feet above mean low water.

In 1957, the commission granted permission to the Sandbar restaurant to place a boat ramp nearby in the Gulf. The same year the Chamber of Commerce was given permission to use the Bay Front Park for a circus and the shooting of fireworks off the City Pier, in conjunction with the new Manatee Bridge celebration.

In 1958, restrooms were built at Bay Front Park, and there was a need for more Tahiti huts to shield beach goers from the sun. Commissioner Frances Livingston complained that a lot was being done for the Bay Front Park, but nothing had been done for the Gulf Park, which ran along the Gulf from Magnolia Avenue to Oak Avenue.

In 1964, city officials said a new city office building was just a dream, but added, when the project reached the planning stage, serious consideration would be given to building it on Pine Avenue near the Community House (now the Island Players).

Jan. 23, 1965, was declared Mitch Davis Day to honor Capt. Mitch as first mayor and commemorate the 40th anniversary of the incorporation of the city. All citizens were invited to the celebration at the Bay Front Park.

The dedication of the new Anna Maria City Hall on May 24, 1967 drew a crowd of more than 100 people. Edward Dean Wyke designed the Bermuda-style structure. The total cost for the meeting room, reception room, offices for the mayor, city clerk, building inspector and chief of police was $30,284.

A dedication address was given by the first mayor Capt. Mitch Davis, who traced the highlights of the history of this municipality from the day it was founded in 1923. At age 80, his memory was remarkable, and his remarks were tinged with humor as he told of his many years operating a fishing boat and as an Island builder. He was responsible for many of the Island's original homes, also Roser Church, the community hall and the old jail.

Mitch Davis was the first mayor of Anna Maria City.

When asked to compare the Island then and now he thought awhile and said, "There is no comparison. Everything was much more abundant then, especially the fish. There were many raccoons, a few alligators, and lots of sharks. The changes are for the better," he added. "But I liked living here before. It costs too much now."

About this time, residents made their own decision not to turn their Island into another Miami Beach, so they outlawed high-rise apartments and duplex buildings as well.

The Holmes Beach Saga

"Few communities anywhere in the world can rival the natural beauty and ideal living conditions of the Town of Holmes Beach and use with impunity the slogan: The Town With A Future!"

This was an introduction to the story of Holmes Beach in the Beachcombers Fair Section of the *Anna Maria Key News* on Feb. 22, 1951, when Holmes Beach was a vacation designation.

Incorporated on March 13, 1950, Holmes Beach became known as the fastest growing home community on the west coast of Florida. In 1951, 180 homes were constructed in a portion of what was formerly a 600-acre jungle. Shortly after residents voted to incorporate, the Holmes family donated land for a city hall. The old structure was razed in 1998 after the present city complex was completed. The Holmes family also gave the city recreational land adjacent to the city hall which was designed for baseball and soccer fields.

The man with the idea for the development was J. E. Holmes, Sr. who first came to the Island in 1907 to work on the construction of the East Coast Railroad from Miami to the Keys. At the close of World War II, he returned to Anna Maria with an idea he had conceived during his sojourn away from the Island. He interested his friend, Frank Giles of Georgia, in the conception of a home community of modest proportions in a luxurious setting designed to attract the retired professional businessman whose work permitted him to spend the whole or part of the year in sub-tropical paradise.

Holmes and Giles spoke to Peder Mickelsen of Minnesota and Francis Karel of Chicago about the project. The four business tycoons merged their talents, and soon the Town of Holmes Beach emerged.

Holmes Beach was named after developer Jack Holmes.

In just one year, more than a quarter of a million dollars in building permits were issued. The swift growth necessitated constant clearing of land. In 1951 two and one half miles of beach was being developed for residents and their guests to enjoy. On the bayside, a series of canals and lagoons and four miles of protected waterfront property were created. Several large apartment complexes were under construction.

The attractive homes being built for the most part were two and three bedrooms, architecturally designed so owners would receive all the benefits from living in a sub-tropical climate. Thousands were lured to Florida and established legal residence to take advantage of the state's homestead exemption. The lack of state income tax was further inducement to build in Holmes Beach, since there was no ad valorem tax levied. It was expected the Town of

Holmes Beach would never have in excess of 2000 homes. Since there were 600 acres in the city it meant each owner would have at least a quarter of an acre.

Jack Holmes said the state road through the Island was as crooked as a dog's hind leg in quite a few places. In January 1952, he went before the State Road Department and offered them a highway through Holmes Beach that would take the curves out of the road. They were impressed with the idea and said when the time came to do something to the road they would act on his idea.

The pace continued through the '50s and '60s. In the mid-'50s Jack built the Holmes Beach marina and yacht club which later became the famed Pete Reynard's Restaurant. In 1952, Jack Holmes built the first shopping center on the Island. The airport he built in the late '40s was used by small planes after the MGM film "On An Island With You" was filmed.

In the early '60s, the construction of Seaside Gardens an affordable waterfront community, took place. The Island Bank was completed in 1960 and the Key Royale Bridge was built about the same time. Homesites were planned for 125-acres overlooking Sarasota and Tampa bays. The Key Royale golf course opened in 1966. In 1945, there were 14 homes in Holmes Beach, and by 1951 more than 200 homes were occupied.

The Town of Holmes Beach celebrated its Fifth Anniversary on Sept. 4, 1955, but the real guest of honor was Jack Holmes, who founded the town and was still a main factor in its growth. Several hundred people from all parts of the county gathered on the patio of the Yacht Club for cocktails. Many toasts were given to Jack, whose vision made it the city with a future. Dinner was served to as many as the dining room would hold. A huge birthday cake with five candles was the highlight of the celebration.

Mayor Maxwell Ingham received many complaints from residents during March 1955 that commercial fishermen were littering the beach with dead trash fish. Town Marshal Phil Carter was informed. An enraged citizen took direct action. A car drove up in the dark and dumped three dead sharks on the mayor's lawn. Asked to comment the mayor, in his usual philosophical manner, did not denounce the vengeful antics but said, "The

Building on 68th Street began in the early '60s

worst way for commercial fishermen to get cooperation from the municipal officials is to leave a lot of dead fish on the beach."

Carter said, "We will get nowhere until we make some arrests." The *Islander's* editor noted, "You could have buried those sharks under your palms. That is good, cheap fertilizer."

The Islander featured a large aerial photograph on the front page of the Oct. 31, 1957 issue entitled "Mid-Island." The filled land behind the cottages shown in the picture, was the Sunrise Park development. Plans were to fill in more submerged land, roughly one-third greater than shown in the picture. The white peninsular near the top of the picture was a matter of great concern to many people. It reached far out into the bay and was close to School Key (Key Royale). If the fill was permitted to go out further it would spoil the view for many residents, but of more importance, it would affect the waterways around School Key. Had a bulkhead law been in effect, it was doubtful if authorities would have allowed this long extension of property into the bay.

Karl Francis Karel presented the Chamber of Commerce an idea for a community center north of the town office in November of 1957. The civic center would be used for a little theater, art exhibits, musicals and conventions. It would be financed by revenue bonds for which the citizens and the town would be responsible. Leased by an all-Island group, it would be available to the Island, Longboat Key, Bradenton and Palmetto. Karel did not ask for any specific action, just enthusiasm for the project. The community center was never built in Holmes Beach, but the Island Community Center in Anna Maria City is thriving today.

An artist's drawing of the General Telephone Company's new Holmes Beach central office was in the Aug. 18, 1960 issue of *The Islander*. The structure would be built on the corner of Gulf Drive and 51st Street. The 4,300 square foot building would be part of a more than $600,000 expansion and improvement program on the Island. The facility would cost $60,000 and was expected to be in service by 1961.

The Town of Homes Beach had become the second largest municipality in Manatee County, according to

Jack Holmes was always promoting the Island. Sometimes his advertisements featured Island beauties. He is seen in the middle of this group.

1965 tax assessment records. Taxable real estate and private property was valued at $12,293,330. This figure represented a $2-million increase since 1960. The surge, which occurred during two years, pointed to rapid expansion of building in this Island community. Permits covered 39 new houses, five duplexes, four apartment buildings, five seawalls, three docks and two pools. Building permits were granted for 21 remodeling jobs.

Polly Archer, city clerk, said Holmes Beach had roughly 3,000 permanent residents in the '60s. In 1950, there were only 65 residents with property valued at $500,000. Property owners had been assessed no municipal tax.

Some 300 of Manatee County's citizens assembled at the Holmes Beach Yacht Club on Jan. 6, 1964 to pay tribute to one of the county's most outstanding citizens in what was believed to be the largest surprise party in the county's history.

John E. "Jack" Holmes was honored in recognition of the most outstanding performance in community development. The occasion also marked Jack's 75th birthday. He was recognized as one of the leading real estate developers and builders in the Gulf coast area and received a gleaming gold plaque. Specifically, Holmes was being honored for the development of his newest project, Seaside Gardens, a $1,500,000 apartment-home waterfront community on 62nd and 63rd Streets. His new concept of easy living on a Florida island combined the economic advantages of co-op construction, minus maintenance costs, and made it possible for purchasers to own the land on which their homes stood because of single-level construction.

State Representative Robert Knowles, the main speaker, said, "If we looked around the county for someone to epitomize our growth over the last 30 years, we'd find none better than Jack Holmes. He played a significant part in the skillful development of land. This is a man with an engineering mind who has applied his skills successfully." He commended Holmes for discovering Pete Reynard, whose Yacht Club restaurant was one of the most successful operations of its kind in the area.

Jack went into semi-retirement in the early '60s, but kept an eye on his sons who continued his work and served in the community. John E. Holmes, Jr. went into banking and served on the Holmes Beach City Council for years. Hugh took charge of Holmes Construction, eventually stepping aside for his son to take over the thriving business.

Jack Holmes and his sons, John, left, and Hugh.

Hugh paid tribute to his father saying, "He gave people the kind of homes they wanted at prices they could afford, and he had the vision to concentrate the commercial development in one small area rather than stringing it out as so many Island communities have done. I believe he made Anna Maria Island the most attractive community on the whole coast of Florida."

In 1974, Island residents were looking up. The Martinique condominium apartments rose seven stories at 5200 and 5300 Gulf Drive. After the first and only multi-story high rise on Anna Maria Island was constructed, all three Island cities passed ordinances limiting the height of all buildings to two stories.

Bradenton Beach Comes Of Age

On Dec. 21, 1951, 84 property owners who lived south of 27th Street, voted to form a municipality and called it Bradenton Beach. With the incorporation, the unanimous election of Bernie Wagaman as mayor, and the type of municipal government they selected, the town took on new dignity, new responsibilities and a more significant place in Manatee County.

It was the hope of many that the incorporation of Bradenton Beach would be a step toward Island unity, a single municipality with individual boroughs and equal representation regardless of size.

Mrs. Mildred Van Hout, chairman of the citizens rally preceding the election said, "Although our numbers are few and community small it is just as important to us as if we numbered in the millions, because it's folks like you and communities like ours that make up these great United States. By your vote and the candidates you elect, the Town of Bradenton Beach will become a community that could be the envy of every city in the entire state of Florida."

The first Bradenton Beach city office was small but efficient.

In 1950, a small group formed The Beachcombers of Gulf Trailer Park and pledged to have fun and frolic, to learn to know each other better and like each other more. A picture in *The Islander* in 1957 showed a small band of Beachcombers holding their certificates as charter members of the club. In 1950, there were few trailers in the park, but by 1957 there were more than 900 residents. Jim Templin, who owned the park, was known as "Skipper of Flotsam," and Dan Reid had the title of "Chief Moocher" of the Beachcombers.

When the garbage collector quit in March of 1952, there was a hiatus of a few days before the newly hired man could take over in a borrowed truck. Mayor Gorsuch said grimly, "Garbage will be collected. If nobody else will do it, I will!"

"Last Sunday he mounted the truck and collected garbage. This was a true spirit of service," according to the *Islander* editor. "He should not do it. We feel that Bradenton Beach got itself a good mayor. We could almost guarantee the spirit of former Mayor Bernie Wagaman rode beside him and made the heavy loads a little lighter."

"State Road Department Sued" was the headline in the Nov. 13, 1952 issue of *The Islander*. The article read: "Some eyebrows rose when a couple of taxpayers brought suit to prevent the building of Island bridges. They claimed the money was not in hand. As partial payment, the county pledged a percentage of future income from gas taxes and tolls from the two Island bridges. The Bridge Street merchants were sponsoring a zoning ordinance which would make the new bridge location residential only. This would eliminate competition among the businesses. It was their hope the Friday shopping migration from the Island to Bradenton would dwindle to a trickle. Off-Island shopping drained money from Bradenton Beach merchants."

Bradenton Beach fought the Gulf in March 1952. Interested property owners and council members decided the Gulf of Mexico must stop encroaching on their property. They called Manatee County Commissioner

The Beachcombers of Gulf Trailer Park planned lots of fun activities

Herman Burnett and ended up assessing themselves $25 per lot. With the help of Burnett and the Erosion Control Board, work began immediately to prevent Gulf waters from damaging properties. Rocks were brought in and jetties constructed.

The council turned down a proposal to purchase a truck and fogging equipment. The Manatee County Mosquito Control Commission agreed to supply a truck and equipment and spraying solution for fogging for $2,800. Bradenton Beach was already operating its own truck at a cost of $5 a fogging. The mayor announced the city had bought 1,000 larvicide bombs which were available to residents for use on mosquito breeding spots. A drainage and paving program was expected to eliminate roadside breeding places.

The new Bradenton Beach Post Office was dedicated on Sept. 6, 1952. The concrete building on Bridge Street was constructed on the site of the old post office. The new quarters were twice as large as the previous building. Glass jalousies and glass bricks brightened and gave a modern design to the structure. Mrs. Bruce Cox, postmaster, said the new facility would allow a much improved mail service for Bradenton Beach. State Rep. J. Ben Fuqua, one of the speakers at the dedication ceremony, said citizens in Bradenton Beach were the most civic-minded people he had ever met. County Commissioner Herman Burnett praised the progress the Island had made in the past three years and cited how much had been done by the Islanders, but also said the county commission had done a good job getting five bridges and Cortez Road constructed.

During the ceremony, Lt. Bill Laney of the Civil Air Patrol, gave an exhibition of stunt flying, and the Manatee High School Band played under the direction of Charles Quarmby.

The first meeting of the Bradenton Beach Fire Department Auxiliary was held Sept.11,1952 at the firehouse. Mrs. J. A. Flanagan appointed Annie Silver chairman of the nominating committee.

There were 233 voters registered for the Nov. 26, 1952 city election. Jack Jones was urged to seek the office of mayor. Charles Hess, city clerk, was seeking reelection, and Robert Martini was running for a seat on the council. Annie Silver, who was described by Mayor Jack Jones as "the most beloved and revered woman on this end of the Island," donated a fifty by hundred foot lot to the people of her neighborhood for two shuffleboard courts in

February 1953. In March, the Annie Silver Shuffleboard Court Club was organized, by-laws were adopted, dues fixed and an ambitious program conceived.

There was no better advertisement for Anna Maria Island, for health and longevity, than Annie Silver. At the young age of 80, she had more spirit and joy of living than some youngsters who felt life owed them easy living. Annie worked all her life and was a successful realtor and grocery store owner. In 1953, she owned four lots with a building on each and managed about 40 properties. She built an attractive office, which she ran with the vim and vigor of a teenager.

Annie Silver was respected by everyone.

Evidently the Town of Bradenton Beach was not content just to pass ordinances. They enforced them. In March of 1953, an offender was brought into court at the fire hall and judged guilty of violating the law of operating a vehicle with the muffler "cut-out open." He was fined $5, and Mayor Jack Jones commented, "The laws of Bradenton Beach will be upheld!"

A new look came to Bridge Street and Gulf Drive in June 1953. The Gulf Terrace Restaurant, where Island folks went for good food and drink, had been completely done over. Large windows replaced walls and gave diners a million-dollar view of the beach and azure Gulf.

In November 1953, an ordinance was passed ordering that numbers be placed on every home and business in the city. Numbers were provided, free of charge, by the city. Failure to display the numbers was punishable by a fine of $25 and ten days in jail, or both.

Residents were looking forward to the time when mail would be delivered to their homes and businesses.

After a resolution by Councilman Todd, the Town of Bradenton Beach voted against any dock being built at the end of a city street. The docks were encroachments and would not be allowed since the town would be liable for accidents and injuries.

In 1954, a series of free band concerts, sponsored by the city, were held on Sunday afternoons during the winter season at a bandstand erected on a lot across the street from the city clerk's office. The 30-piece American Legion Band played rousing selections. Fred Perfect, the leader, announced the concerts would continue through the season since about 500 had attended. Adding variety to the programs, Perfect would often pick up his violin and play unaccompanied except for the sea breeze and rustling palms.

Mayor Jack Jones and his council were congratulated for doing more for Island unity than any other individual group. The mayor explained that when the town was incorporated, the area from the south end of the Island to the town limits was made Residential No. 3. "To put a public beach in a residential zone would be the most terrible thing that could ever happen to the city," he said.

The Bradenton Beach Civic Club, founded in goodwill and dedicated to the welfare of the citizens, expired in December 1955. An *Islander* news item said: "It was murdered by apathy born of the isolationist policies of the majority of people and elected officials. When the subject of incorporating the Island arose, dissension and selfish traits cropped up and dominated the city. The civic club could not thrive under those conditions."

About this same time, Mayor Jack Jones resigned. He sold his Gulf Terrace restaurant and moved to Bradenton. All attending the city meeting heard his parting remarks with shocked silence. He had relinquished the office in the city he loved, and nothing he ever did in office added more to his stature and dignity than his manner of leaving. He felt that because he believed deeply that incorporation of the Island was best for Bradenton Beach his people had turned against him. Jones brought good government and dignity to the city until three of his councilmen turned against him and brought discord of a malignant nature into the council chamber.

The Annie Silver Community Hall had a grand opening on New Year's Day 1956. About 200 people were served dinner followed by card games and a shuffleboard contest. The Ladies Auxiliary cooked four huge turkeys. The new community hall, built and financed by a group of neighbors, would prove to be a fine center for the promotion of goodwill and welfare in the small but devoted section of the community. Annie Silver was too ill to attend the event.

The Ground Corps Observer's Tower, by the Gulf Terrace Restaurant, was built on donated land in September 1956. Jim Zerby, ousted city clerk, assisted by contractor Carl Olsen, put on the finishing touches. The Ground Observers Corps Tower was a watchtower for the Civil Defense Ground Observer Corps. The city was to be complimented on its good citizens who planned the tower and the councilmen who voted to give $300 for materials.

The tower was manned 22-hours a day, and volunteers worked two-hour shifts between 10 a.m. and 8 p.m. A plea went out to all Islanders who were concerned with national defense to render this service to their community and country.

An Island reporter covering the story thought little of civil defense in the area until he heard a New Orleans

broadcaster telling of an approaching hurricane. The local civil defense was prepared for any eventuality.

The Gulf Trailer Park was awarded an approval rating as one of the top mobile home trailer parks in the United States, according to the Mobile Home Manufacturing Company. The announcement was made after 12,525 parks in the country were inspected in February, 1957.

The city leased space in Secor's building on Bridge Street for a city office and meeting room and planned to occupy the new quarters starting September 1, 1957.

On June 13, 1957, *The Islander* carried a picture entitled, "Creating Coquina Beach." The scene was taken from the south end looking north from Longboat Pass. A rock jetty had already been built at the south end along the Pass. Pilings and portions of girders on the Longboat Key Bridge could be seen. The mangrove key was Leffis

Key, earlier known as Coffee Shell Key.

The mile-long area was owned by the E. P. Green Estate, developers of the first Bradenton Beach subdivision, Cortez Beach, on March 14, 1912. The Green Estate entered into an extraordinary right-of-entry agreement with the State Road Department to permit immediate building of the road and bridge over Longboat Pass.

Mayor Dick Connick was mayor for a decade.

After the road and bridge were completed, the Green Estate claimed the new beach. Following years of legal battling, the brouhaha was finally settled in July of 1962. The Green estate sold its title to 110-acres of land to Manatee County for $318,000. The county and SRD also took over ownership of the mile-long beach along the Gulf and Sarasota Bay.

After the construction of the Cortez Bridge, a section of the old wooden bridge from Bridge Street was turned into a fishing pier. In 1964 the pier was in dire need of repair. A public hearing was planned to let citizens decide what course to take because of the cost involved. All agreed the pier was one of the city's most important recreational facilities.

A suit against the operators of the city fishing pier was filed in Manatee County Circuit Court in April of 1964. The suit contended the pier was in need of immediate repair and was in an unsafe and hazardous condition and that the responsibilities were with the lessees of the pier, Howard E. and Belva S. Miller.

The city had originally leased the pier to Frank E. Mellett and John D. Blackmore on Jan. 27, 1959. On September 1 of that year, Mellett and Blackmore assigned their rights to the pier to the Millers, with the city approving the agreement on September 4.

Final plans for shelters, picnic tables, benches, barbecue pits and trash receptacles at the county-owned beach and park at the south end of the Island were authorized by the Manatee County Park and Recreation Commission in February 1964.

County Planning Director William Vines told the beach commissioners that $41,000 had been spent on the new park and he was very pleased "with the mileage gotten out of the money."

Beach Commissioner Walter Hardin estimated that each picnic shelter, including four or five tables and benches, concrete floor and roof would cost about $1,500. Due to the limited budget, he suggested open air tables be installed and permanent shelters be added later.

One hundred twenty-five residents of Sandpiper Mobile Home Park filed into city hall on Nov. 9, 1972 to learn that no matter what action the city council took they would not have to, "hook their cars to their trailers and take off down the road," in Mayor Bill Lindsey's words.

The city wanted the two trailer parks upgraded over the next five years. The crux of the problem was the parks were originally planned for eight-foot wide trailers, and mobile homes were 12-feet wide. Councilman Dick Connick insisted on a compromise and championed the cause of the park owners.

In 1967 Richard Connick, a 39-year-old owner of a Bradenton Beach television repair store, dissatisfied with the way the city council was running, decided to run for a seat on the council. He ran on a no-tax increase platform and called for conservative government. He overpowered the other candidate, and he and his running mate were elected. In his first year on the council he secretly engineered the ouster of the police chief, according to *The Islander*, and was accused of concealing police reports from the public.

Connick piled up 305 votes in a bitter mayoral election in 1973. He swept in two like-minded councilmen, gaining the majority power he would never lose. He began a long feud with Holmes Beach Mayor Jim Zerby over the operation of the Island police radio service. Councilman Roy Marchand tangled with Connick over the city finances. Paving jobs for the mayor and his relatives, allegedly performed by a contractor for the county sewer system, were questioned. The state attorney investigated, exonerated Connick and Marchand dropped off the board.

In 1975, Connick's grip on city affairs moved former Mayor Bill Lindsey to come out of political retirement to oppose him. Lindsey lost, 306 to 179. Connick gained control of the fourth council seat in the election.

David Reid, a 22-year-old waiter, waged an exciting campaign against Connick in 1977, but Connick survived by just 34 votes out of the 896 cast. Charges were lodged by the state attorney that Connick had illegally tapped into county water lines. One charge was dropped and the other thrown out by a judge when a key prosecution witness backed down. Subsequently Connick was removed as chief of the city's fire department in 1978 by the Anna Maria Fire District.

He was elected to a fourth two-year-term in 1979 by default, when no one filed to run against him. Connick attributed his victory to accomplishments such as procuring a stoplight on Gulf Drive at the Cortez Bridge, resurfacing city streets and getting a county ambulance stationed at his store.

Again Connick won in the 1981 election with 403 votes or 64 percent of the votes cast. He felt the results demonstrated the public's approval of his midnight closing of the bars.

After a decade as mayor, Connick turned back challenger Gale Carter to return to office, but only by a 59-vote margin, 364 to 305. Troubles in the police department, and charges by Carter supporters that corruption was rife in his administration were vexing issues for the mayor. One charge was that Connick tried to extort $10,000 from restaurant owners to set up a defense fund for a 1980 lawsuit. At the end of a 10-month investigation by the Florida Department of Law Enforcement, only two of 21 allegations were found to be prosecutable and FDLE declined to prosecute after the mayor repaid $250.

Two candidates announced they would run against Connick in the 1985 election, but dropped out charging harassment by the city. Connick won an uncontested seventh term.

"The people are satisfied with the present administration, so no one ran against me," Connick said. "I think not having an election is a healthy sign because it shows the people are satisfied. We've got a good solid government in Bradenton Beach, and I'll continue to represent the people of this town just like I've done for the past 12 years. Those people that accuse me of being afraid of dissent are just disgruntled ex-city employees or *The Islander* newspaper. People are satisfied, or I would have had opposition."

In 1986, Connick was not up for reelection. It would prove to be his political demise. A group of residents and business people, calling themselves the Sunshine Party, put up three reform candidates for the city council to bring "sunshine into the city."

On December 12, citing health reasons, Connick resigned, and on December 14, three newly-elected councilors elected Barbara Turner mayor for one year. Bradenton Beach residents heaved a sigh of relief, Connick's reign was over.

Incorporation—The Island As One City

In 1950, Bradenton Beach had not been incorporated, and there was controversy about whether to incorporate the Island as a whole, Bradenton Beach by itself, or just leave well enough alone.

Ilexhurst was a subdivision of 160-acres platted in 1901 by Rurick Cobb. It was located on the bay in Bradenton Beach where the Sandpiper Mobile Home Park is today. Those against incorporation were centered in Ilexhurst, and in May 1950 the *Anna Maria Key News* came out with an article entitled "Ilexhurst Secedes."

The new Island phone directory published in November 1950, gave listings under the names of: the City of Anna Maria, the Town of Holmes Beach, Ilexhurst, mid-Island and Bradenton Beach. Ilexhurst did not get away with its secession and was later incorporated as Bradenton Beach.

Early resident Renal Hook said, "When I first visited the Island over the Christmas holidays in 1950, I had no idea about the controversy over incorporation, and I certainly did not realize there were petitions circulating in favor of three new bridges. Had I known, I would have strongly endorsed the replacement of the old wooden bridge, because I was not at all convinced we'd make it across."

The Island Chamber of Commerce sponsored an Island-wide meeting in March in the early '50s at the Island school to explore the subject of consolidating the three Island cities. Harry Varley, editor of *The Islander*, wrote:

"When Islanders have nothing better to think about, they think about consolidation, that is making one city out of the three tiny cities on the Island."

Varley pushed hard for consolidation before Holmes Beach and Bradenton Beach were incorporated in the early '50s. Anna Maria City was incorporated in 1923. A few residents of Anna Maria favored the one-city scheme, but most did not. Time and again a referendum on consolidation of any kind failed. Independent-minded, or self-centered-Islanders would not buy it.

On April 13, 1950, the *Anna Maria Key News* featured an article on incorporation with statements of concerned citizens. Realtor Jack Marshall said, "We have a fast-growing community, which should be brought under one island-wide incorporation at the earliest possible date."

James Forrester, vice mayor of Anna Maria City asked, "What is the big obstacle preventing incorporation? I think it is because the majority of leadership people have not put real democracy to work. They cater to small groups which can't help but end with special privileges. Incorporation to me spells better health, happiness, progress and protection for all."

Robert Pethick, an Island builder, expressed his concern saying, "I hope the people on the Island will not let this question of incorporation slide back into a state of lethargy and finally oblivion. If this happens, the citizens will permit our sectionalized Island to thwart itself and eventually each section will burst at the seams. The Island is too small for separate boundaries."

An article in *The Islander* on Dec. 27, 1950 read: "Incorporation of Bradenton Beach is our greatest hope; incorporation is another step toward Island unity. A single Islandwide municipality where great things can be accomplished is what we want. We might have a bank, emergency hospital, general practitioners, dentist and an Island community center, all big enough for the entire Island. Congratulations to the new town of Bradenton Beach and the first mayor, Bernard Wagaman.

A letter to the editor of *The Islander* in the June 26, 1952 issue read: "I was a G.I. Before that I was a plumber, and since the war I have worked and studied, so now I am a competent, all-around plumber. Reading about how Anna Maria was growing I thought I would start a business for myself on the Island.

"I was told I would have to pay for an occupational license in Bradenton Beach, another in Holmes Beach and another in Anna Maria City. This is ridiculous considering there are less than 3,000 permanent residents on the Island, and with one license I could start in business in a city as big as Tampa.

"I have abandoned the idea of coming to the Island. But why in heaven's name do you have three piddling little cities when the whole Island, filled up, would make one of decent size and one you could be proud of. Must you do everything three or four times? What are you going to do in the future, build three city halls, have three sheriffs – three of everything?

"This outsider sees a lot of petty sectional pride and prejudice preventing your Island from having the glorious future it could have if it was not divided up into absurd government factions. I do not suppose you will print this, if you do just use my initials.

F.F.R. Tampa

On Dec.17, 1954, the Island Committee For Incorporation held their first meeting, and it was decided there would be a referendum vote in each municipality. Since there had been criticism that only elected officials made up the Island Committee For Incorporation, it was decided to appoint a citizen who was not an elected official from each of the communities.

The Island's County Commissioner Herman Burnett said it was his personal opinion the Island would be far better off as one municipality.

"I am whole-heartedly for Island incorporation," said Anna Maria Commissioner Bill Brier. "There are innumerable benefits: financial, savings, police protection, better roads and parks. There isn't anything to lose and everything to gain."

"I am for immediate incorporation," stated R.G. Sherman, Col. USA Retired, a Holmes Beach alderman and member of the Manatee County Planning Board. "Without our realizing it, the Island has outgrown its present organization and now desperately needs benefits that only can be secured by one government municipality.

Among numerous advantages is adequate police protection."

Anna Maria Commissioner Hilding Russell was also in favor of incorporating the Island. "I agree with the form of government suggested by the Committee of Incorporation, where each municipality will be a ward of the all-Island city with two councilmen from each ward elected by the people of the ward."

Holmes Beach Alderman John Holmes, Jr. when asked for his personal opinion on incorporation said, "Having lived on the Island for 29 years, I have heard all the pros and cons about Island incorporation. I have

Many Island residents thought the Island should be one city. Others opposed the idea.

served on the original Committee For Island Incorporation and I feel incorporation is desirable, but am doubtful as to whether this is the proper time."

That was the same doubt Anna Maria Mayor Paul Carlisle had the year before. "It seems to me we are not ready for Island incorporation," he said. "I doubt it would serve any useful purpose at this time. In my opinion the greatest obstacle is the miserable tax situation in Manatee County."

Annie Silver, a much-loved, old-timer, and a power in Bradenton Beach, spoke up in May of 1955. "I signed the petition to exclude Bradenton Beach from voting on incorporation. I am in business, and I realized if I did not sign it might hurt me financially. I knew I could vote, and vote right, when the time came.

"Now I know the facts were misrepresented to me. I have read about the meetings, seen the bulletin sent out by the committee and have watched attacks on Mayor Jones, whom I think is the finest official Bradenton Beach has had or can have. I am hurt and disgusted that a few citizens would attack the mayor. From now on I will work for incorporation. My only regret is there is no way I can erase my name from that petition."

"Annie was a forthright woman who has earned respect and love from all who know her," *The Islander* editor wrote. "With Annie on the side of the right, how can it lose?"

In an inspirational appeal for unification, W. J. Brown's key word was love. "I want to put my whole heart in the Island. I came here a sick man and now I am well. I love the Island. I have not heard one word against incorporation since I came to Holmes Beach. We could all be a better family if we united and the regional fussing would stop. We would have more political strength and voting power. You cannot learn to love your neighbor unless you know him. We should all get together in this and the Island would be a happier place to live."

The Islander editor Harry Varley added: "It would be easy for some obstructionists to be sarcastic and cynical about Mr. Brown's speech; saying it was naïve, emotional, a waste of gentle words to offset the acid verbiage from a scant few."

Another Varley observation emerged in the April 7, 1955 issue of *The Islander*. "Why a fraction of the voters insisted on tacking the word Island to the name of the city is somewhat puzzling to those who believe in the efficiency of simplicity. Think of billions of times the unnecessary word Island must be written and printed from now on, while on all the charts the Island is named, Anna Maria Key.

"If the vote on the referendum is favorable, the name of the city will be the City of Anna Maria Island. That cumbersome name is only academic and should be compulsorily used on legal documents. A letter addressed Anna Maria will reach here as surely as Anna Maria Island."

The nine-man Committee For Incorporation met to hear the rough draft of the charter. *The Islander* article continued: "This reporter was fighting against some weasel-worded paragraphs getting into the charter one of which would give the administrative power to pass vital ordinances by "posting" instead of "publication." Another would tie the hands of future administrations, if ever taxation was necessary and agreed to by the people, by making them swallow, hook, line and sinker, county assessments of property no matter how inequitable they were -- as they do now in Anna Maria City.

"The bill for Island incorporation passed the Senate and now awaits the governor's signature. Voting will be held on the Island in approximately 40 days from the day he signs." This snippet appeared in *The Islander* on April 21, 1955.

"The Deadliness of Delay," was a small headline in the December 21 *Islander* in 1957. "Perhaps the most insidious arguments for not incorporating the Island come from those whose hearts and tongues are in direct conflict.

"They say, we are for incorporation, but not now. The time is not ripe. What they mean is, the longer we can postpone action the less chance it has of becoming a reality. The best way to kill the idea is to preach delay."

A year later there was no report from the Committee For Incorporation. It had ceased to function, because at a meeting a resolution had passed advising temporary abandonment of incorporation and suggesting the merger of Anna Maria and Holmes Beach with a cordial invitation to Bradenton Beach to "come in." After this, the word "incorporation" was seldom mentioned.

Law Enforcement

This Island documentation names Island police up to1950: 1927: Under the Anna Maria City Charter, Marshal H. C. Crandall was paid $1 a day. 1928: Marshal J. H. Minor was assisted by Deputy Marshal Albert M. Davis. 1940s: Marshals in Anna Maria City were: Jesse Ingram, L. H. Dosh, Melvin Davis and Phil Carter. 1950: Special police in Anna Maria City were: Charles H. Pier, William Warttig and Cory Schambers.

In 1956, George Jordan was appointed Anna Maria City's first police chief. In 1965 Gene Stewart became police chief with a staff of three officers.

Bruce Tymeson was named police chief in 1969, a position he held until 1972. Three officers and six auxiliary policemen worked with him.

The City of Holmes Beach was incorporated in 1950. Paul Ford was the first chief of police in 1962. Louis "Humbug" Cobb was marshal until he was replaced by Snooks Adams from the Manatee County Sheriff's Department. Tom Shanafelt and Rick Maddox followed as police chiefs.

Bradenton Beach was incorporated in 1953. Officers who served, beginning in 1961, were Snooks Adams, Paul Fairbanks, Ray Little, David Crumm, Phil Silverthorn, Bill Doss and Paul Ford.

Some folks think it's strange that a seven-mile Island has three police departments but that's the way it is.

The following are a few interesting happenings that were handled by Island police departments and written up in *The Islander* newspaper: Records show on May 17, 1956 Anna Maria Police Chief George Jordan issued the first traffic ticket on the Island. Residents thought Jordan never slept since he was on duty night and day. In September 1969, Bradenton Beach enacted a curfew. On May 14, 1970, the Bradenton Beach police acquired the Cortez Bridge toll building as the police station.

In December 1970, Chief Bruce Tymeson acquired a canine helper named Chief, Jr. and the Bradenton Beach police department had a dog named Lobo. In January 1972, Chief Tymeson captured a fugitive goat known as Lady Astor. The goat, an actor in an Island Players production, was staying at the home of Helen Peters, the director, when it escaped.

In October 1950, two ships caused excitement and speculation among Island residents when they spent the day anchored in the bay about 100 yards off the Anna Maria Bay Front Park. It was rumored that the ships were part of the Cuban Navy, headed for Tampa, with smugglers and Cuban refugees aboard.

Anna Maria Police Chief George Jordan was taken out to the ships by Ed Riley of the Bayou Fishing Center. They went aboard the ships and found the PT boat was The Hawkins out of Morgan City, La. The other was a crash boat or rescue boat with a homeport in New Orleans. The men aboard were reluctant to give direct answers to questions, but did state the ships were being taken to Miami for resale. Another crash boat, anchored off the south end of the Island at the same time, departed when the other ships left Island waters. A total of nine ships were making the Louisiana to Miami trip. They attracted the interest of the border patrol, whose plane was seen flying low over the ships in the bay.

Jess Ingram was city marshal in Anna Maria City in 1950

One day in the early '50s, Dewey Adams, Anna Maria commissioner, was driving to Morehaven to go fishing. He didn't catch any fish, but driving back to the Island he accidentally helped catch an escaped convict. A stolen car, driven by the convict who had escaped from the state road camp near Citrus Center, smacked Dewey's car in the rear. The convict ran, but the highway patrol caught him a few miles away from the scene of the collision. The stolen car was smashed, but Dewey's car was not damaged much. It gave Dewey a good story to tell his Anchorage visitors and habitués.

In October 1953, the entire police force in Bradenton Beach quit. Police Chief Leon Stafford resigned. He was the complete police department. No official reason was given, but it was suspected he was overworked, serving as police chief and Island fire marshal.

Chief Of Police

This is policeman Jordan, of Anna Maria City, who is doing good work correcting traffic violations, reckless driving in particular and at least providing some protection for the people who need it—and will need it more—when the bridges are in operation.

George Jordan was the first police chief in Anna Maria City in 1956.

On a Saturday afternoon in November 1953, a city worker in Anna Maria raised the drawbridge over the canal on Bay Boulevard to oil the mechanism. Along came a car. There was no barrier or watchman. The driver jammed on his brakes when he saw the open bridge, but it was a few seconds too late and his car took a nosedive into the canal. No one was hurt and little damage was done.

The "Raid of 1954" occurred on a Wednesday night about 8:45 p.m. County Sheriff Clyde Crews swooped down on a group of about 70 people who were playing a game and making some money for a good cause. The gambling den of iniquity was the firehouse in Bradenton Beach. Proceeds from the game were going to pay the mortgage on the firehouse which was supported by a volunteer organization. John Engel took the rap and the deputy sheriff took the names. The money was confiscated. The amount was not verified, but an *Islander* reporter heard it was about $28. The game was bingo.

In 1954, a car, driven by a man from Bradenton, emerged from Magnolia Avenue onto Gulf Drive and was struck by a car driven by a youngster from Bradenton Beach. The boy was driving too fast, but the City of Anna Maria had no way of enforcing speed limits. City Marshal Jesse Ingram was a jack-of-all-trades and might have been cutting the grass at the Bay Front Park.

When Dale Wills and a minor tried to sell electrical equipment on the Island, Police Chief Paul Ford of Bradenton Beach hauled them into jail and discovered they were burglars from Melbourne. They had broken into a construction company's warehouse in Melbourne and helped themselves to a bunch of tools. The thieves were held in jail until authorities came for them. An *Islander* reporter wrote: "Only stupid thieves try to get away with something on this one-bridge Island which can be blocked in minutes." The year was 1954.

Two officers were on duty at both ends of the Cortez Bridge during the heavy traffic period of the season. When the drawbridge was raised for more than ten minutes to allow a boat to go through, traffic backed up on both sides of the bridge and drivers often became impatient. Deputy Paul Ford and his officers were courteous but firm and gave out tickets when necessary in this practically crimeless city of Bradenton Beach. It was hoped someday there would be coordinated police protection for the entire Island. The three cities each had a policeman who fortunately had nothing much to do until the bridges were built.

An Islander failed to turn when he left Cortez Road at 1:30 a.m. on July in 1955, and his car plunged though the bridge railing into the water. The car suffered severe injuries. Perhaps the driver was dreaming the new bridge had been built, for the accident occurred near that site.

In 1955, members of the Holmes Beach Businessmen's Club discussed how to get police protection at night. F. P. Stanley said he had paid several insurance claims for malicious damage to Island residents' properties. There were three burglaries at the public beach, Pat and Peggy Holmes' liquor shop was robbed and malicious vandalism such as stealing signs, shooting holes in windows and breaking light bulbs were reported. The business men's club offered to pay part of a night policeman's salary.

In January 1955, a woman in a yellow Oldsmobile drove down Pine Avenue in Anna Maria City and thought the city pier was a continuation of the street. The car hit the end of the pier, broke a wheel and ended up 224-feet out on the pier, inches from the edge. Police Chief Snooks Adams wanted a stop sign or barrier to be set up.

Similar accidents had happened.

About 7 a.m. on Jan.19, 1955, Capt. Lee Taylor and his two crewmen were rescued by helicopter from a shrimp boat owned by K. B. Kimball of Anna Maria. The *Kimtoo* carried a cargo of shrimp valued at $13,000. The boat was heading into the Pass at the North Point of the Island and ran aground on a sandbar in the Gulf, west of the Point, about one mile from shore. The year before the Nancy B was lost in the same spot.

A Coast Guard plane hovered over the shrimp boat in the darkness until there was enough light to bring in the helicopter. Then a basket was lowered to haul the men to safety. The *Kimtoo* was one of four shrimp boats owned by Kimball. The cargo was not insurable. No lives were lost in this incident, however the year before, the captain of the Nancy B drowned trying to swim to shore.

The following accident was described in *The Islander* in 1955: "A car's radiator was pushed into the engine, but the tree, a stout cabbage palm, was not injured. The small black and white terrier in the car appeared to suffer from shock, the driver's glasses were smashed and he sustained cuts on his face. The steering wheel was twisted like a paper clip. The out-of-control car went south on Gulf Drive at 50th street, jumped the shoulder, crossed the street and ploughed through heavy grass until it met the immovable tree with such force it bounced back a few yards. A sign stating 'School, 15 Mile Limit' flew across the road."

On a Tuesday morning in 1956, Police Chief Paul Ford of Bradenton Beach discovered a convict who had escaped from Raiford Penitentiary while serving seven years for forgery, breaking and entering. He had been working on a dredge in Tampa Bay for a week. Ford directed detectives to the Manatee Public Beach where another escapee, who had flown the coop the same day as his buddy, was arrested

On a Monday night in July of 1956, several men decided to go swimming off the new Mira Mar Pier in Bradenton Beach. Warren Kelly, who ran the Gulf Breeze Restaurant, dove off the end of the pier and did not come up. The men pulled him out of the water and called the ambulance. He was in critical condition at Veterans Memorial Hospital with an injured neck and spine and later died.

Bradenton Beach Police Chief Paul Ford saved the life of Deputy Sheriff Clyde Gill in an accident which happened at 1 a.m. in December of 1956. Ford was investigating an accident, involving a trailer truck in Holmes Beach, which had no police at the time. He called the sheriff's department for a deputy. The truck left the Island followed by Ford. Deputy Gill and Ford pulled the truck off the road near the Paradise Trailer Park on Cortez Road. As he and Gill were standing behind the truck questioning the driver, Clifford Randolph and his passenger Sally Hiles, a car coming from Bradenton Beach headed toward the group. Ford pushed Gill out of the way and threw himself on the ground, too late to prevent the car from hitting him and breaking his leg. The speeding car jammed the couple between the car and the truck. Both were killed. The driver, from Auburndale, claimed he was blinded by the headlights of an approaching car.

A jeep stranded in the sand at Manatee Public Beach in 1956 was stripped of a spare tire and wheel, a 10-ton jack, radiator, gas tank tops and a directional light control. Residents agreed incidents like this were certain to increase with more people coming to the Island when the bridges were completed. Some thought there was no need for police protection and night patrols. One prominent official said, "I don't see any need for police. I have nothing to be stolen."

During his many years in law enforcement Snooks Adams was a policeman in each of the Island cities.

A wild party took place in Bradenton Beach in July of 1956. The owner of the Bayside Inn called Police Chief Paul Ford to report that he had made a mistake and sold beer to a minor who claimed to be 23. Ford broke up a group of about 40 teenagers before the party got under full swing on a deserted beach at the south end of the Island. He impounded cans of beer, a full bottle of cheap brandy and a bottle of whiskey. While he was taking the names of youngsters, someone swiped the beer evidence in the chief's car. The owner of the inn was praised, but Ford warned owners of other establishments that selling liquor to the underage could result in losing their licenses.

Speedsters in Bradenton Beach were warned to slow down. Mayor Jack Jones said officials had been lenient, but Chief of Police Leon Stafford had been instructed to bear down on offenders. Parents of teenagers were told to caution their children against reckless drivers. The mayor's program got immediate results. Six violators were fined $10 each.

Don Moore, editor of *The Islander* in the late '60s, wrote a column entitled "The Way We Were." This is an excerpt: "The other week I wrote a column about the Anna Maria City mayor who was arrested by his own chief of police for driving while intoxicated. At the trial the mayor was judge, jury and defendant and found himself not guilty.

"Snooks Adams, the long-time chief of police in Holmes Beach, filled me in on the other half of the story. He reminded me that the mayor in question was the late Bill Brier, who was the mayor of Anna Maria City from 1956 to 1959. The chief who arrested him was George Jordan.

"Snooks recalled that Brier ran his car off the road into the sand at the humpback wooden bridge on North Bay Boulevard that spanned the entrance to Lake LaVista. Snooks said Jordan served the mayor with a summons to appear in court to face DUI charges. However, Snooks said the Anna Maria policeman never saw Brier at the time of the accident. Right after the well-publicized trial, when Brier found himself not guilty, Snooks said there was a city election in Anna Maria and Brier was reelected by a wide margin.

"Immediately after the election, the first thing the mayor did was to fire Chief Jordan. Then he resigned as mayor. The vice mayor became mayor and right away the new mayor reappointed Jordan as chief. Jordan served several more years as the city's only full-time policeman. Brier, who owned the Rod and Reel Motel at the time, sold his holdings on the Island and moved to Bradenton. According to Snooks, he was the part-owner of several bars in town before he died."

In March of 1957, it was near midnight when Police Chief Snooks Adams was patrolling the north end of Anna Maria City. He saw the front of a station wagon sticking out of the pond next to Talbot Brewer's house on North Shore Drive. The occupants had escaped. Then he spotted a soaking wet man in the front of the post office on Gulf Drive and Spring Avenue. The driver had turned into the driveway across the street from the pond and backed into the water. A wrecker was called and no charges were made.

The same month, 81-year-old Carl Youngstrand drove his 1949 Dodge sedan out to the end of the Anna Maria Pier. It was 8 a.m., and perhaps he was looking for breakfast. It was quite a trick to negotiate the narrow pier, but he made it. Those walking on the pier almost jumped into the water to avoid the car. Arriving at his destination, he sat calmly in the car, watched the fishermen and enjoyed the gentle breeze, the sunshine and a fine view of the Skyway Bridge.

When Police Chief George Jordan inquired why Carl chose to drive on the pier he answered, "I just wanted to drive out there, so I did." He was fined $25, and his son soon arrived from Sarasota to rescue him. The highway department had checked Carl's driving qualifications the year before and he passed!

In the January 1957 *Islander* headlines proclaimed: "It's the season! They are here! Wild parties!" The article read: Those tempestuous teenagers, drinking, hollering, stealing signs, racing cars two abreast through the night. Night bathing in the nude!

"The Ole City Jail sign was found on the porch of a Holmes Beach resident, along with other signs. Reports come in daily of various forms of malicious mischief. The sheriff cannot cover all of the Island all the time and authorities will not issue summons for mischief. Residents must look to the calendar for relief from the annoying, annual influx so upsetting to the peace of the Island."

The following article was seen in the June 20, 1957 *Islander*: "Sheriff Baden responded to several calls and five cars patrolled the Island for several nights. Causing most of the trouble were girls who were renting cottages on the beach. The visiting boys were hustled off the Island. Two were sons of prominent Bradenton families. Peace reigned for two nights and then a party on 45th Street broke out again. This time the renters were evicted."

This was in the police report on Oct. 31, 1957: "Deputy Adams smiled when Bill Brier's car was stuck in the sand near the Longboat Bridge last week. This week Adams' car was stuck in the same place."

On Dec. 22, 1957, Police Chief Jordan arrested Neil MacMillan, age 18, a student from Clinton, Ohio, for driving 70-miles-an-hour past the IGA grocery store and the post office. He posted a bond of $25. Drivers were making a speedway of the Island roads, knowing the leniency of the police. The police were instructed to go easy on arrests so the Island would not get a bad name among visitors. With the season about to open, traffic conditions were expected to become more dangerous. There was never a day when drivers were not going 50 to 60 miles an hour from the Manatee Public Beach to Cobb's Corner, near the Holmes Beach Shopping Center. Only the curves in the road from the school to Bradenton Beach kept down speeding in that section. The most fun for off-Island teenagers, with a hot rod and liquor, was to tackle the Island speedway in early morning hours.

About the time the taverns closed, a young man tried to enter the speedway at Cobb's Corner. He missed the curve, hurtled through the triangle, uprooted a palmetto and almost scalped himself. The day after, a block from the public beach, two cars collided. No one was hurt, but a financial blow was suffered by the owner of one car who had allowed his insurance to lapse. Deputy Snooks Adams was on the job up to 15 hours a day and often all through the night. He was on call 24 hours a day, but as good as he was he could only be one place at a time.

A young man, who was a student at Florida Southern College in Lakeland, ran through the tollgate without paying. He was arrested and taken to town, but since he was unable to put up a bond the desk officer released him so he could return in the morning. He failed to appear and was arrested in Lakeland and brought back to the Island for trial. Actually it turned out a girl was driving. The young man took the blame for the real driver who was the daughter of an Island winter resident.

On Saturday, June 22, 1958, Police Chief George Jordan wrote in his official report. "From 1 a.m. to 4 a.m., a motorcade of 127 cars driven by young people celebrating their graduation from high school, invaded the Island. Mrs. Al Robson, not realizing the response, had invited the entire class to come to her home on the Island after the graduation ceremonies.

The arrival of the fleet of cars created much concern to law enforcement officials on and off the Island. After a short briefing about drinking and driving Chief Jordan confiscated one bottle of whiskey and one bottle of vodka. All went well, except the graduates were noisy. The party broke up at 4 a.m., and the cars departed quietly."

Many people awakened by the ruckus phoned the police, and Jordan was roused out of bed. He told the youngsters, "You came on the Island like a bunch of Indians. Please leave like ladies and gentlemen." They did.

Another report by Jordan in June stated, "Several fights were broken up on the North Point beaches. Those attending the late and noisy beach parties were ordered to leave. Anna Maria beaches are wide open to the public day and night. This is wrong! I suggest an 11 p.m. curfew on all beaches. Now people come in late afternoon and stay all night. They do not pay rent or taxes and bother renters and residents."

Sunday night, June 1, 1958, thieves broke into the Mira Mar Restaurant in Bradenton Beach and stole 13 bottles of whiskey and $150 in cash. They left many clear fingerprints for the records. School youngsters, excited about the last day of school, thought it was fun to tear up books and papers and throw them out the windows of cars while cruising the Island. It was not much fun when Sheriff Snooks Adams caught up with them and made them back track and pick up every piece of paper, a three-hour task.

A 226-pound man who had been drinking got tired, parked his car in the middle of Bridge Street and went to sleep. He was awakened by a police officer who fined him $25 for driving while drinking and $10 for illegal parking.

Three cars were racing through the streets of Anna Maria, tires screeching at the corners. Sheriff Adams caught one of the drivers, the son of a prominent Islander. His punishment was, he could not drive for six weeks and he was on permanent probation.

In December 1958, a woman jumped off the end of the Bradenton Beach pier trying to drown herself. The water was so cold she screamed for help and her neighbors pulled her out and brought her to her senses.

Teenagers in Anna Maria City protested the change in the police department from George Jordan to the Manatee County sheriff's department. A petition, signed by 50 teenagers, was presented to the city commission. They wanted Jordan retained as policeman. The petition read: "Police Chief Jordan's services have benefited all of us in many ways, and we appreciate his efforts on our behalf. He is nice when we get in a jam, and he watches out for us at the Teen Club."

It was discovered if the city retained the county sheriff's department it would receive 24-hour service with the use of the county jail for offenders and about $1,450 would be saved. Jordan followed the school bus every day. Mayor Brier said in his 27 years in Florida he had never seen a policeman follow a school bus and it was not necessary since deputies patrolled the highway most of the time.

"Boat Rams Car," was the headline in the July 16, 1959 issue of *The Islander*. According to Police Chief George Jordan, a boat trailer escaped its hitch and the boat crashed into a parked car at the Anchorage on Pine Avenue and Bay Boulevard. Damage to the car was slight, but six feet of aluminum was torn off the boat.

Snooks Adams resigned from the Manatee County Sheriff's Department in August of 1960, a position he had held for five years. Adams said politics was the principal reason. He said he was going to be moved from his Island patrol and was told the move was political. There were rumors he would be fired by the successful candidate for sheriff because of his campaigning for his ex-boss, Roy Baden.

Police Chief George Jordan submitted his resignation on Sept.1, 1963, after 10 years on the job. He had requested a salary increase of $40 per month, and Manatee County Sheriff Ken Gross agreed to pay the sum. Jordan said he would not accept any part of his salary from the sheriff's department. Jordan was getting $275 a month, in addition to a car allowance of $45. When he submitted his resignation to the city commission he gave as his reasons; the differences of opinion about his wages and the fact that the commission had just extended the open hours for the one bar in the city to 2:30 a.m. on Sunday nights.

Sam Adams, one of the first volunteer firemen in Anna Maria, stands on the first fire truck.

John Adams was on the Island during the organization of the Anna Maria Fire Department in the '40s. He wrote "A Look Into The Past" for the Anna Maria Island Historical Society's reenactment of the history of the fire department on its 50th anniversary.

"I am the son of Sam Adams, he was one the first firemen in Anna Maria City. I recall the pavilion fire which occurred after midnight, so very few people were there. I was awakened by Mrs. Bennie Scanio and Mrs. Ernie Cagnina rapping on my window and yelling. I forgot I was in the top bunk and hit my head on the ceiling as I got up. As soon as I recovered, I dressed and ran to the fire.

"We did not have a fire truck. The only thing we had was a horse-drawn, four-man-powered pumper, without the horse. Ernie and Bennie ran to get it from the city garage on Pine Avenue. When they got to the fire, they asked J. Hartley Blackburn and me to join them on the four-man pumper.

"The pump put out a quarter inch stream of water for about 20-feet. Since the pavilion had been constructed of "fat-lightered" pine and contained many cases of beer, flames interlaced with beer explosions, went straight up and were so hot the men were unable to get within range of the flames. The pumper was worthless.

"A Model A truck was donated shortly after the fire. It had a 100-gallon tank of water (without internal baffles) with eight soda ash fire extinguishers in racks on each side of the tank. Soon after it arrived on the Island, the driver Humbug Cobb, executed a fast turn on Gulf Drive onto Magnolia, at the IGA grocery store. Without baffles to slow the water in the truck, it almost tipped over. All the fire extinguishers fell off, and the contents mixed and spewed all over the place.

"The main incentive for organizing a volunteer fire department and getting a real pumper was to lower fire insurance. As I recall, the savings were $25 a house.

"The fire truck was first used on a brush fire on Gulf Drive and Oak Avenue, where the first fire station was later built. Humbug had the hose to the fire before he realized the field was covered with sandspurs. He was barefoot! Humbug was our first fire casualty."

The Bradenton Beach Fire Department was in existence before the city was incorporated. An Island civic group started raising money for a fire truck in 1947. Soon a fire truck, which was used until 1969, was bought for under $2,000. The first fire chief, Leon Stafford, said it was a tough struggle in those days. He made it clear the fire department had no connection with the City of Bradenton Beach. It served all of Bradenton Beach and part of Holmes Beach. The Anna Maria Fire Department served Anna Maria City and half of Holmes Beach.

Dr. M. R. Van Hout wrote the following open note to the editor of *The Islander* on August 14, 1958: "In the early '40s during hurricanes, every man, woman and child battled to save their homes and those of their friends and neighbors. A group of Bradenton Beach women conceived the idea of organizing a ladies auxiliary of the Bradenton Beach Fire Department. Mrs. Bates was the first president. Various money-making projects were undertaken, and all profits were donated to pay off the mortgage on the fire hall.

"Today it is a good hall and houses fire trucks, an ambulance, a disaster boat, a completely equipped kitchen, and is free of debt. During my one-and-a-half years as mayor, we were able to give our firemen $900 to be used as they saw fit. A home was bought next to the fire hall and Mr. and Mrs. Frank Beard are on duty 24-hours a day for fires and emergency calls. During my term in office, the ladies auxiliary never refused any request for help or donations. My wish is that every woman in Bradenton Beach becomes a member of this organization which does so much with so little. Dues are $1 a year. Let us remember our homes are only as safe as members of the fire department are equipped and trained." Van Hout said.

In the event of fire, the Bradenton Beach siren automatically sent out ten blasts. Firemen reported to the firehouse or followed the truck. In 1952, Anna Maria and Holmes Beach were designated as unincorporated areas. A directional signal told the firemen whether the fire was north, south, east or west. Two blasts, from the fire station to the Point; three blasts, from the Point down to the bayou on the bayside; four blasts, south of the fire station.

Island Fire Marshal Leon Stafford urged all able-bodied citizens to help. He said the fire truck and siren-equipped cars had the right of way and all other traffic should pull over and stop until firemen and equipment passed.

On March 9, 1952, all firemen and men on the Island were urged to attend a meeting at the Anna Maria Fire House. William Barnett, superintendent of the Florida State Fire College, taught the latest methods of fire prevention and fire fighting. Fire Marshal Stafford believed that every citizen should know the basic knowledge of fire fighting.

The Island's ability to defend and attack fires was progressing. Two trucks, carrying 1,000 feet of hoses and chemical extinguishers, and a tank truck with 2,000 gallons of water were ready to serve. When necessary, a hose could be connected to the Island Water Company's lines to use the full power of the water company's pumps. Other times, where bay or gulf water only was available, there were lines to carry the water halfway across the Island.

The Anna Maria Island Fire Control District Commission asked the town of Bradenton Beach for permission to enlarge the firehouse in that city on July 10, 1952. Plans with space for two fire trucks, city offices, and living quarters for a resident fireman on the second floor were submitted. To provide space for the two-story building of concrete block and frame it would be necessary to extend the front wall of the present firehouse six feet closer to Second Street. The plans were approved and construction started immediately.

Approximately 100 people attended a dinner at the Bradenton Beach firehouse. Dinner and entertainment staged by the firemen, were in appreciation for the fine work the Ladies Auxiliary had done.

"Where Was The Fire?" the headlines in the August 1952 *Islander* questioned. About suppertime the fire siren sounded and people went out to see the excitement, but no one could find a fire. This was the story:

Leon Stafford said a group decided to have a wiener roast on the south end, beyond where the road ended. This was a desolate part of the Island. Soon there was a roaring fire raging under some dead trees, and the trees started to burn. Someone saw the smoke and called the fire department. No one was hurt, and it gave the firemen a chance to rush to the scene, practicing their ability to get to an out-of-the-way place in a hurry.

"Help Wanted!" was the eye-catching headline of an ad in a local paper. The ad read: "Fire Marshal Leon Stafford needs your help in the worse way and you'd better volunteer. Able-bodied members of the community are needed to work on a 46 by 30-foot addition to the Bradenton Beach Fire Hall. Your pay will be nothing. If you are civic-minded and have a strong back let Leon know."

In August 1953, a property owner wanted to burn off some lots. The owner knew nothing about the

The Bradenton Beach Volunteer Fire Department served Bradenton Beach and part of Holmes Beach.

procedure, but remembered to call the fire marshal. The owner was a good-looking lady. Under Stafford's direction, an eight-foot path was cleared around the lots. The wind was gently blowing in the right direction for the burn. Stafford said every precaution should be taken when burning lots to avoid a brush fire that might get out of hand. There was a penalty for starting a brush fire without the marshal's permission. A pile of raked needles must be contained in a wire basket before burning. Residents were urged not to start fires during dry spells. In May, with high winds and no rain for weeks, half of the Island could go up in smoke.

In the middle of the Bradenton Beach Council meeting on Friday, March 5, 1954, the fire siren screamed. Instantly half of the men ran out of the hall. The mayor recessed the meeting and the *Islander* reporter ran to the fire, two blocks away. Volunteer firemen, volunteer traffic control members, Police Chief Paul Ford and his officers were there in minutes. Extinguishers were on the job and water from the engine pump was available. The fire was in Wallace's Laundry. The city was congratulated on having a splendid fire department, which pledged assistance in all kinds of emergencies.

The Women's Auxiliary of the fire department promised to wipe out any debts owed in the expansion the firehouse. On the eve of St. Patrick's Day, March 16, 1954, the women sponsored a dance at the Beach View Tavern. Admission was a donation of 50-cents per person. *The Islander* promised to publish an honor roll, with the name of every person who bought a ticket. Mr. and Mrs. John Engel provided the list.

Three hundred chickens fed 600 people at Manatee Public Beach in January of 1955. When the hungry men of the Bradenton Beach Fire Department finished cooking and serving the chicken, the only food left was cole slaw and a few buns. Fire Marshal Leon Stafford was the cook with five or six assistants. Profits went to reduce the debt on the firehouse addition.

The Island fire departments planned a dance for June 30, 1955 at the Yacht Club with numbered tickets which were mailed to all Island residents. Prizes were given for winning numbers. The post office discovered the firemen were using the postal service to promote a lottery and stopped it. The fire department personnel did not know they were breaking the law.

The annual Halloween Dance at the Anna Maria Fire Station on Oak Avenue and Gulf Drive was the highlight of the social season. Costumed revelers danced the night away to strains of popular tunes by local bands. There was always a parade of costumes, ranging from the elegant to the ridiculous, judged by the three mayors and other distinguished citizens. Everyone attended, and crowds became so large tables were placed outdoors.

In 1956, the Anna Maria Island Fire District received an ambulance from the Shannon Funeral Home in Bradenton. The free gift, with no strings attached, was stationed on the Island for use in any emergency.

Volunteer firemen in Anna Maria had full time jobs. When they heard the siren, they dropped whatever they were doing and raced to the fire station. The first man to arrive at the station was privileged to drive the truck. The others followed the tracks of water that sloshed out of the tanks.

One day fire broke out before 8 a.m. in the two-story frame house on Spring Lane, Anna Maria, owned by Alfonso Caltagirone. All the firemen responded. Neighbors and firemen removed the furniture from the ground floor. Fortunately, no one was in the house at the time. The fire mainly damaged an outside wall and inside partitions. Firemen thought it started near the hot water heater. One sleepy fireman said there should be a law prohibiting fires before 8 a.m. For 15-minutes, Gulf Drive was crowded like a stock car racetrack with fire apparatus, firemen's cars and curious spectators. The fire was expected to boost donations for equipment on the new fire truck.

It was July of 1958, when the Anna Maria Fire Department was called out to extinguish a brush fire which spread from a pile of rubbish to a nearby house. The fire reached the cabbage palms. A mother raccoon escaped to a tree top with two of her children. Another brush fire sent the firemen to the Bayou Fishing Center. It was quickly extinguished.

After a fire in Bradenton Beach, firemen talked about numerous fire hazards. Small wooden houses had been built so close together that, if one burned and if it was windy, it would be difficult to keep the fire from spreading to the next house. Spaces under some wooden houses were filled with logs for firewood. It was not only a fire hazard, but an open invitation to termites.

"Fire Department Wants Miss Flame," was the headline in the Jan. 16, 1962 *Islander*. The story continued: "A high school student will be selected by the Island fire departments to represent the Island and Cortez in the statewide Miss Flame contest. The Island Miss Flame will be chosen from a group of beauties at the Firemen's Ball in February held at Pete Reynard's Yacht Club Restaurant."

In October 1960, members of the Anna Maria Volunteer Fire Department said their next project would be the sale of house numbers to residents of the city where a system of numbering houses had been completed. The men had already sold house numbers to residents of Holmes Beach where installation of the numbers on houses was mandatory. Officials of both municipalities recommended all residents purchase their house numbers from the firemen.

The editor's note in the September 9,1956 *Islander* summed up how Islanders felt about their firemen. "The fire siren sounds! From every part of the Island men drop their working tools, merchants leave their stores, and no matter where the fire is, the trained volunteers arrive in minutes. Traffic is controlled and firefighters are on the job.

"Side by side, the men who may be at bitter odds in their lives work as comrades. They become part of a united, integrated team. For example, it is certain that Jim Zerby, the city clerk who was discharged, and

Bob Martini, the mayor who fired him, would risk their lives together in fire or flood to save others. Both are volunteer firemen. Islanders should read the Firemen's Pledge written on the blackboard in the Bradenton Beach Fire House."

It read: "To protect life and property against the elements, every member of the fire department assumes a definite responsibility for the lives and property of his fellow men when he becomes a member."

The Anna Maria Fire Hall was a small wooden building on Oak Avenue and Gulf Drive. The members Anna Maria Volunteer Fire Department were: Front row, from left, Rene Caulman, George Jackson, Ed Alder, Pat Cardin, Gary Diffenbaugh, Dave Hiscox; middle row, Mel Robinson, Bob Martini, George Norwood, Tom Angell, David Ross, Hugh Holmes,Jr.; back row, Jim Steenstra, Jeff Willey, Aaron Van Ostenbridge, John Van Ostenbridge, George Wagner, Father Ben Wood, Bill Cipperly and Dennis Mowry.

Post Office Progress

When Eleanor Gill delivered mail in the 1930s there were only 37 mailboxes on the Island. For four years she drove her 1932 station wagon with a .38 German luger and the mail sack on the passenger seat. She not only brought letters, but groceries and other supplies needed by Island residents and an occasional visitor from town.

"You had to help each other out," she explained. "If someone along my mail route needed something I'd pick it up for them in town."

From 1914 to 1941, Anna Maria and Longbeach (Longboat Key) were the only post offices operating on the Keys. On Oct. 14, 1941, the Bradenton Beach Post Office opened with Wendel Longstreth as the first postmaster. In 1940, it became a second class post office.

In June 1952, plans for a new post office in Bradenton Beach were announced. While the new structure was being built, the old frame building continued to operate after being rolled to an area nearby. The new cement block structure would be divided into two units with a total cost of $10,000. Dedication of the new post office in Bradenton Beach was held on Sept. 6, 1952. The building was large and bright with glass jalousies and glass bricks to let in the light. Those working at the new facility were Irma Cox, postmaster, Don Roat and Mrs. Oscar Ritz.

Frances Warttig became acting postmaster of the Anna Maria Post Office in 1943 and postmaster in 1944. She lived in the post office building and ran the post office, with able assistants, as efficiently as possible

Harry Ditmas, better known as Uncle Sam, was one of the first mailmen on the Island.

considering the bewildering changes of addresses as winter visitors came and went. An outstanding member of the community, Mrs. Warttig had many loyal friends. But, she did not fix the brakes on her car when they needed it and ran into her front porch quite a few times. Sam Adams was always there fixing her porch, and one day she said to him, "You're over here all the time so I'd better give you a job."

Alice and Sam Adams worked in the Anna Maria Post Office for a combined total of 21 years. "We came here in 1946 and lived across from the post office," she said. "I went to work at the post office in 1947. At that time, the mail did not leave Bradenton Beach until late in the afternoon. Sam's first job was to go to Bradenton Beach, meet the mail carrier, and get the mail to Anna Maria earlier in the day."

In 1952, the post office could have moved up to Second Class with the sale of a few more dollars of stamps. Mrs. Warttig felt the post office should earn a higher rating only through a natural process or unforced growth.

In 1953, the Island had a permanent population of approximately 3,000 and suddenly expanded to twice that many in the winter season. The post office had to handle the complications of summer and winter addresses, general delivery to hundreds of strangers and incoming and outgoing mail ten times as great.

A postal inspector popped in unexpectedly in June 1953. After spending all day observing many transactions, he handed Mrs. Warttig a document rating the Anna Maria Post Office as 100 percent. Mrs. Warttig was surprised and pleased and gave much of the credit to her assistants. Later she discovered the inspector had been a postmaster for 32 years, and he had never earned the 100 percent award.

Residents in Bradenton Beach heard there was a scheme to close their post office in 1953 and open one mid-Island. They decided to act. Whether it was a rumor or definite plan, they wanted the Post Office Department to know where they stood. Backed by Mayor Jack Jones and the council, a petition was circulated. The petition, with 572 names, was sent to the district director in Tampa.

It was no rumor. Certain people were involved in a plan to close the two Island post offices to have only a central post office. An application had been filled out. The district inspector said he had a directive from the

The early Anna Maria post office was on Gulf Drive and Spring Avenue.

postal department to determine whether such a post office was warranted.

Evidently nothing happened, and in September 1954 it was announced a new post office would be built in Anna Maria City behind the old one, on the same lot. The old building would be razed for more parking spaces. Residents were happy, and Mrs. Warttig's dream for a larger post office came true. About this time Holmes Beach applied for a post office, but did not qualify.

"Holmes Beach Wants A Post Office!" headlines in the Sept. 9, 1954 *Islander* proclaimed. Some residents had visions of a main post office in Holmes Beach receiving and sending mail to and from Tampa by a helicopter which would land on the airstrip and deliver mail in sectional bags to sub-post offices in the area. Anna Maria residents criticized the lack of home delivery. At the height of the season, volumes of general delivery mail took much of the postal workers time.

Holmes Beach residents had mail delivered to their homes from the Bradenton Beach Post Office or they picked up mail from their boxes at the Anna Maria Post Office. Many signed a petition which asked for direct mail service from Tampa to a main Anna Maria Island Post Office with distribution to sub-stations. No immediate action was expected by the petitioners since the success of the proposed distribution plan was contingent on the opening of the proposed new bridges connecting Anna Maria Island to the mainland and

Longboat Key.

Dec. 10, 1955, was "Frances Warttig Day" in Anna Maria. Islanders gathered to celebrate the opening of the new post office on Gulf Drive and Spring Avenue. The Manatee High School Band played a rousing tribute and Rev. Richard Wiggins blessed the building. Mayor Paul Carlisle welcomed distinguished guests and residents. A new flag was raised by the Boy Scouts and Mrs. Warttig received many accolades for a job well done. Her resignation as postmaster had been accepted.

Alice and Sam Adams worked in the Anna Maria Post Office for 21 years.

One year later the entire Island was saddened to learn of Mrs. Warttig's death. Before becoming postmaster, Mrs. Warttig had been the Island reporter for the *Bradenton Herald*. In her news articles she referred to Cortez Beach as Bradenton Beach. The first post office in Anna Maria City was a general store which the Warttigs bought in 1943. She was postmaster for 12 years; before that she was the mayor of Anna Maria City, since no man could be found to tackle the job. The city was in a mess and she brought in good government and kept records much better than her predecessors. A bronze plaque was placed in a small garden near the Anna Maria Post Office. It read: "Long To Remember: A personal tribute from the people of Anna Maria to Frances Warttig, former mayor, postmaster and good citizen. 1956."

A special meeting was scheduled in August 9,1956, to protest the recommendation of Stewart Hawkins for postmaster instead of Harriet Fay, who had worked with Mrs. Warttig for years. The meeting appeared to have been called by a group of citizens, mainly Republican women.

In February 1957, the Post Office Department appointed Stewart Hawkins postmaster to replace Harriet Fay. Many residents protested vigorously in public meetings and by petition that this gross miscarriage of justice should not take place. The blame did not lie with the character of Hawkins, but with the Republican Executive Committee of Manatee County. Hawkins served as president of the Island Republican Club and was promised the postmaster job as a reward. Mrs. Fay had experience in post office work, not only in Anna Maria, but also as a postmaster in Long Island, N.Y.

Frances Warttig was the Anna Maria postmaster.

The October 1957, the *Islander* reported the Anna Maria Post Office building, which was one of the assets in the estate of Frances Warttig, had been sold to Norman Rosedale. It made no difference to the public, at least until the contract with the Post Office Department expired.

On Jan. 1, 1957, the Holmes Beach Postal Station was to open, but since it was a holiday it opened January 2nd with Mary VerMett as the official clerk-in-charge and Frances Hoopes as her assistant. Space was secured between the grocery store and barbershop in the shopping center. Approximately 100 mailboxes were available. For those using the station, the correct mailing address was Holmes Beach, Florida.

In February 1964, the Post Office Department announced the Anna Maria Post Office, at 9908 Gulf Drive, would be enlarged and air conditioned. The contract was awarded to Norman Rosedale, the owner of the building. The contract stated the owner would remodel the building and rent it to the Post Office Department for five years with three, five-year renewal options.

Home mail delivery began May 6, 1964 in Holmes Beach and Bradenton Beach. Homes that were close together would get delivery by carriers who would walk or ride bicycles. In Holmes Beach, where homes were farther apart, a station wagon would be used for delivery.

On June 30, 1973, Irma Cox retired as postmaster of the Bradenton Beach Post Office, a position she had held for 26 years. According to Mrs. Cox, the greatest change in postal service during her time in office, was the expanded city delivery which took care of the tremendous population growth on the Island. An increase of 3,000 in 25 years was reported. Bob Wilson, a 24-year veteran of the Bradenton Post Office, became the new Bradenton Beach postmaster.

For 26 years Irma Cox was the Bradenton Beach postmaster.

Five

EDUCATION

Mrs. Moss's fourth grade in the '50s

The Island School

Marion Colman, granddaughter of the first Island homesteader, George Emerson Bean, penned her memories of the progress of education on Anna Maria Island:

"The beginnings of education on the Island were quite humble, but many things with humble beginnings have become our proudest possessions, and so it is with our school. The first school was a tiny, one-room affair in the locality now occupied by the Gulf Trailer Park (Sandpiper Mobile Home Park in Bradenton Beach). There were six pupils, and the teacher was Miss Gertrude Baer of Palma Sola. The term lasted six months. For four years there was no school, but in 1905 it was re-established in a small building near Cobb's Corner (near the Holmes Beach Shopping Center). But school was not yet continuous. Mrs. Mattie Raymond, one of the early teachers, began her services in 1910. About 1913, a fine cement block schoolhouse was built on Magnolia Avenue in Anna Maria (where the Island Community Center is today). As years passed, the juvenile population ebbed and flowed. During the boom, the building was crowded. For a time it was nip and tuck again whether there would be enough pupils to open the school in the fall. Somehow there always were!

"During the late 1930s and early 1940s, growth on the Island was rapid and continuous. A new room was added, but the building soon became inadequate. Overflow classes were held in nearby houses and in the Community Hall (now The Island Players). Mrs. Lena Phelps was the principal beginning in the early '30s.

"After the war, several barracks were brought in and renovated which solved the problem for a time, but toward the end of the '40s it became evident that nothing would serve but a completely new structure in the

In 2008 Mrs. Moss's fourth graders gathered at her home in Anna Maria to talk about the good old days. From left, back row, Chris Hoffman, Chris Torgeson, James Schambers, Mary Dobbe Love, Jim Slegers, Gary Wagner, John Slegers and Larry Skidmore. Front row Carol Sue Brimmer Ertsgaard, Joan Gunther Pettigrew, Mrs. Moss, Mary Alice Jones Martin and Sandy Marchand Hottman.

middle of the Island. After great planning, the dream became a reality, and the new school was completed in 1950."

The school opened officially on Monday, Feb. 13, 1950 in Holmes Beach. There were just over 100 students, seven rooms, one for each of the six grades, and kindergarten, an ultra modern cafeteria and a clinic. A large overhead gas heater was installed in the cafeteria through the efforts of the PTA in February of 1952. The school board provided the fuel.

Mrs. Phelps was principal, and the staff included: Mrs. Helen Roberts, Mrs. Lucille Sheehan, Mrs. Betty Blackburn and Mrs. Fern Williams. The next year Mrs. Sheehan, Mrs. Betty Mellin, Mrs. Barbara Sherwood and Miss Dorothy Bullock were members of the faculty. Mrs. Robert V. Pethick was in charge of the kindergarten.

There was an active Parent Teachers Association, and fathers of the students cleared the field for volleyball and basketball courts. On Feb. 9, 1950, the first edition of the *Anna Maria Key News* carried the first photograph ever printed of the new school.

Citizenship was taught at the school through actual experience in democratic living. Sixth graders set up schedules enabling them to work more effectually. All grades participated in voting for the Halloween king and queen. Each grade planned menus to be used in the cafeteria. Every child in the school voluntarily signed a card to respect the rights and property of others during the 1951-52 school term.

The Anna Maria School sent out a plea to all parents on the Island and Cortez with children of kindergarten age, or those who knew children who would be five by January 1, 1953, to enroll them in school as soon as possible.

The kindergarten was in jeopardy. There was no assurance that it would continue with the present enrollment. It would not be continued in 1952 unless there was an average daily attendance of 25. To keep that average, more than 25 children needed to be enrolled.

J. Hartley Blackburn of Anna Maria, was principal of the Cortez School where his wife, Betty, was a teacher. J. Hartley was appointed Superintendent of Public Instruction for Manatee County in 1945. He saw the county system grow from 5,464 students to more than 20,000 during his more than 20 years in office. Before the position of superintendent, he had 12 years of public school experience in the county. He was the teaching principal at Manatee Elementary and Walker Junior High School.

Twenty-one children from the Island school were selected to demonstrate primitive camping before 60 park and outdoor officials from many parts of the country in May 1952 at Highland Hammock State Park. J. Hartley Blackburn and Allen E. Crowley, a representative of the Florida Board of State Parks and Historic Memorials, initiated the project hoping that primitive camping would become a part of the school program.

After arriving at the park, the children worked from a set plan where various work was assigned to individuals. They began to eat, work, play and sleep with rudimentary equipment they could find or make. They slept in sleeping bags on army cots in huts made of bamboo with tarpaulin covers. Cooking was done in a firebox, which was a bamboo basket lined with thick green palmetto fronds and several inches of sand.

Island writers, including Wyatt Blassingame and Jack Leffingwell, contributed stories with Island locales for the school library. Writers and artists were asked for contributions by Mrs. Anna Riles, chairman of the book project.

A course in swimming began in July 1952. All children of school age were urged to attend the free course, sponsored by the Manatee County Recreation Department and the Red Cross. Classes were held every afternoon

The annual May Festival was an exciting event. Linda Ingram and Dickie Butterfield reigned over the carnival in the '50s.

Staff of the Island school in 1953 included, from left, Elizabeth Pierce Moss, Eugenia Higgins, Helen Lark, Lena Phelps, Betty Mellin, Dorothy Bullock and Ralph Kleinbeck.

for six weeks in the bay near the Anna Maria Pier. Children waited along Gulf Drive to be picked up by the bus. Later, as part of the countywide program to teach all children to swim, Island children attended swim sessions at Manatee Public Beach three mornings a week during the summer months. In July of 1958, 300 Manatee County school children completed swimming courses at the public beach. When conditions were good, classes were held in the Gulf. Otherwise, the bay in Anna Maria was used.

The children, in costumes, danced around the maypole.

In May 1953, an elaborate May Festival started at 8 p.m. at the school and ran until the younger children could no longer stay awake. An Indian rain dance was presented by the kindergarteners, who made their own costumes, with a little help. Fourth graders performed a Maypole Dance, and Old King Neptune starred in a skit by fifth grade students. The sedate sixth grade class sang five chorus selections.

Lena Phelps, principal, receives a gift from Shirley Brownell. Mrs. Phelps was principal from 1950- 1959.

In 1954, there was an urgent need for more schools in Manatee County. In the original plan, the Anna Maria School would be enlarged by four classrooms. Superintendent J. Hartley Blackburn announced, if funds permitted, an auditorium would be added. Some Islanders said it would be an unnecessary expense since the cafeteria could seat several hundred people.

On the first day of school in 1955, 136 students registered. Two new teachers, Mrs. Eugenia Higgins and Ralph Kleinbeck (the first male teacher) were welcomed. Mrs. Phelps thought when winter residents returned the registration would compare with 1954's high of 208 students.

A reception at the school in December of 1956 honored Mrs. Louis Cobb. She had driven the school bus since 1933 without any accidents. Mrs. Phelps retired in 1959. She was loved by students and staff alike, but was a firm believer in discipline and an age-old method of enforcing it. "Yes, I did use the paddle," she admitted in an interview. "I've paddled sixth graders a head taller than me. A child craves the security of discipline. Children want to be guided, and when they are naughty they are asking for discipline." She was proud to recall that the state school inspector said if he could choose one school in the state to send his children to, it would be Anna Maria.

Mrs. Phelps is remembered to this day by her students who accompanied her on nature walks and field trips. The children learned to love nature and could identify many species of birds. Creating the annual bird

J. Hartley Blackburn was appointed Superintendent of Manatee County schools in 1945.

book was a must for each child.

A retirement reception was held at the school for this dedicated teacher, who through her wide range of interests and depths of enthusiasm enriched the lives of many Islanders of all ages. There were no formal speeches. She received letters and telegrams from friends, former students and their parents from across the country. She was delighted when she opened the gift of a Hi-Fi set which would allow her to indulge her love of music. The climax of the evening came when she and her husband, Clyde, were decked out with fresh leis flown from Hawaii and presented tickets for a 12-day trip to the Hawaiian Islands.

The Anna Maria Island Elementary School was built in 1950.

Sam Schiek was principal from 1959 until 1967. Mrs. Eugenie Higgins, a second grade teacher, introduced reading by words and color in the 1960s. Halloween carnivals were held every October from 1950 to 1957. A king and queen were crowned each year, and awards were presented to children wearing the best costumes in a variety of categories.

In 1956, after the coronation of the king and queen, the PTA provided a chicken dinner, including coffee and dessert. Adults paid $1 and children were charged 60-cents. Those who could not afford the dinner could get a hot dog and cold drink for much less.

The PTA chose as the major project for 1960 to purchase visual aid equipment for the school. A committee was appointed to work with Principal Schiek to survey the school's needs and estimate the amount of money needed. Mrs. Robert Daughaday stressed the need for Gray Lady volunteers in the school clinic.

Anna Maria School principals were, clockwise: Sam Schiek, 1959-67; Jack Dietrich, 1967- 1971; Larry Simmons, 1971- 1972; Tom Walker, 1972- 1974; Jim Kronus, 1974-1999.

When the school year started in September of

1957, the sheriff's office decreed the stretch from the public beach to Cobbs' Corners was no longer a racetrack and lower speed limits would be enforced. Drivers were requested to be especially careful along Gulf Drive because children had to walk in the street. There were no sidewalks.

In April 1957, the Chamber of Commerce passed a resolution favoring an increase of teachers salaries to $1,100 a year. Commander H. B. Barton spoke in favor of the raise, while Jack Marshall opposed it because of the danger of increased ad valorem taxes.

In 1957, a monthly newsletter was published at the school called the *Conch Shell.* Student reporters garnered a variety of interesting school events for the publication.

Pupils of the Island School gave a concert for 59 members of the School Food Handlers Association in 1957. There was a violin ensemble followed by a solo by Gilda Murdock. A mixed chorus of girls and boys from the sixth grade sang several numbers under the direction of Mrs. Phelps.

Registration in February 1957 was 254, the highest on record, and the need for new classrooms was evident. In 1960, two new teachers were added to the faculty; Mary Mott, who taught sixth grade and Wiley Eugene Moss, a science teacher who had taught at Walker Junior High School. "Gene" Moss, a resident of Anna Maria, was well known on the Island. His wife, the former Elizabeth Pierce, was also a teacher at the Anna Maria School.

If Once You Have Slept on An Island

If once you have slept on an Island
You'll never be quite the same.
You may look as you looked the day before,
You may go by the same old name.

You may bustle about the street and shop,
You may sit at home and sew,
But you'll see blue skies and wheeling gulls
Wherever your feet may go.

You may chat to your neighbor of this and that
Or close to your fireside keep,
But you'll hear ships whistles and lighthouse bells
And tides drift through your sleep.

Oh, you won't know how and you can't tell why
Such change upon you came,
But, if once you slept on an Island
You'll never be quite the same.

Rachael Field

This poem was taught to children at the Anna Maria School during the 1950s. They illustrated it with their own drawings and created books.

Ellen Marshall, Editor, Activist and Democrat

Ellen's first home on the Island was the Anglers Lodge on Bay Boulevard next to the Humpback Bridge.

In 1947, friends of a young World War II widow, Ellen Auld, invited her to visit Anna Maria Island. Raised in New York City, Ellen found the Island fascinating.

"I loved it immediately," she said. "The terrain was like Long Island where I spent my youth. The only problem was there was very little to do."

In 1949, she moved to the Island permanently. One of the first people she met was a personable young woman, Harriet Williams. Harriet's mother owned Anglers Lodge. The two-story frame house is still standing close to the Lake LaVista humpback bridge on North Bay Boulevard. Ellen immediately rented a room with a spectacular view of Tampa Bay, and the two women became friends.

That same year, Ellen married Donald Brackin, who was a partner with John Holmes, Jr. in the operation of Holmes Supplies.

Harriet was laboriously putting out a mimeographed newsletter called the *Key News*. The Island Chamber of Commerce had just been formed, and Jerry Cigarran, president, asked her to publish a real newspaper. Ellen joined her on the project.

Jack Holmes gave "the girls" a building in Holmes Beach for their newspaper office.

"It was an extremely courageous thing to do, since I knew absolutely nothing about running a newspaper," Ellen said. "We decided to get a 2,500-pound printing press from a Catholic school in Dade City. The narrow, rickety bridge to the Island almost collapsed under the weight of the mammoth machine. The next step was getting a postal permit and an office. Developer Jack Holmes stepped in at that point.

"Jack would do anything to promote the Island. He said that we had the greatest intestinal fortitude of any girls he ever heard of and offered us a building at 5345 Gulf Drive in Holmes Beach.

"Everything was just beginning on the Island. There were few young adults, so Harriet and I joined all the organizations, and I became secretary for all of them. I loved the Christian Science Monitor, and we patterned our periodical after it. We had no column rule and started, stupidly, with eight pages. The first paper was printed on Feb. 9, 1950, and sold for five-cents. We were workaholics and covered every meeting on the Island. Ads were 45-cents a column inch. The Bradenton and Palmetto papers were not enthused about our podunk paper." Ellen threw back her head and gave a hearty laugh as she recalled the in-town editors annoyance.

Ellen was always on the go in her borrowed pickup truck.

The masthead designed by Island artists, Wes and Yolanda Pritchard, read: "Published on Historical Anna Maria Island, The Anna Maria Key News, Key Resort of Manatee County." A large key was in the background, and the outline of the Island was inadvertently flopped by the lithographer, so the north end was the south.

Ellen turned the mistake into her advantage. It was a conversation piece. When people remarked about the mistake, she reminded them of Wyatt Blassingame's famous quip, which had appeared in a national magazine.

"If you unscrew a screwball anywhere in the United States, blindfold him, turn him around twice and turn him loose, he'll wind up on Anna Maria Island."

The front-page story in the first issue was the dedication of the new Anna Maria Elementary School, accompanied by a six-column picture of the school. Other articles included a story about baseball-great Fred Hutchinson, a picture of him autographing baseballs for Island youngsters, and news of the upcoming Island Players three-act comedy, "My Boys In The Pentagon," with Harold Igo directing.

In other news items, Sam Adams, chief of the Anna Maria Fire Protection Association, was asking $5 from each home and business owner to support the volunteer fire department. Another news story said Anna Maria officials announced all coconut palms arching over Pine Avenue would be removed since they had become a traffic hazard.

In her first editorial, Ellen stated her hopes for the Island. "Like many pioneers of small communities we have a common goal, the planned growth and development of Anna Maria Island."

In this and subsequent issues there were social notes, fishing reports and historical columns by Jack Leffingwell of Bradenton Beach, well known for his part in building the old, wooden Cortez Bridge. On June 1, the front page story was about the groundbreaking of the Island Baptist Church. In August of 1950, the dedication of the Youth Center, the former schoolhouse on Magnolia Avenue, was front-page news. Another story lamented the sad condition of streets on the Island. The opening statement was: "Sand traps and holes make walking a misery, and riding in a car or on a bicycle is actually hazardous."

The big story of the year happened on September 7, 1950. The headline read: "Baby Hurricane Becomes Juvenile." Ellen wrote how an unnamed hurricane flooded the Island, causing considerable damage to Gulf-front properties. She emphasized how Islanders rose to the occasion. Ellen took the *Bradenton Herald* to task for reporting: "Helpless Islanders were scared and grim, and rescuers from the mainland found barefoot women wandering around aimlessly."

It wasn't true she stated, detailing how Island firemen worked for two days and nights securing beach property while volunteers served coffee and soup to residents who took refuge in the community hall.

"We must remember to wear white ties and tails during the next hurricane," she wrote in her put-down.

The major issue in the early months of 1950 was whether the Island should be three municipalities or one city. The City of Anna Maria was incorporated in 1923, and in the wake of the post war boom the incorporation of the southern portion of the Island was called for.

"Whether it is called Bradenton Beach, Anna Maria or Gasparilla Gulch, we need one city on this Island," she proclaimed.

It was a losing battle. In March of 1950, about 70 mid-Island residents met at the Island school and voted 49 to 12 for incorporating separately. The group considered calling the city Coquina Beach, but decided to name it after Jack Holmes, the developer.

It was only a matter of time before residents on the south end formed a city. Bradenton Beach was created out of E. P. Green's old Cortez Beach subdivision.

On Dec. 21, 1950, Bernard Wagaman was elected mayor of Bradenton Beach, and the circulation of the *Key News* was 600. The work was grueling, and many problems faced the two women. The most popular feature was the personal column.

"People wanted to know what everyone was doing and saying. We told it all and used initials. People were dying to know whom we were talking about. If we printed one word that was not a compliment we heard about it," Ellen said. "Many times I heard, if you don't stop writing about me I won't subscribe to your paper. The *Key News* only cost 5-cents, $2 a year. We took stands on everything. Many of my opinions were controversial. It was lots of fun."

Toward the end of the year, advertising waned and the girls could not afford to keep the paper in business. They lost money and never really felt accepted. Ellen and Harriet stopped publishing on March 1, 1951. The last paper had a bold headline, "Damned By Faint Praise," illustrated by two skeletons carrying a coffin.

Harry Varley, a feisty public relations executive from New York, retired on the Island, obtained a permit for a newspaper and named it *The Islander* in 1951.

Ellen kept busy going to city meetings and taking part in Island Players productions. "The city meetings were absolutely marvelous," she said. "People who were not here in the early days really missed the greatest humor and pathos, better than you could ever see in the theater. Some of the funniest remarks I ever heard were at those meetings."

Ellen was photographed dancing with a friend at the popular Sandbar.

Ellen ran for commissioner, but did not get a seat. "I wasn't surprised. My editorials turned a lot of people against me," she said. "All my enemies voted against me," she surmised. One interesting aside on her defeat was that a few voters, intending to vote for a woman, became confused in the spelling and voted for Francis Welsch.

About this time, Ellen now divorced from Don Brackin, met a man-about-town through her association with the Island Chamber of Commerce. Jack Marshall had been director of the chamber for 14 consecutive years and was one of the leading realtors on the Island. They were married in 1954, and she became a partner in his real estate business. "We made a good team," she recalled. "Jack was smart, but I was quick."

Ellen became one of the best-known realtors on the Island. She was a community activist, supporter of the arts and cultural affairs, church worker and one of the original Pink Ladies at Manatee Memorial Hospital in the early '50s.

She raised two stepdaughters, and became a surrogate parent for her two year old great-grandson. Jack opened his first real estate office in Bradenton Beach in the '40s and was credited with naming Bridge Street. This blurb appeared in the August 1,1949 issue of the *Anna Maria Key News*: "Notice: Contrary to scurrilous rumor, I have not yet been run off the Island. I have merely moved, lock, stock and barrel, to my new location at Gulf Drive and First Street in Bradenton Beach. Come see me sometime soon. John W. "Jack" Marshall, husband of *Key News* reporter Ellen Marshall.

Ellen and her friend Frances Livingston were members of the Manatee County Board of Realtors. Frances was a character, very outspoken, extremely smart, and a wonderful fisherwoman. She spent a lot of time on the Anna Maria City Pier and could catch fish when no one else could, but she made a lot of enemies. She would tell people how to fish, what to fish for and scare people away. She would push children, just learning to fish, aside and tell them if they didn't leave the pier she would throw them in the water.

Frances knew how to work hard and was well known throughout the county. She was constantly being quoted and was a good friend to many people.

A keen wit and strong sense of humor endeared Ellen to many on the Island.

"Frances was a WAC during WWII and a widow, so we had something in common and became good friends," Ellen said. "As realtors we got along very well. I've always been a feminist and a workaholic and had admiration for hard-working women who make it on their own. It's a man's world, and it takes a lot of hard work for single women to get along."

In 1985, Ellen closed her real estate business her husband founded in 1945. Members of the Manatee County League of Women Voters were pleading for workers in the new Guardian Ad Litem program. The concept of this vital project was training volunteers who were appointed by a juvenile judge to appear in court as advocates for children who were abused, neglected or abandoned. Ellen signed up.

"Being involved in this program was one of the most stimulating things I have ever done," she said. "I did a lot of hospital work and was one of the first nurses aides in the children's ward of a huge hospital in New York.

"I was always interested in the mistreatment of children due to neglect and abuse. Being an educator and arbitrator for children caught in the middle was important to me. Guardian Ad Litem sort of fell into my lap. I did not want to spin my wheels after Jack died so I got into the pilot program."

For 17 years she guided more than 100 children through the court system as a Guardian Ad Litem. Ellen was the recipient of many prestigious awards for her leadership, creativity, unselfish hard work and enduring dedication to people. She was named the Anna Maria City Citizen of the Year in 1990. In her acceptance speech she explained that she learned to help others from her paternal grandmother, a doctor, with whom she lived as a child.

One of Ellen's most endearing qualities was her keen sense of humor and witty sayings. Even at an advanced age, her memory was sharp, and she loved telling stores of the past, laughing exuberantly at amusing anecdotes.

In the early '40s, Roser Church was a small chapel, and Ellen taught Sunday school and assisted with the first Vacation Bible School. After Jack's death she had time for the administrative work at the church and became the first woman to be appointed chairman of the congregation.

In 1996, at an Island gathering, she received the coveted Heartland Award from Governor Lawton Chiles for her service to the community, especially the children. She was named. "One of Florida's Finest." The governor said, "She's a lady who deserves to be recognized for many years of community service as an advocate for children, Ellen Marshall."

It was a complete surprise. Ellen gasped, flung one hand over her heart, bounced a punch cup off the table with the other hand and shouted, "My God!" The governor apologized for startling her nearly to death.

In a speech to the Island Historical Society, Ellen said she felt like Rip Van Winkle and Rodney Dangerfield rolled into one. She certainly had not been asleep, this energetic woman who worked for others for half a century.

Looking back over her career, Ellen said most of the changes on the Island were definitely for the good. Looking ahead, she believed Anna Maria Island had a "stupendous future." She could foresee Anna Maria City becoming an exclusive community of single-family homes, fine restaurants and boutiques. Holmes Beach would continue as an attractive mixed community of residential and business areas and Bradenton Beach would be the commercial hub of the Island.

"I believe it was fate that brought me to Anna Maria Island," she said. "I've been involved with just about everything here."

Ellen died on Jan. 3, 2003 at the age of 94. A well-attended memorial service was held at Roser Church with the Rev. Gary Batey officiating. On the cover of the bulletin was a picture of Ellen, taken the year before. She was wearing a black beret jauntily cocked over one ear and, as always, her infectious smile.

Harry Varley takes time out to enjoy a game of pool with Merrill Tritt

Varleyism Reigned In The '50s

In 1951, at the urging of many citizens, Harry Varley, the retired president of Schick Razor Company, became the editor of *The Islander* newspaper, a position he held for eight years. During these years, the paper was a mirror of his own views, rather than a sounding board for the three Island communities it served.

The readers said *The Islander* resembled a Revolutionary War paper rather than a small town tabloid. It had a "Give 'Em Hell" attitude straight from the editor's typewriter.

Varley was born in Nelson, Lancashire, England and came to the United States in 1908. After working for a rubber company and writing for a newspaper, he went into advertising and eventually became president of the Schick Razor Company until his retirement in 1950. Later that year, he and his wife, Winifred, moved to Anna Maria Island.

Over the years, the little man with a shock of white hair, a big cigar and a sharp pointed pen had a following that hung on his every word. When Judd Arnett assumed the editorship of *The Islander* in 1959, this is what he wrote about his predecessor:

"During these past seven years, *The Islander* has been cussed and discussed, loved and hated, admired and berated, set upon and defended, damned and dignified. It has never been dull and neither has it been puling when adversity reared its head, nor weak-kneed when storm clouds hovered."

There were readers who considered Varley one of the real individualists on the Island with a rare sense of humor. They liked his ability to carve up those he disagreed with in the pages of his newspaper, with a finesse that has not been equaled by any editor since.

At the same time, Varley had his foes. There were times when it was Varley against the world. Despite the opposition to his views which he might receive from his readers, he never wavered in his efforts to provide people of the Island the "true facts."

In the first issue Varley wrote: "*The Islander* will be written and edited as an entirely independent newspaper, owing no self allegiance to any individual group, sect or organization, and devoted to the entire

The Islander

DEVOTED TO THE PEOPLE OF ANNA MARIA ISLAND

Where Life Is Peaceful . . . and Fishing Is Good

ANNA MARIA, FLORIDA, THURSDAY, MARCH 13, 1958

Where Life Is Peaceful . . .

The Woeful Knight And The Wilful Dragon

Transcribed and delineated from the mind of Ronald McLeod (pronounced Mac-Cloud or Ma-

Harry Varley had his foes. Sometimes it was Varley against the world.

population of the Island."

Nothing could have been closer to the truth. For more than seven years, Varley and *The Islander*, were independent. Varley, who sometimes pictured himself as a quixotic figure in his own editorial cartoons, never gave an inch. He was a leader in a number of fields. While editor, he championed the cause of erosion control.

More than any other person, he fought to see the permeable erosion control groins become a reality. He was founder and first president of the Holmes Beach Board of Aldermen in 1963 and served two terms on the board.

In a column entitled, "More Varley-isms," he enumerated his many contributions: "I kept Cypress Avenue open, full width, when sharpshooters tried to steal strips of it. I prevented a real estate man from asserting ownership to part of Bay Front Park and prevented the payment of $12,000 by the city to clear the title to the park. I proved another man did not own Grouper from Coconut to Pine, and exposed and killed a proposal for the mayor and associates to buy city land, now Bimini Estates, for $20,000.

"I initiated the movement to restore to the three cities 50-percent of the road and bridge tax and started the voluntary tax for mosquito control. Single-handedly, I persuaded the State Road Department to name the bridge from Perico to the Island the Anna Maria Bridge. Before this all drawings and toll receipts read Palma Sola Bridge.

"I spent years, and my money, investigating erosion prevention methods and flew, at my own expense, to Jamaica inspecting and photographing groins. I was able to convince the county to budget an erosion-prevention fishing pier at the county beach.

"There have been many more examples of Varley-isms, but these should be sufficient to confound the critics who would try to make you believe that in giving 12 years of my life to the Island it was, in some mysterious way, a detriment to the place and people.

"For whatever time I have left I shall continue to serve, hoping that Varley-isms will command some small respect, even in the little warped minds of those who now use it as a term of derision."

A born crusader and wordmaster, Varley became the voice of the Island on every issue. He bedeviled the establishment about the bridge. "One good bridge to the Island—NOW!!" was his slogan repeated over and over in every issue of the paper. In 1952, the announcement was made that Anna Maria was slated to get three bridges. The package deal was to be financed by $6-million worth of bonds to be paid off with tolls over a 30-year period. It seemed like overkill to Varley, but he went along with the scheme.

Steve Kimball was of owner-publisher of *The Islander* from 1959 to 1970.

Another feature of his paper was a cartoon of a grim-looking man with a top hat entitled, "His Name Is Mr. Intolerance." The cartoon was made especially for Varley by one of America's great cartoonists, Rollin Kirby, a Pulitzer Prize winner. In the Nov. 15, 1951 *Islander,* the story under the pencil sketch had this caption: "He lives on the Island. He lives everywhere—in the biggest cities and the smallest communities. No longer does he wear the tall hat and frock coat, but you will be able to recognize him by his sanctimonious manner and viciousness of his small soul that looks out through shifty eyes. He is a joy-killer. He is against good things and sometimes, though seldom, against bad ones. Sectarian squabbles are his meat. So are racial fights. Smiles of happiness are to him as a red flag to a mad bull. He is prophet of gloom and doom and joy cannot enter his miserable mind. Watch out for him when you meet anyone who expresses bitter intolerance of other people's way of life, it may be our ancient enemy disguised as a do-gooder. Fight him every time he rears his ugly head. As the serpent dwelt in Eden, Mr. Intolerance crops up

Don Moore was described as "a feisty little editor". He purchased *The Islander* in 1970.

on our Island paradise. Let us keep him in the jungle where he belongs."

Strange and witty headlines often appeared In Varley's *Islander*, such as this story entitled: "Sea Detectives Hunt Jim Brevis. Thirty-odd boats searched for clues to any evidence that would lead to the arrest, conviction and execution of the tiny animal or vegetable that, rightly or wrongfully, has been accused of killing fish and causing the red tide." It should be noted that Jim Brevis is the scientific name for red tide. Red tide is a natural phenomenon which produces an algal bloom environmentally hazardous to marine life. It is called red tide because the blooms make the waters appear reddish brown.

In 1959, after eight years of hard work, Varley gave the paper to Judd Arnett. When Arnett left the Island, Varley transferred the stock to Steve Kimball, who sold *The Islander* to Don Moore.

The Islander Becomes Full-Fledged Newspaper

It was not until Steve Kimball became editor of *The Islander* that the paper started to assume the characteristics of a full-fledged newspaper. For a decade, from 1959 through 1969, Kimball ran *The Islander*.

In his swan song as editor, Judd Arnett who preceded Kimball as editor, wrote, "The Island does have a solid and substantial place for a well-written, well-directed weekly publication devoted to the growth

Jack Egan was *The Islander* cartoonist.

One feature of *The Islander* was the beach beauties, found on the front page of each issue during Don Moore's reign. Marianne Gaba and Kathy Burress, on the opposite page, filled the bill.

and prosperity of the people and area it serves. Steve Kimball is amply qualified to meet that responsibility."

Kimball set the tone of the paper from the outset. In his first editorial in August of 1959, he wrote: "Only county affairs that affect the Island and Islanders will be grist for our mill. Our primary source of news will be the Island and its people."

This policy was the key factor in making the paper great. It didn't try to cover county, state or national affairs. Kimball established another policy when he assumed the editorship, a sense of objectivity. During his time as editor, he developed an editorial page that spoke with authority, but did not try to shout so loud it drowned out other points of view. Considerable space was allowed for letters to the editor.

Like Varley, Kimball voiced his opinions on subjects of importance to the community, but unlike the paper's founder, he limited his subjective comments to the editorial page. During his time as editor, Kimball had many admirers and also a number of enemies. As he wrote in a column about Varley when the paper's founder died: "In the newspaper profession it is axiomatic that an editor- if he is doing a good job- never will win any popularity contest. It is also said that the true gauge of an editor's worth is not necessarily the number of friends he has made, but the number and caliber of the enemies he has made. Harry Varley scored well on both sides of the ledger."

The same could be said of Kimball. He won some and lost some, but mostly he was a winner when it came to producing a sound weekly newspaper. As the Island grew, Kimball focused on hard news and was credited for changing the printing from letterpress to offset printing. In 1966, Don Moore, a University of Florida School of Journalism graduate, joined *The Islander* staff as news editor and part owner. In 1969, Kimball relinquished the editorship. He said he was stepping down so he would have more leisure time to do what he had planned to do when he and his wife first moved to Florida in the '50s. At the urging of a number of residents, Kimball became a candidate for the post of mayor of Anna Maria City and was elected to a two-year term in 1974.

In 1970, Don Moore, along with his wife Roxanne, bought the paper. As editor/publisher, Don had a strong "tell it like it is" style. His "I'm mad as hell and won't take it anymore" editorials did not endear him to many.

"As a very young reporter, working for the *Tampa Tribune,* at that time Florida's finest daily paper, I was marched in to meet the managing editor for the first time," Don said. "Red Newton was a crusty curmudgeon, a man to be reckoned with when it came to his paper's integrity."

"Boy," Newton growled at me, "I've got to tell you I don't want my reporters to be well liked. If they're too well liked by people it's a good indication they're not doing their job."

"I did not forget what Newton said to me. When I became the man in Mr. Newton's shoes in a microcosmic way at *The Islander*, I attempted to run this newspaper as if he was looking over my shoulder, maybe he was. At any rate, it would appear I have had some measure of success in this area judging from the number of politicians *The Islander* has taken on at all levels of government over the years.

"More than any single factor, *The Islander* is a product of the staff that produces it. In my estimation, we've had one of the best newspapers over the years. This point is born out by the fact the paper has won more than 100 awards both national and statewide for journalistic excellence during my tenure. It is also one of the reasons *The New York Times* became interested in buying the paper."

Some people asked, why an Island newspaper? What was a relatively small weekly paper doing in such a competitive market confronted with four daily papers, dozens of TV channels, several shopping guides, numerous radio stations and monthly magazines in the immediate area.

Don answered, "*The Islander* provides news coverage the other media miss. The paper is primarily hard-news oriented and covers the four communities on Anna Maria Island and Longboat Key. *The Islander* reports the day-to-day social activities of its readers, news of clubs and civic groups on the Island and Key, plus fishing news that lets the anglers know what's biting. It has picture coverage of all the beach cities unmatched by any other news media. In short, if it happens on Anna Maria Island or Longboat Key, you can bank on finding it in *The Islander*."

Throughout the paper's history, *The Islander* was the most widely read newspaper on the Island, and under Moore's direction, it became the dominant paper on Longboat Key. The paper's editors championed the cause of erosion control, fought against street closings, supported plans for a better main road and kept a watchful eye on daily events at each city hall. At times, the paper's editorial views received wide support. Other times they were strongly criticized, but at no time was there a shortage of editorial comment. *The Islander* survived and thrived simply because it did one thing better than any other medium. It provided more news of Anna Maria Island and Longboat Key than anyone else.

Don Moore was described in *Editor and Publisher*, journalism's trade publication, as the "feisty, little editor." Steve Kimball echoed that description when he wrote: "Moore was in the paperweight class physically, but his courage, determination and results are far from Lilliputian. He exhibits no hesitancy about taking on the 'big ones' in his editorials, apparently following the theory that sacred cows make the best hamburger.

"Under Moore's leadership, the paper has achieved much additional clout as an editorial force. Recently, because of his stories and editorials about flammable polyurethane foam used in a duplex development on the Island, all four municipalities in the paper's circulation area have adopted measures to abolish the material. Not infrequently, elected officials try to discredit *The Islander* and its editor to make their own inept performances appear better than they really are.

"Scrupulously fair, however, Moore publishes letters that try to disparage the paper and himself, and is particularly careful to print those letters that express views that oppose those of the paper and its staff."

In 1974, *The Islander* became a commercial printing business, and the building, at 314 Pine Avenue in Anna Maria City, was greatly enlarged. In April the public was invited to *The Islander's* open house to view the largest offset printing plant owned by a newspaper within a 50-mile radius.

In 1980, after almost 15 years as editor of *The Islander*, Don Moore sang his swan song in his column, On and Off The Islands. It read: "From this column forward my brother, Colin, will assume total control of the editorial end of *The Islander*. That's very good from my vantage point because he generally believes as I do, editorially speaking. I have to confess my main claim to fame, as far as *The Islander* is concerned, was that I was the person with the good luck to be at the right place at the right time. All I did was follow Steve's game plan for producing a weekly newspaper with some editorial integrity. I printed the truth and generally raised hell with the politicians over the years. Judging from the reaction of the readers, they usually liked what I had to say. Judging from the reaction of the politicians, they didn't."

Moore's sale of *The Islander, Bayshore Banner* and his publishing business to the *New York Times* for $1-million in 1980 came as a big surprise to his readers and his staff.

Island Libraries

Islanders were hungry for books in the early '50s. The only place to borrow a book was Roser Church. It had about 200 books to loan. Anyone could borrow a book and just record it on paper. It was the honor system, and it worked well. "Who knows? This may be the seed from which an Island public library will grow," wrote a pundit of *The Islander* in 1954.

Meanwhile in Bradenton Beach, a movement began to provide a library in the southernmost city for all Islanders. In June 1956, there were 250 books with 150 more promised. A plea went out to residents to donate hardbound books they did not want. Good fiction, classics, reference books and children's books were sought. All the books were classified and lent without charge. The library was in Harvey Memorial Community Church on Church Street in 1957 until a building could be found. An astonishing number and variety of books were donated, and it was certain many more would be given since the library was established in the church.

After four months, the Bradenton Beach Public Library was gaining in size and popularity. The shelves contained about 1,500 books gleaned from many sources.

Island Kiwanis Club members gathered books which were sold from the pavilion at Manatee Public Beach. All proceeds were given to Happiness House in Sarasota, a non-profit organization for children with disabilities.

In the 1970s the Island Library opened in the Holmes Beach Shopping Center. Before that a bookmobile came to the Island once a week.

In 1958, when Helen Swift first came to the Island, the only available book-lending source was the Manatee County Bookmobile. Mrs. Swift graduated from the University of Chicago with a master's degree in library science. When she returned as a permanent Island resident, she volunteered as the bookmobile librarian along with Justine Regan.

Shown from left, Joan Wood, volunteer; Sally White, librarian and Helen Swift, who along with Eleanor Walker, spearheaded the building of the large, modern library we have today.

She persuaded Justine's husband, Larry, to drive the bookmobile to various locations on the Island, including the Anna Maria Community Hall and the IGA parking lot. Every week the bookmobile visited the Island and lent books by the hundreds. Although the bookmobile carried 1,700 books, it was not a large enough selection for Islanders. City and county officials talked about establishing a branch of the Manatee County Library System in Holmes Beach.

The Friends of the Island Library was founded in 1965, and the possibilities of a real library were investigated. On May 17, 1970, the first stationary library was born in a storefront in the Holmes Beach shopping center. Helen Swift and Hope Smith were the librarians. Holmes Beach and Anna Maria City paid half the rent and Jack Holmes paid the other half for the first year. The Friends went to work renovating the small shop, painting and building shelves. The State of Florida and the Carnegie Library in Bradenton made the first collection of books possible.

Over the years, due to rapidly increasing clientele, it was evident a new building was needed. The proposed site was the old airstrip near Holmes Beach City Hall. Eleanor Walker, the first president of the Friends, began a relentless drive to raise necessary funds for a new library. After 13 years of diligent campaigning and with the combined efforts of Jack Holmes and the City of Holmes Beach, which donated the land, ground was broken on April 26, 1982. The feat would have been impossible without state aid, Selby Foundation funds and donations from hundreds of supportive citizens.

The doors of the Island Branch Library were opened on Dec. 15, 1982.

Anna Maria resident H. Patterson Fletcher was the architect. The meeting room was dedicated to Eleanor Walker and Helen Swift, two visionaries whose mission was to build an Island library.

The Island Branch Library opened its doors to the public on Dec. 15, 1982. Many changes have taken place over the years, and most of them can be attributed to the Friends of the Island Library. The Friends established the annual Focus on Florida programs. Begun in 1989, seven free programs each year feature authors, performing groups, and individuals who represent Florida-living at its best. Programs are presented in the Walker-Swift Meeting Room from October through April every year. The Friends conduct annual book sales which are excellent fund-raising projects. Monthly meetings of the Friends Book Club provide stimulating discussions on selected literature and authors. A band of hard-working volunteers support the library's outstanding professional staff. The highlight every summer is a series of the family programs, sponsored by the Friends.

The Island Branch Library has been the heart of the community from the start. It offers access to a countywide collection of books, tapes, DVD's, and a network of computers with access to the library catalog and the internet. The large meeting room is available for special programs, displays of art and meetings of civic groups.

The Island was a close-knit community in the early days. Shown clockwise: Dramas were presented regularly at the Youth Center; Jim Kronus kept the school running smoothly; Little Leaguers attended banquets at Pete Reynard's Restaurant at the end of the season; the Norwood boys were ready for school; Lena Phelps, the popular principal, and her husband Clyde; Bob Ross, director of the Youth Center, oversees a crafts group; a well-known Island couple, educators Elizabeth and Gene Moss; another historical reenactment at the Youth Center.

1967
ART

Six

Places of Interest

The airstrip attracted MGM magnates who agreed the film, "On An Island With You" would be shot on the Island.

The Island Airport

On Anna Maria Island the term "airport" was a misnomer, since there was only a field and no buildings. In 1947, Jack Holmes supervised the construction of an airstrip in Holmes Beach, believing pilots from the war would be interested in using it. Jack had bought 350 acres, mostly mangrove swamps and bay front in the center of the Island and began the development of homesites after World War II. He rented a bulldozer and hired an ex-Marine to clear off 30-acres of jungle. Holmes and flying enthusiast Guy Wimpy laid the concrete strip. The entire project took only 13 days.

Before the strip was completed, Jack Holmes was contacted by Metro-Goldwyn-Mayer. The film giant proposed using the airstrip in connection with production of the film, "On An Island With You." MGM believed that Anna Maria Island would make a perfect setting for the motion picture starring "the million dollar

Hundreds of workers with lights, cameras and miles of cable descended on the Island.

mermaid" Esther Williams and handsome, debonair Peter Lawford. Foliage was placed around the airstrip to make it look like a deserted south sea island.

Holmes used the movie's publicity to promote his new housing project. He produced a brochure which read: "After an exhausting scouting in the Caribbean and other tropical areas, Anna Maria Island was chosen as the spot most perfectly typifying the producer's vision of a romantic tropical island where dashing Naval officer Peter Lawford flies with his kidnapped beauty, Miss Williams. The Island offers every facility for shots. The airport with its 4,000-foot runway can accommodate the Navy bomber. The adjoining yacht basin, where the amphibian plane in which Ricardo Montalban arrives to rescue the heroine, is perfect. In addition to the three principals, the location unit included Director Richard Thorpe and a technical crew of 85."

Hundreds of Hollywood workers descended on the Island with cameras, lights and miles of cable to film the plane landing to bring Lawford to the Island paradise. The film was touted as a mixture of romance, music, rich color and fun. In addition to Montalban, it co-starred Cyd Charisse, who danced to the rumba beat of Xavier Cugat's band, and comedian/singer Jimmy Durante. It was topped off with water ballet sequences of Esther and her expert swimming troupe filmed at Cypress Gardens. The unique swimming pool was constructed in the shape of the State of Florida. Some Island girls were recruited for the bevy of graceful underwater swimmers. Esther was not a great actress, but her languid backstrokes and perfect swan dives kept audiences spellbound. This movie made her one of the top box office attractions in the '40s and '50s.

Esther loved the Island, and some sources say she bought a lot, others think enterprising Jack Holmes gave her the property. Several movie companies have shot scenes on the Island, but none matched the excitement of the filming of "*On An Island With You.*"

Jim Kissick, Naval Flyer

Jim Kissick recalled activity on the Island in the late '40s. He provided the following information and a different version of the airport story. "I was in the Navy Carrier Aviation Division in World War II, got out early and applied for a course at Parks Air College. While back on the Island for about two months, I became interested in Jack Holmes starting his city.

"At this time, MGM was searching along the Gulf coast for the right location for a scene in "*On An Island With You*." It was about a Navy torpedo plane pilot in a squadron which moved from island to island in the South Pacific. Holmes had started his city along the coast, and MGM found the perfect sand flat, surrounded by a jungle of mangrove trees, and large enough to allow a surplus Grumman Avenger (TBF) to land. With Jack's permission, MGM filmed the plane landing across the sand, stopping just short of the jungle.

Jim Kissick

"I was told that once the plane came to the end of its roll, the actress would be whisked into the radio hatch on the right side of the fuselage. Lawford was in the cockpit, and the cameras started rolling. Lawford was seen taking off his cloth helmet. The hatch opened, and out stepped Miss Williams, supposedly having been flown to a South Seas island by her Navy pilot boyfriend, Peter Lawford.

"Holmes gave a party for the cast and handed Esther Williams a deed to a lot near the Gulf. I was told her agent sold it as soon as they returned to Hollywood. As the new city grew eastward, mangroves fell and sand was pumped in. Jack looked at the spot where the Hollywood plane landed and said, 'This is where I'll put an airport.'

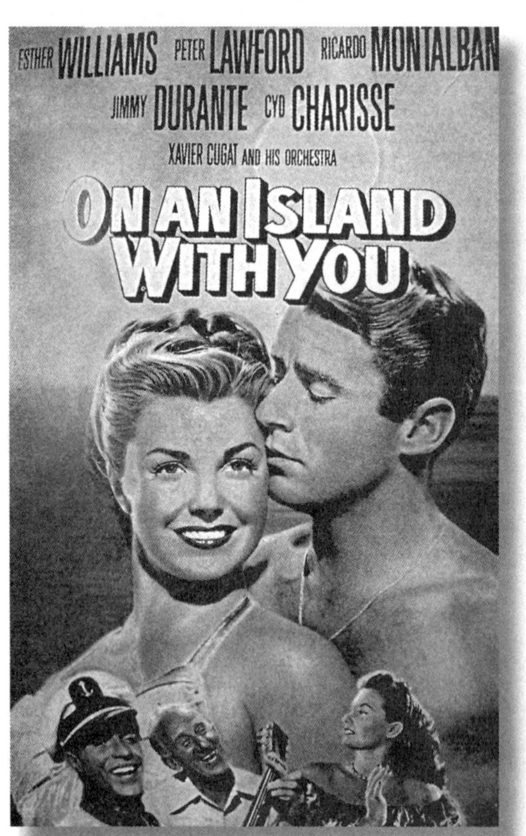

"The grass strip where I landed my Piper Cruise (Cub) and a Jet Ranger helicopter was 1,800 feet long. In the early '70s, Florida mandated all public-use airports had to have a minimum of 2,000 feet of runway. I was asked to join the fight to save it since I had a bachelor's degree in Airport-Airline management. At the northern end, it bottomed against the south end of a short canal. The area to the east of the runway and canal was undeveloped, but Jack Holmes had plans for a residential area. He was approached and asked if the runway could be turned about one degree to the east putting it along the existing canal. The answer was, 'Absolutely not. I plan to put tennis courts there.'

"A short time later, a man flying a Piper 140 low-wing with fixed landing gear attempted to land to the south. He and his friend flew in from Lakeland. The runway could be deceiving. Although only 1,800 feet long, it was very wide. The Piper pilot, unaware of the short length, landed long, and realizing he could not make it, added full power. It was too late. The Piper struck the edge of the roof on a building across the street, did a half roll and ended up between the boat docks west of Pete Reynard's restaurant. That put an abrupt end to any hope of saving the strip."

Anna Maria Island Air Force

By John Adams

My family moved to the Island in the '40s. World War II was over, and a four-year hiatus in home building was aching to be satisfied. At that time there were few homes east or west of Gulf Drive. What is now central

Holmes Beach was a salt flat covered with mangroves and seagrape trees. It was largely under water during extreme high tides.

Shortly after we moved to the Island, a dirt road appeared off Gulf Drive, where the Wachovia Bank is today. We could hear bulldozers working, but could not see them through the seagrapes and mangroves. The vegetation was being cleared for a landing strip. It extended from Cobbs' Corner (now Captains Marina) 1,300 feet north to the edge of the bay at the south end of Key Royale, which was called School Key.

Holmes Beach was a salt flat when John Adams and his father, Sam, arrived in the '40s.

Jack Holmes landed a movie that would use both a wheeled plane and a seaplane. Paul Mantz, arguably the world's best pilot, did the flying for Peter Lawford. I recall watching him make about ten low-level passes, and thinking he could not land the AT6 Bomber because the field was too short. On the 11th pass he landed in an area of about 150-feet, literally stalling the plane to a perfect landing. As it turned out, the previous passes were for various takes of filming.

The movie stars stayed at the Orange Blossom Hotel in Sarasota, because it had the only air conditioning in the area. They were flown back and forth in a little Grumman Widgeon seaplane. If you saw the movie you will remember the seaplane taxiing to shore and Peter Lawford, dressed in a starched white uniform, stepping out and wading to shore to rescue Esther Williams who had been kidnapped by the natives. He looked a bit like General MacArthur returning to Bataan, only MacArthur's uniform was not white.

Hydroplane races attracted crowds along the bay.

The first take did not happen that way. Peter stepped out of the plane and sank out of sight. His hat floated away. He was blustering, and the director did not know whether to laugh or cry. Since the water was deep, sand was filled in while Peter was flown to Sarasota to get his uniform washed and pressed.

After the war ended, ex-GI's could take flying lessons on the GI Bill. To develop the airport, Jack Holmes hired a fixed-base operator named Bob Grey. He was one of the finest pilots I've ever flown with.

Bob brought in about seven airplanes, a Piper Super Cub, an Aerocoupe and four Piper Cubs. John Holmes, Hugh Holmes, Percy Simpson and Johnny Jackson were some of the Islanders who learned to fly with the Anna Maria Island Air Force. All of the planes practicing touch and go landings on Sunday afternoons were a sight to see. I had the job of washing and refueling the planes, and when the GI's didn't have time to take their lessons, Bob would teach me free of charge. I quickly learned, but I was not pilot material and never completed my training.

Three episodes stand out in my memory. There was a French beautician, Pierre Duba, who built three small buildings near 47th Street in Holmes Beach. He asked to rent a plane but had forgotten his logbook and license. Life was freer then, and Bob said he would take a test ride with him. If Pierre could fly the plane Bob would let him rent it.

Pierre could fly the Aerocoupe, which had an open roof. Bob unfastened his safety belt, slouched back in the seat and proceeded to read a comic book. Pierre landed the plane on the short runway with water at each end. He touched down at the tip of the runaway where the sand was still soft from the morning high tide. The wheels sank deep, flipping the Aerocoupe on its nose. Bob slid out on the sand still holding the comic book.

Other amusing incidents were watching student pilots make their first solo take off and landing. Johnny Jackson shot a perfect landing and the plane was only 50-feet off the ground. The Piper Cub just stopped, fell to the ground and bounced rather high a number of times on its flexible landing gear. Humbug Cobb ran to see if Johnny was hurt. Johnny's first question was, "Has the plane stopped bouncing?"

While shooting pool on the City Pier, we would brag about our flying skills to the pier regulars. We talked about flying between the pier and the telephone wires overhead where numerous pelicans and seagulls sat.

One Sunday morning the Anna Maria Air Force took off all together and headed for the pier at a very low altitude. The closer we got, the closer the wires looked to the pier and the more apprehensive the fishermen became.

I was in the lead plane piloted by Hugh Holmes. When we got close, Hugh stuck his head out of the Aerocoupe to look back and see if everyone was following. When he stuck his head out, the wind ripped off his glasses and he promptly pulled up over the wires. There were a number of fishermen getting ready to jump in the water.

John and Hugh Holmes rented Piper Cub airplanes from the airport to fly Bennie Scanio and Leon Stafford to Camp Blanding so they could inspect war surplus fire trucks. It was a bumpy ride all the way home, and John pulled a joke on Bennie. The exposed wing struts came through the cockpit and crossed over the passengers heads. As the wings flexed, the struts would move back and forth. John told Bennie the wings were going to break off unless he could hold the struts so they would not move. When John landed the plane Bennie was white as a sheet and swore he would never fly again."

Hugh G. Holmes, Sr.

Recollections

by Hugh G. Holmes, Sr.

When I returned to the Island in early June of 1946, I had just been discharged from the Navy. The airstrip had already been cleared with two runways. The longest runway was from north to south, and the second runway intersected it and angled to the west through what eventually became the Seaside Gardens development. My father, John E. Holmes, Sr., owned the property in partnership with Frank Giles. Giles was also a resident of this portion of Anna Maria Island, which was to become the City of Holmes Beach in 1950.

When the property had been sufficiently cleared so that the sand and shell runways could be used, a major movie picture company contacted my father and asked if it would be possible to use the field for shooting some scenes for the movie, "On An Island With You." They reached an agreement, and shortly thereafter the scenes were shot.

Paul Mantz, a well-known test pilot, flew a Navy torpedo plane in and landed it on the airstrip. This was the plane in which Peter Lawford brought Esther Williams to the island. Several scenes were shot around this action. Other scenes were shot with Ricardo Montalban flying in on a small Navy seaplane and landing on the shoreline just east of the south end of the airstrip. This was the area just to the north of the entrance into the present boat basin. My father later built his home on this property, and my son lives there at the present time.

During the shooting of the film, I was asked to supply a small surplus military truck with a boom and winch

to move equipment, if needed. It could also to be used as a prop. I supplied the truck, with myself as the driver, so I could have an opportunity to watch the filming in progress. When the filming was completed, the Navy plane was flown out, and that was the end of that chapter in the life of the airstrip.

My father was soon contacted by Robert Grey, a recently released instructor from the Army Air Force. Bob was interested in starting a pilot training program and an air taxi service at the newly constructed airfield. They proceeded to have the airfield licensed and certified for this purpose. As soon as the proper approvals were received, they proceeded to build a residence on the adjacent property with provisions for a classroom for student instruction. The first group of students consisted of myself, my brother John E. Holmes, Jr., John Jackson, who had been recently discharged from wartime service in the Merchant Marine, and later became the owner and operator of Jackson Plumbing Company in Holmes Beach. A friend and business associate of mine, Alan (Percy) Arnold, was also in the group.

My actual flight training started on March 16, 1947. I made my first solo flight on April 4, 1947 and had my check-out flight for my private license on May 23, 1947. Then I flew on a regular basis until October 28, 1947. On that date I flew my father to West Palm Beach to a real estate convention. After I dropped him off, I returned to the Island. This ended my career as a pilot due to financial reasons, and the fact that my time was occupied with courting my future wife, Jean Messersmith.

During the early years of the operation of the airport the most interesting things I recall are a few minor mishaps. One of the pilots flipped a plane over on the north end of the runway, with no injuries and only minor damage to the plane. A student pilot made a rough landing and damaged the landing gear of the plane he was piloting, and a visiting pilot stalled while coming in for a landing and dropped his plane into the boat basin on the south end of the airstrip.

While I was actively flying, the things that stick out in my memory mostly were my cross-country flights to Tallahassee, Gainesville, Winter Haven and West Palm Beach. Another interesting flight was to the Bradenton/ Sarasota airport, just prior to a hurricane.

The storm reports were getting worse by the minute, and the wind was picking up considerably. Bob Grey called the airport and made arrangements to store his planes in one of the hangars. He asked if I would be willing to take one of the planes up. I said sure, and then I learned of the difficulty of flying in strong winds in a small plane with limited horsepower. You may want the plane to go one way, but the wind usually has a different idea. I made it, however, and had to land on a taxi strip right in front of the hangar. There were ground crew members on hand to grab the wings and hold the plane on the ground.

Bob continued to run an air taxi service and light package service for several years, but he could not generate enough income to keep operating. Charlie Whittaker, a commercial pilot, started a commuter service for passengers and freight with a twin-engine plane covering local airports within the state, but that also turned out not to be feasible.

Eventually the property was given to the City of Holmes Beach to be used for municipal purposes. With airport regulations becoming stricter, the city felt it could not meet the new government requirements, and the airport was closed in the mid '70s. Today there are city offices, a public library, a fire station, a ball diamond, tennis courts, a basketball court and other recreational facilities on the land. This was a much better utilization of the property.

A Popular Attraction

In Jack Holmes' brochure we read: "Anna Maria Island may be reached by plane or boat or a ten-minute automobile drive from Bradenton. An air taxi service is available to meet any incoming plane. It's easy to get to Anna Maria Island, but it's hard to make up your mind to leave."

A painting of a modern home was the front-page picture in *The Islander* on Jan. 10, 1952. The story proceeded to tell about the Wimpy family's house which was the subject of a painting by Earl K. Haag. "There's not another like it on the west coast of Florida!" the reporter exclaimed. "Perhaps not in the entire state."

The home of Mr. And Mrs. A. J. Wimpy and their children was across the street from the present Island Library. On the ground floor was a hangar that accommodated their four-passenger Beechcraft Bonanza plane. The house was built on the edge of the airport, so the Wimpys could land their plane and drive it right into their hangar. On the other side of the house was a small harbor where their boat was tied. This was an ideal Florida home, according to the writer.

A photo in *The Islander* in December of 1960 shows A. G. Wimpy, a flying contractor, fueling his plane at Huffines' Standard Service Station on Marina Drive.

The caption under a photograph of the airstrip in the June 21, 1956 issue of *The Islander* read: "One of the advantages of having friends who own planes is they may drop down from the skies anytime, land on the airstrip and give us the pleasure of their company. After lunch, pilot Lee Taylor took this reporter in his plane, a little bigger than a bathtub with wings, and we were able to see all the Island from a new perspective. We wished those who refer to the Island as 'the beach' could have been passengers to see all the developments underway.

"In 1952, a blue Beechcraft Bonanza, four-passenger plane swooped down to land on the airstrip. Inside were

The Wimpys' home, on a canal near the airstrip, had a hangar for Wimpy's four passenger Beachcraft Bonanza plane.

three passengers who were wintering in Fort Myers. Harry Schaeffer was so intrigued by the picture he had seen of the Wimpys' hangar-home that he and his friends flew to the Island to see it and to make inquiries in the hopes of building the same structure. Harry said a landing strip adjoined his home in Michigan and a set-up similar to the Florida one would be ideal.

The reporter continued writing that Holmes Beach had much to offer. "It's a short walk to the beach. Each lot to the east of the landing strip has access to the airport on one side and a boat harbor on the other. On the west side there will be a highway. Schaeffer asked Frank Giles if the landing strip would be permanent and was assured it would be. Actually, it is becoming very popular. Planes land here frequently and there is no doubt the use of the strip will increase in the future. It gives the Island a certain cachet."

Kenneth Lewis of Washington D.C. was touring Florida by plane in 1952. He landed at the Holmes Beach airport and looked in the area for an apartment, but found everything filled.

"The only thing I have is a roll-away bed in the garage," Mrs. John Prothero told him jokingly. Lewis left in quest of other accommodations. A little later, the Protheros found a bundle of clothing and a man's shoes beside the roll-away. The owner had gone to the beach. When he came back from the beach he said it was the best offer he had on the Island, so he decided to accept it. Mrs. Prothero felt so sorry for him, she put the roll-away in the kitchen. It was the first time she had rented her kitchen.

Bill and Helen Genung came to Holmes Beach after he retired in the '60s. He designed and built the Blue Water Beach Motel. Then he bought a Cessna Skyhawk and was a frequent user of the Holmes Beach airstrip. His last flight was in 1983, when he flew a Sweitzer sail-plane from Chicago to California.

In September of 1958, Governor Luther Hodges of North Carolina and friends flew to the Island airstrip and stayed at the Clement home in Holmes Beach while enjoying two days of fishing. A picture in *The Islander* shows the plane parked in the front yard of the home.

A plane owned and piloted by Bill Hochstetler was seen in the front lawn of the Hochstetler home. It provided a background, incongruous but homey, for photos taken by Bill's friend, photographer Tom Wortley in 1957.

Mrs. Peter Karr of Anna Maria met her son, Jim, at the airstrip. He picked her up in a jet helicopter and took her to his home north of Tampa. It was the first visit of a jet helicopter to the Island and spectators were impressed with its power, speed and maneuverability.

In 1956, U.S. Border patrol pilot, Ralph Cole checked the airport's station log with Carl Gulat while on the Island during a routine check flight. The Border Patrol was taking special interest in small planes that were arriving from or departing to destinations in Cuba. There was a concern that the planes might have been carrying unauthorized passengers or contraband merchandise, arms or similar items.

A freak accident was reported in the *Key News* on Aug. 10, 1950. A storm with high winds hit the Holmes Beach Yacht Basin and two planes were damaged. Prior to the storm, Capt. Lou Meyer had checked the planes and saw they were fastened down. Meyer said a gust of wind could do amazing things to an object weighing less than 1,000 pounds. The wind was so freakish, at the height of the storm, that boats moored to their slips in the yacht basin barely moved. The water was calm and John Miller and K. B. Kimball, who owned planes about 200 yards from the damaged planes, said their planes never budged.

Flying School and Air Taxi Service

The Grey Flying Service came into the world of flight instruction during the winter of 1946. Bob Grey started the school with three planes, but went bankrupt in May of 1948. Bob taught about 50 students during this time. He also picked up a newspaper route for the *St. Petersburg Independent* in 1947 to take up the slack of the flight school business. The *Independent's* slogan was: "If the sun don't shine, the paper's free".

In 1964 James Howell started an air taxi and charter plane service on the airstrip.

"Needless to say, we didn't give away many papers," Bob told a reporter of the *Island Sun* in the March 29,1989 issue. Bob's wife, Rhetta, and her pet raccoon were treated like royalty on the planes. The raccoon made many trips from Holmes Beach to Athens, Georgia, where the Greys had a home. Bob flew Rhetta to a Clearwater hospital when she was in labor with one of their children. He landed on a street near the hospital. Years later, Bob broke all the rules when he flew his plane under the Skyway Bridge just before the ribbon cutting ceremony.

"Living on the Island and running a flight school was dangerous in those days," Bob said. "But it was fun and exciting. One of the requirements for a flight student to get his license was to practice flying at night. In order for the planes to land safely, the runway had to be lit. We begged, borrowed or stole any lights we could find."

Rhetta and Bob were considered rebels by their parents for leaving an established lifestyle in New York and coming to a primitive Island. "We were the hippies of the '40s," Rhetta recalled.

The Island was especially susceptible to power failures and blackouts. Power lines were strung up in the trees and would often blow down during storms. A hurricane and tidal wave in 1947 blew the power lines down and temporarily closed the only bridge to the Island.

"We thought we would make a fortune that day," he said. "The surging seas and powerful winds caused people on the Island to evacuate." Since the bridge was out, the ideal way to get to the mainland was in one of Grey's planes. The few residents living on the Island used the planes to escape from the rising Gulf. Everyone made it to safety before the water literally covered the Island. Because there was sparse vegetation and few trees the water totally engulfed the land.

This plane overshot the runway and ended up in the canal

"It was scary," Bob said about the lack of protection during severe storms.

Millions of fiddler crabs once roamed wild on the dry, dusty airstrip. When a plane swooped in for a landing a trail of dead fiddlers could be seen.

Bill Laney had an air taxi service in 1953. He met regular airline planes in Tampa and dropped Island passengers off on the Holmes Beach airstrip, thus avoiding the 120-mile round trip by car. He charged by the hour or trip and could also teach anyone to fly. His company, named Airmotive, was located in Bradenton.

A new air taxi and boat charter service was initiated by Charters, Inc. with veteran Island pilot Carl Gulat heading the operation in the '50s. His company was located at 505 56th Street in Holmes Beach on the south end of the airstrip. The company owned a Model 182 Cessna, four-passenger plane, which was quartered on the airstrip and used for air taxi service. In addition, Charters, Inc. had twin-engine planes available for charter or ambulance work. Three charter-fishing boats, docked at the yacht basin, were in operation south of the Holmes Beach Yacht Club. Plans for a license to operate a taxicab service on the Island were being formulated at that time.

On December 7, 1953, a Trans Eastern Airways Cessna 195 set down on the airstrip, inaugurating the first regular plane service to and from the Island. This was definitely a step forward for the Island and revealed the foresight of those few who reserved the land for an airstrip. The new service linked the Island with all points in Florida, originating at Pinellas International Airport with stops at Tampa International Airport, Anna Maria Island and Venice. The fare from the Island to Tampa was only $5.25 plus tax and took about 20 minutes. There were two flights a day, at 8:15 a.m. and 3:50 p.m.

"The Holmes Beach Airport has been in operation for more than 20 years." This was the first line of the article in *The Islander* on September 3, 1970. The headline for the article was: "Island Airport Needs Runway Improved—NOW!" The story read: "During this time there have been close calls with airplanes taking off and landing on the grass and shell strip. Planes have overshot the runway, wheels have collapsed, and propellers have been damaged. On August 22, 1970 a man and his 20-year-old son taxied to the south end of the runway in a single-engine rented Cessna. The younger man was at the controls, there was light rain, but no wind. By the time the plane was off the runway it was barely off the ground. It hit pilings in Watson's Bayou, at the north end of the strip and crashed. Many people who live in homes near the airport want to see it closed because they say it is not safe. There are those who are in favor of the airport and consider it a real asset to the Island. They want to see the runway improved and lengthened. The Holmes Beach Board of Aldermen control the airport and have not made any effort to improve the runway. The only thing the aldermen have accomplished is to mow the grass portion of the field every few weeks."

The series of accidents made local and state officials pessimistic about the airport's fate. In 1965, a single-engine plane hit a power line near the Island Bank, flew the length of the strip, and flew away without being identified. The death knell for the airport sounded in the early '70s with the crash of a single-engine plane. Two people suffered injuries when the right wing of their Beechcraft Musketeer clipped the corner of the Gateway Marina at the south end of the runway in an abortive landing attempt. The plane cut off the top of a rubber tree at the rear of the building, struck some outriggers in a cabin cruiser in the bayou next to Pete Reynard's Yacht Club restaurant, and cartwheeled tail first into the water. It was sandwiched between the restaurant's seawall, a row of houseboats and other boats in the yacht basin. A Bradenton man jumped in the water and swam to the aid of the pilot, Gerald Strouse, age 36.

The fate of the airstrip had been hanging by a thread. Although the voters in Holmes Beach voted to keep the airport, the state aviation department said it did not meet their standards. Now, after this crash, residents thought it would be only a matter of weeks before the airport closed.

The August 16, 1973 issue of *The Islander* explained a plan to keep the airport alive operating the field as a heliport. Officials at MacDill Air Force Base in Tampa thought it was an excellent idea. It would be possible for pilots to fly in and out in emergencies.

After a battle about regulations, the Department of Transportation (DOT) closed the airport in October of 1973 to everything but helicopters landing at the airport. The simple fact was the airport failed to meet standards. The DOT gave the city six months to bring it up to code. The DOT spokesman said it would cost more than $500,000. That disclosure killed chances for keeping it open as a conventional airport. Several councilmen still hoped the field could be turned into a heliport.

"Holmes Family May Want Portion Of Airport Returned," was the surprising headline in the December 6, 1973 *Islander*. A couple of years before, the family deeded 177-feet that once was the north end of the municipal airport with the understanding it would remain in the city's ownership as long as the airport was in operation. "Since the DOT forced the closing of the airport the Holmes family may be considering asking the city to return the land to them," according to an *Islander* reporter.

John Holmes, Jr. said the city was stopping people from driving across what was once the northern end of the airstrip between the Holmes developments of Seaside Gardens and Shell Point condominiums.

"We deeded the property to the city to be used as an airport," he noted. "Now it's not being used as an airport, so why can't I drive across it?"

Not much was written in the papers about the airport in 1974 except the 177-feet was still being debated. The question of who owned the airport came to a head in October of 1974 when the Holmes Construction Company constructed a roadway across the airport extending from 63rd Street to a construction project on Shell Point. The airport's demise was in early 1975.

Building Bridges

The Cortez Bridge, the first and only link to Anna Maria Island, opened in 1922. The span of clattering wooden planks was barely wide enough for two cars to pass. While the bridge was being built in 1921, a devastating hurricane hit and much of the work was obliterated by the late-October storm. The story of the first bridge is told in the first Anna Maria Island history book, *"The Early Days."*

By the '40s, the bridge became more rickety, and was so narrow that all traffic had to be stopped so school

On March 3, 1957 the Cortez Bridge was dedicated. A crowd of 4,000 was on hand to watch the official bridge opening.

buses could traverse the swaying structure. The bridge moved with the wind and waves. Cars would make the boards bounce and bang which sounded like shot guns going off.

The Island population was about 800 at this time. Residents loved the solitude of their island and smiled while they waited for the hand-operated drawbridge on the Cortez Bridge to open for boats. The ritual of hand-cranking the cross arms stopped the cars. The turntable span was cranked by the bridge tender walking around and around while pushing his arms and chest against a crude wooden gear handle. The entire routine was done every time a boat passed through

A letter to the editor of *The Islander* in 1953 seemed to express the thoughts of many. "We rattled over the decrepit Cortez Bridge, which sounded like castanets of an inebriated Spanish dancer - only amplified a thousand times. As usual, men were replacing rotten boards at an annual cost probably as great as the interest on a new bridge. What new bridge? The one everyone talks about but nobody seems to do anything about. The shopping center signs at the approach to the bridge amused me. One says the only complete shopping center is in Bradenton Beach and another says an incomplete shopping center is in Holmes Beach."

Aspiring governor Leroy Collins drove across the old bridge in 1954. His reaction was, "This is terrible! This bridge must have been obsolete 20 years ago. It should be replaced without a day's delay. I do not see how the people around here tell if it's thundering or a car coming across. This is the worst bridge in the State of Florida."

Motorists were frustrated as they waited impatiently for the bridge tender to go through the long operation. When the bridge was open, a line of waiting cars could be seen the full length of Bridge Street down to Gulf Drive. It took about 15-minutes for a small boat to pass through. A tugboat or barge could take half an hour. Manatee County residents who would have liked to enjoy the public beach would not risk crossing the rickety old bridge with the death rattle in its boards. "Will Islanders be angry enough to get together in a mass meeting and make their voices heard in Tallahassee?" an *Islander* reporter queried.

In a 1955 issue of *The Islander,* a photograph of J. W. Bennett, the bridge tender, was shown hammering down large spikes which were sticking up on the bridge, a menace to tires of vehicles crossing. There was a sign stating,

“Load Limit of Six Tons.” Busloads of children crossed the bridge every day. Large machinery, concrete trucks and other heavy loads up to 18-tons used the bridge every working day.

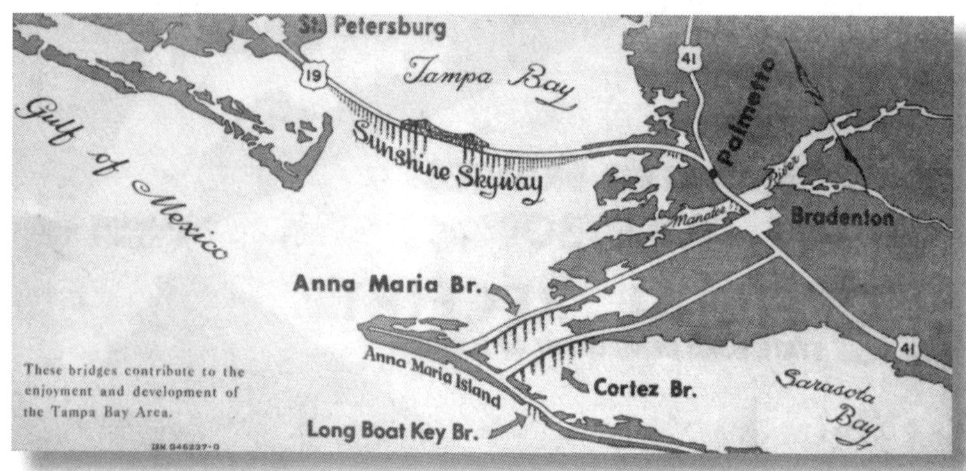

Tolls were discontinued in April of 1964.

Bennett was notified that he could keep his job when the new bridge was built. He had pushed the bascule draw six times a day, more than 2,000 times a year, thousands of times tramping around like a mule circling a well. Possibly in the future he could press a button.

A story in the *Bradenton Herald* on Jan. 18, 1955 reported that mainland filling station operators were being accused of unwittingly causing hard feelings between Bradenton and Anna Maria Island residents. They were discouraging tourists from visiting the Island because “the Cortez Bridge was liable to fall down.”

Headlines in the March 3,1955 *Islander* read: “Reporter Hits Bridge.” Bob Hanscom, a reporter for the *St. Petersburg Independent*, was driving to the Island to attend a meeting of the Manatee Press Club. He started through the draw of the decrepit Cortez Bridge and was met halfway by a huge truck, which took up most of the bridge. In a frantic effort to avoid the truck, he turned abruptly to the right and escaped with a dented fender. The truck went merrily on its way. Hanscom had a few unpleasant things to say about the narrow bridge and the truck driver when he arrived at the meeting at Holmes Beach Yacht Club.

When World War II came to an end everyone was eager to attract northern tourists and open Manatee County to development. A loud clamor began for good bridges. The Sunshine Skyway Bridge opened with great

The new Cortez Bridge can be seen in the center of the picture. The old Cortez Bridge is on the right.

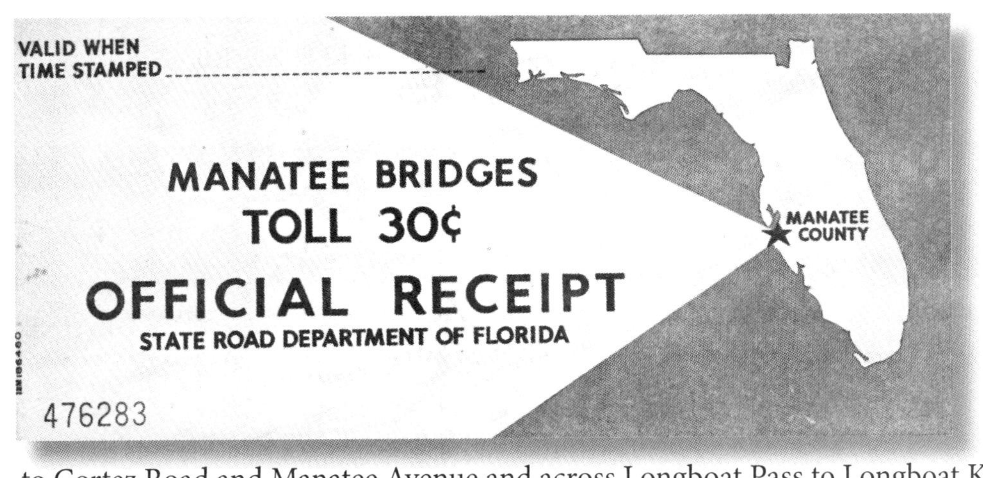
VALID WHEN
TIME STAMPED ______________

MANATEE BRIDGES
TOLL 30¢
OFFICIAL RECEIPT
STATE ROAD DEPARTMENT OF FLORIDA

476283

MANATEE COUNTY

fanfare in 1954, bringing promises of a new era of growth for the west coast of Florida.

In the '50s, the chairman of the state road department said they were doing everything humanly possible to get bridges to the Island. He said bonds had to be validated and sold for bridges to Cortez Road and Manatee Avenue and across Longboat Pass to Longboat Key. Finally, a decision was made to float bonds which would be paid off by tolls.

An *Islander* article on June 30, 1955, entitled, "Trouble Brewing On Mid-Island Bridge," stated a bridge would have been built in the '40s on the proposed Manatee Avenue site if a petition, signed by 60 Islanders, had not killed the project. Again in '55, petitions were prepared for the county commission and the state road department asking engineers to change their plans from a causeway and bridge to a bridge only. Petitioners wanted the road over the water to the bridge span to be built on pilings giving the water freedom to come and go. Most of the water was exceedingly shallow and under normal conditions less than a foot deep for hundreds of feet, especially from Perico Island.

Objectors to the causeway were old timers Tink Fulford, Louis Cobb and Elmer Raymond, who knew the waters and conditions and had experienced the 1921 hurricane when much of Anna Maria Island was inundated with a couple feet of water. The hurricane wiped Cortez Beach clean. Boats, fish houses and net dryers were destroyed. Perico and School Key were partially covered with water. In Holmes Beach Sportsman's Harbor, where

A crowd of 17,000 watched the Great Arturo Wallenda walk on a tight rope across Longboat Pass to celebrate building of the Longboat Key bridge in 1940.

St. Bernard's Catholic Church is located, the water reached the top step of Capt. Jones' house and drowned many of Mrs. Jones' ducks.

In 1954, the State Improvement Commission was threatened with a lawsuit if the mid-Island bridge was to lead directly into Manatee Avenue. At the end of 1955, city officials were confident that the construction of the new bridge would start within 60 days. All preliminary surveys were complete. The program would include five new bridges in Manatee County: Anna Maria Bridge would span the bay and end at the public beach; a bridge would replace the Cortez Bridge, another would be between Anna Maria Island and Longboat Key. A bridge across the Manatee River would relieve congestion on Green Bridge and a bridge would be built across the Braden River at Arcadia Road. The mid-Island and Cortez spans would be toll bridges and the others free. The cost of the five-bridge project was estimated at $6,000,000.

Legal obstructions were cleared, and the Cortez Bridge began to take shape in 1956. The location was a few hundred feet north of the old bridge. Concrete and massive steel pilings were driven down into the bottom of the bay.

Harry Varley, editor of *The Islander* in the '50s, was known to be a bit verbose in his ramblings. He wrote: "Prosperity may come to Anna Maria Island riding in over the new bridges, but there will be other passengers. Hoodlums and crimes will follow as close as shadows with the increasing wealth. There is nothing to worry about, but surely something to get ready for.

"While the Cortez Bridge remains the only exit from the Island, there is little inducement for outside gangsters or crooks to come here for their nefarious purposes. In a matter of seconds a roadblock could bar escape. The drawbridge could be opened in minutes.

"With three bridges and a larger, richer population more stores and greater accumulations of money on our bankless Island, we shall become more desirable to crooks. In our three-divided corporate area, there is little chance of planning law enforcement on an Island–wide basis with any hope it would work well.

"The county sheriff would cooperate, but could only furnish limited help. Too much time would elapse before the highway patrol could get to the location of the trouble, especially at the north end.

"This is one good reason for all-Island incorporation before all bridges come. Not only law enforcement, but all other subjects of government could be discussed and plans made to meet the needs of our fast-growing Island. There should be a huge leap forward and incredibly fast progress when the bridges are built."

There was an astounding amount of misinformation published over the years about the bridge project and the bond issue. Another note of discouragement came from those who had worked and fought so hard for the bridges. Once the bridges had been assured, there was more criticism than ever from sources strangely silent when the battle to get the bridges was in progress.

Islanders were fed up with talk about bridges. They felt whatever measures could be employed, no matter how drastic, they should be initiated to make the powers-that-be transform words into action. One bulldozer or pile driver at work would be more convincingly satisfactory that 10,000 words.

Nevertheless, two concrete and steel bridges opened in 1957, and a third link to the Island, the Longboat Key Bridge, followed in 1958. On March 3, 1957, the Cortez Bridge dedication was held to the delight of everyone on and off the Island. It was the largest celebration those on the Island had ever seen. A crowd of 4,000 was on hand to watch the official bridge opening. A carnival, encompassing the entire Island, included street dancing, circus acts and a water ski show. Airplanes soaring over the Island and costumed dancing girls were something to behold. Bathing beauties from the Christiani Brothers Circus, riding elephants were the first to cross the bridge. They were followed by a caravan of officials and a steady stream of hundreds of cars traveling bumper-to-bumper.

Bridge Street was the scene of many festivities. Music from an American Legion Band filled the air and dancing went on until midnight. Another carnival, with a Ferris wheel and roller coaster, was going on in Holmes Beach. At Manatee Public Beach, performances by the Sarasota High School Sailor Circus and a wax replica display of the Last Supper attracted throngs.

In Anna Maria City, the Bradenton Water Ski Club put on a show between the Rod and Reel Pier and the

City Pier. A spectacular fireworks display lit up the sky in the evening. Boat parades, airplane sightseeing and moonlight sails continued the festive atmosphere into the night.

One of Florida's favorite native sons, former judge and governor, Senator Spessard L. Holland, cut the ribbon declaring the Cortez Bridge open on March 3rd and dedicated it to the people. At a luncheon, held at the Gulf Terrace Restaurant, more than 100 state and county dignitaries heard Senator Holland reminisce about the many summers he and his wife had spent on Anna Maria Island. "Good fellowship prevails on this Island," he said. "I'm glad to see they made the span wide enough with protected areas for fishermen." The bridge was 2,629 feet long with a vertical clearance of 17.6 feet.

A few days later, the disintegrating old Cortez Bridge was torn down. About 670-feet were saved on the western end for a fishing pier. In two weeks 82,820 vehicles, each paying a 15-cent toll, had crossed the new bridge.

The Admiral charter boat was one of the first ships to go under the new bridge.

On the back of the toll receipt for the Cortez Bridge was a sketch of the surrounding area designating the mid-Island bridge as Palma Sola Bridge. The Bradenton and Anna Maria Island Chambers of Commerce requested the new bridge be known as Anna Maria Bridge. Their argument was the name would be historically significant and the best promotion of the Gulf beaches.

Many asked if there would be a yearly rate for residents, such as monthly commuter tickets like railroads issue to passengers. It was recommended a straight toll charge per vehicle, every trip, in each direction be made. Pedestrians, including fishermen who passed the tollgate, would be charged the vehicular rate. The State Road Department tried to work out a plan where the tolls would be removed in five or six years.

The fire marshal asked that fire vehicles of the Anna Maria Island Fire Control District be given free passage on the bridges. On April 25, 1959, headlines appeared in the *St. Petersburg Times*: "Heavy, Heavy Toll Hangs Over Anna Maria's Head. The 30-cent round-trip toll to Anna Maria Island looks about as perpetual as death and

The Humpback Bridge replaced "Hangman's Bridge" on Bay Boulevard.

taxes!"

The majority of Islanders were willing to pay tolls for a safe bridge, and to be free from the daily menace of the worn-out span which could have been smashed to smithereens in a moderate storm. There were grumblings, especially among older residents, of paying tolls when other communities were getting toll-free bridges. After all, *The Islander* editor wrote, "Islanders pay a high tax on gasoline which should entitle them to vastly more consideration than they have received."

At precisely 3 p.m. on Sept. 4, 1957, the Anna Maria Bridge, which ended at the Manatee Public Beach, was open for traffic. There were no ribbons, trumpets, drums or elephants, and not one governing official from the Town of Holmes Beach or any other town was on hand.

On April 28, 1964, the collection of tolls on the two Island bridges was discontinued. Harry Varley, editor/publisher of *The Islander,* had the distinction of paying the first toll when the Anna Maria Bridge opened on Sept. 4, 1957 and paid the last toll collected on that bridge. A ribbon was cut, opening the bridge to free traffic, and rousing music by the Manatee High School band marked the end of an era. A black casket and wreath of old toll receipts were placed beneath the sign, "Rest In Pieces." Almost immediately State Road Department employees started dismantling the toll plaza.

Discontinuation of the tolls was made possible by the refinancing of the balance of a $6-million bond issue which provided funds to build the two bridges to the mainland, plus the span to Longboat Key.

Land for sale tripled in value on the Island because of the new bridges. Developers who had bought huge tracts of land for a few hundred dollars a lot were selling them for $3,000 and up.

The wooden bridge to Longboat Key was less than a year old when the hurricane of 1926 swept up from Miami and damaged the structure linking the southern end of Anna Maria Island to Longboat Key. In 1932, following two weeks of constant winds which raised the water level in the bay, one of the most devastating spring storms in the history of the west coast swept the bridge into the bay. For the next 26 years, there was no bridge. In 1958, the drawbridge was completed and the Town of Longboat Key was formed.

In 1940, a scheme to build a toll bridge between Longboat Key and Anna Maria Island was conceived by a group of men from Tampa and a super-salesman, Eugene M. Elliott. He gained fame when he raised $1-million to build the Gandy Bridge between Tampa and St. Petersburg in 1924.

According to Ralph Hunter's book, *From Calusas to Condominiums*, the group engaged one of the top bridge builders in the country, got permission from the War Department and planned a grand celebration to commemorate the event. Some bought shares of stock hoping the bridge would stimulate tourism. In October of 1940, advertisements appeared in area newspapers promoting a free barbecue on March 14, 1941.

The *Sarasota Herald-Tribune* reported there were 17,000 people at the celebration. "The hillbilly rhythm of the Gulf Coast Cracker Band had folks dancing. All ages took part in a jitterbug contest. A golf exhibition was in full swing, and the essay contest had many entrants. Powerboats cruised on the Gulf of Mexico, and planes circled overhead. Enthusiastic crowds ate thousands of pounds of barbecued meat with all the trimmings and saw the Great Arturo walk on a tight rope across the Longboat Pass. The program was opened by Bradenton Mayor Charles W. Ward who said, "This bridge, built upon rock, will remain a permanent structure. In this time of war, when billions are bring spent on destruction, it is a pleasure to witness this event."

Crowds gathered to watch as the ceremonial concrete was poured. It was reported later no one had paid for the concrete. According to Ralph Hunter, the men who were going to build the bridge disappeared, taking the stock money with them. To this day no one knows what happened to the men or how much money was stolen. The stock buyers would not admit they fell for the scheme.

In the City of Anna Maria on North Bay Boulevard near the City Pier, a primitive bridge of planks was constructed by Sam Adams in 1946. The water flowing from Tampa Bay to Lake La Vista was known as "the ditch." Later a drawbridge was built. In 1952, Chief of Police George Jordan printed a sign stating the drawbridge on Bay Boulevard had been condemned. He said the city commissioners had condemned the bridge. However, when asked by an *Islander* reporter the commissioners said they knew nothing about it. Since several planks needed to be replaced, the bridge was closed for repairs. Despite the fact it was risky for two cars to pass on the 15-foot bridge, the side rails were loose and the bridge was no longer functional as a drawbridge, drivers were assured they could cross at no danger of dropping into the canal. It was known as "Hangman's Bridge" because the rope and pulley system resembled a hangman's rope.

At a city meeting in June of 1952, H. B. Miller presented a drawing for a humpback bridge on Bay Boulevard to replace the drawbridge. He stated this type of bridge would enable the opening of a yacht basin which would benefit the city. A mishap occurred the next year when a workman left the bridge open while working on the mechanism that controlled the raising of the bridge. A driver saw the open span too late and his car took a nosedive into the canal. No one was hurt and little damage was done.

In August of 1954, *The Islander* reported men were repairing "Hangman's Bridge." The editor of *The Islander* stated vehemently it should not be repaired. "It should be abolished. It is an eyesore, a civic atrocity and a useless piece of mechanism. Not once has it been raised to permit passage of a yacht. A rowboat cannot go under it at high tide unless occupants push up against the bridge."

In February of 1958, several newspapers carried photographs of cars driving across the new bridge on North Bay Boulevard. This bridge, as envisioned by H. B. Miller, replaced Hangman's Bridge and exists today. Captions under the photographs read: "Though the bridge is open to traffic it cannot be paved and finished until the fill has settled." Work was also underway on another bridge that would span Crescent Drive, in Anna Maria City. The developers were from Clearwater.

The May 31,1956 issue of *The Islander* told of the construction of a bridge to the mosquito-filled mangrove swamps of School Key, which later became Key Royale. The bridge, which would be high enough to permit passage of any craft using the channel beneath, would connect Key Royale Drive to the 150-acre School Key, east of Anna Maria Island.

The *Bradenton Herald* carried this exciting news on Feb. 14, 1960: "Heavy machines have begun to dig the first of 12 canals which will transform the jungles of School Key into one of the finest residential communities on Florida's west coast."

On The Bridge

Written by Marion Colman in 1939

Jaunty little sail boat floating down the bay!
Hurry up, you slow poke. We can't wait all day.

Motors lined up by the draw waiting just for you
As if there wasn't anything in all the world to do.

There's that load of lumber for Billy's garagettes,
Candy for the corner store, bread and cigarettes.

Matters of great moment awaiting all of us;
Some are even trying to catch the morning bus.

Saucy little sailboat, who do you think you are
That you should take precedence over a motor car?

You who have no motor nor even any oar,
Lift your skirts and scurry through and bother us no more.

Marion Colman, granddaughter of George Emerson Bean, the first homesteader on Anna Maria Island, was known as the Poet Laureate of Anna Maria Island.

Commercial fishermen caught tons of fish in their nets.

Fishing Spots

The motto of the early *Islander* newspaper was: "Anna Maria Island- Where Life Is Peaceful and Fishing Is Good." Over the years, the Anna Maria City Pier, built in the early 1900's at the end of Pine Avenue, continued to deteriorate, but somehow it held together until the mid-1970s when two-thirds of the dock walkway was carried off in a storm. The city had to pay $30,000 to replace the missing section. There is probably not a stick of the original wood left, but the City Pier has retained its 1912 look of "the way we were." The pier embodies the spirit and character of Anna Maria Island.

John Adams remembers in the early '50s he and his friends would get old meat from the IGA grocery store and put it on the roof of the pier to rot. When it was good and ripe, they baited a shark hook with it, added a chain leader, several hundred feet of heavy rope and a bunch of tin cans.

"At night we would go out to the Anna Maria Pier, throw the baited hook out and tie the end to a bench seat that was nailed to the pier. Then we'd go inside and shoot pool. Shooting pool on a swaying dock required considerable anticipatory skill. When we heard the tin cans rattle we would run out and pull in a good-sized shark.

"One night we ran out and saw the bench and a number of planks from the pier heading up the bay. We never saw that shark, but we knew it was a good one."

In 1954, Lefty and Wanda Miller took over the restaurant on the end of the City Pier. With her reputation as a cook and his as a fisherman, they were sure to make a success of this new venture. Pier expenses became a bone of contention in August of that year. The city paid about $2,500 a year to run the pier. Some thought the city should not support it since visitors used it more than residents. At a city meeting, C. M. Bayless said if the pier was destroyed they might as well put a headstone at the North Point and a footstone at the south border of Anna Maria City, because there would be a dead city in between.

This aerial picture of the Rod and Reel Pier and the City Pier was taken in the early '50s.

One commissioner stated there was another pier, the Rod and Reel Pier had just been built. Commissioner Bill Brier said nothing. It was his own private pier for the use of those who rented his Rod and Reel Motel units.

The mayor changed the discussion to the City Pier and hinted that the city might get help from the county for maintenance of the City Pier. He said his board had come up with the idea of charging 25-cents admission to the City Pier. Bayless thought the city should borrow enough money to put the City Pier in good condition, so it would need no annual maintenance expense. "They keep patching a worn out, leaky roof when they need a new roof," he exclaimed.

Lights and flags were installed on the City Pier in 1958, so storm warnings could be flown day and night. In 1969, Lefty lost the franchise to operate the pier to another bidder.

In 1974, a storm washed away 200-feet of the walkway and damaged the remainder. The bait house and restaurant weathered the storm. In 1988, Tropical Storm Keith damaged the pier again. Broken pilings were washed away and large areas of the deck were destroyed. Most of the floor of the restaurant was gone and the interior was exposed to water and weather. The restaurant was torn down, and pier aficionados were looking forward to a new look of the old landmark. "Fast Eddie" Porter leased the restaurant. The same year members of the Anna Maria Civic Association worked to get the pier on the National Registry of Historic Places. After being reviewed in Tallahassee it was turned down.

Over the years, the historic Anna Maria Pier has been the most popular place on the Island to fish. Old timers tell of the "tons" of fish they hauled in. Now the pier is more of a place to meet friends and chat about the good old days. Fishing is slow, but it's a lovely walk out to the end to see dolphins roll, gorgeous sunsets and the picturesque Skyway Bridge in the distance.

It was March 1953, and what a sight along the Gulf beaches. In the water were dead fish by the millions. The skies were full of birds, diving into the schools of fish and on the shore were happy anglers. Bathers, a few feet from shore, could not help stepping on schools of fish. Father Kniveton, vicar of the Church of the Annunciation, borrowed a neighbor's shovel and lifted some jacks up between the rock groins in front of his home. He could have shoveled many more. Bob Cable brought several king mackerel weighing 20-pounds and more to the *Islander* editor. A beach cleaning party, to remove the fish carcasses from the beach, was formed at the Clever Cottages in Anna Maria City, with F. W. Cooper in charge.

In 1974 a 48-foot sperm whale washed ashore south of the City Pier.

That same year Frances Livingston, a realtor and avid angler, landed a whopper of a tarpon on the flats near the bay. The big fellow was on display at George Wagner's Bayou Fishing Center. It was five-feet long and 124-pounds, and gave five giant leaps, but Frances knew how to land it.

In November of 1954, Bay and Gulf waters were alive with mullet. Commercial fishermen were hauling them in, along with sizable sport fish, by the ton. The water boiled with mullet in the canals. Residents demanded the cities take steps to enforce the ordinance against commercial net fishing within 1500-feet of a municipality. Some fishermen came into bayside residents' front yards, which was annoying by day, but worse at night since strong lights were used.

There were many reports of good catches of king mackerel moving into Island waters in April 1955. Three men aboard a small boat caught 74 kings averaging 10-pounds each.

Dr. Ralph French and Frank Cavendish are pictured with the 1,386 pound, 17-foot hammerhead shark caught off the Rod and Reel Pier in 1960. Doc French made an incision in the shark and 143 baby sharks were released into the water.

Ever since John Stanley got the idea in 1947 to build a 500-foot- long fishing pier adjacent to his motel, the Rod and Reel Pier weathered the times and defiantly stretched its arm into Tampa Bay. Records say the pier was built in 1950 by Capt. Dewey Adams and Jim Hackney, and completed Feb. 10, 1950. The pier had many owners since Stanley, but the best remembered were Nel and Frank Cavendish who took over in 1962 and operated it for 20 years. Every day a new adventure awaited anglers who frequented the popular pier.

Nel did the cooking and Frank provided real character to the pier. Frank never wore shoes, and every day at 3 p.m. he would dive off the top deck for a swim to entertain the tourists. The presence of large sharks never discouraged Frank from swimming from one end of the pier to the beach every afternoon. It was a night swim that stopped the ritual.

"All of a sudden I saw this "old boy" heading for me," he told a reporter. "I curled up in a little ball so he couldn't bite my legs. He turned away from me, but swatted me with his tail. A shark's tail is like sandpaper. That tail peeled me like an orange. It took four Manhattans and a box of Band-Aids to get over it."

With Frank at the helm there was always something going on. He had kids fishing tournaments and used the pier as a weigh-in station for the Annual Tarpon Tournament. The Island Privateers organization was founded on the top deck. In the '60s and '70s, Frank would throw out large hooks baited with huge fish when he left at night. In the morning it was not unusual for a monster shark to be thrashing around at the end of the line.

An account in the *Island Herald* stated Cavendish caught 779 sharks weighing 160-pounds or more. On June

George Norwood is pictured throwing the net he made off the City Pier.

28, 1973, Frank spent the night on the pier. He wrapped an old tire around a piling to absorb the shock and let out 40-feet of stout rope, eight–feet of chain, and an enormous hook with a 15-pound stingray for bait. The entire pier shook when a monster shark hit the hook in the middle of the night. The next morning Cavendish waited for the pier regulars to appear and help him get the huge hammerhead shark up on a pulley.

Ralph "Doc" French dove into the water and wrapped a rope around the shark's tail. The shark was too tired to attack. They finally got it up and found it weighed 1,386-pounds and measured 17-feet. This record has never been broken. A pair of hammerheads, more than 13-feet long, and the 17-foot giant, got Frank's name into the record books. When he caught a big one, he would call all the local watering holes and proclaim he just caught the biggest shark of the season. Word would spread all over the Island and the pier would be crowded with the curious who were also thirsty for beer and hungry for tasty hot dogs. The cash register never stopped jingling.

"My grandfather (Frank Cavendish) stopped shark fishing when the movie, "Jaws" came out," recalled Rodney O'Quinn. The jaws of the mammoth hammerhead were displayed at Pete Reynard's Yacht Club restaurant for years. Island dentist, Dr. Jack Richardson, crowned several of the teeth with gold. The jaws can now be seen in the Anna Maria Island Historical Museum, 402 Pine Avenue, Anna Maria. One day a nine-year-old boy baited a hook on the Rod and Reel Pier and caught a hammerhead shark that measured 48-inches between the eyes. Island writer Wyatt Blassingame always liked the old pier.

"The pilings were cracked and rotting, and Old Man Cavendish was gone," he said. "But the man who tosses out a hook baited with a generous slab of stingray still has a good shot for a shark.

"When I first came out here we'd sit on the pier, play poker and fish for sharks," said Wyatt, who lived on the Island for over 50 years. "We'd throw out bait and wrap the line around the bucket while we played cards. Every once in a while, you'd hear the bucket clanking and you'd know you had a shark on. Shark jaws fascinate me," he said, admiring the impressive dentures of a 6-foot dusky just caught on the pier. "Look at those teeth. Not one row, but four or five!"

Jeff Klinkenberg, a columnist for the *St. Petersburg Times*, interviewed Wyatt on the pier. Wyatt had just completed a four-month study of sharks, and his latest book, *The Wonder of Sharks*, had just been published. His interest in nature was more than a hobby. Wyatt Blassingame was a well-known writer who in 54 years produced 600 magazine articles, four adult novels and 57 books, most of them about natural history for young readers.

In 1975 shark fishing came to an abrupt halt. The public's fascination in sharks was evident after the scary film "Jaws" came out. Frank said after the thriller was released, if he were to hang another shark from the pier, 2,000 people would come out to see it, and the pier would fall into the pass.

The *Islander* reported 10,000 reds were caught at the Rod and Reel Pier in six days. Frank Cavendish was quoted as saying, "We were standing three deep at the end of the pier and pulling in so many fish that they had to close the windows in the restaurant to keep the fish out."

What causes sharks to attack? No one really knows. There have been no attacks reported in the waters around Anna Maria Island. Holmes Beach Police Chief W. H. "Snooks" Adams was born and reared in the fishing village of Cortez. His parents and their families, the Fulfords and the Adamses, were commercial fishermen who had almost daily contact with sharks all their lives on the west coast of Florida.

"In all those years I never heard of any commercial fisherman losing his life to a shark," Snooks said. "Fishermen constantly get sharks in their gill nets with all the trash fish and stingrays. It is common to herd out the trash fish through an opening in the net. I've guided sharks out by taking hold of their front fin. I was never bitten, and I don't know any commercial fisherman who was. The sharks are after fish, not man."

Anglers from across the United States and some foreign countries have spent many happy times relaxing on the City Pier where an excellent view of the Sunshine Skyway Bridge and the North Point of the Island can be seen. In 1980, Frank sold the Rod and Reel Pier, and he passed away in November of 1987.

During a rain squall in 1974, a 48-foot sperm whale washed ashore just south of the City Pier. As the whale lay on its side, hardly moving in the water, its big eye seemed to be watching the men as they circled close in boats less than half the size of the giant sea creature. Jack Bass of Holmes Beach maneuvered his open boat within a few feet of the sperm whale's tail as the dying monster rested on its side near the pier.

What made the sperm whale special to scientists around the country was the fact that it was alive when discovered in the bay off the Island. Veterinarians from the St. Petersburg Aquarium performed an autopsy. The doctors struggled to climb on top of the whale to extract blood with a hypodermic syringe. They said it was a full-grown male sperm whale.

The protected waters of Florida's Gulf Coast were not its natural habitat. Although whales are found in tropical waters, they are sometimes spotted well off the coast in the middle of the Gulf. These whales are plentiful off the Atlantic and Pacific coasts. Another thing that was most unusual about the whale washing up near shore to die is that whales normally die in deep waters. Island boats hauled the immense carcass to Egmont Key.

On March 3, 1957 the modern steel and concrete, $1-million Cortez Bridge opened to great fanfare. Islanders were ecstatic. It was the largest celebration ever on the Island. In July 1957, there was a chance the old bridge would be given to Bradenton Beach. Robert Hall wanted to make the existing end of the bridge a pier named Holiday Marina. He anticipated boats tied alongside the pier in rented slips and seats along the railings. Fishermen could haul in fish without paying a bridge toll. Hall could foresee a building containing an oyster bar and snack counter and a float which would be equipped with gasoline pumps and other marine supplies.

The mayor and councilmen were opposed. The mayor was afraid of the expense of maintaining the pier. But the public demanded a pier. Finally Hall agreed there would be no expense to the city, and the council agreed to accept the free pier. In the meantime, the men who had agreed to put up money for the project dropped out. However, there was some satisfaction. Had it not been for Hall's dream it was doubtful if the city would own a free fishing pier.

Here's a whale of a tale from Don Moore, editor of *The Islander,* written in 1973: "Residents and visitors gawked in disbelief as they drove past the city barn near the foot of Cortez Bridge. The city's sanitation crew and volunteers strained, pushed and pulled a huge black carcass, lowered it with the help of a wrecker, and managed to load it into the rear of a garbage truck. The 17-foot, 2,000-pound denizen of the deep had washed up dead on the beach between two erosion jetties at Seventh Street South in Bradenton Beach." The story did not identify the monster sea creature.

First Public Beach

In 1947, a mid-Island stretch of land from Gulf Drive to the Gulf of Mexico, was created by a special legislature act and ratified by voters to be known as Manatee County Public Beach. Permission was granted by the National Production Authority.

Bids came in during May 1951 for the construction of the first unit of buildings. Cost of the building, which would include restrooms, lockers, showers and a small concession stand, was estimated at $18,000. Plans called for a structure 80-feet long and 38-feet wide, with a roof hanging over the sidewalk at the base of the building. The roof would double as a sun deck. A tax of one mill for five years financed the project. After building restrictions were lifted, plans to build an auditorium, restaurants, swimming pool and pier with a combination groin were made. The structure was designed by Bail, Horton and Associates.

The Public Beach officially opened Sunday, Dec. 16, 1951 with a ceremony at the pavilion. Tribute was paid to a large group of dedicated volunteers who had worked closely with members of the Beach Committee for the public beach and the proposed Manatee Avenue Bridge; both were major developments on Anna Maria Island. It was hoped the building would be equal to and even exceed any others on the west coast of Florida.

Mr. and Mrs. Percy Gabert, the first managers, were in charge of making the facility available to the public for parties, dances (which would be held on top of the pavilion) and other socials.

One of the highlights at the beach during the '60s was the rousing Beachcombers Fair. Starting in 1951 this was an annual event, and a great many activities took place at the same time in various spots on the Island. "There's A Big Day Coming!" was the headline under a photo showing a wide expanse of sand at the Public Beach in *The Islander* in March of 1952. The second Beachcombers Fair, a weekend of fun, was in full swing. "Swim, sing, dance, chat with friends, greet strangers," the article read. The Lions Club boasted that Melvin Davis, the finest chef on the west coast, was on hand to cook delicious barbecued meats. Island women baked a

A ceremony at the pavilion on Dec. 16, 1951 officially opened the Manatee County Public Beach.

glorious assortment of mouth-watering pies, cakes and cookies.

Young folks danced on the deck of the pavilion under sunny skies or stars. The latest fad was surf dancing. The girls wore pedal pushers and the boys rolled up their pants and they danced along the water's edge. The more orthodox dancers could be seen on the roof of the pavilion, sometimes called the Beach House, which had been polished and waxed for the occasion. Danceable tunes by the Tea-Bags Orchestra, of radio and dance hall fame, set the mood.

The official Beachcombers headgear was a raggedy straw hat, symbolizing the carefree spirit of the Island beachcombers. Everyone wore one, the shabbier the better. The Manatee High School Band played all Saturday afternoon at the pavilion. Contests for the kids were hilarious. They tried to climb the greased pole to get the $5 bill on top. There were pie eating contests, target throws, obstacle, foot, spoon, and sack races. Prior to the boat races in Tampa Bay, a group of nefarious Beachcombers came ashore searching for buried treasures. Fishermen from one end of the Island to the other entered the Island-wide fishing contest. Dewey Adams judged the biggest and best catch. The Beachcomber costume parade and the baby parade were hits.

By July 1952, the Manatee County Public Beach was well-known throughout the county as the most popular gathering place. Organizations planned all sorts of festive events on the beach. The most popular events were the frequent fish fries attended by most of the Island residents and visitors. By October of 1952, the beach was open from 10 a.m. to 6 p.m. daily, and Bob Pennstrom was the manager.

The county commission approved an extension of the pavilion roof in January 1953, and a patio breezeway was added.

"What this beach needs most is a good bridge to get to it," a news article stated. "The Beach Committee will take care of everything else." In August, Public Beach manager Pennstrom was quoted as saying it had been a "whopping summer."

A three-day carnival was planned for the Island in August 1954 in celebration of the opening of the spectacular Sunshine Skyway Bridge. Public Beach manager A. J. Norman was the organizer. Plans were made for a baseball game, dances, circus, bathing beauty contest, anglers tournament, water skiing demonstrations and round-the-Island tours. To encourage visitors, many of the motel and rental unit owners offered a weekend family rate of $15.

Three outstanding citizens received awards of merit at the Beachcomber Fair held at the newly built Manatee Beach pavilion. Thomas Baggs, left, a member of the Beachcomber Club, presented the awards to Jack Holmes, Sr., who developed a model community; Richard B. Ernest, mayor of Anna Maria, who helped make the Youth Center a success and Bernard Wagaman, who was responsible for the incorporation of Bradenton Beach.

During the summer months, the Red Cross Water Safety program was held at the Public Beach with all Manatee County School children participating.

The Island Kiwanis Club took over the operation of the Public Beach in November of 1954. The Kiwanians bought a piano and a heater for the room in the pavilion where they held meetings. In December, Santa Claus arrived on a bright red fire truck at the beach to the delight of the children who received toys and goodies from the jolly old man.

Close to 500 attended the band concert and chicken barbecue at the Public Beach in January 1955. The Bradenton Beach Fire Department served more than 1,000 chicken dinners and turned in a large profit to help pay off the debt on the firehouse. There were more people at the Public Beach than ever before. It was June in

January, but the water was a chilly 62-degrees.The crowds were a forewarning of what was going to happen when the bridge to the mainland was completed.

A helicopter landed on the public beach in September of 1956. Islanders were surprised and concerned about the Public Beach becoming an airstrip for helicopters. Their fears were laid to rest. It was an Army plane carrying agriculture observers of medfly operations and they had dropped down to refuel.

The Christiani Brothers' three-ring circus came to the Public Beach on Oct. 31, 1957 and presented exciting

Special events at the annual Beachcomber Fair attracted crowds to the Public Beach in 1952.

afternoon and evening performances. Sponsored by the Island Junior Chamber, more than 100 performers from around the world drew large crowds. The Christiani bareback riders were recognized as the royal family of the circus world. Kids of all ages were entranced with the Siamese elephants, aerialists, jugglers, aerial bears, dancing palominos, trained dogs and ponies, beautiful girls and hilarious clowns.

A full time lifeguard, employed by the county beach commission, was on duty from 10 a.m. to 5 p.m. daily in December of 1957. Additional lifeguards were employed when crowds increased. An unsinkable fiberglass boat, which could be launched by one man, was near the lifeguard stand. It was equipped with ropes on each side to offer a handhold to those being rescued.

Rules and regulations were posted: No dogs, no fires and no bottles. The library, run by the Kiwanians, brought in monies which were distributed to local charities, and a staff of 12 fulltime employees was assisted by Kiwanis volunteers.

Parachutists thrilled crowds at the Public Beach on Saturday afternoon in April of 1958. Merritt Hurlbert, foreman of the Visioneering Company of Sarasota, and his brother, Larry, put on the sky-high show for employees of the company who were enjoying an afternoon lunch at the beach. The men were members of the Tampa Sky Divers. They bailed out of a small plane 3,000 feet over the public beach, but a south wind carried them north where they touched down.

No one questioned the statement that the Public Beach was Manatee County's greatest asset. The county commission decided to take immediate steps to protect what was left of the beach after the June 17, 1959 storm that gouged out many feet of beach. A plan was prepared for artificial nourishment of 1,300 feet of beachfront and installation of three groins. The possibility of federal aid and securing sand from dredging the channel of the West Coast Waterway was explored.

Following the damage caused by tropical storm Brenda at the end of July, a comprehensive program of artificial renourishment was recommended by Jay Langfelder, an engineer from Florida Coastal Engineering Laboratory at the University of Florida. The renourishment was not a one-time undertaking. Sand would be continually lost, so the renourishment would be repeated time and again.

In 1964, a new anti-erosion pier was constructed at the Public Beach, 460-foot in length. A build-up of sand was apparent at the shore end of the pier. The pier and groin were designed as a beach stabilization measure by world-famous, Sydney Makepeace Wood. It was the first of its kind in Florida.

South End Public Beach Opposed

In 1954, the citizens of Bradenton Beach were vocal in expressing their views of a public beach in their city. They were against it. They were good Americans, and did not want to deprive any citizen of any rights because of race, color or creed. It was not a question of segregation. They just did not want a public beach of any kind in the City of Bradenton Beach. Mayor Jack Jones said it would be a terrible mistake to create a public beach at the south end of the city.

"There is no more dangerous place to swim," he stated. "The distance around the Pass between Anna Maria and Longboat Key is highly hazardous. There are strong currents and powerful undertows."

The *Bradenton Herald* reported: "The location of a Negro public beach on the south end of the Island has been tentatively approved at a meeting of the Public Beach Commission."

It had also been approved by the Negro Civic and Businessman's League of Manatee County. How a Negro beach could be established with public money was unclear since the anti-segregation ruling by the U.S. Supreme Court.

The editor of *The Islander* asked, "Why on Anna Maria Island, when there was not a single colored taxpayer or resident living here?"

Who was responsible for this decision? Chairman J. Pope Harllee, Jr. said, "We have to put a Negro beach somewhere, or eventually let Negroes use the existing Public Beach in Holmes Beach."

Anna Maria Mayor Paul Carlisle assured the delegation the proposed beach at the southern end would be "admirably suited for a public beach."

Realtor Jack Marshall stated, "This is the most serious situation our Chamber has ever faced. A Negro beach on the Island would mean the end of high property values. The Negro agencies would attempt to force the sale of Island property to Negroes. It would open the Island to them. It would be against our way of life and the future growth. No Negro beach on Anna Maria Island!"

Should the south end become a public beach was the biggest problem the Island ever faced. From 13th Street in Bradenton Beach to the Longboat Bridge was nine-tenths of a mile. This was about 150-acres, not including the right of way for the road and nearly two miles of Gulf and Bay beaches with no buildings. The owners, since 1912, were represented by Dan Blalock of Wyman, Green and Blalock of Bradenton. The all-important question was if the state could take personal property with erosion control as the reason. Prior to building the road, pumping in most of the present land was an expenditure of $750,000 for erosion control. This section of the Island was a tangled mass of jungle, a mosquito breeding swamp and the road was impassable for cars. The entire shoreline was prey to the Gulf which was constantly eating away the land. As it stood it was uninhabitable.

In July 1954, the Public Beach Commission abandoned its attempt to make a segregated beach at the south end of the Island. A new public beach would be near the end of the causeway leading to the Sunshine Skyway Bridge.

Members of the Anna Maria Citizens League voted again to ask authorities for a public beach at the south end of the Island in October of 1958. However, legal rights to the area were in doubt. Bradenton Beach Mayor Van Rensselaer was adamantly opposed to the south end becoming a public beach. He suggested giving the land to the Blalock interests with the hope that "by building large hotels, apartment houses and fine residences a large amount of tax revenue would be brought into the county."

Looking north from the newly completed Longboat Key Bridge the southern end of the Island can be seen. This is now called Coquina Beach.

In the early 1900's, E. P. Green, a real estate man, bought most of the southern end of the Island. When condemnation suits on the south end were filed by the State Road Department (STD) in 1956 none were filed on Green's property. The STD got a right of entry letter from the Manatee National Bank, trustee for the estate. Then the Green heirs claimed the beach belonged to them. The result was a lengthy legal battle, with the county and SRD pitted against the Green descendants. The case dragged on for five years until an out-of-court settlement in 1962. The land was sold by the estate to the state and county for $318,000. The Greens stipulated the property (appraised at more than $1 million) forever remain in the public domain.

In March of 1964, Manatee County officials dedicated the new beach pavilion at the county-owned southern end of the beach. Officials who had assisted in acquiring the south end for the county spoke. Vice chairman Mike Klemmer said, "This is a great day because one of my dreams has come true. My dream was to see this Island property dedicated to the people of Manatee County for their enjoyment."

Later, a contest to name the beach was held. Coquina Beach was chosen.

Seven

Major Events

How World War II Affected The Island

In December 1941, a radio announcer broke into a program with this incredible news flash: "A devastating Japanese air strike has been made on the U.S. Naval Air Base in Hawaii. America is officially in a state of war."

Florida was already at war. President Roosevelt, who believed air power would be the key to defeating Hitler and Tojo, was turning wild, untamed Florida into a vast training ground for airplane pilots.

The largest airfield was MacDill Air Force Base in Tampa, constructed by Roosevelt's Works Progress Administration (WPA) in 1940. Air cadets, training at a Florida air school, picnicked on Anna Maria Island beaches with their families before leaving to defend their homeland.

By the end of 1941, folks on Anna Maria were used to seeing vapor trails crisscrossing the skies and planes zooming down to drop practice bombs on Mullet Key and Passage Key. It did not take a stretch of the

This group of sailors was stationed on the Island during WWII.

imagination to picture German planes bombarding Tampa Bay and deploying waves of paratroopers floating down on Island shores.

In Anna Maria City a radio tower went up at the west end of Pine Avenue to be near the post office, one of the few places on the Island with a phone.

For two years men in Company C met in town at the Bradenton Armory, but it was difficult to keep their interest. The company commander chided absentees in his newspaper column. He wrote: "None of us want to be under German or Japanese domination, but few are willing to work while the sun is up. Many men have expressed a desire to have their names on lists, but when danger comes these men will be more in the way than if they did not come at all."

It all changed after December 7,1941. The turnout was spectacular. Company C burgeoned with 600 members. Most of the volunteers came from Bradenton. Anna Maria, Bradenton Beach and Cortez were lumped together in one unit referred to as the Beach Company. Holmes Beach did not exist. The beach group was the smallest with only 25 members. Later, a Women's Defense Council (WDC) was organized. Anna Maria was Precinct 14. The WDC was a formidable group. With so many able-bodied men overseas, the women left behind picked up many volunteer duties crucial to the home front war effort. The WDC was supervised by the Manatee County Civil Defense Council (CDC). One of the first things the CDC did was to map locations for plane-spotting towers to be manned by civilian volunteers. The Army's top brass were aware that MacDill Field and the shipbuilding industry in Tampa could be likely targets for German bombers.

The Civil Air Patrol (CAP) began operations the week before Pearl Harbor, but saw little action. The Navy could not see a way to use them until the situation became desperate. Tampa Bay's CAP unit was first stationed on Davis Island. CAP pilots had the dangerous duty of target-towing over the Gulf. The Army equipped planes with reels to wind and unwind cables attached to target sleeves, many of which were decorated with caricatures of Hitler and Tojo. It took strong nerves to keep the small planes steady on a course while fighters roared around them with guns blazing. Ninety aircraft went down with 26 fatalities and seven serious injuries.

Remember ration books, war bond rallies, posters of Uncle Sam warning civilians to watch for enemy spies? Women rolled bandages for the Red Cross and worked in factories. Everyone collected foil and metal and grew victory gardens. The country pulled together as a team for the war effort.

The year of 1942 was a crucial one for Anna Maria Island, according to the Roser Memorial Church publication, *Our Church and How It Grew.* This excerpt was taken from the booklet: "United States was in the grip of a life and death struggle with its enemies. Americans, including some Island men, were in combat all over the world. At home tight restrictions on travel and demands of war work kept many northern winter residents from making their annual trek to Florida.

"Anna Maria was a peaceful, quiet Island except for the hum of airplanes and muffled sounds of the Coast Guard patrolling the beaches. War was a reality for the Island community since many of the men were gone.

"Members of the church published a monthly newsletter called the *Anna Maria Messenger* which was distributed on the Island as well as to the boys in service. It contained news from home and from the men and women in the war zones. It was a great success.

"One of the Island boys, Steve Raymond, was captured in Manila. He survived the Bataan Death March and was held in a Japanese prison until the end of the war. His liberation brought much rejoicing throughout the Island."

In 1944, Lorna Schiek recalled the Community Hall, on the corner of Gulf Drive and Pine Avenue, was a meeting place for soldiers stationed on the Island. It was the Island USO.

"The men working at the radar station on the North Point lived in houses along Gulf Drive," she said. "Some were married and had their families with them. Island families provided refreshments at the Community Hall. Wyatt and Gertrude Blassingame invited men to their home on Maple Avenue for dinner. It was a popular home to visit and became known as Gertie's Place."

Mrs. Blassingame and her daughter, Peggy, were interviewed by Roy Hoopes for

A sailor meets an Island girl in 1942.

his book, "Americans Remember The Home Front." The following is part of their story:

"I was 11 and sitting in the living room. Mother was listening to the news on the radio. All of a sudden she started to cry and screamed. 'The Japanese have bombed us. It's war! It's war!' My friend Polly Moore and I ran down to the beach to tell my father. I was scared," Peggy said.

Members of the Anna Maria Island Veterans of Foreign Wars Post 8199 were active in the community in the '50s and '60s.

Mrs. Blassingame recalled the day her husband, Wyatt, came home and said he had applied for a commission in the Navy. "I felt so alone when he was sent to Rhode Island. Then he was sent to Hawaii and Okinawa. I followed that battle on the radio and the map. I learned to depend on myself and had no fears. We didn't even have a key for our front door. There were 80 men working at the radar station on the North Point and they were all invited to our house on holidays."

Peggy remembered how wonderful her father looked in his sparkling white lieutenant's uniform. "I was too young to have a serviceman for a personal friend," she said. "When they whistled at me and said things, I wanted to slug them with my pocketbook!"

At 14, Peggy recalled hearing scary rumors about a U-boat in the Gulf. "Polly and I were plane spotters. We were assigned to a station on the Gulf between Pine Avenue and Spring Street. We worked a couple days a week, two or three hours at a time. We had charts and were taught how to recognize shapes and silhouettes of planes and how to tell distances. It was confusing at first, and we were lucky to distinguish between a seagull and a plane. As soon as we saw planes we reported them to headquarters. We were terribly confident, but saw only domestic planes.

"I remember standing in long lines to buy canned food with coupons. We could not get much meat, and shoes were rationed. Before my father went into the service he was an air raid warden on the Island. One night he was patrolling and saw a bright light. He ran toward it getting madder and madder. Then he realized he was heading toward our house. I was in the bathtub and had forgotten to pull the shades down. I was grounded for a month, and I missed some great movies."

Mrs. Blassingame remembered the end of the war vividly. "My neighbor came over screaming the armistice had just been announced. I grabbed my daughters and cried I was so happy. It was about three months before Wyatt came home from the Pacific."

Annie Silver came to Island in the '20s. In 1935 she bought property in Bradenton Beach and opened a grocery store and real estate office. During the war Annie always had cold drinks for the Coast Guard men who patrolled the beaches. Her granddaughter, Dorothy Wagner, said at night black shades were drawn and very dim lights were used. On hot nights the lack of ventilation was unbearable.

"My grandmother was asked by the Coast Guard to go out on the beach at regular intervals during the night with binoculars and report any lights or unusual happenings. On several occasions I went with her. She often made calls to the patrol when she got home. Once there was a writer from Europe who escaped to this country to write a book. Government agents asked Annie to secretly rent him a cottage. His name was Jan Valtin, and the book, well known during the war years, was, "*Out of the Night*," Dot recalled.

Snooks Adams was the first law enforcement officer on the Island in 1953 and then police chief in Holmes Beach from 1964 to 1979. He joined the Navy a week after the Japanese bombed Pearl Harbor and spent four years in the service, surviving some of the most horrendous sea combat battles in the Pacific.

Maude Holmes was head of the Island Observation Post.

In a 1998 interview Snooks said, "My family served in every war from the Civil War to Bosnia. There were six of us, my brothers and me, serving at once in World War II. Four of my brothers were in the Navy, one was with General Patton, and my other brother was in the Air Corps flying B-17's. He was shot down and ended up as a prisoner of war in Germany. During the war, mothers hung American flags on their porches. My mother had six flags flying." The late Governor Lawton Chiles honored the six heroes in the Adams family and the tribute can be seen in congressional records.

Bob DeVane served in the Seventh Armor Division as a medic. When he arrived on the Island in 1957 he was active in the Anna Maria Island VFW 8199. For years the VFW conducted Memorial Day services honoring Gold Star

The Fiske home at 808 South Bay Boulevard was next to the Bayou Marina.

Mothers and placed wreaths under the flag at the Island Elementary School in memory of veterans who served their country so courageously.

"When America entered the war in 1941, my father closed his office and joined the defense effort by traveling around Florida building barracks at Army Air Corps bases," Hugh Holmes, Sr. said in a speech to members of the Island Historical Society.

"My mother, Maude, did her part in the war effort. The Air Corps had an observation tower near the Sandbar restaurant, and she was head of the observation post. She had a special line to Tampa, and if we heard an airplane all the kids would go out and spot it, and she'd make a report to Tampa.

"There were fears of German U-boats in the Gulf and attacks from enemy planes. The Island was completely blacked out every night. A Signal Corps training station and barracks, protected by barbed wire, were built near the Island's north tip. Members of the Coast Guard patrolled the beaches.

These sailors were stationed on Anna Maria Island.

"Passage Key and Mullet Key were used for target practice by U.S planes, and the kids on the Island, including me and my brother, would sit on the City Pier and watch the fireworks. One of my most vivid memories was the time, shortly before D-Day, when an armada of bombers rehearsed for the invasion of Europe. It was a sight I will never forget," he said. "There were about 500 of them. They covered the sky, almost blacking out the sun."

Before the war's end, Maude said goodbye to her sons and they went off to join the troops along with many other Island youths.

Jack Fiske began his story in 1942, when planes from MacDill Air Force base started to use the waters around the Island for practice bombings and target shootings.

"My folks built a home at 808 South Bay Boulevard in the '40s. This area was the center of all the practice bombings and target shooting. Since I was nine years old all the action had my rapt attention. I was intrigued with the planes when they dropped dummy bombs and would shoot the other planes as targets. Passage Key was the main target. It was a large island then with a lake in the middle and dense vegetation. Now it is a sandbar between Egmont Key and the northern tip of Anna Maria Island. They bombed with100-pound bombs and skip bombs. The planes overhead dragged targets for other planes to shoot with machine guns. You could hear the rat-a-tat-tat of the guns on Anna Maria.

"It was reported U-boats were in the area, so Coast Guard cutters were stationed in the passes at night. There was an Army crash boat at the City Pier to pick up downed fliers. Army barracks were near the site of the present Rod and Reel Pier. The Corps of Engineers would not allow any buildings near the barracks, so there were no houses on Bean Point.

"During the hours of bombing on Passage Key, planes would come from MacDill Air Force Base and fly along the Manatee River toward Passage Key and strafe bomb the Key. After the bombing run, they would bank up over the Gulf to the south and fly over Anna Maria, back to the river and continue the same circle.

"Island residents were restricted in all activities. Lights in homes were kept dim and curtains closed at night. Only parking lights on cars could be used, and fishermen could not fish at night. We could feel the repercussions when bombs fell on Passage Key. The ground was shaking. One morning everything was shaking so much we had to push dishes way back on the shelves so they would not fall and break. It was a very trying time for Island folks.

"We could see huge plumes of water spouting up in the bay where bombs had dropped. The man stationed at the City Pier in a crash boat would hightail it out of there when the bombs got too close. One bomb did land on the Island near the Hasslets house. The Waterfront Restaurant is there now. A retired Irish policeman lived there and the bomb damaged his home severely. He had it repaired and went on living there for some time. The same bomb shook our house so bad the roof began to leak. Fortunately, a crew came down from MacDill and fixed it.

Serviceman considered the island a choice assignment

"One afternoon a fighter plane was flying toward the Island over the Gulf at a very low altitude right over our house. We were just leaving when we noticed two silver objects jettison from under the wings of the plane. We were shocked to see them fly over our roof and land in the bay. I was a curious boy so I waded out to see what had dropped into the water. It was two fuel tanks. They were filled with holes which allowed them to sink.

"On Mullet Key there was a quarantine station, an air strip and a hospital. We saw damaged ship going up to the Tampa shipyards for repair."

For awhile resort owners on the Island tried to keep their businesses going. The new Gulf Park Trailer Park in Bradenton Beach advertised: "We cater to the more fastidious tourist with a house on wheels who prefers a more exclusive location. We are famous for our socials and dances in our commodious club house."

Trying to entice tourists, the new Bradenton Beach Civic Club boasted about the town's new street lights and noted the Cortez Bridge had been widened and paved with a smooth asphalt surface for better driving. Cortez Road to Route 41 had been widened, smoothed and lined with "vegetable gardens, fields of gladioli, orange groves and pretty tourist cabins."

Tourism finally slowed down. Visitors could put up with the rationing of sugar, gas and food and the annoyance of military planes flying over the beach. But when German submarines began torpedoing ships along the Florida coast, they headed home. The new streetlights in Bradenton Beach were blacked out for the duration.

Two men who served on Anna Maria Island during 1943 and 1944 were reunited years later on the Island. They discussed their tour of duty with the Signal Corps Battalion, attached to the Army Air Corps, the forerunner of the U.S. Air Force. Roy Fulton and Pat Clark were both assigned to watch for enemy airplanes on the Island. There were no gun replacements at the small military installation near the site of the present Rod and Reel Pier, just the Army radar tower, two radio towers and a water tower.

"I remember we had a mock invasion pass overhead one day," Clark said. "We picked up the planes on the

radar from 150-miles away. Our planes would practice bombing Passage Key, and every once in awhile someone would not make it and go down in the bay. I don't know how many planes crashed, but I saw a lot of them. We had a lot of inexperienced pilots. The Coast Guard would pluck them out of the sea."

At this time there was no bridge to Longboat Key and only the rickety, wooden bridge to the mainland. The main road on the Island ran through Bradenton Beach.

"We were young and rough," Clark recalled. "We ate our meals in the rain outdoors. There were mosquitoes, scorpions and sand fleas."

Whenever the men had a chance, they went into the mainland, frequenting the Bradenton bars. They remembered Todd's Bar in Bradenton Beach and one popular watering hole in Anna Maria, named the Anchorage. For recreation they went to the beach, floated for hours on air mattresses spotting dolphins and strolled along the beach looking for shells. They did not have time to fish since the Army kept them busy during the day.

"We had six hour shifts and those who got the midnight shift would usually fall asleep," Clark said. "When I was on duty if I found men asleep I would tell them they get a court martial. They would stir for a few minutes, and when I came back again I would find them asleep."

After the war was over Clark went back to Detroit. Years later he remarried and returned to Anna Maria in 1955. He and his wife loved the Island and returned several times. Fulton moved back to the Island in 1954 and worked for Jack Holmes in the '70s. Both men now live in Bradenton and were glad to visit the Anna Maria Island Historical Museum for this interview in the '90s.

The Porpoise

By Jack Leffingwell

It was the beginning of World War II and Henry Smith, like most Island boys, was a regular "fish" in the water. Once, on a bet, he swam from Ilexhurst (Holmes Beach) to Longboat Pass. Late one evening Henry was sitting on the beach near the Gulf Terrace Restaurant when a Coast Guard boat came up the coast and anchored about half a mile offshore.

Henry knew the men on the cutter and decided to visit them. Shucking his scanty clothes he waded out in the Gulf and swam toward the ship. He had nearly reached the vessel when the anchor went up and the boat headed northwest.

Henry's shouts were to no avail as the noise of the engine drowned out his voice. By this time it was quite dark and the boy was at least half a mile offshore. Realizing he was in a serious predicament, Henry turned to shore. But where was it? There was not a light visible, because of the wartime "lights out" regulations. He did not know which way to swim. For a time he was frightened and tired himself needlessly swimming. Then he began to float and watch the sky, hoping he would be able to orient himself by the stars.

As he floated, suddenly something brushed against him. At first he thought it was a shark, but soon found he was surrounded by a school of porpoises. They began pushing and nudging him in one direction and one of them actually got under him and more or less supported him. Henry had often heard these strange mammals would push the body of a drowning man to shore, so he kept quiet and let them work.

He later said the porpoises worked with him for a long time until they were interrupted by the return of the Coast Guard boat and he was rescued. This is a true story told to me by a reliable resident of the Island.

I also had a strange experience with these weird creatures. When returning to the Island from an excursion to Egmont Key, I saw a great commotion in the water off the starboard bow and changed course to investigate. Upon arriving on the scene I found two porpoises entangled in a gill net. You know if a porpoise cannot get air it will drown.

With the help of a boat hook and a machete I managed to free the creatures and after they found they were free they put on a show of the art of swimming all around the boat. They followed me all the way to the mouth of the river.

I learned the scientists at Wood's Hole Laboratory in Massachusetts, by the use of under seas microphones, found porpoises talking to each other by means of grunts, thumps, whistles and twittering noises. I believe the two I rescued must have spread the news for even now when I am out in the boat any nearby porpoises begin to roll and flip their tails at me in a most friendly manner. Truly they are strange creatures. This article was in the *Anna Maria Key News* on December 28,1950.

Note: Porpoises are related to whales and dolphins. They are distinct from dolphins. The word "porpoise" has been used to refer to any small dolphin, especially by sailors and fishermen. The most obvious visible difference between the two groups is that porpoises have flattened, spade-shaped teeth, distinct from the conical teeth of dolphins, and shorter beaks.

According to Steve Davis of the Mote Marine Laboratory, dolphins are in the Gulf of Mexico. The most common species is the bottlenose dolphin. There are many stories of dolphins rescuing swimmers and protecting swimmers from shark attacks.

In 1953 Jack Holmes built the first swimming pool on the Island at his new home on 56th Street. The house and pool were proclaimed to be "The Showplace of Anna Maria Island."

Firsts on Anna Maria Island

Mr. and Mrs. John Holmes, Sr. held an open house in September of 1952 to show off their new home on 56th Street and their ultra-modern swimming pool which was on the bay. This was the first pool on the Island. One of the most amusing events of the day happened when Holmes Beach Mayor Y. H. Taylor welcomed the Holmeses to the town of Holmes Beach. Although Mr. Holmes was one of the main forces in the development of this part of the Island which bears his name, until he and his wife moved into their new home they lived in Anna Maria City.

In the early '50s the first television set was in the home of Mr. and Mrs. John Holmes, Jr. Everyone went to their house to watch this new invention. It took forever for the test pattern to go off, but it was worth it.

The Islander publisher, Harry Varley, had this to say about the new electronic device in 1952. "It has been the experience of other sections that when television arrived the crooks and frauds came with it. On the new market, all kinds of television sets were dumped in a wide range of prices. Butchers, bakers and candlestick makers became dealers although they barely knew how to turn them on.

"The result was serious loss to many innocent people who thought buying a television set was similar to purchasing a toaster. It is vastly different!

"Our warning! Do not buy any television set unless expert service is available. They are highly complicated instruments. Until the set is worked on little things can black out the picture and kill the sound. It may cost only pennies for an expert to correct the trouble, but until he does, the set is dead.

"Should you buy a cheap set it may not be possible to have it repaired. The main tube, which is quite costly, could be a used tube with a limited number of light hours left. Pay enough to have the name of one of the top leaders of the industry on your set. Then your investment will pay you net dividends of unbroken entertainment and enjoyments."

In 1947 the first Anna Maria Island beauty contest was held on the Fourth of July.

Island beauties paraded in front of jovial judges and throngs of Island residents. Everyone had a great time at the beauty contest.

In the 60's Island storms delivered wonderful waves for local surf contests

Storms, Disasters and Surfing Delights

Storms passed close to the Island in 1944 and 1945. One demolished First, Second and Third Avenues in Bradenton Beach and chewed about six feet under Fourth Avenue at Sixth Street South. Those streets were on a knob of sand that stuck out into the Gulf starting just south of Bridge Street and coming back to shore at the south end of the Island where the north end of Coquina Beach is. Another slow-moving storm passed northwest of Tampa with 60mph winds. Tides in Tampa Bay rose more than six feet above normal, the highest since 1921.

Joe Webb in perfect form is captured exiting a beautiful storm swell.

Jim Kissick went off to war in 1942. When he came home he found many of the homes in Bradenton Beach were missing.

Sam Adams recalled the time he went fishing with the Moores of Moore's Seafood Restaurant on

Longboat Key. "There was quite a storm," he recalled in an interview with an *Islander* reporter. "We rode it out but we were overdue. The Coast Guard sighted us and called in. When the boat came back the whole town of Anna Maria turned out to greet us. Businesses were closed. One man got off the boat and kissed the ground."

Jim Brady drops in on a 60's storm swell.

"Gulf Storm Tears Up Roads On Anna Maria Island," was the front-page headline in the *Bradenton Herald* on Sept. 5, 1950. "The wind and rain steadily built up toward the climax which was the high tide at 3:30 a.m. Waves roared in with an increasingly powerful assault and rain poured in torrents as the high tide neared. Islanders had only their indomitable spirit and bare hands to hold back a vicious sea that seemed bent on beating, lashing and pounding every structure and terrain that stood in the way of its relentless force.

"Red Cross leaders and volunteers worked through the night. Red Cross officials pushed the evacuation of beach residents from danger points, kept a stream of information going by phone and radio and helped reunite members of families who had become scattered."

"Baby Hurricane Becomes Juvenile Delinquent," was the headline in the newly published *Anna Maria Key News* on Sept. 7, 1950, "Anna Maria Bloody But Unbowed!" The article went on the say civic leaders and citizens were disturbed by accounts in the daily papers. "We were not grim and scared as a result of the hurricane," the reporter insisted. "Instead we were talking about how lucky

Houses near the beach were destroyed. Several floated out to sea.

we were compared to residents of devastated Pinellas county beaches."

Islanders found it highly amusing to read, when the weather cleared we had fled by the hundreds into the sheltering arms of the Red Cross and "begged" for further assistance.

Still another interesting and hilarious anecdote, outlined in the daily paper, was that during the height of the storm bars were doing a good business while women wandered barefoot through the streets.

"Actually heroic citizens worked 76 hours without rest. Children of 7 and 8 years of age filled sand bags. It was only the weight of the bags that kept them from being blown off their feet in the high winds. Teenagers drove trucks, hauled sand bags and ran errands. Men and women stood chest deep in the Gulf while waves crashed over their heads as they worked to secure strategic points. Many patrolled the Island offering information and assistance. Women brewed gallons of coffee. It was truly a superb performance by all."

Editor of the *Key News*, Ellen Brackin (Marshall) quipped, "We must remember to wear white tie and tails during the next hurricane, and it is hoped that someone who recognizes formal dress will be sent to cover this poor, sniveling, waterfront crowd.

This road in Bradenton Beach was undermined by the pounding surf.

"Island residents would like to know what impression was being attempted in stories colored in such fashion. Quite obviously the person who wrote this had not ventured very far beyond the bridge because if he had he would have noted the fire stations at both ends of the Island were on 24-hour duty for two days and nights. He might have peered into the Gulf and recognized men working against the forces of nature and actually winning in many cases."

Editor Brackin conceded, "If the writer did not have knowledge the news report becomes so much verbiage, one that might be termed chicanery. Civic leaders and citizens alike were disturbed by the idiotic ramblings in the local daily paper.

"In Anna Maria it might have been observed the Anna Maria Community Hall was open day and night as volunteers served coffee and soup to soaked citizens whose only reason for braving the elements was they were good neighbors and solid citizens," Ellen wrote.

Repeated reports from a Bradenton radio station said that the Miami Weather Bureau stated the Island had been evacuated. The broadcast continued by saying the hurricane had turned and winds had diminished to 65 miles an hour.

"We had all lived through a great deal worse that that," Brackin wrote. "Few if any would have left the Island if they had not received the wrong report. It was not only ridiculous, but dangerous to get traffic started over the washed out roads and the frightful Cortez Road, which was under construction. In the future there must be a clearing house for the Island so that both ends know exactly what the situation is."

The following newspaper account was sent to George Harris, Jr. from Hildegard Bell of North Carolina. Her concern for the Island was justified from accounts she read in the *Asheville Citizen News*. One read: "A lone bridge leading from Anna Maria Island washed out leaving four-fifths of the Island isolated and hundreds marooned. To the south, Sarasota rescue teams removed inhabitants out of the little fishing village of Cortez."

Ellen Brackin, with her usual sharp wit, exclaimed: "A resort filled with grim citizens is not attractive to tourists and prospective visitors from North Carolina. They might feel the four-fifths of us who were isolated and marooned might possibly develop cannibalistic tendencies by December!"

When the water rose, these boys took a canoe ride on Holly Road in Anna Maria.

In October 1953 a storm hit the Island, damaging seawalls. Sandbags saved the seawall at the Gulf Park Hotel. A small cottage near the Cove Hotel sunk without a trace and another house careened at an odd angle. Two houses were converted to waterfront property.

Plate glass doors at the Island Pharmacy in the Holmes Beach Shopping Center departed for parts unknown. Trees were uprooted on the Clyde Phelps' property and Peter Sosa's beachfront. Streets were inundated with turbulent water. When the storm passed, a few cottages were closer to the water. Many houses had not moved, but part of the beach had gone out to sea.

In 1954, Bradenton Beach organized an emergency committee with Mayor Jack Jones at the head. Police Chief Paul Ford was in charge of traffic, and each councilman checked his ward and reported to the headquarters at the fire station. Fire chief Joseph Mallot was in charge of the firemen. Reports were sent by two-way radios to volunteers. All merchants were asked

Damage to the Anna Maria City Pier was extensive.

to keep businesses open so supplies would be available. Women of the auxiliary agreed to make coffee.

Hurricane Flossy hit a deserted beach near Fort Walton with 100mph winds and eight were killed. A storm report on Sept. 26, 1956 stated very little damage was done on the Island by high water and strong winds as the

Streets were flooded during the storms.

edge of Flossy stirred up the elements. The water was the highest in five years. There were washouts behind a seawall on Fourth Street in Bradenton Beach. Water crossed the Island between the Mira Mar and Gulf Terrace Restaurant leaving a four to six inch deposit of sand on the road. A house in Anna Maria was threatened by the wild Gulf waters on a Sunday. People came to help in their church finery. Women and children held sand bags open while the men filled and placed them. Some men installed pilings to shore up flagstones on the terrace and prevent water from undermining the house.

Soon officials arrived and erosion control members appeared with trucks filled to the brim with rocks, and a huge dragline was used to build a wall of rocks in front of the house. The house was saved! It proved emergencies on the Island united all the people. When there was an urgent need, men, women and children came running to help.

Upon investigation, it was revealed the Gulf had flowed across the Island about half a mile from the southernmost house in Bradenton Beach. At low tide there was less than 50 yards from Gulf to Bay and at high tide the waters met. The wash of the Gulf across the road at the narrowest and lowest part of the Island showed how vital it was to get a good bridge to the Island so people could leave in case the Island was in the direct path of a hurricane.

In May 1954, this strange headline, "Spume-Drift In The Night," appeared in *The Islander*. About 11 p.m. drivers heading south on Gulf Drive suddenly swerved to the left near North Fourth Street in Bradenton Beach to avoid a "snow" drift looming unexpectedly in the beam of their headlights. A strong southwest wind had blown all day and foam had collected against the rock groins. Great masses of spume had piled up, overflowed the groins and blown across the road. The glare of headlights gave the startling impression of snow piled up.

A tidal wave swept over the south end of the Island on Feb. 14,1958. The editor of *The Islander* stated to call it a tidal wave was a gross exaggeration. The wave was estimated to be only two feet high, which would have made it the smallest tidal wave to ever hit anywhere.

The widely publicized Hurricane Donna, with winds up to 150 miles per hour, hit the Florida Keys and went up the Gulf coast on a Saturday in September of 1960. Donna subjected the Island to lusty winds and rain for hours. The canals were nearly dry and the grassy bottom of the Bay was visible. More of the wreck of the old molasses barge, off of Bradenton Beach, could be seen. Starting Thursday, newspaper, radio and television bulletins advised residents of coastal, low-lying areas to evacuate. Many Islanders prepared to escape Donna's crippling blows by evacuating.

Most of them made reservations at Bradenton motels. Early Saturday, Manatee County Civil Defense officials advised residents to leave, and by midday all residents were ordered to evacuate the Island. Beginning Saturday afternoon the wind velocity increased to 75 mph and continued until early Sunday. During the height of the storm it was impossible to stand without holding on to a sturdy structure.

The most serious damage was a roof torn off a home in Anna Maria. Shingles were torn off of many homes, uprooted trees and broken limbs cluttered streets and yards. The Island Water Company experienced a break in service, and Sunday morning a gas-driven auxiliary pump was used. Most Islanders who spent the night on the mainland returned home in the morning to discover Bradenton sustained more damage than the Island.

"Hurricane Alma Lashes Island" was *The Islander* headline on June 9, 1966! The storm skirted the Island

causing havoc during the early morning hours. Despite high winds and rough seas, there were no injuries. At the height of the storm, between midnight and 1 a.m., residents estimated the winds were blowing between 85 and 100 mph. Luckily the tides were low when the wind reached its peak. Many of the newly planted palm trees flanking the south side of the pavilion on Coquina Beach toppled. Telephone and power repair crews were on duty early the next morning.

Front page headlines in the Nov. 14,1968 *Islander* blared: "Tornado Hits Anna Maria." Damage at the Bayou Marina was more than $500,000. The tornado swept across the Island ripping roofs off of homes on White

Avenue, Anna Maria, and damaging homes and trees along 82nd and 83rd Streets in Holmes Beach. Mayor S. A. Hutchinson's home on the bay was damaged, and the Bayou Marina on South Bay Boulevard was left in shambles.

It did not last 40 seconds, according to Norman Franklin, owner of the Bayou Marina. "I heard it coming and saw one of the roofs of the boat shed ripped off. I ran to my house and when I opened the front door I was blown right down the hall."

The roof of the Franklin home was ripped off. His wife, Marie, and their three-year-old daughter, were in the house but were not injured when the twister hit.

Franklin said just about every one of the 68 boats moored at the marina was damaged. The only person injured in the freak twister was Terry Wells, 13, of Wauchula who was struck by flying debris while standing in the parking lot. The boat of Clyde Sasser was damaged. He was on his boat when the tornado passed through. "The rain and wind were blowing and then there was a sudden change in the tone of the wind. I looked up and saw the roof leaving. By the time I ducked down in the cabin of my boat it was over."

A couple of years later, a giant tidal wave swept across sections of Anna Maria Island, Longboat Key and Lido Key causing extensive damage in the millions. Gigantic breakers struck along a 40-mile stretch of coastline from St. Petersburg to Siesta Key.

A wall of water, more than five-feet in height, hit beaches without warning at 11a.m. Saturday, Feb. 15, 1969. Homes, motels and businesses along the Gulf and the main roads were flooded. Tornado warnings had been sounded for this section of the coast early in the morning. About 10:30 a.m. a squall line began moving along the beaches. As the low-pressure system passed over, high winds and heavy rain commenced. High waves washed across sections of the Island leaving rocks and debris strewn along the road. The worst of the storm was over in five minutes.

Flooding was reported in the Gulf Trailer Park and southward. Bill Lindsey, owner of Lindsey's Diner in Bradenton Beach, suffered a broken wrist when he tried to close the door of his restaurant as a wave rushed in.

A garage apartment in Bradenton Beach collapsed on a car. A large glass sign at Trader Jack's Brigantine restaurant was blown out by the force of the wind. Shorty O'Connell, who managed Coquina Beach at the south end, said he had never seen anything like it in 20 years.

Coquina Beach, the mile-long county beach at the south end of the Island was completely covered with water. Logs, used to mark the parking area, floated around like matchsticks. Mrs. Loyd Greene, who lived on Gulf Drive, said five tremendous waves hit her house. "It was something I had never seen before," she recalled.

Colony Beach Resort on Longboat Key was the hardest hit of all the motels on the Key. Ten units were flooded. The large plate glass windows in the dining room, that provided a grand view of the Gulf, were knocked out by palm trees that were hurled through them by the force of the waves.

Erosion Threatens

The urgency of the erosion became apparent to everyone on the Island, not just Gulffront property owners. An erosion committee held immediate meetings to formulate plans to finance work to secure the entire Gulf front with rock groins.

The Islander reported 11,000 tons of rock had been brought to the Island for the immense erosion project. In addition, by August 1952, 17,000 additional tons had been moved to the beaches.

In March of 1952, it was reported that beaches on the southern end of the Island to half a mile north had been disappearing. Much of the sand had been deposited on the North Point.

The north end of the Island had been referred to as the North Point. A report on erosion studies from Washington, D.C. called this site Bean Point, to perpetuate the memory of George Emerson Bean, the first homesteader who acquired all the land from the northern tip to Magnolia Avenue. In 1956 a request was made to Mayor Bill Brier that the name be preserved with a sign at Bean Point carrying the legend of George Emerson Bean.

H. B. Miller, chairman of the erosion committee, hoped the construction of 100 rock groins would be started as soon as the $150,000 bonds, voted on by freeholders, were validated. Native rock was best because of its availability. The cost was only $12 a foot compared to $100 a foot for rock imported from Miami.

John Adams was an advocate for the renourishment of the Island beaches.

When it came to a realistic knowledge of tides, currents, erosion and everything pertaining to the waters and shores of Anna Maria Island the words of Louis Cobb, "Sugarfoot" Raymond, "Tink" Fulford and Mitch Davis were more respected than others.

The following observations were written by an unknown philosopher: "The relationship of cause and effect of the tides seems so obscure that nature appears to be fickle and capricious and it may seem to our casual observation that she is not complying with her own basic laws. We can have no well grounded hope for success in our endeavor to combat erosion on shore lines fronting large bodies of water if our planning does not aim toward and result in a structure that will cooperate with those mighty forces turned loose by wind and storm. If we insist on building near the water we must learn to deal with it when it goes on a rampage."

Sydney Makepeace Wood came to the Island to study the shoreline, location needs, currents, underwater contours, effect of winds and many other factors involved in erosion prevention methods and building beaches.

There was powerful opposition from those advocating nourishing beaches by pumping in bay-bottom sand which would vanish at the first high water. The proponents of solid walls and groins were against Wood's designs.

The Island Erosion Control District Commission wanted no part of Wood's increasingly permeable groins and piers and refused to believe their eyes and ears when shown photos and told about the results.

When asked how long before the groins would have a visible effect, Wood replied, "Often the beach will build up as quickly as the groin is being installed, so that, before the end is reached many feet of beach have been established and hundreds of cubic yards of sand are deposited."

John Adams, longtime Island resident and civil engineer, called a Beach Info Forum in 1996 to give a briefing on the erosion of beaches on the Island. He stated there was a unique opportunity to improve, protect and maintain them for the next 40 years. He outlined Island erosion history from 1913 to 1989. Referring to the 1921 hurricane, he said 36 percent of the city was lost north of Pine Avenue in that disaster. Rebuilding took more than five years. If a similar storm hit today it would wipe out 212 homes, three motels, a pier, miles of paved roads, sewers, water, power and telephone lines. His answer was that Anna Maria City was offered 40 years of beach maintenance and repair by the state at no cost to the city. He urged residents to vote for the renourishment.

The Scourge of Red Tide

Red Tide is a common name for a phenomenon known as algal bloom, an event in which estuarine, marine or fresh-water algae accumulate rapidly in the water column or bloom. These algae are microscopic plant-like organisms which form dense, visible patches near the water's surface. Certain species contain photosynthetic pigments that vary in color from green to brown to red. When the algae are present in high concentrations, the water appears to be discolored or murky, varying in color from purple to almost pink, normally being red or green.

The most conspicuous effects of red tide are the associated wildlife mortalities among marine and coastal species of fish, birds, marine mammals and other organisms. The term red tide is often used in the United States to describe a particular type of algal bloom common to the eastern Gulf of Mexico, also called "Florida red tide."

It is unclear what causes red tide. The occurrence in some locations appears to be entirely natural, while other red tides appear to be the result of human activities. No deaths of humans have been attributed to Florida red tide, but people experience respiratory irritation such as coughing, sneezing and tearing, when red tide organisms are present along the coast and winds blow toxic air onshore. Swimming is safe, but skin irritation and burning is possible in areas of high concentration of red tide.

Records show the Island never experienced red tide before 1947, when the great red tide plague struck and Islanders were overcome with the acrid, gassy smell and stench of dead fish on the beaches.

Headlines in a 1953 *Islander* read: "Putrefying Mass In Bay Prompts Emergency Action In Bradenton Beach and Health Department Acts To Dispose Of Fish Killed By Red Tide." Tons of dead fish along the Bradenton Beach bayfront prompted a special meeting of Dr. John Neill, county health officer and the Bradenton Beach City Council.

Dr. Neil commandeered work crews and equipment from Bradenton. Dead fish floated throughout Sarasota Bay, piled up around the bridge and small docks. Mid-Island residents reported quantities of decaying fish washing up on bay shores, but most of the fish were going out with the tide. U.S. Fish and Wildlife Service and the Coast Guard planned to test the value of copper sulfate to kill the red tide organisms. A similar test off the Fort Myers beaches, during the 1952 outbreak was effective, but too expensive for widespread use.

In 1957, the Holmes Beach airstrip became the headquarters for agencies sending planes to locate and fight red tide. Waters of all local passes were sprayed with copper sulfate to kill the microscopic organisms. In November, the abominable red tide came within a few miles of the Island's Gulf shores. High winds and choppy waters permitted the gases to escape and dead fish were blown ashore. A curious note: All the fish were trash fish and most of their heads and insides were missing. Anna Maria Mayor Bill Brier said the fish were small, bottom feeders and that was why they died from the vicious organisms.

Eight

Civic Pride

Youth Center cheerleaders: Back row from left, Nancy Welch, Shirley Tobe, Debbie Poe, Heather Bartling, Patricia Tebbetts. Front from left, Gigi Cobb, Jill Arnold, Michelle "Peanuts" Bernard, Peggy Bass and Lisa Corrigan

Island Community Center

The most important building on the Island in 1952, according to a writer for *The Islander*, was the Youth Center in Anna Maria. An Island-wide organization, it was geographically in a bad location for mid-Island and Bradenton Beach youngsters who had to pay 15-cents on the bus to come and go.

The building on Magnolia Avenue and Crescent Street was originally the first schoolhouse. It was designated as the Anna Maria Beach Public School and erected by the school board in 1913 in recognition of the rapid growth on the Island.

Later, it was known as the Youth Center after the elementary school was built in Holmes Beach in 1950. Sponsored by the Island Lions Club, the Youth Center was run by Mr. and Mrs. Richard Ernest and a few

In 1956 land was cleared for a ballpark at the Youth Center. Shown, from the left, Bennie Scanio, Warren Spahn, Anna Maria Mayor Paul Carlisle and Frances Livingston.

devoted workers. On January 28, 1952 there were 72 children in and around the center. Outside, young boys were learning the rudiments of baseball from Fred Hutchinson, a former pitcher for the Detroit Tigers. Stew Hawkins and Johnny Holmes were working with another group.

The Youth Center was always in need of volunteers to work with the girls and boys on Saturdays. "It's not like baby sitting," the newspaper article said. "You may pick up a child that has fallen, take sand spurs from another's socks, show little ladies and gentlemen to their respective salons of relief and button up a back or two."

On Saturday nights teenagers played games, sang and watched movies for ten cents. Volunteers sold soft drinks and candy. Where would the children go if there was not a Youth Center? This was a question pondered by many Island families.

In June of 1952, the old building served on Saturdays as the Youth Center, and on Sundays it became a church. Monday nights it housed some fancy poker games. About this time Mr. and Mrs. Fred Hutchinson and

Award winning Tarpons: From left, John Norwood, Dale Johnson, Jim "Crazylegs" White, Dan Lease and Chuck Wickersham.

The Fighting Tarpons traveled to Naples to play the Naples Optimists in 1966

Bennie Scanio appeared before the city commission to point out that land for a public playground was getting scarce, and unless something was done promptly it might disappear altogether. The commission agreed. A deal was made with the school board allowing the school property to be used as a playground. City land that had been used as a garbage dump was swapped for land adjoining the school. Walter Hardin donated a lot. Captain Bill Davis swapped land he owned for some elsewhere. The entire block containing the school building was set aside for the Youth Center and playground.

Dr. Roy Gunther, a member of the Teen Club Adult Council of the Youth Center, explained the financial situation of the center. He said the recent merger of the Teen Club and Playground Association formed the Anna Maria Island Youth Center. The new addition cost about $15,000 and approximately $2,000 was needed for immediate work on the building. Bills would be presented to the county for improving sanitary facilities, painting, screens, carpentry and a public address system. Dr. Gunther praised the work of the directors, Mr. and Mrs. George Engel and volunteers Mr. and Mrs. Fred Frost. In concluding, he said that the greatest need for funds would be for maintenance.

Fred Hutchinson, who had been active in the development of the center, said the Youth Center was an outstanding facility for the Island, and he felt it was worthy of the support of every person on the Island.

The following was taken from an article entitled "*Youth Center History*" by Wyatt Blassingame: "In the late summer of 1959, following the tragic death of his son, Benji, Bennie Scanio, brother-in-law of Ernie Cagnina, began what was by no-means a one-man drive to improve the Youth Center. He was certainly the greatest single contributor to it. Backed by Fred Hutchinson and Dr. Roy Gunther and various center sponsors, he worked at raising money by every means. From auctions, with donations from the Atlantic Coast Line and Seaboard Railroads, to fish fries, the coffers grew. The old Manavista Hotel in Bradenton was being destroyed. Bennie personally bought hotel timber and hauled it to the Island in his own truck. The old Ringling Brothers Circus winter quarters in Sarasota was being abandoned and Bennie knew the man to see. Some of the light poles on the Youth center baseball field once toured the world as circus tent poles. The backstop was once a part of a lion cage. The barbecue grill was a bear pen and part of the fence once circled monkeys rather than youngsters in Anna Maria.

"Meanwhile, Al Robson contributed plans to enlarge the old building. Plans allowed for small additions aiming toward a complete plant sometime in the near future. But things were rolling too fast for piecemeal work. Frank Blount of Florida Limestone Company in Palmetto poured $2,000 worth of cement into foundations and floors with nothing but a verbal promise of maybe, when and if. Island contactors and carpenters donated materials and labor. There was no time for fishing on Saturday afternoons and Sundays.

"On July 2, 1961, the Anna Maria Youth Center was officially dedicated. It was well used. A good part of the year the joint was jumping with baseball, tennis, dancing and parties. By 1968, football, as well as baseball, were being played where sandspurs had reigned supreme. But football was expensive, and there was too much travel involved. When the Island kids went to Palmetto to play they wore sneakers. The Palmetto players had cleats on their shoes. There was a brief standoff—and then everybody played barefoot. The next week Patsy Hutchinson bought shoes with cleats for the entire team. There were other expenses such as travel, insurance and heavy equipment.

Ernie Cagnina organized this baseball team in the early '50s. Front row from left, Ernie, unknown, Melvin Davis, bat boy Jack Fiske, two unknowns, Tom Larson. Back row, from left, Charlie Jones, Percy Arnold, Richard Wiggins, Hugh Holmes, John Holmes and Jimmy Selman.

"Then someone mentioned soccer. It was popular in Europe and South America, but to most people on the Island it was little more than a name. On the other hand, all that seemed to be needed was 11 kids to a side, boys or girls. They could all play together in shorts and shirts with a comparatively cheap ball and open space. In 1972 football gave way to soccer and the program expanded every year. A few years later 150 youngsters from six through 18 took part in the Florida State Soccer Association, playing games from the Skyway Bridge to Venice.

"Baseball held its own. New lights were added on the field and a concession stand was built with donations from the ladies auxiliary. The center hosted an annual Rotary Invitational Baseball Tournament each June with teams from Manatee and Sarasota counties.

"In 1976, adult programs were added to make better use of the building, when it was not being used by the youth, and to serve the community. Volunteers gave free Medicare and income tax help. In 1977, the charter was amended to change the name to the Anna Maria Island Community Center. It was hoped that federal funding might be available for such as project. Unfortunately that did not work out.

More than 20 boys and girls, between the ages of 7 and 15, learned the art of sailing, racing and water safety as members of the Island Pram Fleet in the early '60s.

"Meanwhile, the old building, despite painting and patchwork continued to mellow and mold. The old porch had been enclosed for an office. The old office was a storeroom. The kitchen was locked since it had neither roof nor floor. There were termites which nobody dared disturb. If they departed, the building might collapse. The wiring was ancient and no new appliance could be added without disconnecting an old one. To completely refurbish would be prohibitively expensive.

"The Board of Directors, all volunteers, worked diligently to raise funds for the new Community Center so it would be ready by the fall of 1983. The slogan, "Center For Me In '83," was heard throughout the Island. The committee believed the spirit of cooperation, which started the whole thing, still existed on the Island. Islanders would see a new Island Community Center in which they would all take pride."

Among the many sports offered at the Youth Center was field hockey. Everything was free for the Island kids.

The tennis courts were marked, back-stops finished and a Teenage Tennis Club was formed in

Players on the Island Merchants softball team in 1974, were: Back row from left, Bill Shelton, Lane, John Norwood, Chris Larios, Joe Bernard. Front, Steve Tucker, Randy Bricker, Jon Spencer, Al Cascarano, Bob Smith.

October 1956. Appeals for contributions went out to the three cities. Fred Hutchinson was planning to have an all-star exhibition baseball game in January at the Braves field to benefit the Youth Center playground. Plans for a baseball dinner were underway. "Hutch" garnered a great deal of credit for the playground. He helped start the idea and was the spark plug for years.

In 1957, tennis lessons were offered by Eugene Nolan, a tennis pro from Baltimore, who had organized a junior tennis program in the suburbs of Baltimore. Nolan was interested in bringing young people from fifth grade through high school to the Island courts for a series of ten, one-hour tennis lessons at a cost of $5 for the full series.

The Anna Maria Island Youth Center joined the District III Teen Council in October of 1960. The council had members from Tampa to Sarasota. Mrs. George Engel, director of the Island Youth Center, attended a meeting of district groups in Bradenton. There was a "bop" session and Dean Edwards of Anna Maria was the panelist in the discussions. Objectives of the council were to bring recreation and teen centers leaders together and exchange ideas on improving all the centers.

Herbert C. Teel was hired as director of the Youth Center in 1964. The center was open 30-hours a week during the winter and 40-hours a week in the summer. The annual salary for the director was $3,600. Teel said he planned a more active program at the center and planned to start baseball practice for Little Leaguers.

Womens Clubs

The Island Woman's Club was one of the earliest and most active clubs on the Island in the '50s. The theme of the November program in 1950 was honoring the former presidents of the club, which was formed in 1941. Mrs. L. H. Dosh, the first president, spoke of the early days and how hard the members worked to get the club going. Mrs. Oscar Russell, the second president, said the work really got underway in 1945. Many projects were

The 1950 Anna Maria Island Woman's Club executive board.

held to raise money to improve the Community Hall, on Gulf Drive and Pine Avenue, where the meetings were held. This was the year the membership increased so the club was able to apply for membeship in the National Federation of Women's Clubs.

Mrs. J. M Stiffler, president from 1946-47, told of Christmas bazaars, card parties and dinners and generous contributions given to charities. Mrs. Allen Brown succeeded in arousing the interest of club members in a bird study which had been of value to club members years before.

Miss Marion Colman, president from 1947 to 1948, spoke of the many donations given to Happiness House during her tenure in office. In 1948, the club inaugurated a plan to have school children take part in bird book contests. She said the funds raised from a successful Hollywood breakfast assisted in sending some pupils from the Anna Maria School to the Safety Patrol Convention in Washington, D.C.

The president, from 1949 to 1950, was Mrs. J. T. Thomsen who said that year should be called the Award Year since the women were fortunate to receive prizes at the national convention for their club scrapbook and a poem written by Miss Colman. One feature of the season was the Welcome Travelers program with Mrs. William B. Young as mistress of ceremonies. The Community Hall was decorated for the occasion, and each speaker appeared framed as though talking from a portrait.

Mrs. George Clark, the president in 1950, said members should remember they are not joined together by personal fame or individual credit. The main idea was teamwork and to give assistance where it was most needed in the community, state and world.

Lions Club

Island Lions Club members were selling mops and brooms, made by the blind at the Lions Lighthouse in Jacksonville in July of 1952. The money raised in this project was used to for Lions activities on the Island.

On Saturday evenings the Lions Club members staged movies which attracted large crowds. One guest speaker, Alvin Pluff past president of the Lions in Rochester, N.H., said the Island club was the finest he had seen. One fact was the high attendance at the meetings. He made all the Island members realize what a fine place their Island was and had only one word of criticism, the ubiquitous mosquitoes.

The Anna Maria Readers Club was organized in 1942. From left, front row: Mrs. Johnson, Mrs. Louise Patzke, Marion Colman; second row, Franc Hydorn, Zipper, the pup, Mrs. Barlett, Louise Tamm, Mrs. Louis Dash, Lula Colman, Carrie Parrish. Back row, Mrs. Alfred Blair, Mrs. J.D. Brownell, Irene Gaskiell, Mrs. Peder Mickelsen, Florence Luckenbill, Mrs. Alfred Dybdock, Mrs. Thomas Thomen, Mrs. William Hathaway, Mary Hall, Mrs. Elmer Raymond and Mariam Murphy.

The Lions were known far and wide for their annual Minstrel Shows held at the Anna Maria Community Hall. Back in the '50s, everyone wanted to see the show. Seating was hopelessly inadequate and dozens of chairs were brought in from the Youth Center. In 1952, George Morris directed the show, Ted Tripp was the interlocutor and Mrs. Norman Rosedale provided the music.

Members of the Island Lions Club, at a meeting in October of 1960, voted to assume as one of their principal projects, the sponsorship of the Island Youth Center.

Civil Air Patrol

In 1952, the Holmes Beach airport was the base for maneuvers of the Civil Air Patrol (CAP). Units from Orlando, Tampa, St. Petersburg and Bradenton participated under directions from the Tampa Civil Air Patrol. Cadets formed ground forces consisting of an armed guard, a first aid station, and rescue teams for land and water. The Guard Squadron was under the command of Jack Leffingwell of the CAP. Part of the program included parachute jumping. Seven boys and two girls from the Island were members of CAP.

John L. Leffingwell, Sr. was appointed to organize the squadron of CAP in Manatee County. CAP Wing Headquarters in Orlando stated the organization, which was being formed in Manatee County, was the only active civil defense organization in the area.

In July, Holmes Beach hosted the Manatee County Civil Air Patrol. Twelve planes arrived at the Holmes Beach airstrip. Seventy-five flyers participated in a flying circus and were guests at a luncheon given by the Holmes Beach Council. Crowds of Islanders came out for the air show.

Readers of *The Islander* were interested in an article in the March 1955 issue entitled, "Serve Your Country,

Become A Plane Spotter". In 1955, the Island CAP advertised for a couple of old trailers, or wheels and axles. They were needed to mount two, 3,000-watt, motor-driven generators which had been donated by the government for emergencies. One was stationed in Anna Maria City, another in Bradenton Beach, and one was available in Holmes Beach, owned by Hugh Holmes.

Connie Zerby, one of the volunteers, described the system of spotting, reporting and recording planes. Fifty to sixty planes were seen every day. Using a simple code, planes were described by symbols and reports were phoned to Miami immediately.

William O'Connell was in charge of the Ground Observer Corps Tower in Bradenton Beach in July of 1957. He and Major Pinney had carried the burden of guarding the area far beyond the call of duty. From July 11 to July 27, 449 aircraft were logged at the Ground Observer Corps Tower. Observer hours totalled 461 during that period with only 13 observers. O'Connell issued a request for more observers so hours could be increased to 24 hours a day. Persons with normal vision, hearing and speech were urged to get involved.

When I was working as a reporter for *The Islander* in the early 70's I went on a mission with the Sunset Patrol. The patrol members were looking for ships in distress in waters around the Island. We spotted a small boat far from shore and reported the find to the Coast Guard. It turned out to be friends of my sons who had gone fishing and run out of gas. The Island boys were brought safely home by the Coast Guard.

Two men who were staying at the East O' The Sun cottages in Bradenton Beach saw a plane in trouble. They said the plane hit the ground, bounced and then plunged into the Gulf. They reported the mishap to Jim Templin who alerted the Civil Air Patrol and Deputy Sheriff Snooks Adams. Help came from all sides: the highway patrol, the sheriff's department patrol cars, planes, a helicopter and Coast Guard boats. They searched for hours. A check with all airports and Air Force headquarters revealed no planes missing.

Finally the search was abandoned with all the experts agreeing whatever the men saw was not a plane. An old timer suggested they might have seen a waterspout. After a tube-shaped cloud of a waterspout has become invisible, the water at the base kicks up for some time. It appears as a huge splash, similar to the effect of a large object plunging into the water. Another expert thought it could have been a large stingray.

Although it was a false alarm, it showed how quickly all concerned responded to an urgent call for help. Jim Templin was extremely proud of members of the CAP who helped in the search of the ghostly airplane and many other mishaps.

Island Churches

Roser Memorial Community Church, built in 1913, was the first church on the Island.

Roser Memorial Community Church
512 Pine Avenue
Anna Maria

A succession of ministers have come and gone at Roser Memorial Community Church over the years. In the early '40s, the Rev. W. Bradford Maskiell from New York, increased the membership, especially among the youth. Then Dr. James Madison Stifler, a retired minister from Evansville, Ill., served until 1948. Under his leadership the church made great strides such as: obtaining property, becoming incorporated, and adding transepts on each side of the original building.

The Wiggins family: The Rev. Richard and Mae Wiggins, Becky, Ricky and Nina.

The Rev. Carl Elmore from Englewood, N.J. initiated "practical" preaching, increased the congregation and made many improvements. A large parking lot, a Hammond organ, a parish house and a pastor's assistant, Mrs. Olivia Maskiell, were also added. The church maintained a thriving Sunday School, Youth Fellowship, Woman's Guild, Couples Club and was planning the first Vacation Bible School. Carl Elmore became the winter preacher and said when the church asked, he would occupy the pulpit "whenever the spirit moved him."

Marion Colman, a faithful church worker, said: "In remaining undenominational, the attitude of Roser Memorial Church is not isolationist, it is ecumenical or all inclusive of the world-wide nature of Christianity."

In 1953, more space was needed and church officers asked the congregation for $22,000 in contributions. An educational building had been the dream of the growing membership for many years. A garage was erected by volunteers to house several Sunday School classes. Rapid development of work with teenagers and young married couples had made the building inadequate.

In September of 1953, the cornerstone of the $24,000 educational building was laid. A metal box enclosed in stone contained a Bible, the history of the church, a list of charter members and contributors to the building fund, a copy of the church constitution and covenant and copies of local newspapers with stories about the new edifice. On Jan. 3, 1954, the formal opening of the educational building took place during the 11 a.m. service. A new bell replaced the old, corroded cowbell in the bell tower. The bell was a gift from a railroad company.

The Rev. Charles Lease, who lived in Wisconsin, received a call from Roser Church in April 1954. He had been advised to go to Florida for his health and the timing was right. He, his wife Mary, and their two children moved to the Island. When asked about his belief in non-denominational churches he answered, "I think the non-denominational church is one of the greatest, forward-looking movements in the Christian faith today. I believe life in such a church represents about the highest and most practical sort of Christian living. We like Anna Maria Island, love the kind, neighborly people, and we are honored to serve historical Roser Church."

On a sunny Sunday in 1957 ground was broken for the Roser parsonage on Jacaranda Avenue.

After the untimely death of Rev. Lease, the Rev. Richard K. Wiggins became the resident pastor in 1955. He was the church's second full-time minister. In his first year, a monthly newsletter, edited by his wife Mae, went out to all church members. Gas heaters were installed in the church. Members voted to buy El Rancho Motel and the name was changed to Rosemere Court. The four duplexes and an office were located across the street from the church on Pine Avenue. Members agreed to operate the motel to finance payments on the mortgage.

Rev. Wiggins conducted the first Christmas Eve Candlelight Service, which became a tradition. An early Sunday morning service was added and potluck suppers became popular. In October 1957, ground on Jacaranda Avenue was broken for a church parsonage. The Roser Men's Club was founded in 1959, and Sunday School attendance soared to 180. The Golden Anniversary of the church was celebrated, and a long-range concept of extension was adopted. Membership hit 400.

In 1965, Rev. Wiggins left the church for a position with Manatee Community Services in 1965. The Rev. Samuel Beaty from Ohio was chosen as the minister and began his duties in February of 1966. About a month after the Beaty family moved into the parsonage on Jacaranda Avenue a young woman in her thirties and her toddler daughter appeared and moved into the Beatys' house.

Sara Marshall, who contributed to the church history book, *"Our Church and How It Grew,"* referred to the woman who moved in with the Beatys when she wrote: "She was blonde, a little plump, and a very pleasant woman with a slight lisp. She obviously wielded a great deal of authority over the Beatys, personally and professionally. Their relationship was an enigma to us. We did not know where she came from or why she was here. People began to talk, not only in the church, but in the community. Church members took sides. Some insisted she should be asked to leave, or the Rev. Beaty be asked to leave. Others, deferring to the minister as a man of God, refused to listen to anything that would dishonor him. Others merely sat back, passing along gossip and waiting to see what would happen. There was confusion in the church and disharmony. Attendance began to drop off."

Members of the Roser Youth Group were involved in many church and community activities

According to Marshall's story: "An outside evaluation team, specializing in church analysis, was called to appraise the situation. After three days the team left with no statement except that they were totally baffled by the whole situation and had never encountered anything like it. The Rev. Beaty was called before the deacons to make an accounting of himself. There was nothing to explain, he said."

Finally, the situation became intolerable to everyone, with the exception of Rev. Beaty. In March 1967, just thirteen months after he came to Roser, he submitted his resignation effective June 1. It was a great relief to everyone, even those who liked him personally.

The Rev. Albert Butterfield was called to be the third full-time minister at Roser Church in February of 1966. The highlight of his time at Roser was the building of a new sanctuary. Ground was broken in 1973. On Nov. 2, 1975, the Sunday worship service began in the small historic chapel (Circa 1913) and moved to the new spacious sanctuary. After 11 years the Rev. Butterfield retired and the Rev. Frank Hutchison and his wife, Sylvia, and daughter, Jeanie, moved into the parsonage in 1978. The Rev. Hutchison was a charismatic preacher and his attractive wife brought bright colors into the parsonage and the Sunday School rooms. He started sunset services on the beach, in addition to regular Sunday worship services. Most exciting, at this time, was the church's adoption of the Lams, a refugee family from Vietnam. In November 1979, the Lams moved into a small apartment on the church grounds and church membership hit an all time high of 700.

Sara Marshall ended her church story on a high note: "At the dawn of a new adventure which integrates foreign and home missions, a new minister who seems well-suited to our needs and plans for growth and an ever-expanding program for the future, we close our present history."

The Church On The Island
Written by Fannie Heron Wingate in the 1930s

There's a church on the Island in the southland,
Between the Gulf and the Bay,
It stands like a friend by the side of the road
And ever seems to say.

This chorus is repeated after each stanza:
Oh come, come, come, come
Come to the church on the Island
Oh, come to the church on the Bay,
There's a message for you and work to do,
Hear the call of the Master today.

And its bell peals forth a message
Across the balmy air.
Come one, come all, oh heed my call,
Come join in praise and prayer.

The mockingbirds sweetly are singing
In the sunshine's golden glow.
The palm trees wave their graceful arms
And whisper soft and low.

The dear old church stands waiting
Like a friend by the side of the road,
And it seems to say, "Come enter here
And lose your heavy load.

Island Baptist Church
8605 Gulf Drive, Anna Maria

Ground breaking ceremonies for the Island Baptist Church were held on May 28, 1950.

Baptists on the Island appealed to the Rev. Frank T. Anderson, pastor of the First Baptist Church of Bradenton, for an Island church. He responded wholeheartedly by bringing his choir and some of his congregation to a service held in the Anna Maria Community Hall. This was the beginning of services which would be continued until a permanent church could be built. In the meantime, faithful Baptists met for prayer in island homes. In March 1950, the Baptist Training Union was organized under the direction of members from Bradenton. The Cooperative Missions Department of the Florida Baptist Convention sent the Rev. and Mrs. A. D. Dawson to the Island to establish and build a Baptist chapel. Temporary officers were elected. Mr. and Mrs. James Forrester donated the ground, and plans were designed by the Rev. Dawson and drawn by William Bayless, the builder.

Ground breaking ceremonies for the Island Baptist Church were held on May 28, 1950. Located on Gulf Drive at the entrance to Anna Maria City, the white concrete edifice was set off by two large palm trees which gracefully came together at the front entrance. At night, floodlights illuminated the scene which was called one of the most serene and striking sights on the Island. In 1951, the first Baptist Bible School on the Island was held with 85 children attending, ranging in age from 4 to 15 years. In 1952, a new building was in progress to accommodate Sunday School classes

The Island Baptist Church was not entirely self-supporting. It continued to be a mission of the First Baptist Church of Bradenton. The Rev. Malcom E. Smith was pastor and in July of 1952 the Rev. H. A. Gross came from Foley, Florida to be the first pastor of the Island Baptist Church.

Episcopal Church of the Annunciation
4408 Gulf Drive, Holmes Beach

A one-car garage was the Episcopalian Chapel of St. Michael, the Archangel, the first unit of the Annunciation Parish. Above it was the vicarage of the Rev. Burket Kniveton, vicar, his wife and daughter.

The "chapel" was on Spring Lane in Anna Maria.There was no organ, but majestic music came from the surf which was a stone's throw away. The incense was from the oleander, jasmine and other flowering bushes near the house. A simple altar, with its ever-burning light and sacred vessels, completed the air of sanctity. Not many could be seated, but the faithful could gather around the always-open door for the daily service.

In 1948, some devout Episcopalians asked the Rev. Henry I. Louttit, Bishop of South Florida, to start a mission. Not many were interested so the plan failed.

As the Episcopal population increased, Mrs. George Harris of Holmes Beach drew up a list of 120 names. Again, the help of Bishop Louittit was sought. This time the Rev. Kniveton was called from St. Mark's parish in Venice, and the possibility of building a parish on the Island was studied. On the first Sunday in May 1952 regular Divine Services were initiated in the Youth Center with a congregation of 53 and 27 children in Catechism.

More than 100 people turned out for the ground-breaking ceremonies of the Episcopal Church of the Annunciation.

In September, the Bishop impressed with Father Kniveton's work, said work could begin on a permanent Parish of the Annunciation on Anna Maria Island. In June 1953, the first confirmation call was held with 14 communicants.

Even before the altar was installed, the Tabernacle had been donated. Within it perpetually was the consecrated Host for worship and emergencies. If a person died in the middle of the night, they could receive the Blessed Sacrament.

Gifts from members poured in. All the sacred vessels of gold and silver, altar cloths and vestments, made by the women of the church, a statue of St. Michael and a bronze bell were donated.

In November 1952, a service was held in the Community Hall with 65 worshippers. By March there were 105 members. A woman's auxiliary was formed. It was decided the church would become an independent parish, self-supporting, within a year. Two lots were purchased north of the public beach and Mrs. Alexander Carleton donated an adjoining lot.

The ground-breaking ceremony took place April 19, 1953. More than 100 people turned out for the event. The women of the church marked the site with white string and the sod was turned with a golden shovel. Children received sweet cakes, an ancient Old Testament rite.

The women of the church began tireless, never-ending efforts to raise money at dinners and various other events. The actual construction started June 1, 1953. Father Kniveton was optimistic about the future of the Island Parish of The Annunciation.

A dedication service was held in the completed edifice in September of 1953. In accordance with the ancient ritual, the Rt. Rev. Martin J. Bram, DD, suffragan bishop of the Diocese of South Florida, knocked on the door of the church and demanded entrance. He and his entourage were admitted by Senior Warden George Harris, Sr. The blessing of the altar was followed by music and bell ringing and the first High Mass at the altar was celebrated by Father Kniveton.

Fred D. Ball, who retired from active life in civil welfare, devoted his time to woodcarving. He carved seven religious plaques which he donated to the Church of the Annunciation. They were displayed on the walls of the new church.

On March 1, 1956, the Rev. Burket Kniveton left the church for a ministry in the Bahamas. A simple, but impressive service was held at the water's edge. The Rev. Kniveton's boat was blessed, according to the ritual of the Episcopal Church. The boat was purchased through donations of many, but the greatest contributors were boat builders Louis Cobb and his son, Humbug. They gave hours of hard work to remodeling and equipping the vessel. Many people on the Island felt the loss of Father Kniveton, but they knew thousands of people in his new parish would be blessed. The stout little ship, "Star of the Sea," carried the blessings of all Islanders who were privileged to know the Vicar Kniveton at the Church of the Annunciation. Friends and neighbors gathered around and the choir sang as the "Stella Maris" departed for the Bahamas. Col. R. D. Sherman volunteered to pilot the boat on the first leg of the journey.

The Rev. Gerald Kenneth Lowe was appointed Vicar of the Church of the Annunciation by the Rt. Rev. Henry I. Louttit, Bishop of South Florida, on March 1, 1956.

For two years Father Lowe had been Vicar of St. John's Church in Brooksville. From 1936 to 1944 he served as Dean of Christ Church Cathedral in the Falkland Islands Dependency. In World War II, Father Lowe held a captain's commission in the British Army, serving as chaplain and assistant chief censor to the forces. He, his wife and their four children became popular with Islanders right away.

Gloria Dei Lutheran Church
6608 Marina Drive, Holmes Beach

Gloria Dei formally became a congregation of the Florida Synod of the United Lutheran Church of America on Feb.1, 1958, and the first service was held on August 3 of that year in the Annie Silver Community Hall in Bradenton Beach.

Ground was broken on August 20, 1961 for the construction of Gloria Dei Lutheran Church.

The Rev. Frank E. Lyerly was called to Anna Maria Island by the Board of American Missions of the United Lutheran Church of America. He had served for three years as pastor of a Lutheran church in Maiden, N.C. He and his wife, Barbara, came to the Island in 1958 to help establish the new Lutheran church. There were almost 100 Lutherans on the Island at that time.

In 1959 the adult charter membership totaled 107 and the childrens charter membership was 20. Pastor Lyerly, the mission developer, was called to be the first pastor.

Three acres of land were purchased and ground was broken on August 20, 1961. Construction of the church, at 6608 Marina Drive in Holmes Beach, began. The unique building was the only one of its kind in the Lutheran

Church of America. It represented a total investment of $175,000 for the site and building. The imposing building, erected on the triangular site, was designed by Victor Lundy of Sarasota, an internationally acclaimed architect. A number of his churches were featured in publications such as *Architectural Record* and *Architectural Forum*. Lundy, commissioned by the State Department, had worked on foreign embassy buildings. Stanley Lujack of Bradenton was the contractor.

The church had a seating capacity of 296 with overflow capacity of 250 with the use of the parish hall. Two educational wings were added at a later date. The original building included a pastor's study, sacristy and a conference room. A central heat pump system allowed for cooling and heating.

Normal procedure in the building of churches in the United Lutheran Church was to build a parish hall first. An exception was made for the Island church. This was only the sixth exception in ten years.

Pastor Lyerly said the trend among Lutheran churches was to depart from the conservative, traditional buildings which he felt had become "over-Gothic" in design. Newer Lutheran churches featured modern architectural styles, which he felt expressed the Lutheran faith, which was "alive and dynamic." He said the triangular design of Gloria Dei was symbolic of the Holy Trinity, an important tenet of the Lutheran religion.

The first worship service in the new edifice was held on May 13, 1962. The next year Pastor Lyerly left the Island. Pastor Lester M. Utz was the second pastor beginning on Jan. 1, 1964. A Service of Dedication began with a procession of the congregation led by the pastor, Rev. Utz. Rev. Harry H. Beidleman gave the sermon entitled "The House of the Lord." Children of the church carried palms, and members of the church council carried Bibles, altar service books and sacramental vessels. The church choir was under the direction of Mrs. Harry Frazee, who sang a solo, "The Holy City," based on the text of Psalm 122:1. More than 300 attended the dedication service and received a special dedication program and a picture of the church.

Following Pastor Utz's resignation on May 31, 1967, Pastor Franklyn S. Lambert became the third pastor to occupy the pulpit at Gloria Dei. When Pastor Lambert left, due to poor health, Pastor Lyerly came back to begin his second term of ministry at Gloria Dei from July 11, 1974 until his retirement. Pastor Danith L. Kilts was installed as the fourth pastor on April 18, 1993.

Christian Science Church

The First Church of Christ, Scientist in June 1971.

5314 Marina Drive, Holmes Beach

In 1963 a group met to discuss holding Christian Science services on the Island. Soon informal Sunday evening services were held at the Manatee County Public Beach pavilion in Holmes Beach. Services moved to the Community Hall in Anna Maria and testimony meetings were held once a month on Wednesday evenings.

The group decided to form a society on Dec.11, 1964, and on April 25, 1965 this recognition was granted by the Mother Church, The First Church of Christ, Scientist in Boston.

The first lecture took place in the Anna Maria Elementary School on Jan. 21, 1968 to an overflowing audience. Contrary to popular belief, Christian Scientists are not forbidden to go to doctors. The choice is left up to the individual.

A storefront was rented at 5314 Marina Drive, in the Holmes Beach Shopping Center. Men in the congregation turned it into a Christian Science Reading Room which was open to the public starting Jan. 2, 1971.

Meanwhile, plans were drawn for a church. Ground was broken at 6300 Marina Drive, Holmes Beach on June 3, 1971. Hugh Holmes, the contractor, said the church should be completed by mid-October. The 2,400-square-foot building, designed by Bradenton architect Dean Wyke, would seat 125 parishioners and include an office and Sunday School rooms.

Members of the church held the first meeting in the new church on Nov. 3, 1971 and the first Sunday service on Nov. 7. Since it was founded in 1962, the church had been known as the Christian Science Society of Anna Maria Island. When services moved into the new church building, it was known as the First Church of Christ, Scientist of Holmes Beach. The name change denoted the local society had met all the requirements of the Mother Church.

On Nov. 11, 2003, the membership voted to dissolve the church. Declining membership was the reason for their decision. Many parishioners changed their membership to the First Church of Christ, Scientist in Bradenton. Items from the Island church were given to the Bradenton church, including the organ and stained glass windows. It sold for $1.825 million. The building was demolished in 2004 and the land cleared. Six, three-story condominiums replaced the church.

The main part of Harvey Memorial Community Church was built in 1948.

Harvey Memorial Community Church
300 Church Avenue, Bradenton Beach

The Rev. Joseph C. Harvey of Philadelphia retired from the ministry in 1940 and moved to Bradenton Beach, the southernmost city on Anna Maria Island. He was unable to find a church nearby, so Rev. Harvey began holding services in the recreational hall of the Pines Trailer Park. This continued until the main part of a new church building was built in the summer of 1948. The building was named the Bradenton Beach Church and Social Service Corporation.

The main portion of the building had been Army barracks used during World War II on the North Point of Anna Maria. The barracks were knocked down and reassembled under Rev. Harvey's supervision. One account said, "The Army barracks were moved from behind the Great Ribs and More Restaurant."

In a speech Marion Colman gave to the Star Club in 1945, she said, "The Army Signal Corps was stationed on the North Point. It was top secret and no one was allowed to walk around the Point. After the barracks were sold and moved away some became dwellings and others were used for temporary school rooms, before the new school was built.

"One was moved to Bradenton Beach and used as the community hall during the week and a church on Sundays. Later it was called Harvey Memorial. I remember Rev. Harvey and his daughter. He was a man of strong convictions and much courage and perseverance. He started religious services in the Pines Trailer Community Hall on Feb. 7, 1943 and worked hard to build a congregation. It is now a community church and a member of the Florida Fellowship of Community Churches."

In the 1950s many services were held in the bare structure which had the sides and framing exposed. Friends of the church labored to finish the inside of the building. The only cost were the materials.

Rev. Harvey's last year at the church was in the winter of 1951. He died in 1953 at the age of 90. Residents recalled how he had preached in nearby trailer parks, and his untiring efforts and great devotion resulted in the founding of Harvey Memorial Church. He was one of the most beloved citizens on the Island.

The Rev. Arthur Simms became pastor in 1951, and the name of the church was changed to Harvey Memorial Church. The Rev. Harvey was appointed Pastor Emeritus at the first fall meeting in 1952. The sign on the church read, Community Church, which was retained at the Rev. Harvey's request. It was his wish that the church be used as a community meeting place as well as a church.

Sunday School and adult social evenings started in the fall of 1952. A gas stove was installed the same year. In the summer of 1953 the Bradenton Beach City Council began holding monthly meetings in the church. The caption under a picture of the church in *The Islander* read: "The fact that it is a church seems to have little effect on the behavior of the councilors and citizens attending, although each meeting is opened with a prayer. There is hope!"

Civic organizations also made use of the building for meetings. Col. Lemp donated $500 toward a new organ in 1954 as a memorial to his deceased wife. Sunday, January 9th was a red-letter day for the church. A dedication service for the new Hammond organ was held, and an organ recital by Walter Kimbell of Sarasota was enjoyed by all who attended.

In 1955, the kitchen was remodeled. The same year, the building was enlarged due to the increased congregation during the height of the tourist season. The City Council donated $500 toward this improvement. This added twice the seating capacity. At an open house in the fall of 1957, the Women's Church Group was organized. Through their efforts, the kitchen was remodeled and redecorated, and a tile floor was installed. All the improvements cost very little since the volunteer work was done by members and friends.

St. Bernard's Catholic Church
248 South Harbor Drive, Holmes Beach

In 1947 Kathleen Donovan Jones gave a 150 by 250 foot lot on 43rd Street in Holmes Beach for the construction of a church. The church became St. Bernard's Catholic Church. The gift was a memorial to her parents, Capt. John R. and Sophie E. Jones. Originally from Canada, the Joneses homesteaded a large tract of land near the center of the Island. Two years later Miss Kathleen sold an adjoining tract, 250 by 370 feet, to the church for a token price of $250.

Before a building was constructed Masses were celebrated in private homes, the Bradenton Beach Fire Hall and the Anna Maria Elementary School.

In 1955, Archbishop Joseph Hurley expressed his desire for an Island church, however, the parish only had $9,600 in the bank. The Rev. Robert Schieffen, administrator of St. Joseph Parish in Bradenton, gave the go-ahead and plans were drawn for a provisional chapel to serve until the bridges were built.

The bridges were vital to the Island in the early days. Archbishop Hurley designated St. Bernard of Clairvaux as the patron of the new church. On Jan. 29, 1956 services began in the uncompleted building. There was no ceiling and studs were exposed. Plastic covered the windows and rough sheeting covered the exterior.

The exterior could not be finished until a shipment of red cedar arrived from Oregon. The first load was ruined by floods that inundated the northwest early in 1956. Father Schieffen celebrated the first Mass, and the second Mass was offered by the Rev. Francis Welsmiller, who became the parish priest.

The St. Bernard Mission of St. Joseph's Church in Bradenton was completed in 1956. This was the beginning of St. Bernard's Catholic Church in Holmes Beach.

In February of 1956 the church remained unfinished. There was a debt of $52,000, and furnishings were needed in the priest's living quarters. The congregation consisted of 61 families.

Dedication of the church was held on March 8, 1956. The theme of the dedication was: The church belonged to Anna Maria Island. It was announced that Hernando DeSoto, a Catholic, landed nearby in 1539 and this new "outpost" would continue his Catholic tradition.

The parish grew in size and in May of 1958, when the Longboat Pass opened, Catholics from Longboat Key added 30 families to the congregation.

In 1970, Bishop Charles McLaughlin dedicated the new St. Bernard Activity Center. There were 320 families from the Island, Longboat Key and Cortez in the parish. In 1972, Father Welsmiller, who had been pastor of the church for 17 years, left with his father to open an orphanage for boys in Mexico.

Easter Sunrise Services

One of the oldest traditions on Anna Maria Island since the '50s has been the Easter Sunrise Service held at dawn on Easter morning. The following was an article in *The Islander,* written in 1953: "Many Attend Sunrise Service. Each year the attendance is greater than the year before. Hundreds gathered on a beautiful, but cool morning, to hear the words and songs and watch the sun come up in a cloudless sky.

"As was the custom, clergy from all the Island churches took part in the service held at Manatee Public Beach in Holmes Beach. As the sun came up F. D. McDonough played one verse of "Up From The Grave He Arose" on his cornet. Rev. A. W. Simms, pastor of Harvey Memorial Church, led the group in prayer. The Rev. John Lockyer, associate pastor of Roser Church, read a message from the Bible. The congregation sang, "All Hail The Power of Jesus' Name," under the leadership of Roger Stonehouse. All Island choirs were invited to "amalgamate" on the roof of the Beach House. The benediction was pronounced by Rev. A. J. Gross, pastor of the Island Baptist Church."

"Our Triumphant Faith" was the title of the message Rev. Richard Wiggins, pastor of Roser Church, delivered on Easter Sunday in April of 1956. Combined choirs of the Island churches sang "Easter Hope" directed by Mrs. O. W. Harpold, music director of Roser Church. The Rev. Edward Jackson, pastor of the Island Baptist Church, gave the prayer and read the scripture. The Rev. A. W. Simms of Harvey Memorial Church pronounced the benediction. The annual sunrise service continues as the most inspiring hour of Island life for the people who come from as far as the North Point in Anna Maria to unite in worship in darkness and see the glorious sunrise of a new day."

The Roser Youth Group was ready for a summer camping trip when this photo was taken.

The Island Players

"One evening in 1949 Harold and Sara Igo were walking around Anna Maria City when he spotted an old building on the main road. 'You know that would make a good theater,' Harold said, as he pointed to the community hall. His wife laughed, but Harold was not discouraged. He made some connections, read his plays to anyone who would listen and eventually a meeting was called to set up a theater on the Island. A dozen enthused people attended and Harold Igo was chosen director of the new community theater." This article appeared in the *Bradenton Herald* on December 12, 1949.

"Harold Igo, a distinguished playwright, actor and director is nationally recognized as a man of importance in the American theater. A newspaper man, he sent his first play to Yale and was immediately accepted in the university's writing and directing course. Eventually Igo wrote and produced 14 long plays and eight short ones. Nine were produced at the Pasadena Playhouse, two were Off-Broadway, one was seen in Cincinnati and one played in Chicago. Several were staged at the Island Playhouse."

Almost as soon as the founding group was organized the Anna Maria Island Woman's Club asked Igo to stage a play. The play, "The Preacher Takes A Wife," was for the club members only. It was a hit, and the women insisted plays should start in the theater immediately.

"We are encouraged to make our debut, not to strut our stage, nor to be impressive, but to afford a source of entertainment for the whole Island using the abundant talent of Island residents. There are many difficulties, such as problems with inadequate lighting, paucity of scenery and costumes, but they are minor. Outside the window, leading from the primitive dressing room, sits a chair. To pass unseen from one side of the stage to the other, the actors climb out the window, grope for the chair and scurry around to the back door. When a group hurriedly begins their journey there is a peril to limbs and costumes."

Founders of the Island Players, Sara and Harold Igo.

These were the words of Roger Stonehouse, the Island Players first president, spoken at the initial performance of the Island Players in 1949.

With no money, props or other tangible assets, but rich goodwill toward each other and loyal admiration for the director, the Players started their first year. They were enthusiastically supported, and the year's end found them with cash in the bank, some scenery, props and costumes which they stored in the Old City Jail.

"The Mail and the Manicurist" was the Players first production in the 137-seat theater and it represented half the fare for the 1948-49 season. They also produced a Christmas play. Within several years the group was producing three plays a season.

In an interview, Harold Igo told of the beginning of the Island Playhouse. "There was absolutely nothing backstage. The wind whistled through the cracks in the wall. It was cold in the winter and hot in the summer. There was no heat or air conditioning in those days. We would string a sheet up for a make-shift dressing room. The actors were dedicated and had lots of courage. In one play there were 35 actors and we had to rent a trailer for a dressing room."

Harold's wife, Sara, was a talented portrait painter. She designed sets, supervised costumes and was the makeup artist for the actors during the 17 years Harold was affiliated with the Players. Sara recalled her days with the Island Players: "I wanted to act, but I forgot my lines twice so Harold said I had to stay backstage. Twice I painted portraits of leading actors that were hung on stage and they became an integral part of the play's plot. I think the best play was 'The Waltz of the Toreadors' in 1959. That was 10 years after we started. It was artistically the best and everything went perfectly. Harold liked to cast Island residents whenever he could. He thought

This large cast was in a popular play in the '60s.

people on the Island would like to see people they knew on stage. And I think he was right."

The Island theater was Harold's greatest joy. In the early days he wrote a few of the plays. Summing up the years he spent as founder and director he said, "Looking over the years is like reading a bundle of love letters, for the theater is a love affair. If you love it, nothing matters, neither heat nor cold, hunger or thirst. There were times when the theater was colder than a New England barn and times it was hotter than a steam bath. Meals were missed, actors dashed in after a hard day's work, with grime of toil as their makeup. There were delays, discomforts, but always there was fun and excitement. To our old friends we express our deep gratitude and to our new friends we say the best is yet to come."

At the Anna Maria City Commission meeting on Dec. 1, 1951, several members of the Island Players board protested against the city's ruling that the Players must pay one dollar every time they used the community hall. They explained the Island Players was a non-profit organization, dedicated to providing cultural benefits for Island residents. They did not see why they should be penalized one dollar every time they used the hall. Members of the Island Woman's Club, who had done so much for the hall, were equally disturbed. In later years the Players were charged one dollar a year.

In March of 1953, a very different play "Sand Dollar Circus" was in rehearsal. Igo wrote the play for a large cast in the little theater. He was undaunted working with 30 people. Some of them had never been on the stage before. He chose a modern, intricate form to delineate his ideas and promised the play would entertain, provoke arguments, discussions and give the audience plenty of laughs.

Since those days, in addition to presenting numerous Broadway successes, the Players made many improvements to the hall on Pine Avenue and Gulf Drive by replacing antique equipment and furnishings. This added to the enjoyment of those using the historic building. It originally was owned by the Gillette family of Parrish in the early 1900s. The house was cut in half, barged down the Manatee River and across the bay to Anna Maria. A team of horses pulled it up Pine Avenue.

The Island Playhouse was transformed into a quaint community theater. The speaker's platform was amplified and strengthened, and wiring and lighting were improved. Exits were enlarged and lighted. There were dreams of a theater/auditorium that would expand the Island's opportunities for entertainment and attract small conventions to the Island.

At the annual dinner in 1954, Evelyn Kermode, president of the Island Players said, "Five years ago the Woman's Club asked Harold Igo, a visiting playwright, to stage a performance as a special event for them. From this successful presentation came an insistent demand for local little theater with our brilliant Harold as director. After his gracious consent our wonderful Island Players came into existence. We started without money or props. When our first year ended with all the bills paid, we had a tidy show of profit. The Players moved forward with each succeeding president and we have just completed a highly successful season under the leadership of Milton Collion.

Helen Peters was a talented actress and an excellent director.

"As your incoming president I won't promise a new Cortez Bridge, or the elimination of red tide, but I do pledge myself to initiate some practical steps toward our greatest necessity, a true theater building of our own."

Harold Igo spotted an eye-catching blonde on the beach in the early '50s. It was Helen Peters, and he recruited her on the spot for his upcoming play. A resident of Minnesota, she held a bachelor's degree in journalism and a minor in theater from the University of Minnesota. She was a recipient of the McKnight Fellowship from the Tyrone Guthrie Theater at the university, and she taught radio drama at the U of M and drama to several theater groups. Helen also had a Sunday "View and Do" television show. Occasionally she opened refrigerator doors in commercials.

After her first appearance she was cast in numerous Players production to rave reviews. In 1962, Helen moved to the Island permanently and Harold Igo hired her as a guest director. When illness forced him to retire in 1966, his legacy was continued by this talented lady, a position she held for 12 years.

Helen worked hard to make all the plays she directed as professional and realistic as possible. She managed to get a real goat for "Teahouse of the August Moon." The city refused to let her keep the goat on the Island, so she hid it at her home on North Shore Drive and towed it to the theater each night until the play closed.

In a speech for an Island club, Mrs. Peters told of the little theater she grew to love. "The Island theater fascinated me. There was less than a seven-foot proscenium. The audience sat on wobbly folding chairs placed precariously on risers. It was so hazardous. Sometimes a chair would slip off the end during a performance. The actors were wonderful. I didn't know the meaning of the word "can't". Upstage was the outside of the building with holes for windows. Of course, there was no air conditioning. We used fans in the summer and oil space heaters in the winter, but it was still too hot and too cold. Our light board was two small dimmers worked by hand, and they did not always work. The curtain was a 50-year-old brown velour donation, which sometimes would not open or close.

"The audience was so close an actor could reach out and touch them. It was disconcerting. But even more so were the comments from the audience which were plainly heard on stage. 'Is that real mink?' Or the woman who repeated every line to her hearing impaired husband. The stage was so small I could not cast tall men. I would bar hop to find actors. My real concern was the people. If I can help just one person develop an interest in the theater, then it's all worthwhile," she said.

One of Helen's finest actors was Sara Marshall. Sara recalled this incident: "Betty and Hartley Blackburn were my neighbors. In one play I swept onto the stage in heavy makeup and regal robes as Queen Elizabeth. Betty and Hartley were in the audience and started waving at me. That was typical in the Island Playhouse."

Sam McDowell became a much-loved veteran of the Island stage. He remembered "Streetcar Named Desire" as one of the more successful productions. "Sara played Blanche DuBois, but we were worried how the Island audience would receive it since Tennessee Williams was a little raw for the Island audience. It was a tremendous effort by the cast and the audience received it well," he said.

The theater building languished for years and by 1970 was in sad disrepair. The Island Players hoped to have their own theater constructed. When the city granted them permission to make repairs and install better seating they got to work. This brought complaints from others who used the building. The objectors said the Players were taking over. Mayor Harry Cole said the city was faced with a dilemma—what to do with the old building that was gradually being eaten by termites.

"The public should be delighted that the Players are willing to maintain the building," Cole said. "It would be a liability without the support of the theater group."

Although most residents thought the community hall had a certain amount of nostalgia, from a practical point of view the old white frame building was quickly becoming a white elephant. Older residents considered it an historic landmark, while others thought it had outlived its usefulness. The city commission was confronted with the problem of what to do. They admitted it would either be a painful or costly decision.

Several years later, the city gave the Players exclusive use of the hall. In 1973, Helen Peters organized the Off Stage Ladies, a support group for the theater. The women hustled to make money. They purchased curtains, lighting equipment, dressing room mirrors, air conditioning and heating and 140 seats attached to the floor. Board members, concerned with every aspect of the theater, worked on and off stage. Only the director, lighting technicians and musicians were paid.

In 1988, numerous fund rising projects were staged to raise $50,000 for renovations. A veranda was added to the front of the building, the box office was enlarged and a sewing room and a workshop were built. A kitchen and a new lighting room all transformed the ancient building into jewel on the corner of Gulf and Pine. It was set off with the Island Walk, signature bricks that swelled the coffers, and Florida landscaping by Michael Miller and his volunteer helpers. The acoustics were excellent and the coziness and charm of the early days remained. Five shows a year were directed by a rotating group of guest directors. With the backing of local subscribers and supporters, ever-increasing ticket sales and grants, the theater consistently operated in the black.

The Island Players Theater is now ranked highly in area publications, among such notables as the Asolo Theatre in Sarasota. Actors come from St. Petersburg, Venice, Bradenton, Longboat Key and Sarasota to act on the Island stage. Harold Igo would be astounded see his theater today. It would surpass his wildest expectations.

In the early days the Island Playhouse was the Community Hall.

Nine

Businesses

The first business on the Island was Cobbs' Marine Ways.

Early Business Establishments

In the early days, businesses on the Island were mainly fishing, farming and boat building. Sam Cobb founded Cobb Marine Ways at the curve of Gulf Drive in Holmes Beach, which was known as Cobbs' Corner. This was the oldest continually operating business on the Island. Sam came to the Island from New Jersey and opened the boat works about the time of the Spanish American War. With the gradual increase in population on the Island, a few small stores soon appeared. In November of 1947 there were 908 permanent Island residents, 469 houses and 88 trailers. A headline in *The Islander* on July 31, 1952 proclaimed: "Business Is Good On Anna Maria Island."

"No Vacancy!" was the headline in a February 1952 *Islander.* The story went on to say how wonderful it was to see no vacancy signs up all over the Island and how sad for visitors who would have liked to stay.

"There is not an available bed on the Island at this time," the article read. "Countless people have been turned away. Even friends cannot be accommodated. If realtors and business people grumble it is only because of their hard work and the heavy burden of money pouring into their pockets.

"The season will be good for all. Next year will be even better. That is the nature and measure of Anna Maria Island's growth."

Jack Holmes contradicted gloomy reports in a December 1954 *Islander*. Some mainland papers claimed that business was "awful" on the Island. Jack Holmes, Sr., the incurable optimist, handed out the following proclamation to the press:

The unique feature of the Silver Dollar Bar in Bradenton Beach was hundreds of silver dollars that were embedded in the bar.

"The contractors and real estate men in Holmes Beach report the best fall season in history. New homes are being built and sold. Old houses and lot sales for the past three months have amounted to a total of $591,200. Rental management offices report rentals are approximately 80-percent full at the present time. Inquiries are coming in way-above-average. Merchants on the Island are well pleased. One merchant said the old bridge was a blessing in disguise as more people are trading at home."

Another exciting headline appeared in the June 19, 1952 issue of *The Islander*: "Holmes Beach Plans Shopping Center!"

In the same newspaper, pictures of a group of cottages, designed and built by Roger B. Hall were shown. The paper did not give an address, but attested to the fact the Anderson Haven cottages were ultra-modern in design, with ceilings that followed the roof pitch. Hall wanted to get away from the cracker-box square and rectangular shaped homes.

Real estate ads in the newspapers were unbelievable. In 1952, realtor Jack Marshall advertised a bargain home. The new cinder block house had tile floors, a modern bath, two large sunny bedrooms, large closets, new furnishings, a carport and a sundeck. The 100-foot front lot, in the top residential section of the Island, was up for a quick sale. The price was $9,800.

George Wagner offered a house with a million-dollar view of Tampa Bay on a fully landscaped lot. The two-bedroom, bayfront home offered an excellent strip of beach and sold for $17,000.

One of the first grocery stores on the Island was Silvers Grocery in Bradenton Beach. Annie Silver

The IGA Foodliner opened on April 13, 1946.

ran the store from 1939 until 1947 when a heart attack made it necessary for her to sell the store to James Longnecker. In 1950, Richard Wagner became the owner for several years. In 1955, the store was sold to Mr. and Mrs. Kenneth Bailey of Bradenton who planned to turn it into a modern grocery store.

The IGA, A Family Business

Meanwhile in Anna Maria City, a family had moved from Tampa and opened a grocery store on the corner of Gulf Drive and Magnolia Avenue. Born in Tampa, Ignazio Ernesto Cagnina was the oldest of nine children. His father was a cigar maker. The family often visited Anna Maria Island to enjoy the beach. As a young boy, Ernie would save his money to buy round trip tickets to Anna Maria Island on The Plant, a popular excursion boat. Ernie worked in a shipyard in Tampa before he was drafted into the Army. When his military service ended in 1946, he bought the grocery store in Anna Maria and moved his family to the Island.

Ernie and Josephine Cagnina, above, Bennie and Antoinette Scanio were the proprietors of the IGA.

"When I first came down here you could shoot a rifle down Gulf Drive and not hit anything," Ernie said. "There were about 600 people on the Island. There was a filling station, a novelty store and a post office. The wooden bridge on Cortez Road linked the Island to the mainland, and the city of Holmes Beach had not been established. I had a relative who ran a store in Bradenton Beach. He told me about this store in Anna Maria. He thought I should buy it. At first I said no, then I talked it over with my brother-in-law, Bennie Scanio. We bought the store, became partners and I've been here ever since."

The IGA Foodliner officially opened on April 13, 1946. Through the years, Ernie Cagnina was respected as a capable businessman. He was one of Anna Maria's first volunteer firemen. Reflecting on what had happened years before, Ernie found humor in a story that didn't seem too funny to him at the time.

Johnnie Cagnina stood outside the IGA dressed as the Phillip Morris mascot.

According to Cagnina, the first fire truck was bought from the MacDill Air Force Base for $500. It was parked at the home of the fire chief, Melvin Davis, on Pine Avenue.

"About eight of us were at Melvin's home during a storm playing poker. Melvin mentioned it would be bad if they had a fire because of all the wind. Then we got a fire call. A house in Holmes Beach was on fire. When we got there we found we didn't know how to operate the truck. Because of the water pressure, it took three guys to hold the hose. We finally put the fire out, but the damage was done. The house burned all the way down," Ernie said.

Ernie knew many famous celebrities in politics and sports. "I knew Al Lopez in Tampa," he recalled. "We played ball on the same team. I was about 16 at the time, a second string catcher and Al Lopez was catching most games. If Al got hurt or couldn't continue, I took over for him." Unfortunately, Cagnina's ball-playing days ended with an arm injury.

Ernie Cagnina became the most popular mayor in the history of Anna Maria City and secured a place in the hearts of many of his constituents. At first he was reluctant to enter the political arena because he was a grocery store owner.

Ernie Cagnina served six consecutive terms as mayor of Anna Maria City.

"People kept asking me to run," he said. "I had never run for office. I thought it would hurt my business, because as mayor you are going to step on somebody's toes at times. I did not want to run.

"I got into politics because an older couple came to me and said 'Ernie, you gotta get this mess straightened out.' The mess was the police department. I did it for them and for others who thought I was a leader. My wife died in 1973 and I had time to spare," he explained.

The police department was a problem for several years. When Ernie dismissed the police chief, the entire department resigned. The departing chief stood up at a city meeting and announced the city was without protection. Cagnina, while vigorously chewing on a cigar, declared that was true for five minutes. In a short time five deputies from the Manatee County Sheriff's Department arrived in Anna Maria to keep the peace.

Ernie was just as adamant about condominiums and beach renourishment. Issues like these kept Cagnina returning to the political arena, cigar clenched firmly in his teeth, ready to roll up his sleeves and go to work.

The genial, cigar-chewing mayor had an unprecedented reign, serving six consecutive terms from 1975 to 1988. He always won by a landslide victory and three times returned to office without opposition.

He was a political follower, and for decades was a respected figure in the Manatee County Democratic Party organization. Gov. Lawton Chiles called Ernie his mentor, and former President Jimmy Carter invited him to his 1977 inauguration in appreciation for hosting him as the unknown presidential candidate at the Island Youth Center in 1975.

Many dignitaries were present when Governor Chiles kicked off his bid for re-election. Ernie was singled out and honored above them all. Governor Chiles said: "I just want to say a word about my mayor, Ernie Cagnina. I don't go anywhere without my mayor. Ernie has been my mentor and spiritual leader for as long as I've been coming to the Island. He looked after me and my kids, and now he's looking after my grandchildren."

The close-knit family team who ran the IGA were Josephine and Ernie Cagnina and Antoinette and Bennie Scanio. Josephine and Antoinette were sisters. Anyone who traded at the store knew the friendly, more-than-normal service they gave in their own inimitable style. The public never knew of their numerous good deeds. Working from early morning to late at night, they would go out of their way to get a customer what they wanted at a fair price. One time they were short four hams which had been promised to a customer on a certain day. Bennie flew to Tampa, hired a car, drove to the warehouse and flew back with the hams which were delivered on time. Ernie and Bennie had philosophical views of business and life. They did not desire to make a fortune. They wanted to serve people, and that's exactly what they did for almost 50 years.

Ernie would deliver telegrams and emergency groceries to Island homes. When customers were low on funds, the store owners would carry them through until they could pay their bills. They accepted and delivered telegrams. Cashing checks and locating people were other services. Doors opened at 8 a.m. and closed at 9 or 10 p.m. The many hours of work never interfered with their devotion to their community. No request from an organization was ever turned down by Ernie or Bennie. They were good storekeepers and fine citizens.

Every Christmas the store was open for the Annual Children's Christmas party. Island children received candy and presents from the generous store owners. A miniature carousel was outside the store, advertising Pepsi Cola, and the kids could have free rides.

From behind the counter Ernie watched Island families grow up and leave and then return with their new families. He and Josephine raised two children, Johnny and Carmen, in a large frame house on a large lot behind the store. Bennie and Antoinette shared the house. They had two daughters, Marie and Rosemary and a son, Benji, who died at an early age.

In 1957 the IGA Foodliner was remodeled. This resulted in new departments, more shopping space and an enlarged parking area. The caption under the picture of the store in *The Islander* read: "It is doubtful if there is a larger, finer store anywhere in a community this size on an island."

Tony Conboy, who ran unsuccessfully for mayor against Ernie in 1975 said, "I always hung out in the store.

Ernie reigned over the poker games in the back room of his store.

Everybody loved the mayor, including me. But how can you run against Santa Claus?" Despite his age, Ernie refused to retire at 84. With his trademark, a 10 Perfecto Garcia cigar, hanging out of the corner of his mouth, he still bagged groceries, greeted customers and delighted in his old habit of handing out lollipops to the children.

"Ernie had a uniqueness," said Mayor Ray Simches when he heard of Ernie's death in 1994. "He was a caring, kind and gentle man who left an indelible stamp on the history of Anna Maria and fond memories for all who knew him."

J. D. Webb opened a modern drugstore on Marina Drive in 1963.

Pharmacies

The first drug store on the Island was located in Bradenton Beach in the early '40s. It was owned and run by the Askew brothers, Ben and Jim. Located on the southeast side of Bridge Street, it was later moved to the middle of the block on the north side of the street. Folks said it was progress to have this super store. Along with pharmaceuticals, it offered beachwear, household items and a soda fountain. Billie Martini worked at this "nerve center of the Island."

J. D. Webb and Birdie Tebbetts discuss current events at the drugstore soda fountain.

"We had up-to-the minute news of what was happening on the Island and opinions on what we figured was about to happen in the future," she said.

In 1953, the Askew brothers leased the choicest location in the new Holmes Beach Shopping Center, on the corner of Gulf Drive. They offered pres-cription service and quick delivery by a special messenger.

Joe Webb was an accomplished surfer.

J. D. and Jackie Webb and their eight-year-old daughter, Paulette, moved from Atlanta to the Island in 1954, and J. D. became the pharmacist at the Island Pharmacy in the Holmes Beach Shopping Center. In 1963, he opened a new 6,200 square foot drug store on Marina Drive across from the Holmes Beach City Hall. An affiliate of the Arcadia Drug Company of Arcadia, the new store was named

Ben Webb takes aim.

Webb's Island Pharmacy. It featured modern fixtures for displaying merchandise, a large stock and a 50-seat restaurant. At this time, the Webbs had lived on the Island for eight years and had two sons, Ben and Joe.

An ad in *The Islander* implored residents to elect J. D. "Doc" Webb as their pharmacist. The ad read: "My pledge to you: See your doctor, then phone Webb's Island Pharmacy, and your prescription will be called for and delivered. I am consistent with quality, won't be undersold, and I will give you S & H Green Stamps too!"

Holmes Beach Shopping Center

On October 30, 1952, *The Islander* featured an architect's rendering of the new Holmes Beach Shopping Center. It was the vision of Jack Holmes. The builder was Holmes Construction.

This was another first for Jack who had more firsts than anyone on the Island. He had just put in the Island's first swimming pool, built an airstrip and did more advertising and promotion of the Island than anyone. 'This is progress!" the reporter declared. The drainage and storm sewage had been completed and the foundation was underway in the construction of the $200,000 shopping center in the heart of Holmes Beach. A new corporation was formed by the officers: John Holmes, Sr., Frank Giles and Ray Perrine.

The new shopping center, in operation in 1953, can be seen in the upper left of this aerial photograph.

The project was financed by the Island Shopping Center Inc., composed of John Holmes, Sr., Frank Giles and Ray Perrine. Located geographically in the center of the Island, leases were made almost immediately with a variety of businesses including a barbershop, drug store, electric appliance store, realtor and an antique shop.

Three acres of land were planned for the shopping center which was expected to be in operation by Jan.1, 1953. Plans for a series of modern, flexible, double-fronted stores facing Holmes Boulevard and 54th Street were formulated. The entire property, a portion of which was designed for parking 350 cars, was between Marina Drive on the east and Holmes Boulevard on the west, Gulf Drive on the south and 54th Street on the north. Sidewalks, protected by an overhang from the buildings, and a 12-foot roofed walkway bisected the stores.

The buildings were owned by the corporation and leased to the shopkeepers. Giles said plans to set rents as low as possible would be an inducement for developing the community shopping center.

In 1969, groundwork was laid for a chain supermarket and drugstore to be located in a new shopping center located in the cutoff that ran south of Manatee Avenue and tied back into Gulf Drive below Manatee Public Beach. Representatives of C & H Enterprises, the Miami firm that planned to build the shopping center, said construction should be completed by the fall of 1970.

Al Fresco Beauty Shop

Beauty treatment under the sun was the theme of Pierre's Studio in Holmes Beach, across the street from the elementary school. It opened to great fanfare in 1955. The salon had a unique feature, an open-air beauty parlor. Pierre and Paula Duba were innovators of the terrace-type, crescent-shaped studio consisting of a 2,000-square foot outdoor patio. It was equipped to give hair and beauty treatments, with the exception of facials and shampoos which were done in the main indoor salon. The patio was designed for use in nice weather, for sun lovers to get a natural tan along with beauty treatments. Pierre had a flood of requests from operators who wanted to work on solar haircuts. Patrons came dressed in everything from street clothes to wet bathing suits.

First Financial Institution

A $40,000 modern building housed the Island Bank, located close the Holmes Beach Shopping Center on the corner of Gulf Drive and Marina Drive. Future expansion was in the plans for the building with glass lobby walls. Construction of the Island Bank had reached the final stages in April of 1961. Officers of the bank announced that an open house would be held later in the month. Paul Krone, architect, said the bank had the latest and best equipment. A drive-in window, a night depository, a meeting room and safe deposit boxes were just a few of its many services. Clarence E.(Cotton) Brewer, who had moved from Pikeville, Ky., was president and F. P. Stanley and Robert Moses were vice presidents. Melvin Akins was the cashier. The bank opened for business in April 1961.

The Island Bank was open for business in the spring of 1961.

In 1969, the bank had doubled in size. In addition to the expansion of the building, parking facilities were enlarged and more landscaping added. Approximately 4,900 square feet of space was added when the new addition was completed. Plans called for the expansion of the first floor and the addition of a second floor. Most of the space on the second floor would be used for the trust department. The additional room on the first floor would provide space for an enlargement of the safe deposit vault, expanded bookkeeping, a proof department, additional lobby space and teller windows.

In eight years the bank's assets grew to approximately $8 million and served more than 5,000 customers in various departments.

Shortly after arriving on the Island, Paul Carlisle and his wife, Norene, purchased the Anna Maria Motel.

First Motel

Shortly after retiring from DuPont in 1949, from a career as a chemical engineer, Paul Carlisle, and his wife, Norene, of Wilmington, Delaware, discovered Anna Maria Island. Not content with a life of leisure, they purchased the Anna Maria Motel from the builder. This was the first motel on the Island and it was located at the northern tip of Anna Maria on Bay Boulevard and North Shore Drive. The genial couple made many friends and every morning motel guests would discover the daily paper and a juicy Duncan grapefruit on their doorstep, all for a mere $5 a night. The Carlisles ran this ad in the Island paper: "Anna Maria Motel - At The Tip of the Point - Efficiency Units and Cottage - You Will Like It."

Anna Maria Mayor Paul Carlisle

It was not enough to keep Paul Carlisle busy, so he earned a real estate license and set up an office in the motel. Soon he became president of the Island Chamber of Commerce in 1953 and 1954. Along with other Island enthusiasts, Carlisle was responsible for the construction of three bridges to the Island.

As one of Anna Maria's biggest boosters, he took an active part in the city's growth. He was there for the ground breaking of the Youth Center field and in 1954 was elected mayor of Anna Maria City, the city he loved. After a brief illness, Paul died on

July 3, 1956. Norene continued to operate the motel with the help of her daughter, Margaret Chapman. Norene died in 1982 at the age of 91. Margaret remodeled and managed the motel until it was sold in 1989.

Gulf Park Hotel and Trailer Park

Gulf Park Hotel in its heyday.

The first largest real estate transaction on Anna Maria Island took place in April of 1954. Mr. and Mrs. Henry J. Templin of Michigan bought the Gulf Park Hotel and

Trailer Park from Mr. and Mrs. Dick Dodge, who had owned the Island landmark for more than eight years. The article in *The Islander* did not reveal the price.

Rurick Cobb, one of the first Island homes- teaders, built the Clubhouse in 1909. He was backed by German-Americans who were in the phosphate industry in Tampa. The Clubhouse was a three-story building featuring a huge dining room, shower stalls on the first floor and bedrooms on the third floor. Since there was no bridge to the Island, Cobb built a 1,100-foot pier from the hotel to Anna Maria Sound to enable an 11-passenger motorboat to bring guests from Tampa.

The first residents in the Gulf Trailer Park were carnival folks.

In 1914, at the onset of the war, guests did not come to the complex, and in 1915 the mortgage was foreclosed by Howard Zewadski. He sent Frank Farrel to manage the hotel and the Ilexhurst Hotel was born. In 1921 the hotel withstood a devastating hurricane. In the early days Ilexhurst surveyors were paid off in property in lieu of cash. At that time Island lots were a dime a dozen.

Anna Maria Cobb Riles, whose claim to fame was being the first white baby born on Anna Maria Island, said the section was called Ilexhurst because of the buttonwood, or ilex trees, that grew there. During the Great Depression, business fell off and the property around the hotel became overgrown with the trees. The hotel was deserted and the pier fell apart.

Slowly business revived with the influx of Midwestern farmers, who came south in 1940 to escape the bitter cold. Cortez Bridge was built and more tourists came. A colored postcard, during this early period, featured an aerial photo showing Bay-to-Gulf development. A sizeable pier was on the bayside where steamers discharged passengers going to the hotel.

"Years ago the Clubhouse was a respectable place," said 81-year-old Anna Maria Cobb Riles, who was the original builder's niece. Interviewed by a *Bradenton Herald* reporter in February of 1979, she explained that the building started out as a private club. It was a party place with a rumpus room on the first floor and upstairs there were comfortable chairs and large tables for games and dining. Later it was opened to tourists, providing them with a place to swim, sunbathe and fish.

Through the years many interesting characters stayed at the hotel or frequented the beverage area. George Simeon, a famous French author, was one. It was said that he had more works published than any writer of his time. He brought Gerald Kersh, a novelist and short story writer for the *Saturday Evening Post* and other magazines, to the Island hotel. Kersh produced the first Island newspaper in 1947. This was the *Bradenton*

Fun times at the Gulf Trailer Park in the '40s.

Beachcomber, according to one account. There was only one issue of the paper and it became a collector's item. In it was a photograph of a gala party in the hotel. Gerald Kersh was pictured looking like a Spanish conquistador, with a mustache and beard, and pretty ladies and male companions were grouped around him.

It was about 1940 when Mrs. Zewadski started the Gulf Park Trailer Park across the street from the hotel. The park catered to tourists and winter visitors. The hotel was renamed Gulf Park Hotel and the pier was rebuilt. The trailer park grew rapidly. There was a community hall, and all who lived in the bayside park became a close-knit community.

According to an *Islander* story in the Feb. 24, 1955 issue, there were 174 trailers in Gulf Trailer Park and capacity was 198. Peace, pleasure and camaraderie reigned. The spirit of the genial owner, H. J. Templin, was evident throughout the park. In 1957, the park was notified it had been awarded an approval rating as one of the top mobile home trailer parks in the United States, according to the Mobile Home Manufacturing Company. The announcement was made official in a publication after 12,525 parks in the country were inspected.

During World War II, the U.S. Coast Guard stationed a company in the hotel and later built a Coast Guard Station in Cortez.

In 1945, Mrs. Zewadski leased the hotel to Dick and Betty Dodge who later bought it. Two men leased the hotel from the Dodges in 1950 and planned to turn it into a modern restaurant with 12 rooms for transients, several cabanas and two pavilions. The main business was the bar.

However plans did not materialize, and in 1954 the hotel and trailer park were sold to Jim Templin of Michigan. He turned the ground floor into a barbershop, submarine sandwich shop, an ice cream parlor, grocery store and a bar. In 1960, the third floor was condemned. Templin sold the hotel to Bill Britt and Gerald Vorbeck in 1972 and in 1976 it was sold to Wayne Rickert. It became a hangout for the younger set. Noise and parking became problems and Mayor Dick Connick threatened to close the bar.

In the '70s the hotel was nothing but a bar and was given a controversial name, The Oar House. It became a popular drinking place for the Island youth. David Reid and Warren Jerrems managed the bar for owner Wayne Rickert. The managers had constant problems with residents of the trailer park across the street, which had been renamed the Sandpiper Mobile Home Park. Trailer park residents objected to the all-night noise from the drinking crowd. At times more than 200 people were jammed into the watering hole listening to popular rock musicians. The Oar House gained a reputation for having big-name entertainers such as Gregg Allman, Dickey Betts, Leon Redbone and Tom Waits. Wayne Rickert requested the city let him raze the aging structure and build a condominium, but his request was denied.

Dale White wrote this description of the historic Gulf Park Hotel in the *Sarasota Herald Tribune*: "In its declining years the Oar House turned on, tuned in and dropped out. Surprise concerts by the Allman Brothers Band converted the old hotel into Manatee's Mecca of rock music. Hippies and bikers considered it the place to party. Nearby residents complained about the loud music and disruptive behavior of the Oar House clientele. Acting on neighbor's complaints, Mayor Dick Connick vowed to close the hangout."

In the early hours of Feb. 22, 1979, bartenders and patrons smelled smoke and saw flames billowing out from the abandoned second floor. A short circuit in the heating system was blamed. Beer cans exploded, glass bottles shattered, coins in pinball machines bubbled up in what fire officials estimated to be 1,800 degree heat. Managers David Reid and Warren Jerrems were able to save the cash register, most of the records and several cases of beer before the heat became too intense. Later, contents of one of two safes were salvaged from the smoldering ruins. People on the mainland could see the flames which raged for nine hours. The building that represented 70 years of Island history was reduced to ashes.

Mayor Connick and David Reid were contenders in a mayoral election. Reid lost by a slight margin of 40 votes. It was well known the two did not get along. Ironically, it was Connick, in his role as fire chief, who fought the Oar House fire with members of the Anna Maria, Bradenton Beach and Cortez fire departments.

Don Moore, a former editor of *The Islander*, wrote, "An old friend just went up in flames. When I was a kid growing up on the beach during World War II the old Gulf Park was the northern boundary of my microcosmic world. A bunch of us played in an area from Gulf Park to Surf Point, a group of small wooden cottages that once stood at 22nd Street and the Gulf in Bradenton Beach.

"Gulf Park was the most formidable building in my little world. Even three decades ago the ancient bar did not look much different than it did minutes before it burned. It was falling down in 1944, the first time I can remember laying eyes on the place. About the only difference is that in those days the bar had a third story that had been removed in the early 1960s because it was about to collapse from disrepair and termites.

"From a child's point of view Gulf Park was a huge old building with large verandas around all four sides of the second floor. At the ground level, in those days, it looked pretty much like it did up until last week- a dark, dingy dive where one could find all kinds of people. During the war it was an Island nightspot that seemed to be eternally open.

"Even in those days people would say if the termites in Gulf Park ever stopped holding hands the whole place would fall down. About the only thing that changed was the management. Most recently a couple of young fellows were running the bar and from all indications breathing new life into the old place. Now it's gone. Gulf Park is no more. Another Island landmark has perished. It was a tie to the past on a sleepy little island where everyone knew everyone and no one was in a big rush to be anything but neighborly."

A Funeral Home

In 1959 plans for a funeral home to be constructed on Marina Drive in Holmes Beach were complete. Griffith-Cline of Bradenton purchased the site from Jack Holmes. The mortuary of white brick-crete contained a chapel and living quarters for the mortician.

Holmes Beach Yacht Club Becomes Pete Reynard's

This was the exciting headline in *The Islander* on February 26, 1953. The artist's sketch showed a building 60 by 100 feet on the peninsula southeast of the Holmes Beach shopping center, across from the yacht basin and a few yards from the airstrip.

"There is a channel leading from the bay," the reporter wrote. "It is fearfully and wonderfully made and clearly marked."

The club would be owned by a group of stockholders. Small membership fees would entitle members to voting privileges and the board would supervise social affairs. Plans called for a modernistic building with private clubrooms, a main dining room, a cocktail lounge, a kitchen and service facilities. The cocktail lounge and dining rooms would be open to the public with a seating capacity of 300. The larger dining room would be available for use as an auditorium. Docking facilities for boats and plans for a swimming pool were formulated. Due to upcoming financial problems the pool was never built.

Pete Reynard put Anna Maria Island on the map.

In November of 1953, the kitchen and bar were being installed. The all-stainless steel kitchen had two charcoal broilers. It was a fine kitchen, according to Chef Pedro Perez who had a wealth of experience in restaurant cooking. From Lake George, near Saratoga, N.Y., he was famous for his tasty smorgasbords.

Almost immediately 100 memberships were purchased. F. P. Stanley, treasurer, said only 500 memberships would be accepted. The fees were $25 for family, $15 for individuals and $10 for winter visitors. Members would be permitted to bring guests. The formal opening was set for New Year's Eve of 1953.

Times were tough and the club had trouble making ends meet. In 1954, Jack Holmes announced the yacht club had been built a few years ahead of the economic possibilities of a private club breaking even financially. He gave Mike Vertich, who had vast experience managing restaurants, the concession for the restaurant and bar. Vertich, who was originally from Hamilton, Ohio, previously owned the Mira Mar in Bradenton Beach. Jack Holmes said it was up to club members to organize and formulate plans to utilize the club, subject to wishes of the owners. Always optimistic, he was sure the club had a bright future.

The Compass Room.

At one point negotiations were underway for a merger with the Bradenton Yacht Club. An *Islander* reporter wrote in June of 1953, "If negotiations weather the storm, a substantial number of members and boats will be seen at the Yacht Club. It bothered Islanders that the name of the Holmes Beach Yacht Club would be changed to the Bradenton Yacht Club. The Bradenton group was registered with Lloyd's of London, a factor of significance in yachting circles throughout the world."

In October of 1954, Islanders were surprised to read in the newspaper a new manager was coming to the Yacht Club. Pete Reynard from Clearwater bought the concession for the bar and restaurant from Vertich. Jack Holmes had the novel idea it could be a private yacht club for three months and public restaurant and community hall the other nine months of the year. Pete Reynard had other ideas.

A Greek immigrant with a French name, Pete turned the failed club into a fabulously successful restaurant, which put Anna Maria Island on the map. He was just 16 when he signed on as a seaman aboard a freighter, which his uncle captained. Pete's first voyage took him across the Atlantic to New York. The ship docked on the Jersey side of the Hudson River overlooking the famous Palisades Amusement Park. The summertime fun was irresistible to the young man who watched from the deck of the ship. When the ship steamed out of the New York Harbor, Pete Reynard was not on board.

Pete and Eleanor Reynard received an award for their work in the community from Gene Page of the Bradenton Herald.

His uncle failed to report Pete to the United States immigration authorities, so Pete was able to procure a working permit. He started as a bus boy in a New York restaurant and worked his way up the ladder to head waiter. It was a proud day for him when he became an American citizen.

Pete was fascinated by show business and signed up for ballroom dancing classes. He became an expert dancer and was soon touring the country with various partners in the '30s and '40s. While he was entertaining troops on a USO tour during World War II, a severe attack of pleurisy ended his dancing career.

Pete bought the Star Dust Restaurant in Clearwater, and it was here he met his future wife, Eleanor. They were married on Aug.17, 1954. Friends told them about a new restaurant on a small island, bordered by the Gulf and Sarasota Bay, which needed new management.

"We knew it was premature to open one here," said Eleanor in an interview with me in 1989 for *The Islander*. "There was a large room, a kitchen and a lounge. Jack Holmes was the owner. We came across the old rickety wooden bridge and our dogs, miniature dachshunds, were scared to death."

Nevertheless, on Oct. 26, 1954, the Reynards entered into an agreement with Jack Holmes to lease the business. They had a crew of 10. Pete was a great promoter and advertised on television several times a week. He would cook steaks, which became the most popular item on the menu, with his inimitable flair. Television made him famous. Everyone recognized him by his pencil thin mustache, black hair and broad smile. Eleanor was a perfect hostess, with a knack for remembering names and details. She had a fondness for people. Joe DeMaggio, Joey Burns, Fred Hutchinson, Birdie Tebbetts, Warren Spahn and their families were regulars. When the Sunshine Skyway Bridge and the two Island bridges were built, folks from nearby counties streamed to the Island mecca.

A fire destroyed the restaurant in 1965.

The restaurant became Pete Reynard's Yacht Club and diners came by car and boat. Bordered by canals on three sides, the establishment boasted a variety of innovative features which gained acclaim from far and near.

In 1960, a revolving salad bar was installed, one of the first in the area. Even today, although many restaurants have salad bars, few revolve. You could stand in one spot and load your plate with tempting delicacies. Compartments on the bar were kept filled by hands behind a curtain.

On March 17, 1965 tragedy struck. A fire during the early morning hours destroyed the entire building except for two concrete walls. The Reynards were not discouraged and started to rebuild immediately. The entire restaurant was enlarged and the revolving Compass Room was added. The entire seating area in this room revolved which gave approximately 50 diners an excellent view of boats, picturesque canals and activities around the water.

But it was the Mermaid Room that became the most sought-after spot in the restaurant. Mermaids could be viewed in a 50-gallon tank of water and diners were spellbound as they watched the graceful swimmers execute a water ballet. In reality, it was a film shot at the Miami Hall of Fame featuring bathing beauties with excellent aquatic abilities.

The Captain's Room, enhanced by a nautical décor, was used for club meetings, private parties and was especially popular for wedding receptions. Weekly luncheon and dinner meetings of the Anna Maria High Twelve Club, the Island Rotary Club, plus monthly Welcome Wagon luncheons, kept the facility humming with activity. Following the expansion, almost 600 diners could be accommodated. For many years Pete Reynard's was regarded as one the best eating spots on the west coast of Florida. It was a pleasant place for boaters to dock and spend the night.

Pete Reynard greeted the newly-crowned Miss Florida, Chris Torgeson.

Casual dress was as acceptable as formal wear for grand dances booked by social organizations. Bands attracted those who loved to dance the night away. It was a friendly place with tasty food and drink.

"My best memory of Pete's is that I met my wife there," said Snooks Adams, Holmes Beach police chief, who celebrated his retirement there in 1975. "Liz was working there and driving a Ford with Kansas license plates. I went in the kitchen and told her if she was working there she had to get Florida tags. It was the law. She asked why I was arresting people who were working. I said that's how I make my living, arresting people. A couple days later we got together and married soon after."

Wes Rudolph was a longtime Island musician who regularly played the organ at Pete's. After his death, friends and family met at Pete's and scattered his ashes nearby. Even in death, he was near the many friends he had come to love over the years he worked at Pete Reynard's.

Eva Pringle worked at Pete's and recalled when two men got into a fight at the salad bar. One thought the other had cut in front of him. The salad bar revolved which made the issue of a line moot.

Loretta Yearwood Hopps was a waitress at Pete's in the '60s. She remembered Pete as a very caring man. "At Easter and Christmas he would give all his employees' children complete outfits. The boys would get suits and hats and the girls would get complete ensembles, even underpants. He was wonderful.

"Pete would walk around the dining room visiting with everyone. When there was a problem in the kitchen, he would walk slowly to the kitchen. When the doors swung shut, he would run to the source of the problem and make sure the cooks got the message." Loretta worked at Pete's for about seven years before she opened a beauty parlor on the Island.

Former Holmes Beach Mayor Carol Whitmore went to Pete's on her first date. "It was the first time I ever ate in a revolving room," she said. "For anything special we always went to Pete's."

Sandy Haas-Martens first went to the restaurant in 1970 when her parents 35th anniversary dinner party was held there.

Jackie and J. D. Webb were about the first customers at Pete's when it opened in October 1954. "The food was delicious. Saturday night was always Pete's restaurant for us. I always had the "Sizzler," a large steak on a sizzling platter," Jackie recalled.

Fire Chief Andy Price said the first time he went to a restaurant with his folks it was Pete's. "I was a kid and I couldn't understand the revolving room. Every time I looked up it was all different. The restaurant was the venue for countless fire department functions and Little League banquets."

The first time my husband and I went to Pete's was in 1957. Our mouths watered when we saw the steak platter. It was $3.95, and it took us a while to save up enough money to go to dinner and pay a baby sitter. It was a big deal to go to Pete's.

An old menu, printed in the '50s, included a lobster entrée for $2.50; spring lamb chops, $1.95; fisherman's platter, $2.25. The most expensive item was prime New York cut sirloin steak with onion rings, vegetables, and salad bar for $3.75. Cocktail prices were 65-cents for Cuba Libre, 85-cents for Planter's punch and 90-cents for a sidecar. Beer and ales cost 40-cents for domestic brands and 60-cents for imports.

Pete Reynard reached the highpoint of his career when he was named Restauranteur of the Year by the Florida Restaurant Association. He received many plaques from organizations over the years attesting to his excellence as a restaurant owner.

Al Grossman, who was Pete's theatrical agent during his dancing days in New York, moved to Florida. One evening he went to dinner with friends at Pete Reynard's. After dinner he casually asked the owner if he had ever been in show business, Pete replied, "Al Grossman, don't you remember me? You used to book my act."

Every year Pete and Eleanor returned to Pete's homeland. It was on Greek soil on Sept. 26, 1975 that Pete sustained a heart attack and died. He was 72. He was buried in Greece, but hundreds attended his memorial service held at Roser Church in Anna Maria City. The entire Island was saddened. Eulogies were delivered by Holmes Beach Mayor Jim Zerby and Pete Reynard's fellow restaurateur, Trader Jack Pearsall. Al Grossman credited Pete with keeping the South Florida Museum going. For six years Pete held a $100-a-couple banquet for the museum at his restaurant. It was always a huge success.

Trader Jack Pearsall and his wife, Pauline.

"If it hadn't been for Pete we could not have kept that museum open," Al said. "He gave a lot and didn't make a dime on it. I have never worked with anyone as cooperative as Pete. He had a big heart. Manatee County, and especially the Island, has lost a very, very dear friend."

Eleanor came back to the Island and decided to keep the restaurant going. "I had a full, competent staff that I could depend on. Everything went fairly smoothly," she said.

On Jan. 22, 1979, Eleanor married Tony Tatakis, a Greek restaurateur from Sarasota. Pete Reynard's continued to thrive as the Island's population increased, especially during the tourist seasons.

On Oct. 31, 1988, Tony and Eleanor sold the business for more than $2-million to Davis Rittoff and Rocky Carroll, who had been the general managers since 1982. The new owners never recaptured the magic of Pete Reynard and the restaurant floundered.

The entire structure was torn down in 2002 to make way for the Tidemark complex. The Island lost another historic landmark.

Mira Mar Transformed to Trader Jack's

The Island's most popular restaurant and night club, rivaled only by Pete Reynard's, was near the Cortez Bridge. Built in 1946, the Mira Mar was managed by Mike Verdich.

"I have fond memories of the old Mira Mar," said Billie Martini, whose husband, Bob, was mayor of Bradenton Beach in the early '50s. "We celebrated our second anniversary there in 1952 and Mike served us a big spaghetti dinner. I caught a big tarpon off the molasses boat that sank there in 1940. When the boat broke up in the middle of the night, one man drowned. Everybody on the Island was on the beach watching them rescue the others."

"The Island Lions Club met at the Mira Mar in the '50s," said Ted Tripp, mayor of Anna Maria in the '50s. "We wanted a good place where we could eat. It was a family place and you could get a good meal there. We played hand shuffleboard and had a lot of fun."

Jerry Cigarran, who was prominent in Island politics in the '40s and '50s said, "Two guys from Tampa built the Mira Mar. Their idea was to turn it into a gambling casino. I got them to talk to the governor and sheriff about a casino, but nothing ever came of it."

Verdich ran the Mira Mar until the mid-1950s. It was purchased in 1962 by a show business couple, Bob and June Sheldon. They acquired the property for $50,000 from Verdich, kept the name Mira Mar, and turned it into a nightclub.

The Sheldons had a comedy act. Music was provided by Romeo St. Cyr on piano and drums and Marie on her fiddle and "Golden Sax." They constructed a stage and dance floor and put on shows Friday and Saturday nights. There was no air-conditioning. The windows were opened and

June Burnett and Bob Sheldon staged an entertaining comedy act.

the Gulf breezes blew through. Anyone could get in the show if they could sing, whistle, play the harmonica, or do anything else entertaining. The Mira Mar was a popular spot for Islanders and tourists.

In an *Islander* interview June Sheldon told the reporter, "We had a gut bucket. That's a washtub rigged up with

The building on the beach is Trader Jack's.

a string tied to a broomstick. People loved to twang it and sing. There was one big, heavy gal named Frances who would sing, and her prim and proper friend would take her false teeth out, put them in her bra, and bang away on my cocktail drum. Bob called them the Cherry Sisters. That was the worst act on Broadway.

"We had such fun. My son Bobbie came in when he was 12 and started playing the clarinet. He taught himself to play and learned all the numbers by ear. Later he became a composer and a band director for an area high school.

"We had hootenannies on Sundays and the crowds were unbelievable. The biggest attraction was the outdoor bar that wrapped around the north end of the club. Sometimes the awnings leaked, but no one cared. It was known as the Monkey Bar, because of the bizarre collection of stuffed monkeys, all shapes and sizes, which hung from the roof and ceiling. Our weekday business really took off after we opened the Monkey Bar. Bob called a pet store and tried to get a real monkey, but that didn't turn out, so I put up the monkey dolls. People sent us monkeys from all over. Some were made of stockings, others were stuffed."

"Jack Pearsall bought the Mira Mar in June of 1968, but before he had the grand opening, Hurricane Gladys came and almost wrecked the building. Then we were glad we had sold it," June said.

Arthur Courville and Eugene Carpenter invested $5,000, leased a strip of land near the restaurant, and built a brick hamburger stand. They called it the Mira Mar Drive-In. It opened on the Fourth of July in 1964 and hamburgers sold for 19-cents.

"There were such crowds we thought we were going to have to call the police," Carpenter recalled. "People went to the Monkey Bar and then came to our place. On Saturday nights people would be standing six deep waiting at the Monkey Bar. That was a jumping place. Our Mira Mar Drive-In made $45,000 the first year - $65,000 the second and $75,000 the third – not bad for a $5,000 investment! We sold out before Jack Pearsall bought the Mira Mar. When he bought the restaurant he closed the Monkey Bar and tore down our place. My partner laid a funeral wreath on the remains after it was knocked down."

"The Monkey Bar was my idea," Bill Coder said. "At first Bob Sheldon didn't go for it. Then he agreed it would be a good idea. I gave Bob the first monkey. It was named Monkey Bar because people go to a bar and make monkeys of themselves. I cooked for the Mira Mar and the drive-in. Gene Carpenter and Art Courville didn't know much about cooking. We served smoked hot dogs. Everyone wanted to know how we smoked them. I told them we did it at night. All I really did was put a few drops of liquid smoke in the cooking water. I had one guy who came in every week for a 10-pound box of them.

"I worked two years for Pearsall. He was the hardest person I ever worked for in my life. He paid big, but rode hard. I cooked everything, but if anything went wrong he would come back and bawl me out. It got to the point where he'd cuss me out and I'd cuss him back. After that, we got along pretty well until we had a set-to and I quit. The winter I quit, Jack put on a Christmas party and forced me to come. He told me if I didn't come he would come to Bradenton and get me. And he did. He gave me a $100 Christmas present."

"When the Sheldons had the Mira Mar they put on quite a night club act. Romeo could really play the piano and drums," Dorothy Wagner, early Bradenton Beach resident recalled.

In 1968, Jack Pearsall, who owned 27 restaurants in his lifetime and operated the Coach House Harbor Restaurant in Pompano Beach, bought the entire complex from the Sheldons. He had been in the restaurant business since 1933 and was lured to the Island by the most famous restauranteur, Pete Reynard. Pete told him the Island could use another good restaurant and he would rather have him than someone else. He enlarged and renovated the Mira Mar, and changed the name to Trader Jack's Brigantine. He claimed he spent $100,000 on nautical and marine items to decorate the bar and dining room. On the wood paneled walls were old time sailing ships, gigantic shells of sea turtles, several huge lobsters and crayfish along with quaint signs such as, "Beer 5 Cents." A coral wishing well, fossils of sea creatures, and ships in bottles were all fascinating to the diners. A large antique diving suit greeted people as they walked in the front door. Adding to the nautical theme, patrons could view through large windows the old molasses barge that sunk in 1940 in the

Trader Jack's sustained damage during violent storms.

Gulf. Several hundred feet off the beach parts of the ship could be seen, especially during low tide.

Jack closed-in the outdoor Monkey Bar and created the Wheelhouse Lounge. One conversation piece was a large sign hanging over the bar, which read: "Where everyone knows what everyone else is doing, but still reads the local newspaper to find out if they got caught."

Trader Jack was one of the Island's favorite characters. Tall, with a full white beard and a hearty laugh, he was a shrewd businessman who created a unique atmosphere where locals could feel comfortable and tourists could talk about the Mira Mar when they got home.

The restaurant, which seated 350, was a phenomenal success. Trader Jack had charisma, smart advertising methods and good food. Going to Trader's Jack's was a must for tourists. "It is a family operation," Pearsall stated, "informal and inexpensive."

Special events during the year attracted throngs. The Halloween party with cash prizes for the best costumes brought out the most elaborate costumes ever seen on the Island. The St. Patrick's Day and Christmas parties drew hundreds, and annual shows were legendary. In October, employees performed circus acts. Christmas in July featured shows such as "Cabaret" and "Showboat."

Trader Jack's was the first restaurant on the Island to offer early bird specials. Diners who arrived between 4 and 6 p.m. could get selected meals at reduced prices.

A fire in 1987 destroyed the popular restaurant.

One of Pearsall's strengths was his employees. Many worked at his restaurant for years. He expected a lot from them, but he was fair and took care of them with incentives such as Christmas bonuses.

"It was like a big family," Scott Moore said. "Employees liked each other and were happy working there. That was good for business and the customers could see it."

"Jack Pearsall hired some show business people," recalled Dot Wagner. "They were waiters and bartenders. A couple times a year all the employees would put on a circus show. It was really good, quite professional. It was splendid when Trader Jack owned the restaurant. It was the place on the Island to go and dance. All three of our kids worked there."

In 1977 Pearsall sold out to Phil Fayette who did well for eight years despite harassment from city hall. In 1985, the restaurant was closed after Fayette pleaded guilty to charges of income tax evasion stemming from a cigarette tax counterfeiting operation on the premises of his former fruit and grocery business in Vermont. The sale of Trader Jack's was supposed to close in June 1987, but a fire a week before, which authorities believed was set by an arsonist, left the once renowned restaurant a burnt-out shell.

Suzanne Stedecke, a Bradenton Beach resident, described the scene as a "big ball of fire." She said flames were visible for miles. "I just freaked out!" she exclaimed. "I used to eat there all the time. I could not believe it." Dozens of horrified residents watched the raging inferno. Nothing remained of the Island landmark but ashes and concrete blocks. Bradenton Beach Mayor Barbara Turner summed it up by saying, "When you lose something like this it is devastating. We've lost a lot of history today."

Authorities investigating the fire said at least one arsonist used gasoline to start the blaze that destroyed the $500,000 building.

Islanders mourned the death of Gwynne "Trader Jack" Pearsall in June of 1997. They had happy memories of an era when Trader Jack's was one of the most popular spots on the west coast of Florida.

"He drew people here and made Bradenton Beach happen," said Scott Moore, a local backwater fishing guide who worked at the restaurant for 14 years. "People came from Tampa and stayed all night at local motels so they could dine and dance at Trader Jack's."

The Shady Cove

Back in the 1940s, a popular drinking spot was The Cove on Gulf Drive across from Bradenton Beach City Hall. Miles "Brownie" Brown was one of the first owners of the two-story, frame building which was built on stilts. He ran a good bar, and stakes at the poker tables were high, which attracted professional gamblers. Girls in the upstairs rooms attracted a different clientele. Island folks spoke about The Cove in whispers. No one ever admitted going there. As the population on the Island increased The Cove changed. Gamblers and prostitutes left, but regulars still came to the bar.

Then the building was torn down, and instead of a beach bar, a family-style restaurant named The Patio appeared. Island workers and fishermen stopped for food and drink. The menu included clam chowder, shrimp, hamburgers and hot dogs. In 1978 The Patio was torn down to make way for the expansion of the adjacent Harbour House Restaurant. Islanders shook their heads, another historic landmark was gone. Today the Beach House restaurant sits on this site.

The Anchorage

In the early 1900s, the Anna Maria Beach Company made land sales from an office at the foot of the City Pier on the corner of Pine Avenue and Bay Boulevard. Long after the office disappeared, Lola Mae Hackney and her husband, Jim, built a two-story frame building and called it The Anchorage. During the '40s they sold sandwiches and beer to homesick servicemen manning the radar station on the Island during World War II.

In post-war years it was the favorite place for residents to relax, have a snack and watch the crowds parade back and forth on the historic City Pier.

As the years rolled by, the bar attracted a rough crowd. In May 1975, lawmen swooped down on The Anchorage and arrested more than a dozen patrons. However, no one was convicted of anything. Rumors flew around the Island about the arrests and citizens were angry about the entire event.

In 1953 a new cocktail lounge, The Anchorage Annex, opened. Since numerous requests were heard for the privilege of the "first drink" Mrs. Hackney issued a policy of "first come, first served."

One evening the skipper of a 60-foot shrimp boat strolled into The Anchorage saying he was lost. He had a huge catch of fish aboard his boat, but was low on ice and fuel. He pleaded for help. Dewey Adams, who lived upstairs with the Hackneys, gave him directions to Cortez where he stayed for the night and got supplies. In the morning he headed to his homeport in Fort Myers.

The Anchorage was under new management in 1955. John Weiss planned to install a larger, modern kitchen and remodel the rundown place. He renamed it the Coral Cocktail Lounge, and served seafood, steaks, chops and snacks.

Dewey Adams was asked what he would do with his time. "Go fishing," he replied. To the same question, Mrs. Hackney said she would live in her house on Spring and Bay Boulevard and go to city meetings.

Roser Church members vehemently objected to the expansion of The Anchorage in 1956. A delegation, headed by Fred Archer and a group of teenagers, protested the remodeling of The Anchorage since it was too close to the church. Mayor Bill Brier said two men from the beverage commission had measured the distance between the main entrance of the church to the restaurant and found it was farther that the legal requirements of 500 feet. Francis Welsch and Hilding Russell checked and found it to be 542 feet. C. M. Bayless said, " I think the people are knocking on the wrong door. They should see the health and fire departments." Since there were no violations, the expansion began. Years later the decrepit Anchorage was torn down and Fast Eddie's Place went up, but that's another story.

Duffy's Tavern

In 1936 a young Midwestern couple, Carl "Skinny" Freeman and his wife, Janice came to Florida on their honeymoon. They traveled throughout the state, but were so impressed with the west coast they vowed to someday come back and open a business near the beach.

Sixteen years later they arrived on Anna Maria Island with their two young children. They found a commercial building lot in Holmes Beach and planned to build a drive-in near the beach. Construction started in 1952. The front of the building faced Gulf Drive. It was straight across from the Manatee Public Beach. They found curb service would not work since it was too hot in the summer and too many mosquitoes. Business was slow for the first few months, but eventually the Mid-Island Drive-In became popular with locals. It was the only privately-owned commercial building in that area. A dense jungle surrounded it. Water came from a point well, and there was no sewer system. Islanders, tourists and baseball players on spring training discovered the drive-in. The owners put in long hours serving breakfast, lunch and dinner. Then due to family problems, they were forced to close and return to the west.

The business was leased to a couple for a short time and then to Claude Whiteman, who was known as Duffy. Claude was a trumpet player during the Big Band Era. He named the cracker shack Duffy's Tavern, after the popular radio show of that time. In the 13 years Duffy leased the business it became well-known. After he retired, an Island resident, Pat Geyer, took over the management of the business. To say she was successful would be an understatement.

Pat bought Duffy's Tavern in April of 1972. Duffy stayed around for a while and then he moved on. Notable people from all walks of life passed through the squeaky, weathered door. Write-ups about Duffy's Tavern could be seen in all the local papers and USA Today. *Travel & Leisure* magazine, a publication that featured exclusive places where jet setters visited, also featured an article on Duffy's Tavern. It was a drastic contrast to swank restaurants on the picturesque coasts of Greece or Africa where the water was so clear one could see the label on a beer can 50-feet down.

Morgan Steinmetz who penned a "Keeping Up" column for the *Sarasota Herald Tribune* wrote, "Imagine my surprise and delight when I saw an article in *Travel & Leisure* entitled 'Backwater Florida.' It was all about our part of the state from Tampa to Punta Gorda to Arcadia. What particularly delighted me was the paragraph about Duffy's Tavern in Holmes Beach."

Pat Geyer became the proprietor of Duffy's Tavern in 1972.

"The headline said, '*Travel & Leisure* visits Duffy's Tavern. No passport. No Visa. Neither does Duffy's take American Express. If you are up for a real cracker encounter,' the article said, 'Open the rickety screen door at Duffy's across from Manatee Beach.'

"The magazine could hardly do justice to Duffy's in a few sentences so I went out to Holmes Beach to talk to the owner, Pat Geyer who operates the place with her daughters, Peggi, Patti, Penni, Polli and Pam, six days out of seven," Steinmetz wrote. "Geyer rules Duffy's with sangfroid suggestive of a Supreme Court justice."

Pat produced a copy of the *Travel & Leisure* article from behind the counter. "The fellow who wrote that must have been here a long time ago," she said. "He wrote about the rickety screen door and I replaced it with a solid door 10 years ago. I don't have black bean soup, like he said. I have navy bean soup."

Geyer had devoted clientele. Once people discovered Duffy's, they didn't forget. "I come here for the good atmosphere and the good food," said a young man in his early '30s. "I grew up around here and I used to come in after surfing, with salt water and sand running out of my shorts. Now that I am older, I come in to drink a few beers and just think about surfing."

Duffy's was always famous for its cold beer, Bud On Tap was served in a frosted mug. Geyer said her delicious cheeseburgers came from the best meat and were cooked on an old, well-seasoned grill. Seating capacity in Duffy's Tavern was 28 and there was standing room.

The inside of the eatery was festooned with baseball caps, football and baseball pennants, bumper stickers, old license plates and conversational signs. One sign read: "Lost Dog: Three legs, blind in left eye, missing right ear, tail broken, recently castrated, answers to the name of Lucky."

Don Moore, editor of *The Islander* in the '70s, supported Pat when she was running for a seat on the Holmes Beach City Council. He said because she was the owner of the most popular hangout on the Island she had her finger on the pulse of the community. Pat was successful in her bid on the council and went on to become mayor of Holmes Beach from 1990 to 1994. She also sat on the council for years.

After losing the lease in 2002, Duffy's Tavern relocated to Marina Drive across from the Holmes Beach City Hall. The beer and burgers are still great, and natives and visitors still love it.

The Sandbar

The early Sandbar featured a bathhouse.

When crowds came to the Island before the first bridge was built in 1921, they arrived by steamer at the Anna Maria Dock, which is now the City Pier. The "day trippers" strolled up Pine Avenue for a day of fun and frolic on the Gulf beach.

The most popular place to go was The Pavilion which was directly on the beach. There were rooms for changing into bathing attire and snacks were sold. In 1946, a mysterious fire burned The Pavilion to the ground. The famed Bucket Brigade fought the blaze, mostly to protect nearby buildings. Rumors spread that the owners did not waste much water on the fire. Soon, two old Army barracks replaced The Pavilion, and the Sandbar Restaurant was born.

In the '30s, a diving platform on pilings was erected out from the Sandbar, about 100-feet offshore. It was connected to the beach by a cable to minimize chances of swimmers falling prey to sharks and other creatures of the deep. Old timers still talk about the platform and

the wire, which is now marked by three submerged pilings. They are sometimes visible at very low tide.

Changes were made to the building in the ensuing years. Mrs. Bernice Eno, the owner in the late '40s, added a dance floor, which made the Sandbar even more popular.

In 1950, a hurricane caused extensive damage to the building, and the diving platform disappeared. Mrs. Eno rebuilt a much sturdier building. In the early '60s, she sold the Sandbar, and a string of owners took over.

The bar was removed from the south side of the building in the early '70s. A new and larger bar and lounge were added on the north side.

The Sandbar Restaurant was purchased by the present owner, Ed Chiles, the son of the late Governor "Walkin" Lawton Chiles, in 1979. "It is my intention to remain here for years to come," Ed said. "We can achieve that goal by constantly providing good food and polite, courteous service."

Ed has strived to retain the natural historic charm that has made the Sandbar one the landmarks of Anna Maria Island. In August of 2008, a deck, parking lot, bathrooms for the handicapped, a front façade and gazebo were added. Extensive landscaping, using mainly native plants, updated the restaurant while retaining its allure.

"Our commitment in preserving the historical nature of our restaurant, while providing first rate customer service, the best local seafood and a memorable experience for our guests remains our primary goal," Ed Chiles stated.

Blue Water Beach Apartments

In January 1959, a gala party dedicating the "magnificent" Blue Water Beach Apartments in Holmes Beach was front page news in *The Islander.* Invited guests totaled 200, but area newspapers called it an Open House. This lured many freeloaders.

"An array of food the likes of which has never been seen on the Island was displayed on a 40-foot long table," the reporter wrote. "Stuffed lobsters, chicken Jeanette, a huge whole fish, salmon and sandwiches cut in triangular wedges were served. A pheasant, complete with feathers (this might have been a table decoration) and many exotic dishes to tempt the most particular diner were enjoyed by those attending."

The large, luxurious complex was called the largest single achievement on the Island. After its completion, the owners requested the city council rezone property across Gulf Drive to allow building a restaurant and cocktail lounge to seat 200.

5400 Gulf Drive Apartments

The former home of renowned columnist, Walter Lipman of Holmes Beach, was torn down to make room for an apartment complex which would be known as 5400 Gulf Drive.

Larchmont Development Corporation announced the first of the completed apartments would be open for inspection on January 30,1964.

The most outstanding feature of the apartment complex was the 306-feet of beach frontage affording owners easy access to a private beach and an excellent view of the Gulf. The owners explained the 100 percent co-operative plan by saying when 85 percent of the apartments were sold the property would be deeded to an association of owners. This nonstock, nonprofit membership organization would have membership confined to owners of the apartments.

The First and Last High-Rise

The only high-rise structures on Anna Maria Island are the two Martinique Condominium buildings, completed in 1970 on the Gulf at 53rd Street in Holmes Beach. After the $1-million, seven-story buildings were constructed, the three Island municipalities passed ordinances limiting building heights to two stories.

Sidney Wilkinson, the Bradenton architect who designed the first building, said the contemporary design would accommodate 48 two-bedroom, two-bath luxury apartments each with its own balcony. Each apartment would have individual air conditioning and heat and would cost approximately $30,000. The ground floor was designed to have a pool, recreational facilities, a terrace and parking. A. L. Sainer and Joseph Blum, the owners, were New York attorneys with homes in Sarasota.

Telephone Building

At a special meeting held at the Holmes Beach City Hall, plans were approved for the erection of a telephone building at 51st Street and Gulf Drive in Holmes Beach. This would be an automatic exchange with no regular employees other than occasional maintenance men. Construction began in 1958.

Island Doctor Builds Island Medical Clinic

Mention the name of Dr. Edgar Huth to longtime Island residents and they will agree he made exciting contributions to Anna Maria Island. The son of two teachers, Dr. Huth was raised in the suburbs of Milwaukee. He graduated from the University of Milwaukee Medical School in 1931 and in 1932 took over a general practice in a small town in northern Wisconsin. He recalled what life was like back then in an interview with this reporter in 1985.

"It had been a lumber town, but became so poor the county treasurer did not have enough money for his own salary. During the three years we were there, I delivered 512 babies, with 506 home deliveries. I received almost

Dr. Edgar Huth and the new Island Medical Center.

nothing until the government set up a federal relief office in town. Then I received $15 for each delivery, 75-cents for an office call and $1.50 for a house call. I did receive 25-cents a mile for house calls. That often amounted to more than the $15 delivery," he recalled.

Ed and Lillian Huth had two sons, John and Dan. One time Dan and John were huddled in the back seat of their father's car while their brave father calmly walked toward a farmer who was holding police off with a shotgun. The courageous doctor eventually talked the farmer into giving up the gun.

To get to a stroke victim the intrepid doctor drove as far as he could in his car and skied the remaining six miles through a howling snowstorm. His progress was covered by the local radio station and tracked by farmers who would phone in when he passed their houses.

One Christmas in the '50s, the family decided to vacation in Key West to escape the brutal northern winter. Dr. Huth recounted their adventures:

"We had an idea we'd like to retire in Florida, but then decided if we could find a suitable place we'd move right away. I took the Florida state boards and Lil rode up the west coast to find a spot where medicine was needed. We ended up in Naples, but the hospital was 46-miles away in Fort Myers."

They headed north toward Anna Maria Island."We drove over the old, rickety bridge to Bradenton Beach. The skies were so blue and the sand so white, it was wonderful. We drove up a winding sand road and stopped. Sitting on the sand dunes under the Australian pines we decided this was it.

"There were no doctors on the Island. We went to Jack Marshall, a realtor, and bought the land for our house and a lot behind the Holmes Beach Shopping Center for an office. In April 1953, the modern, fully equipped Island Medical Center was completed. We made a good choice and were never sorry we moved."

At this time the entire Island population on the Island was barely 1,000, not enough to support a doctor. Dr. Huth discovered many trailer parks along the road he took to the Bradenton hospital. In a short time the campers learned a doctor passed twice a day. Soon he was making house calls as he drove in and out of town. Sometimes he would work until 11 p.m. Office calls increased at such a rate he hired another doctor.

Trav Brown arrived to be Dr. Huth's assistant. "Summers were quiet on the Island, but when the season opened in October we were busy all day," Dr. Huth said.

A general practitioner, Dr. Huth delivered babies, did major surgery and was trained in anesthesiology. Mrs. Huth was her husband's receptionist and bookkeeper. One day she was unable to work, so Ruth Taylor, a registered nurse, filled in. She was compassionate and well-liked and stayed for 27 years, until her retirement.

Dr. Rex Lee, the first Island dentist, opened his office at the northern end of the medical center. His wife was his assistant and receptionist. In 1957, the medical center was enlarged. The blueprints for the expansion were signed by Ed Huth, architect. "I was an engineer before I became a doctor," he explained.

Another of Dr. Huth's accomplishments had nothing to do with medicine. He was the one who spearheaded the project to get rid of the mosquitoes that plagued the Island. Details are covered in this book in the chapter titled "Mosquitoes."

Dr. Huth retired from active practice in 1960. Dr. John Deam took his place at the Island Medical Center. Dr. Huth spent time treating indigent patients at the Manatee County Health Department. He developed innovative surgical techniques and invented finger scalpels and tools used in some of the world's first open heart surgeries.

Dr. John Deam

Dr. and Mrs. Huth traveled abroad and volunteered their services at a new mission hospital in Liberia. For three months he was the only surgeon at the hospital deep in the jungles of Africa. He operated on a heart or diesel generator with the same meticulous expertise. The jungle tribe named him Para-mount, which meant Chieftain-Chief Of All Chiefs. Dr. Huth died in 1998 at the age of 92.

Meanwhile, Dr. Deam was busy at the Island Medical Center. He arrived with his wife, Alice and three children, David, Donna and Douglas. A graduate of Albright College in Reading, Pa., Dr. Deam received his medical degree at Jefferson Medical College in Philadelphia. He interned at Tampa General Hospital and practiced for a year in Tampa. Mrs. Deam, a graduate of Pennsylvania State Teachers College, taught at a school in Tampa while living there. The Deams moved back to Pennsylvania, where he set up a general practice, before accepting the position on Anna Maria Island.

Property Sales Booming

In 1955 realtor Ruth Mahar made the largest sale on the Island since the boom days in the early 1900s. The property she sold fronted 200-feet on the Gulf. The price of $80,000 included furniture and furnishings. The two acres included six one-family cottages, a shuffleboard court and several barbecue pits. The buyers also purchased a home site on Palma Sola Bay. That block of lots was two blocks north of Manatee Avenue.

The last sizable piece of property on the Island, outside of parks, was sold to Lacios and Lardas for $6,280. Known as Fiddlers Flats, the 24 lots ran from Spring Avenue to Magnolia Avenue. A $5,000 performance bond accompanied the bid to assure the land would be filled, cleared and graded to the level of adjoining Bimini Bay Estates, which was five feet above the mean low water line.

The Island Water Company

In the early days, artesian wells supplied water for Island residents. After 1912, when the Anna Maria Beach Company started laying the foundation for the city, there was a municipal water system. Residents of Anna Maria City, who used the system, paid 50-cents a month per house and received water from five flowing wells owned by the city. There was no pressure, so consumers needed auxiliary pumps. Wells and pipes were added through the years.

"A new water system is a necessity," was stated an article in the *Key News* in 1950. "No one is obliged to use the system if they prefer to drill a well point or shallow well of their own."

Then Karl Francis Karel, a banker and developer from Riverside, Ill., appeared on the scene. He had just bought property on the Island and offered to arrange financing for a water system for Anna Maria City. In 1950, the city commissioners voted to give him the franchise for 30 years. Karel agreed to give the commission the right to purchase the system and run it themselves at any time.

It was hoped the new water works would eventually extend to Holmes Beach and Bradenton Beach. Anna Maria Mayor Richard Ernest told a *Key News* reporter in 1950, that granting the water works franchise to Karel and Associates of Chicago was the third boom in Anna Maria City in three years. First, the fire department was formed, next, the city streets were resurfaced and then the new water system.

About 100 residents voted in favor of the 30-year franchise after hearing the many advantages. After Anna Maria Mayor Ernest went to Bartow to receive a permit for the water works of Anna Maria, a ditching machine started laying pipelines. Due to the poor condition of the casings in city-owned wells, it was decided to dig a new well to the south of the Island Baptist Church. In order to maintain pressure, another booster station would eventually be constructed in the vicinity of the Anna Maria Yacht Basin. Water, pumped from the city well into a concrete pressure tank by two electric pumps, was aerated and chlorinated. The basic monthly rate was $2.50 for the first 2,500 gallons to 4,000 gallons.

"City Water Runs When Lights Fail," was a headline in the Dec. 27, 1951 *Islander*. "If you are a user of city water you need not worry if electric power fails. Karl Karel, the water magnate, says he has a gasoline pump which takes over when power is unavailable."

"I start the pump if the lights are off as long as five minutes," Karel said. "If I'm not around the engineer does it."

There were 275 houses being served by city water. The system at that time was capable of taking care of up to 500 houses.

"It's like running an Island newspaper," Karel continued. "We don't make any money now, but if we live long enough and the place keeps growing we may break even someday."

The Island Water Company ran this ad in area newspapers in March 1952. "Water, the cheapest thing you can drink. Our deep well-water contains fluoride which helps prevent tooth decay in children. It is also chlorinated for your protection!"

These accolades, bestowed on Karl Francis Karel, appeared in an April edition of *The Islander*: "His name will always mean 'water' to our people. He brought water from wells 400-feet deep in the cool bedrock into homes on the Island. He formed the Island Water Company. He has hundreds of bosses and critics. City, county and state authorities are holding their official thumbs over him, ready to turn them down on the slightest provocation. Karel guarantees pure water, free from contamination. The state checks regularly to protect him and its citizens."

In May new rates for people building homes or preserving gardens were announced. The yard beautification rate minimum was $5 a month for the first 10,500-gallons. To obtain the special rate, customers were required to sign up for a year. The tap-in charge for new customers was $15 for a line from the water main to the property line.

On May 8, 1952, a photo of the Holmes Beach City Hall and adjacent waterworks appeared in *The Islander*. "What a handy arrangement," the caption read. "Gen. H. Y. Taylor, mayor of Holmes Beach, can wield his gavel with one hand and, as manager of the Island Water Company, can turn on pumps with the other. After the water company spoiled its customers by allowing unlimited water at a flat rate, they were compelled to install water meters. Before the meters, 300,000-gallons a day were used and after meters were installed between 50,000 and 70,000-gallons were consumed."

The Manatee County Water Company announced the beginning of business as a corporate organization on Jan. 1, 1953. The company took over businesses formerly operated as the Whitfield Estates Water Company on the South Trail in Bradenton, and the Island Water Company in Anna Maria and Holmes Beach.

Officers of the newly established company were Karl F. Karel, president; (Ret.) Brig. Gen. Y. H. Taylor, vice president; and K. B. Narans, secretary-treasurer. Charles R. Schuh was given a 30-year non-exclusive franchise to operate a water plant in Ilexhurst. Permission was granted for laying and maintaining water lines under county roads by the county commission in June 1953.

The Manatee County Water Company notified users that a new higher rate would go into effect in May of 1956. There were 500 users on the Island and one day, at the height of the season, 270,000 gallons were used.

Islanders wanted more and better water, and the experts believed there was better water on the Island and it would be only a matter of a few years when water would be brought from the mainland. The Island water did not measure up to standard in quantity of chloride.

Water lines were being installed to the Bayou Fishing Center at the south end of Bay Boulevard in Anna Maria City and lines extended on the main road in Holmes Beach, south to 27th Street in the Ilexhurst area. Two miles of pipes were laid. Before crossing the border between Holmes Beach and Bradenton Beach it was necessary for the water company to obtain a franchise from the City of Bradenton Beach.

The company built a 160,000-gallon reservoir in 1957 near the water company office, adjacent to the Island Baptist Church. This meant plenty of water, under pressure, regardless of storms, electrical or mechanical failures. It appeared when the Island became more populated, water from shallow wells would no longer be potable or safe.

A major expansion program was announced by the water company on May 16, 1957. New wells were drilled and more than 15,000 feet of new mains were laid. Now serving more than 700 customers in Anna Maria, Holmes Beach and Whitfield Estates, the program cost in excess of $60,000. New wells were drilled on the company's plant site at Gulf Drive and 85th Street in Holmes Beach. Water was aerated as it was pumped into the reservoir to eliminate traces of sulphur.

Karl Francis Karel, on the left, caught the largest fish in an Island Fishing Tournament in the early '50s.

In 1961 the Island Fire Control District installed a 30KW, three-phase generator at the plant to insure adequate water for fighting fires in the event of a power failure. George Norwood, a volunteer fireman, became manager of the water company. A new deep well was connected to the Island water system, which served Holmes Beach and Anna Maria in 1964.

George Norwood was manager of the Island Water Company.

"This brings immediate relief from the severe water shortage," said Holmes Beach Mayor Elmer Twist. "We are continuing our efforts to find new wells so the supply can keep pace with the fast growing population. The water has been fully approved by the Manatee County Health Department. Plenty of water and some to spare is the ideal condition toward which we are working constantly."

Plans for extending the $20-million county water system to the Island were firming up by March of 1966. County Attorney Richard Hampton said the franchise agreement would be drawn up as soon as possible. He said the county would draft a contract to purchase the Island Water Company for $395,000. The water company was serving about 1,100 customers in Anna Maria and Holmes Beach at this time. All three Island cities passed a resolution to purchase county water. Manatee County would pay about $1.4-million to purchase the Island Water Company and extend mains to the Island.

Ten

An Island Paradise

The By The Sea Dancers entertained at the historical society's popular historical pageants

Change Is Inevitable

Residents of Anna Maria Island like the slow and easy pace of living. For example, if you go out on the City Pier and watch cars go over the humpback bridge on Bay Boulevard you will see they move as slowly as the sea turtles. Some drivers are looking out over the expanse of Tampa Bay to the distant islands, others peer out the car window to make sure the driver coming toward them is not too close.

Some say Anna Maria is the only island community in Florida to retain an idyllic quaintness and a small-town ambience that most island communities lost back in the '50s. In recent years the Florida Department of Transportation has proposed a 65-foot fixed span bridge to replace the Anna Maria drawbridge on Manatee Avenue. The plan was not in sync with the pattern Island residents were accustomed to, and the majority rejected the project emphatically.

The drawbridge, which lifts frequently for boats to pass through, is inconvenient for visitors and symbolizes the slow pace of Island residents who don't mind stopping to observe sea life and the boats.

In the '50s the three cities considered straightening the main road on the Island. But, many thought the curved road was more asthetic, furthermore the curves cut down speeding. Residents liked the road to follow the curves of the beach and they enjoyed the scenic tour.

On Nov. 13, 1952, *The Islander* carried an article about the rapid growth of the Island being a source of joy to tax assessors and collectors. Most inequitable assessments were in Anna Maria City for the simple reason there was much that was old and an astonishing number of new residences. In Bradenton Beach there was a vast preponderance of old buildings and in Holmes Beach, which was new in the '50s, the odious comparisons were few in number.

"It seems to be the policy of the assessor to consider old assessments sacred no matter how much out of line they were. When property changed hands the assessor's pencil was sharpened to a needlepoint and the buyer was hurt. The same pencil was employed in assessing new residents," the *Islander* reporter wrote.

Judd Arnett wrote an article in the *St. Petersburg Times* in 1957 captioned: "Will Success Spoil Anna Maria?" He stated,"It will be intriguing to see what happens out there when the influx of new residents and business activities, promoted by the three new bridges, reaches its peak. Surely it is coming, for if there is a community on the West Coast directly in the path of the wave of the future, it is Anna Maria."

Don Moore, editor of *The Islander* in the '70s, came to the Island when he was a boy in the mid '40s. "Many changes have taken place," he said. "Most have been made in the name of progress. Progress to most people seems to be anything different and relatively new. Contractors call it progress to erect new buildings. Land excavating companies say it's progress when they bulldoze all the wild palms, palmettos and mangroves. City fathers believe it's a sign of progress when they boast of newly paved streets, central water and systems, more homes and businesses going up every day.

"But, is it progress, I wonder. When I was a boy a kid could trap coons in the underbrush along the bayside or roam the mangrove thickets and fields of needle grass in search of pirate treasures. Most of the raccoons have been driven away or killed by cars and the fields have been cleared for more homes.

"Years ago, long before the three concrete bridges were built, there was an old wooden bridge linking the Island with Cortez. It clattered and shook with every car and truck that rolled over it. Every once in awhile a boat or barge would hit the draw and put it out of commission for a day or two. No one worried too much about the inconvenience - it was a way of life.

"It's ironic that with every passing day the concrete jungles and traffic jams of the north, which most vacationers and residents think they are escaping when they come to Anna Maria, are becoming more of a reality here. The metamorphosis from a sleepy little Island, with a few homes scattered here and there up and down the beach, to a mid-20th century community with expensive homes, well-manicured lawns, roads without ruts and all the modern conveniences, has been made under the guise of progress."

Among the noticeable changes on Anna Maria Island in the past 30 years are three stop lights, Pete Reynard's restaurant is gone, the Anna Maria Post Office is on the bay and fishing and shelling are not what they used to be.

In 1947 there were 908 residents on the Island, 469 houses and 88 trailers. In 1968 the population was 5,077. In 1970 a total of 5,206 people lived on the Island and in 1980 there were 7,155 permanent residents on Anna Maria Island.

In 2009, when this book was written the total population of the Island was 8,574. There are 1,875 permanent residents in Anna Maria City, 5,107 residents in Holmes Beach and 1,592 residents in Bradenton Beach.

Ode To Anna Maria Isle

By Genevieve Alban

The early morning breezes stir
Frothy fringe on waves of blue,
The sun begins its stately rise
With rays of glorious hue

The sea gulls call, the sea oats sway
While sandpipers march in a row,
Sand dollars and the starfish wake
To join in nature's show.

The palm trees wave a proud salute
To pelicans as they fly,
While dolphins rise and dip again
As they go gliding by.

The ibis and the herons prance
With stately charm and grace,
While sea and sand and azure sky
Melt in a fond embrace.

A turtle lumbers back to sea
Leaving tracks that mark its way,
Where eggs are buried safe and sound
To hatch another day.

Of all the places here on earth
Of every kind and style.
The one that nature blessed the most
Is Anna Maria Isle.

Genevieve "Gen" Novicky Alban came to the Island in 1982 from Boardman, Ohio where she was the clerk/treasurer for the Township of Boardman. An artist, poet and teacher, she founded the Artists Guild of Anna Maria Island in 1989 to promote and support all Island artists, and develop an artistic community on the Island.

George and Carolyne Norwood in the Anna Maria Island Historical Museum

About The Author

Carolyne Norwood co-founded the Anna Maria Island Historical Society in 1990. She served as director for 15 years and wrote her first book, *The Early Days 1893-1940*, in 2003. During her tenure, she gave speeches in school, churches and civic organizations, bringing intriguing Island history to all ages. She wrote five historical plays about the first homesteaders, the first church, the Island school, the founding of Holmes Beach and the first volunteer fire department.

Originally from Baltimore, Maryland, she and her husband, George, and their three children, pulled up roots and settled on Anna Maria Island in 1956. Their fourth child was born in 1957. Her beloved husband died in 2002.

Carolyne still lives in the home they built in 1960, near the North Point of Anna Maria City with her faithful dog, Lulu. She has a summer home at the foot of Grandfather Mountain in Linville, North Carolina. She has seven grandchildren and eight great-grandchildren. All live in Florida.

Chris Torgeson, Miss Florida 1966.

Looking West-Bradenton Beach, Fla.

BRADENTON BEACH, FLA.
VIEWED FROM THE AIR

Comments

"This is a very informative read. Happy memories of the past flow through your mind like the waves over the beaches of Anna Maria Island. There were happy and sad times, but all were rolled into one unique experience called Island Times."

Jack Dietrich, Anna Maria Elementary School principal 1966-1970

" Outstanding! Marvelous! A tour de force exceeding my expectations. The cover and photo quality is excellent. Carolyne is to be commended for all her work and effort. "

Linda Kinnan, Manatee High School English teacher, retired

" Carolyne has done a superb job of scouring newspaper accounts, interviewing old timers and combing through the archives of the Anna Maria Island Historical Museum to bring you, "Tales of Three Cities: From Bean Point to Bridge Street." It is a Herculean book that details the Island's colorful history from 1940 to 1970. In it you will learn how the Island rid itself of mosquitoes, thanks to a doctor; the origin of Island institutions, what happened to the Island airport, how the Islander became a real newspaper, the fight for a public beach at the south end, famous restaurateurs who put the Island on the tourist map and much more. It is sure to fascinate and delight you from the first page to the last. "

Pat Copeland, co-founder of the Anna Maria Island Historical Society and Museum, Island journalist

It seems every person who ever set foot on Anna Maria Island and most of the events that have taken place on the Island in the past few decades Carolyne Norwood writes about in her latest book. "Tales of Three Cities." From the title page to the author's biographical sketch it is a joy to read. This is a tremendous effort by Carolyne. It gets better and more fascinating the more you read. I like the animal stories and the education chapter, since I was a teacher at the Island school in the '50s. I marvel at Carolyne's ability to gather this information. All would be forgotten if she had not written this masterpiece. Thank you, Carolyne, for this magnificent book! What memories it stirs.

Eizabeth Pierce Moss, who first came to the Island by boat as an infant in 1917. Still lives in the same Gulffront house her parents purchased in 1943. The frame home was built in 1924.

"I realized I was laughing while I was reading. The memoirs of old timers were especially amusing. I think it's most unusual to discover a funny history book."

Elizabeth McCloskey, home health worker

The Cover

The aerial photograph, taken in 1940, shows the Island from the North Point or Bean Point, looking southward. The Rod and Reel Pier had not yet been built. The City Pier, at the end of Pine Avenue, juts out into Tampa Bay. The pier was built in 1911, before there was a bridge to the Island. It was the hub of all activity on this seven mile strip of land. Steamships docked at the pier bringing visitors and supplies. The background is the original deed of the tract of land homesteaded in 1839 by George Emerson Bean.